BBC BUSINESS ENGLISH

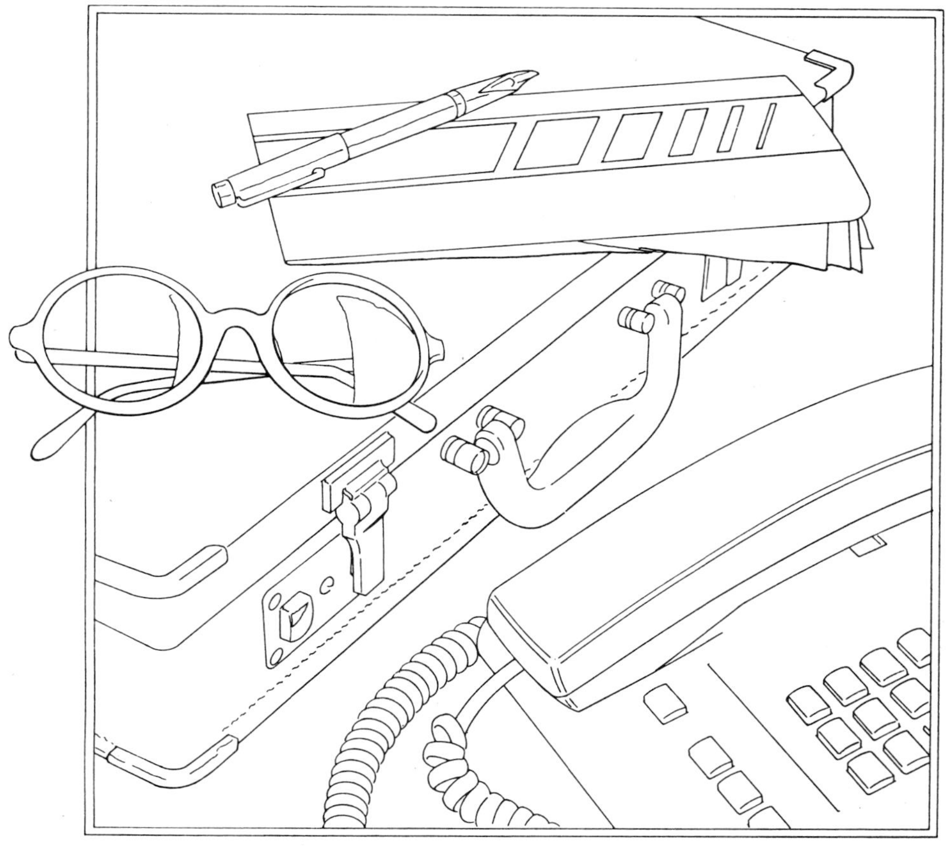

ROGER OWEN

BBC ENGLISH

Published by BBC English 1992
Reprinted 1993, 1994, 1996

BBC English, 80 Wood Lane, London W12 0TT

BBC Business English

Pack	1 85497 239 1
Book	**1 85497 237 5**
Audiocassettes (3)	1 85497 238 3

Prepared for publication by Stenton Associates

Illustrations: JMJ Design

Cover design: Jim Wire

Recordings produced by Martin Williamson, Prolingua Productions

Printing: Butler & Tanner Ltd, Frome and London

The business situations in this book feature fictional characters, organisations and events. No resemblance to real people or companies is intended.

Author's acknowledgements
Among the people who have helped and advised me in the writing of these materials, I should particularly like to thank Arinee Methasate, Frederick and Nola Allen, Robert Sykes, Irwan Owen, Russell Sunderland, and my meticulous, long-suffering editor, Adrian Stenton.

I should like to dedicate this book to the people who taught me most about the English language – all my past students at the City of London Polytechnic and,long before that, at the English Departments of Gajah Mada University and Sanata Dharma Teacher Training Institute, Yogyakarta, Indonesia.

Contents

Introduction

BBC Business English will help you to improve your English. It is suitable for anyone who has studied English to intermediate level or above, and who wants to use English at work. It is designed for people who want to study English on their own, in their spare time or while they are travelling.

The book

This book contains 24 units arranged in nine sections. Each unit contains a business topic, theme or problem. The companies, countries and characters involved change from section to section. This means that you can choose which unit to study, to review a particular skill or language point. You do not have to work through the book from unit 1 to unit 24, although this is a good way to use the materials.

In each unit there is: an introductory page explaining what you will find in the unit; three double-page 'spreads' of dialogues, documents and exercises; and an answer key and commentary. On pages 6 and 7 you will find some reduced-size pages with notes on the materials they contain and how to use them.

Business terms and everyday phrases are explained in the units or in the index and glossary at the end of the book. You will also need a good dictionary while you are working through the book. The exercises in the book are of many different kinds. Some have correct answers, and you will find these in the answer key at the end of the unit. Others are more 'open' – for example writing a memo – and for these exercises you will find a 'model' answer in the answer key. Sometimes you are asked to look or listen for a particular point; in this case, the answer key will give a short commentary so that you know whether you have understood the material properly.

The answer key also contains a 'study record'. Make a note of the date when you try an exercise for the first time; come back to it later and see how much you remember. If you make a note of when you complete an exercise, and when you revise it, you will be able to see how much progress you have made.

Study record	
10.1	7/9, 14/9, 5/10
10.2	7/9, 14/9
10.3	

The cassettes

The three cassettes contain the recordings of the dialogues in the book, and some other material for listening and speaking practice.

This symbol in the book means that you should be ready to play the cassette when you have read the instruction and understand what you are being asked to do.

When you work through a unit for the first time, you will need to use the book as well as the cassettes, as the book guides you through the course. But once you have completed a unit or section with the book, it can be very helpful to play the cassettes on their own, perhaps in a car or personal stereo. You can practise listening for meaning and listening for pronunciation. Listen to how the dialogues are spoken, to the rhythm and intonation of the speech. As you get to know the dialogues, try saying the words along with the speakers.

Some advice on study

Try to spend twenty or thirty minutes a day with **BBC Business English**; this is worth far more than having a two-hour period once a week. Keep the book with you so that you can look at it when you have five minutes to spare during the day; play the cassettes when you are travelling to and from work.

When you begin to study a unit, read it carefully and listen to the recording – several times, if you like. Then work through the documents and dialogues in detail. Use the word notes, the index and glossary and your dictionary to make sure you understand what you read and hear. Do the exercises, and use the answer key – not only to check your answers, but to check your ideas. The exercises are not to test you, but to help you to learn, so you are not 'cheating' if you look at the answer key before you have finished the unit.

Refresh your memory by re-reading and re-working units you have already studied. Use the 'study record' in the answer key to keep notes on when you first do an exercise, and again when you revise it. A good method is to revise a unit after a week, then go back to it a month later. Keep a notebook for **BBC Business English** so that all your answers and notes are in the same place. Plan your work – either following the order of the book, or choosing the topics or language that are most useful to you – and make a record of your progress. Find a way of using the study materials that suits your needs and the time you have to spend. Above all, get to know the dialogues and documents as well as you can – and enjoy learning with **BBC Business English**.

A note for teachers

Although **BBC Business English** is designed for self study, it offers a wealth of realistic business situations, language and exploitation which can be used as a basis for group work. The book and cassettes can be used as the starting-point for class activities such as role play, listening for gist, listening for detail, writing letters, memos and reports, building vocabulary, practising grammar and focusing on particular areas of difficulty such as using figures and dealing with social situations.

The course presents English as the language of international business transactions, and the wide range of settings, companies and types of work it features will give students a good basis for building their business knowledge as well as improving their English.

How to use this book

On this spread are reduced pages from the book. They show the different kinds of material the book contains, with notes on how to use them.

You will progress much more quickly if you regularly revise what you have learned. Study a page and do the exercises. Then revise the exercises a week later to see how much you can remember. Revise them again a month later. Remember to mark your progress in the study record.

This symbol [cassette symbol] means that you should be ready to play the cassette when you have read the instruction and understand what you are being asked to do.

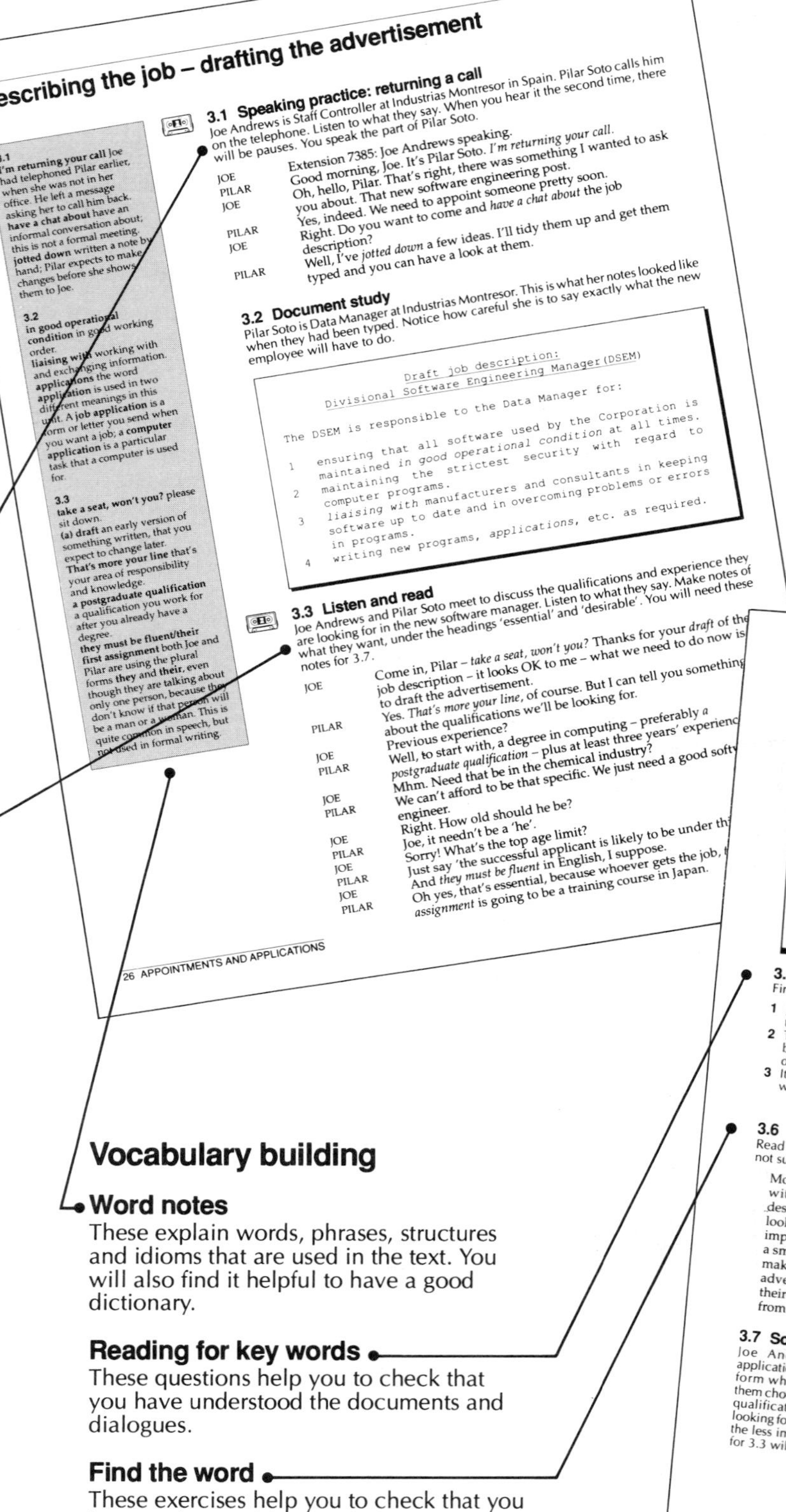

Describing the job – drafting the advertisement

3.1 Speaking practice: returning a call
Joe Andrews is Staff Controller at Industrias Montresor in Spain. Pilar Soto calls him on the telephone. Listen to what they say. When you hear it the second time, there will be pauses. You speak the part of Pilar Soto.

JOE Extension 7385: Joe Andrews speaking.
PILAR Good morning, Joe. It's Pilar Soto. *I'm returning your call.*
JOE Oh, hello, Pilar. That's right, there was something I wanted to ask you about. That new software engineering post.
PILAR Yes, indeed. We need to appoint someone pretty soon.
JOE Right. Do you want to come and *have a chat about* the job description?
PILAR Well, I've *jotted down* a few ideas. I'll tidy them up and get them typed and you can have a look at them.

3.2 Document study
Pilar Soto is Data Manager at Industrias Montresor. This is what her notes looked like when they had been typed. Notice how careful she is to say exactly what the new employee will have to do.

Draft job description:
Divisional Software Engineering Manager (DSEM)

The DSEM is responsible to the Data Manager for:
1 ensuring that all software used by the Corporation is maintained *in good operational condition* at all times.
2 maintaining the strictest security with regard to computer programs.
3 *liaising with* manufacturers and consultants in keeping software up to date and in overcoming problems or errors in programs.
4 writing new programs, *applications*, etc. as required.

3.3 Listen and read
Joe Andrews and Pilar Soto meet to discuss the qualifications and experience they are looking for in the new software manager. Listen to what they say. Make notes of what they want, under the headings 'essential' and 'desirable'. You will need these notes for 3.7.

JOE Come in, Pilar – *take a seat, won't you?* Thanks for your *draft* of th job description – it looks OK to me – what we need to do now is to draft the advertisement.
PILAR Yes. *That's more your line*, of course. But I can tell you something about the qualifications we'll be looking for.
JOE Previous experience?
PILAR Well, to start with, a degree in computing – preferably a *postgraduate qualification* – plus at least three years' experienc
JOE Mhm. Need that be in the chemical industry?
PILAR We can't afford to be that specific. We just need a good soft engineer.
JOE Right. How old should he be?
PILAR Joe, it needn't be a 'he'.
JOE Sorry! What's the top age limit?
PILAR Just say 'the successful applicant is likely to be under th
JOE And *they must be fluent* in English, I suppose.
PILAR Oh yes, that's essential, because whoever gets the job, *assignment* is going to be a training course in Japan.

3.1
I'm returning your call Joe had telephoned Pilar earlier, when she was not in her office. He left a message asking her to call him back.
have a chat about have an informal conversation about; this is not a formal meeting.
jotted down written a note by hand; Pilar expects to make changes before she shows them to Joe.

3.2
in good operational condition in good working order.
liaising with working with and exchanging information.
applications the word application is used in two different meanings in this unit. A **job application** is a form or letter you send when you want a job; a **computer application** is a particular task that a computer is used for.

3.3
take a seat, won't you? please sit down.
(a) draft an early version of something written, that you expect to change later.
That's more your line that's your area of responsibility and knowledge.
a postgraduate qualification a qualification you work for after you already have a degree.
they must be fluent/their first assignment both Joe and Pilar are using the plural forms **they** and **their**, even though they are talking about only one person, because they don't know if that person will be a man or a woman. This is quite common in speech, but not used in formal writing.

26 APPOINTMENTS AND APPLICATIONS

Listening and speaking

Speaking practice

1 These short dialogues help you to practise speaking natural English. Start by listening to the dialogue on the cassette.

2 Let the cassette play on. You will hear the same dialogue, with pauses. You speak the part of one of the characters. After that you will hear what the character said.

Listen and read

1 Listen to and read the dialogue as many times as you like.

2 Listen to the pronunciation, the rhythm and the intonation. Notice how people group their words together when they speak.

3 Practise 'shadowing' each speaker – say the words at the same time as the speaker says them, and in the same way.

Vocabulary building

Word notes

These explain words, phrases, structures and idioms that are used in the text. You will also find it helpful to have a good dictionary.

Reading for key words

These questions help you to check that you have understood the documents and dialogues.

Find the word

These exercises help you to check that you have understood the vocabulary for a business topic. All the words that you need to fill the gaps are given in the box.

Reading and writing

Document study

These give you practice in reading business documents in English. They will help you to write your own business letters, reports, memos, etc. When you read a document, notice how it is presented, its layout and punctuation, and how the material is organised in paragraphs.

Information from the text

There are many different exercises in the book which ask you to find information, and often to explain it or express it in a different way. Many of these exercises ask you to read, speak, or explain figures, or to make simple calculations. In most cases you can either speak or write the answers – or do both, on different days.

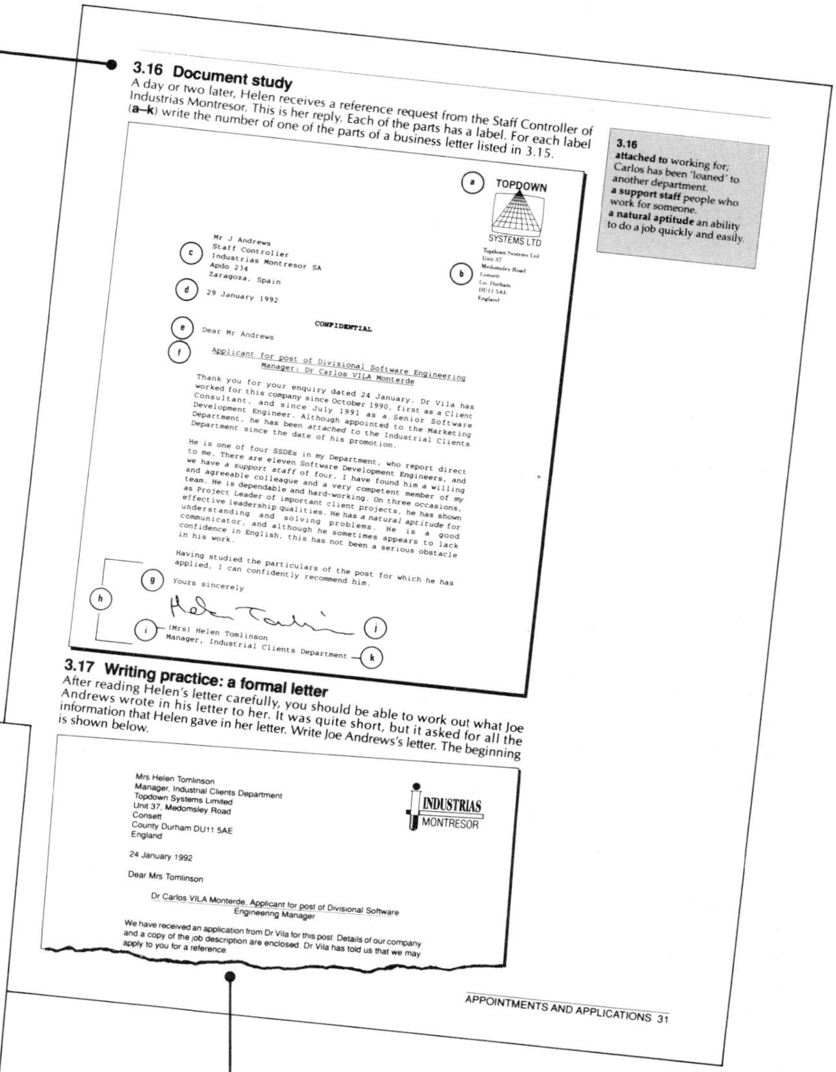

3.16 Document study

A day or two later, Helen receives a reference request from the Staff Controller of Industrias Montresor. This is her reply. Each of the parts has a label. For each label (**a–k**) write the number of one of the parts of a business letter listed in 3.15.

TOPDOWN SYSTEMS LTD

Mr J Andrews
Staff Controller
Industrias Montresor SA
Apdo 234
Zaragoza, Spain

29 January 1992

CONFIDENTIAL

Dear Mr Andrews

Applicant for post of Divisional Software Engineering Manager: Dr Carlos VILA Monterde

Thank you for your enquiry dated 24 January. Dr Vila has worked for this company since October 1990, first as a Client Consultant, and since July 1991 as a Senior Software Development Engineer. Although appointed to the Marketing Department, he has been attached to the Industrial Clients Department since the date of his promotion.

He is one of four SSDEs in my Department, who report direct to me. There are eleven Software Development Engineers, and we have a support staff of four. I have found him a willing and agreeable colleague and a very competent member of my team. He is dependable and hard-working. On three occasions, as Project Leader of important client projects, he has shown effective leadership qualities. He has a natural aptitude for understanding and solving problems. He is a good communicator, and although he sometimes appears to lack confidence in English, this has not been a serious obstacle in his work.

Having studied the particulars of the post for which he has applied, I can confidently recommend him.

Yours sincerely

(Mrs) Helen Tomlinson
Manager, Industrial Clients Department

3.16
attached to working for; Carlos has been 'loaned' to another department.
a support staff people who work for someone.
a natural aptitude an ability to do a job quickly and easily.

3.17 Writing practice: a formal letter

After reading Helen's letter carefully, you should be able to work out what Joe Andrews wrote in his letter to her. It was quite short, but it asked for all the information that Helen gave in her letter. Write Joe Andrews's letter. The beginning is shown below.

Mrs Helen Tomlinson
Manager, Industrial Clients Department
Topdown Systems Limited
Unit 37, Medomsley Road
Consett
County Durham DU11 5AE
England

INDUSTRIAS MONTRESOR

24 January 1992

Dear Mrs Tomlinson

Dr Carlos VILA Monterde, Applicant for post of Divisional Software Engineering Manager

We have received an application from Dr Vila for this post. Details of our company and a copy of the job description are enclosed. Dr Vila has told us that we may apply to you for a reference.

APPOINTMENTS AND APPLICATIONS 31

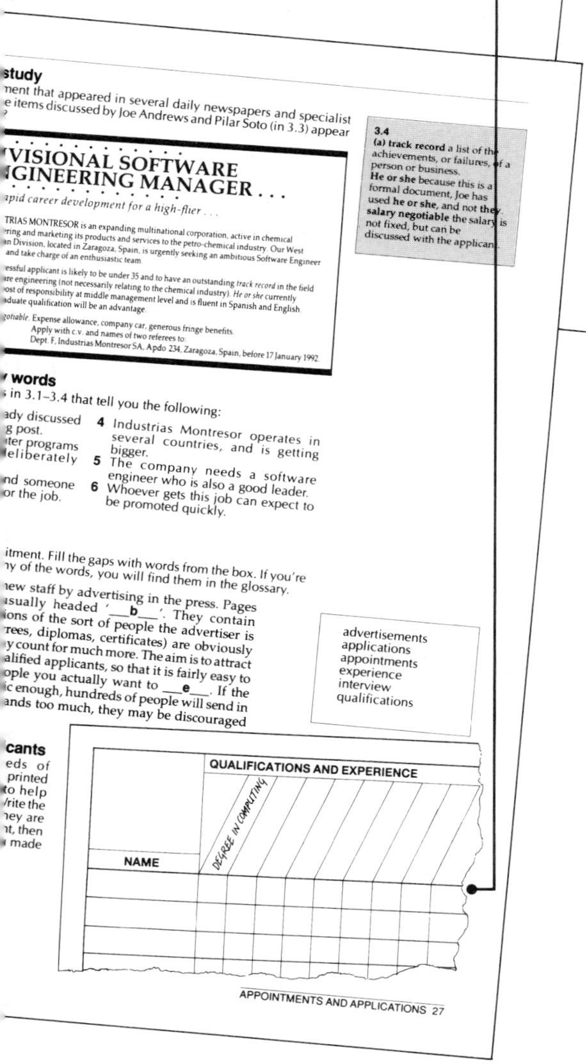

study
ment that appeared in several daily newspapers and specialist
e items discussed by Joe Andrews and Pilar Soto (in 3.3) appear

VISIONAL SOFTWARE
GINEERING MANAGER . . .

apid career development for a high-flier . . .

TRIAS MONTRESOR is an expanding multinational corporation, active in chemical
ring and marketing its products and services to the petro-chemical industry. Our West
n Division, located in Zaragoza, Spain, is urgently seeking an ambitious Software Engineer
and take charge of an enthusiastic team.

essful applicant is likely to be under 35 and to have an outstanding *track record* in the field
are engineering (not necessarily relating to the chemical industry). *He or she* currently
post of responsibility at middle management level and is fluent in Spanish and English.
aduate qualification will be an advantage.

gotiable. Expense allowance, company car, generous fringe benefits.
Apply with c.v. and names of two referees to:
Dept. F, Industrias Montresor SA, Apdo 234, Zaragoza, Spain, before 17 January 1992.

3.4
(a) track record a list of the achievements, or failures, of a person or business.
He or she because this is a formal document, Joe has used **he or she**, and not they.
salary negotiable the salary is not fixed, but can be discussed with the applicant.

words
in 3.1–3.4 that tell you the following:

ady discussed
g post.
ter programs
eliberately

nd someone
or the job.

4 Industrias Montresor operates in several countries, and is getting bigger.
5 The company needs a software engineer who is also a good leader.
6 Whoever gets this job can expect to be promoted quickly.

itment. Fill the gaps with words from the box. If you're
y of the words, you will find them in the glossary.

new staff by advertising in the press. Pages
usually headed '__**b**__'. They contain
ions of the sort of people the advertiser is
rees, diplomas, certificates) are obviously
y count for much more. The aim is to attract
alified applicants, so that it is fairly easy to
ople you actually want to __**e**__. If the
c enough, hundreds of people will send in
ands too much, they may be discouraged

advertisements
applications
appointments
experience
interview
qualifications

cants
eds of
printed
to help
rite the
ey are
t, then
made

NAME	QUALIFICATIONS AND EXPERIENCE								
	DEGREE IN COMPUTING								

APPOINTMENTS AND APPLICATIONS 27

Writing practice

Many of these exercises do not have only one possible answer. The answer key gives a 'model' answer which you can copy, or you can write your own answer.

Some of the written exercises give you some help, either with individual sentences or with the document as a whole.

If you find that a written exercise is too difficult, don't worry. It is better to study the model answer carefully and try the exercise again some time later.

If you are studying with a friend, read each other's work and try to improve it; or work together to produce the best possible version.

Unit 1: A tour of the factory

SITUATION

In this unit, we meet two companies: Keypoint Security (UK) Ltd and Midland Furniture Limited. Midland have just bought a factory in the South Midlands of England, about 150 kilometres north of London. It is in an industrial area where there are many other factories and offices. At the moment the building is empty. Midland have asked Keypoint to look at the building and to make sure that it is safe and well protected before they move in.

CHARACTERS

Sarah Street	is Marketing Director for Keypoint Security Ltd.
Receptionist	at Midland Furniture Ltd.
Irena Phillips	is Client Services Manager for Keypoint Security Ltd.
Jeff Jones	is Production Manager at Midland Furniture Ltd.
Peter Jackson	is a management trainee at Keypoint Security Ltd.

All of these characters are British.

LANGUAGE

Vocabulary	Factories and offices; what the different areas inside a building are used for; words for describing and measuring spaces and areas.
Skills	Dictating; greeting somebody; introducing yourself; introducing somebody else.
Structures	As you ... know ... ; Do you know ...; estimating figures; a/an/the.
Documents	A memo; a factory plan; architects' instructions; a report.

Visiting a factory

1.1
a memo a short written message to someone in your own company; **memo** is short for **memorandum**.
a preliminary survey an initial examination; a more detailed examination will be made later.
premises the buildings belonging to a company; the word **premises** is always plural, even if there is only one building.
(a) site a place where a building is, or where it will be built.

1.2
a management trainee someone who is learning to be a manager.

1.1 Listen and read

Sarah Street is Marketing Director for Keypoint Security Ltd. She is dictating *a memo*. Listen to what she says, and write the words missing from the typed memo below.

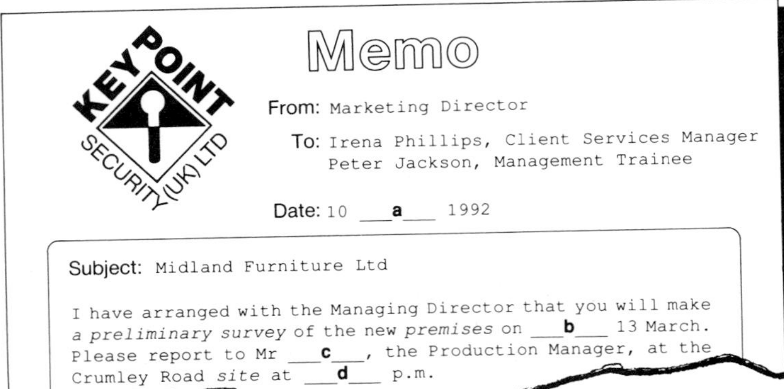

KEYPOINT SECURITY (UK) LTD

Memo

From: Marketing Director

To: Irena Phillips, Client Services Manager
Peter Jackson, Management Trainee

Date: 10 ___a___ 1992

Subject: Midland Furniture Ltd

I have arranged with the Managing Director that you will make *a preliminary survey* of the new *premises* on ___b___ 13 March. Please report to Mr ___c___, the Production Manager, at the Crumley Road *site* at ___d___ p.m.

1.2 Listen and read

Peter Jackson joined Keypoint a few days ago as *a management trainee*. He is with Irena Phillips, the Client Services Manager, on a visit to a client, Midland Furniture. Listen to what they say. How do they greet each other? How does Irena introduce Peter to Mr Jones?

RECEPTIONIST Good afternoon. Can I help you?
IRENA Good afternoon. My name is Phillips, Mrs Irena Phillips of Keypoint Security. My colleague and I have an appointment to see Mr Jones at 2.30.
RECEPTIONIST Thank you. I'll tell him you're here. [She telephones Mr Jones's office] Hello. I have Mrs Phillips, of Keypoint Security, in reception. Thank you. [To Irena] If you'll take a seat, Mrs Phillips, Mr Jones will be right down.
IRENA Thank you.
. . . . . .
JEFF Mrs Phillips? How do you do. I'm Jeff Jones.
IRENA How do you do, Mr Jones. Can I introduce a colleague of mine, Peter Jackson.
PETER How do you do.
JEFF I'm pleased to meet you, Mr Jackson. Yes, Mr Irving told me you'd be coming. Well, welcome to Midland Furniture! Shall we go straight round to the new premises? I'll tell you more about them on the way.

1.3 Speaking practice: greeting people

Listen to this conversation. When you hear it the second time, there will be pauses. You speak the part of the man.

RECEPTIONIST Good morning. Can I help you?
MAN Good morning. My name is Wilson, David Wilson, EMC Electronics.
RECEPTIONIST Yes, Mr Wilson?
MAN I have an appointment with the production manager.
RECEPTIONIST Mrs Smith? That's her, over there. I think she's coming over.
MAN Oh yes, I see her. Thank you.
. . . . . .
WOMAN Hello! Are you looking for me?
MAN Yes. Mrs Smith? I'm David Wilson from EMC Electronics.
WOMAN How do you do, Mr Wilson. Susan Smith.
MAN How do you do.
WOMAN Let's go to my office, shall we? Did you bring the report with you?

1.4 Listen and read

Jeff Jones drives Irena and Peter to the new premises. He tells them about the company. Listen to what they say. What are the advantages of the new site? How many buildings are there on the site?

JEFF As you may know, the company is planning to expand its sales overseas, so we had to find a bigger factory. This place we're going to, on the Farm Lane Industrial Estate, isn't, in my opinion, ideal, but it's quite big, it's got good access to the motorway and it's fairly cheap. *From the security point of view*, though . . . well, I'll be interested to see *what you make of it*.

. . . . . .

JEFF OK, here we are. We've got this large building that you see in front of you, plus a separate, much smaller, building round the back.

PETER You said it was built in the 1930s?

JEFF Round about then, yes. It's old, but it's in good condition.

IRENA Do you know who owned it before you?

JEFF It was a printer's for about twenty years, but they've just *gone bust*. That's why it was cheap, and the board *reckoned* we could afford it. Right, if you'd like to come along with me, I'll show you round the site.

> **1.4**
> **From the security point of view** if you consider the security aspects.
> **what you make of it** what your opinion of it is.
> **gone bust** closed down because they lost too much money.
> **reckoned** believed.

1.5 Structure practice: giving and asking for information

Jeff Jones says 'As you may know, the company is planning . . . ', to Irena and Peter (1.4) because this is a polite way of giving people information when you are not sure if they do or don't already know it.

Rewrite the sentences below, using 'As you . . . know, . . . ', and one of the words from the box. Notice that you do not use 'that' in this structure.

> may
> might
> perhaps
> probably

1 We have just bought a new factory.
As you may know, we have just bought a new factory.
2 We're going to look at the site.
As you ______ know, ______
3 Keypoint specialises in security services.
As you ______ know, ______
4 Midland Furniture is planning to expand.
As you ______ know, ______

Irena says 'Do you know who . . . ', because this is a more polite way of asking people for information when you are not sure if they will know the answer. Rewrite the questions below using the more polite form.

5 When was the factory built?
Do you know when the factory was built?
6 How old is this building?
Do you know how old ______ ?
7 Where will the trucks enter?
Do you know ______ ?
8 What does Midland Furniture make?
9 Which countries do they export to?

Walking round the factory – 1

1.6 Listen and write

This is an architect's plan of Midland Furniture's new factory. It shows what each part of the building will be used for. As you listen to the rest of this unit (1.7, 1.9, 1.11 and 1.13), make a note of where on the plan of the factory Jeff, Irena and Peter are standing as they are talking – **A**, **B**, **C** or **D**.

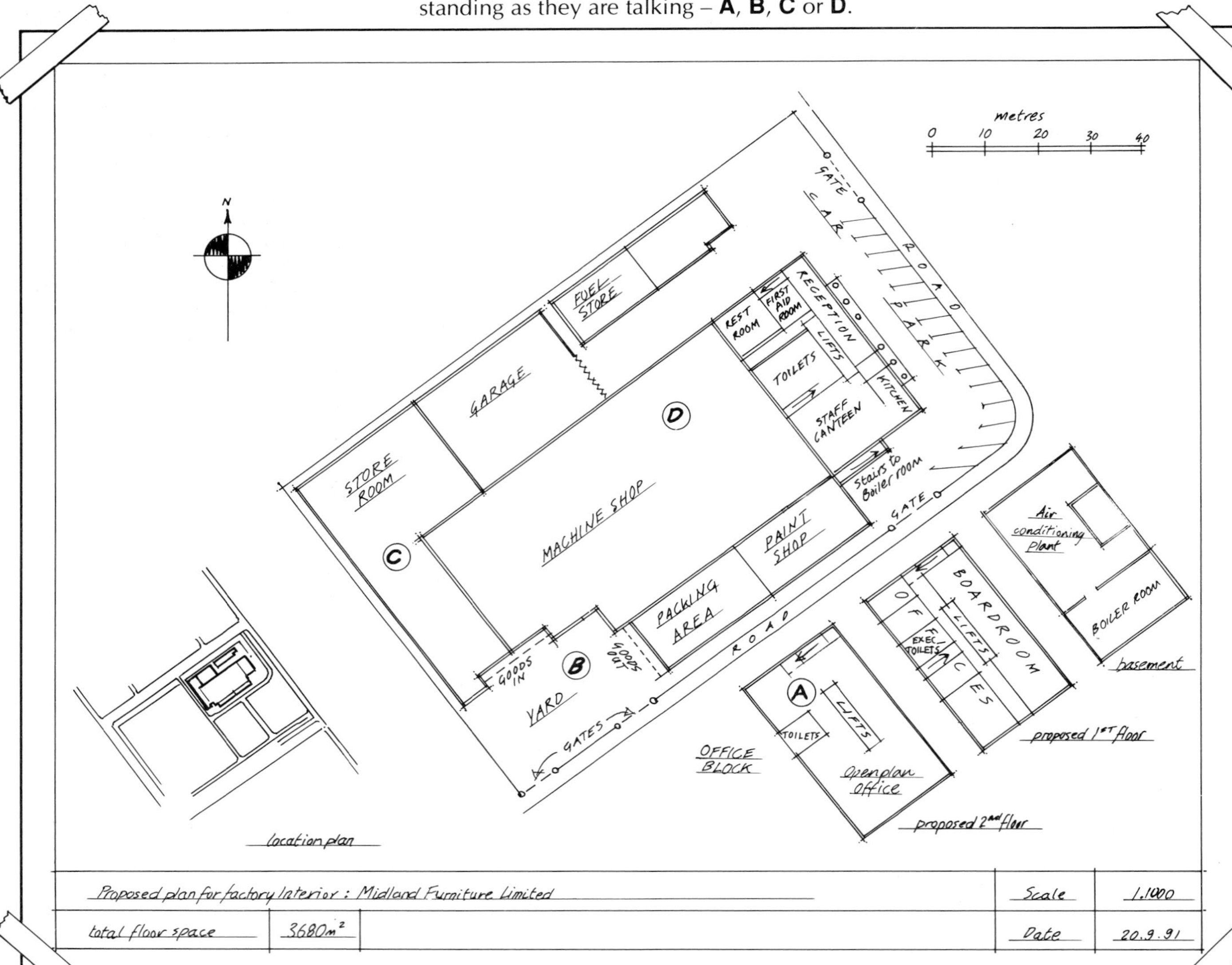

1.7 Listen and read

As they walk round the factory, Irena and Peter comment on some of the security problems. Listen to what they say. What problems do they see? Remember to note where they are on the plan (1.6).

> **1.7**
> **Yeah** an informal form of 'yes'.
> **That's a point** that's something I hadn't thought of.

JEFF Now, if I can just find the right key. Ah! There we are.
PETER These gates are really massive, aren't they?
IRENA *Yeah*, but you're going to need a good strong fence as well.
JEFF At the moment of course the whole building is just an empty shell. This is where the trucks will come to load and unload.
IRENA *That's a point*. There'll be a lot of trucks going in and out. Will they refuel here?
JEFF Yes. The garage and the fuel store are round the back.
PETER There are a lot of outside pipes, and outside doors. You'll need security guards on duty here twenty-four hours a day.

1.8 Find the word

The directors of Midland Furniture have instructed a firm of architects to design the inside of the new factory. This is an extract from their instructions. Look at the plan opposite and find the words missing below.

The existing factory is of single-storey construction, except for the office ___**a**___ , which is on three ___**b**___, with a basement beneath.

The *ground floor* of the office block is to be used as a reception area and staff ___**c**___. There will also be a first-aid ___**d**___, rest room and ___**e**___.

The basement below the office block will continue to house the boiler ___**f**___ and air-conditioning *plant*. On the first floor we require a boardroom and at least four ___**g**___ for senior executives.

Floor space in the factory should be allocated as follows:

Store ___**h**___:	900 m^2
Machine ___**i**___:	2000 m^2
Paint *shop*:	380 m^2
Packing ___**j**___:	400 m^2
Total:	3680 m^2

1.8
(a) floor all the rooms of a building on the same level; a storey; in British English the floor at street level is the **ground floor**, and you go up to the **first floor**; in American English the **first floor** is the floor at street level.
plant machinery used in industry; **a plant** can mean a factory.
(a) shop a place in a factory where things are made or worked on.

1.9 Listen and read

Peter and Irena ask Jeff questions about how the factory will work. Listen to what they say. How does Jeff show that he is not giving exact figures? Remember to note where they are on the plan (1.6).

PETER According to the plan of the factory, this is going to be the store room, is that right?

JEFF Yes, the sawn timber will come in here, through the unloading bay – it'll be checked in and stored on racks until it's needed.

PETER How long will it stay in the stores, on average?

JEFF Not long. Just a few days, normally. Stock turnover's very quick. Timber's expensive stuff these days, *you can't have it hanging around.*

IRENA And what's likely to be the total value of your stock, roughly?

JEFF Well, very roughly, three, three hundred and fifty thousand pounds, I should think.

1.9
you can't have it hanging around you can't afford to have it not used; the wood is too expensive to store for a long time.

1.10 Speaking practice: estimating figures

Read the questions below, and write down your answers. You don't need to be exact. Use the 'estimating' words from the box and information from this unit in your answers. Then listen to the questions, and speak your answers. Don't worry if your figures are not exactly the same as the ones you hear.

1 How old is the building? – About sixty years.
2 What's the length of the corridor between the boardroom and the offices?
3 How far is it from the garage doors to the road?
4 What's the size of the boardroom?
5 How many cars could you get in the car park?
6 What's the total value of the timber in the store room?

about around
approximately
roughly

Walking round the factory – 2

1.11
automated done by machines or robots.
(an) assembly line an arrangement in a factory where each worker makes only a part of a product before it is passed on to the next worker.
the finishing's done by hand the final work is done by people; usually when the initial work is done by machine.
(a) flat-pack, self-assembly kit a set of parts which the customer makes into a product, and which can be packed into a small size for delivery; this is a good example of how English creates a complex meaning by combining simple words.
keep an eye on things watch the factory and the workers to make sure that everything is working properly.

1.13
a closed-circuit TV camera a camera that is part of a television system within the factory, so that the security guards can see what is happening at different places.
you name it and anything else you can think of.
(an) executive suite a set of offices for a senior manager; Jeff thinks that the Managing Director's office is bigger and smarter than necessary.

1.11 Listen and read

Irena and Peter continue their tour of the premises with Jeff Jones. Listen to what they say. How do Irena and Peter show that they are uncertain about what they are saying? Remember to note where they are on the plan (1.6).

JEFF	This will be the machine shop. We're putting a lot of money into new equipment, computer-controlled, everything *automated*.
PETER	A sort of *assembly line*?
JEFF	Well, not exactly. It's all going to be organised on what they call the 'just-in-time' system. We only build furniture that people have ordered.
PETER	I see. So you won't have to keep a lot of surplus stock. And everything's going to be assembled by robots, I suppose?
JEFF	Oh no. All *the finishing's done by hand*. We're very proud of our tradition of craftsmanship. Although actually, our new range of furniture is all *flat-pack, self-assembly kits*.
PETER	I imagine they're easier to transport.
JEFF	Precisely!
IRENA	Mm, I'm sure it'll all be very impressive. Could we have a look at the office accommodation now?
JEFF	Yes. You see those big windows overlooking the factory floor? My office is up there, so that I can *keep an eye on things*!

1.12 Structure practice: *a*, *an* and *the*

You can use 'a' or 'an' with nouns which can be counted: 'a factory', or 'a table'. These are called countable nouns, and they are usually marked [C] or [nc] in dictionaries. They can be used in the singular or the plural: 'He is making a table' or 'He is making tables'. But many nouns in English cannot be counted: 'He is making furniture'. Nouns like 'furniture' are called uncountable nouns, and are usually marked [U] or [nu] in dictionaries.

You can use 'the' with either countable or uncountable nouns, when you want to refer to something you have already talked about: 'The table is finished' or 'The furniture is finished'.

Write the words missing from the text below. Use 'a', 'an' or 'the', or nothing. If you are not sure whether these nouns are countable or uncountable, check in your dictionary.

> Midland Furniture have recently bought ___**a**___ new premises in Crumley Road. It is ___**b**___ large site, which they will use for making ___**c**___ furniture.
>
> They will bring in ___**d**___ plant from their other factories to set up ___**e**___ assembly line for ___**f**___ furniture.

1.13 Listen and read

Jeff shows Irena and Peter round the offices. Listen to what they say. What offices and rooms does he list? Remember to note where they are on the plan (1.6).

JEFF	Well, down on the ground floor there'll be the reception area, staff canteen, toilets, rest room and first-aid room. Upstairs, here on the top floor, there'll be a big open-plan office for all the secretaries and computer operators.
PETER	There's a splendid view from up here. You can see the whole site.
IRENA	Yes, it'd be a good place to put *a closed-circuit TV camera*.
JEFF	Then on the first floor, the boardroom, which will also be used for management meetings, sales presentations, Christmas parties, *you name it*. On the other side of the corridor, as I showed you, overlooking the machine shop, will be my little place, offices for two other department heads, and the boss's *executive suite*.

1.14 Writing practice: a report

On Monday morning, Irena is back in her office preparing her report. First she writes down the headings for each paragraph. Then she makes notes under each heading, and finally she writes the report. When it's been typed, the introduction looks like this:

REPORT ON FACTORY PREMISES AT FARM LANE ESTATE
Client: Midland Furniture Ltd

1 Introduction

On 13 March 1992, following the Marketing Director's instructions, I carried out a preliminary survey of these premises with Mr Peter Jackson of Keypoint Security and Mr Jeff Jones of Midland Furniture. This report is a summary of my first impressions. It does not attempt to consider the security requirements of the site in detail. However, it raises a number of points that Keypoint Security and the client may wish to consider before proceeding further.

1. Introduction
2. Location and general description
3. Proposed use
4. Security: strong and weak points
5. Recommendations

The notes below will help you draft short paragraphs for the rest of Irena's report. Each paragraph should be presented in a businesslike way, but remember that good business English can be quite simple and informal.

2 Location and general description

Read sections 1.4, 1.6, 1.7 and 1.8 again. Say where the site is, and what the buildings are like.

The factory is located ______
There are two buildings ______

3 Proposed use

Read sections 1.7, 1.8, 1.9, 1.11 and 1.13 again. What will the factory make? What actions will happen inside the factory and in the grounds?

The factory will be used for ______

4 Security: strong and weak points

Read sections 1.7, 1.11 and 1.13 again, and make a list of all the strong points and all the weak points in the security of the site. Remember that when you present a list, all of the points should be listed in the same way. You can number your points, and you can write them as phrases or as full sentences, as long as they are all the same. This makes the list easier to write and easier to read.

4.1 Strong points:
1 massive gates
2 . . . . . .
4.2 Weak points:
1 poor fence
2 . . . . . .

5 Recommendations

You now have to decide what recommendations to make. Look again at the plan in 1.6, and at the list of security points you made above. Again, you can list your recommendations:

5.1 The property should be surrounded by a strong fence.
5.2 ______

Study record	
1.1	
1.2	
1.3	
1.4	
1.5	
1.6	
1.7	
1.8	
1.9	
1.10	
1.11	
1.12	
1.13	
1.14	

Answer key and commentary for unit 1

1.1 Listen and read

a March **b** Friday **c** Jones **d** 2.30

1.2 Listen and read

The receptionist and Irena greet each other by saying 'Good afternoon'. Jeff, Irena and Peter greet each other by saying 'How do you do'.

Irena introduces Peter by saying 'Can I introduce . . .'.

1.4 Listen and read

The advantages of the new site are: 'it's quite big'; 'it's got good access to the motorway'; 'it's fairly cheap'.

There are two buildings on the new site: 'this large building that you see in front of you, plus a separate, much smaller, building round the back'.

1.5 Structure practice

1–4 are model answers; there are a number of possible answers.

1 (Answer given in text.)
2 As you may know, we're going to look at the site.
3 As you might know, Keypoint specialises in security services.
4 As you probably know, Midland Furniture is planning to expand.
5 (Answer given in text.)
6 Do you know how old this building is?
7 Do you know where the trucks will enter?
8 Do you know what Midland Furniture makes?
9 Do you know which countries they export to?

1.6 Listen and write

In 1.7 they are standing in the yard, **B**, when Jeff says 'This is where the trucks will come to load and unload.'

In 1.9 they are standing in the store room area, **C**, when Peter says 'According to the plan of the factory, this is going to be the store room, is that right?'

In 1.11 they are standing in the machine shop area, **D**, when Jeff says 'This will be the machine shop'.

In 1.13 they are standing on the second floor of the office block, **A**, when Jeff says 'Upstairs, here on the top floor, . . . '.

1.7 Listen and read

The problems are: 'a lot of trucks going in and out'; the position of the fuel store; 'a lot of outside pipes, and outside doors'.

1.8 Find the word

a block **b** floors **c** canteen **d** room
e toilets **f** room **g** offices **h** room
i shop **j** area

1.9 Listen and read

Jeff shows that he is not giving exact figures by saying 'Just a few' and 'very roughly'. Also, the way he gives the number 'three, three hundred and fifty thousand' shows that he is not being exact about the value of the stock, and he emphasises that by saying 'I should think' afterwards.

1.10 Speaking practice

1 (Answer given in text.)
2 About thirty metres.
3 Around sixty metres.
4 Roughly thirty metres long and ten metres wide.
5 About 15.
6 Roughly three hundred and fifty thousand pounds.

1.11 Listen and read

Irena and Peter show that they are uncertain by saying 'sort of', 'I suppose' and 'I imagine'.

1.12 Structure practice

a (nothing)
b a
c (nothing)
d (nothing)
e an
f the

1.13 Listen and read

Jeff lists eleven offices and rooms: the reception area, the staff canteen, the toilets, the rest room, the first-aid room, the open-plan office for the secretaries and computer operators, the boardroom, Jeff's office, two offices for department heads, and the boss's office.

1.14 Writing practice

These are model answers; there are many possible answers.

1 Introduction
(Answer given in text.)

2 Location and general description
The factory is located on the Farm Lane Industrial Estate. It occupies a corner site of about 4000 square metres. There are two buildings, the main factory and a small fuel store round the back. The main building is of single-storey construction, except for the office block, which has three floors and a basement.

3 Proposed use
The factory will be used for making furniture. Midland will use a lot of new computer-controlled equipment. Trucks will deliver wood to the store room, and then furniture to the customers, often as kits.

4 Security: strong and weak points
4.1 Strong points:
 1 massive gates
 2 whole site visible from top floor of office block
4.2 Weak points:
 1 poor fence
 2 many outside pipes and outside doors; easy to climb onto roof or break into factory
 3 fuel store too close to garage
 4 large numbers of trucks going in and out

5 Recommendations
5.1 The property should be surrounded by a strong fence.
5.2 A closed-circuit TV camera should be used to check that people are not trying to enter the building.
5.3 The fuel store should be moved away from the garage, or it should be made fireproof.
5.4 There should be security guards on duty at the site at all times.

Unit 2: The firm

SITUATION

In this unit, we look in more detail at Keypoint Security (UK) Ltd, and especially at the organisation of the company. Peter Jackson, the young management trainee, is given the task of finding out how the company works. We look at how decisions are made and how information is communicated within the company, and at some aspects of its finances. We also look at how meetings are arranged and conducted.

CHARACTERS

Irena Phillips

Peter Jackson

Sarah Street

Secretary at Keypoint Security Ltd.

Michael Vincey is Managing Director of Keypoint Security Ltd.

Bert Field is Production Manager for Keypoint Security Ltd.

Harry Dent, Andy Scuff, Jane Parget and Mary Wilford all work at Keypoint Security Ltd.

All of these characters are British.

LANGUAGE

Vocabulary	Company departments and managers; shareholders and directors; shares, investments and takeovers; incentives.
Skills	Giving instructions; making an appointment; running a meeting; writing a company profile.
Structures	Figures with decimal points; each/every/all.
Documents	An organisation chart; a financial report; an agenda; notes.

Finding out about company organisation

2.1
a week or so a week or a little longer.
a company profile a short description of the company.
I tell you what I've just had an idea.

2.2
I'll pencil it in I'll write it in pencil in case I have to change it later; the secretary has to check the meeting with Mr McTam before she can confirm it with Peter.

2.3
reports to is responsible to; if Peter reports to Irena, then Irena is his manager.
a director someone elected by the shareholders to run a company; a director may also be a manager.
the board the group of directors of a company; also called **the board of directors**.
R&D research and development.

2.1 Listen and read

Irena Phillips is in her office talking to Peter. Listen to what they say. What instructions does Irena give Peter?

IRENA Now, Peter! Management trainees are supposed to make themselves familiar with every department of the company. As you've only been with us *a week or so*, I think you might find it useful to write *a company profile*. Visit all the department heads. Introduce yourself. Find out everything you can about how the company's organised, how each department operates. *I tell you what*. How would you like to write a short report for me, say by the end of the week?

PETER Yes, of course. How long should the report be?

IRENA Oh, two thousand words should do it. Would you like to make a start now, and I'll get on with my report on Midland Furniture!

2.2 Speaking practice: making an appointment

Peter has to make appointments to see all the department heads. To do this, he telephones their secretaries. Listen to what they say. When you hear it the second time, there will be pauses. You speak the part of Peter.

PETER Good morning. My name's Peter Jackson, I'm the new management trainee. I wonder if you can help me. I'd like to make an appointment to see Mr McTam.

SECRETARY Let me have a look at his diary. How long will this meeting take?

PETER It shouldn't take more than half an hour, I don't think.

SECRETARY Well, if it's only half an hour I could fit you in at half past three this afternoon. How would that suit you?

PETER Oh, I've already got a meeting this afternoon. Could he manage Monday at half past eleven?

SECRETARY Yes, I think so. *I'll pencil it in* for 11.30, and confirm it with you when I've spoken to Mr McTam.

PETER OK, that's great. Thank you very much!

2.3 Document study

The chart below shows the organisational structure of Keypoint Security. Study it carefully, and re-read 2.1. Then write the words missing from the text.

Irena Phillips is the Client Services Manager. She *reports to* the ___**a**___ Director, who, as *a director* of the company, ___**b**___ to the ___**c**___. The ___**d**___ Managers report to the Production Manager, who is their ___**e**___ head, but who is not on *the board*. He therefore reports to the ___**f**___ Director, Michael Vincey, who is also the company Chairman.

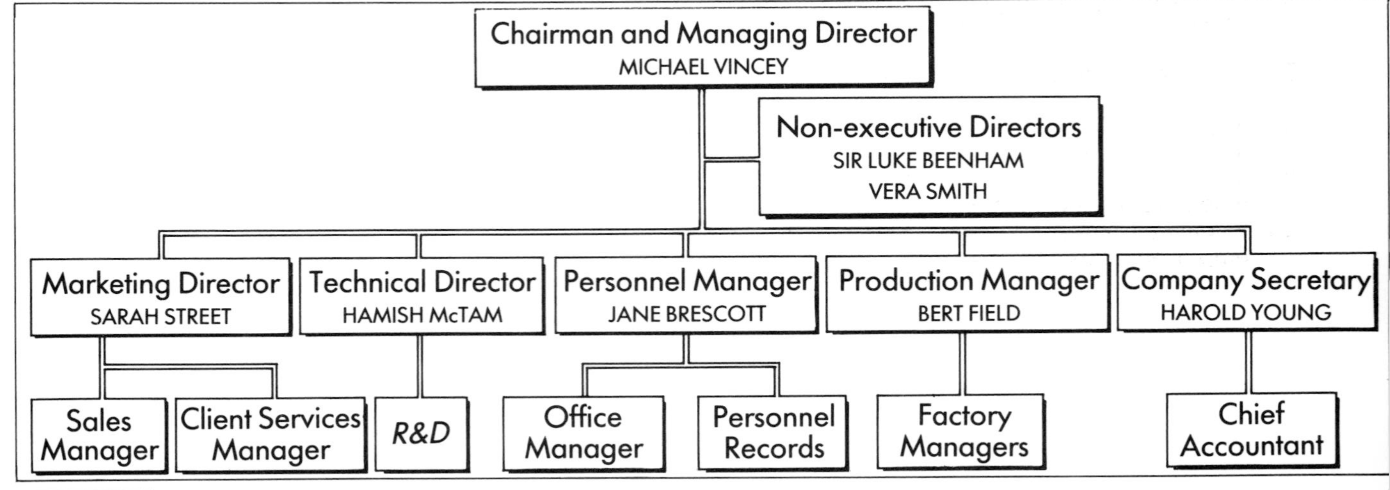

2.4 Listen and read

Sarah Street shows the chart to Peter, but she also explains to him how she thinks the company could work more efficiently. Listen to what they say. Notice how Peter questions Sarah to try to find out exactly what she means.

SARAH We ought to be thinking in terms of little groups of people, each group doing one particular job, and all the groups interlocking.

PETER But each group must have a leader, surely?

SARAH Yes, but that's the whole point! Not necessarily the same person all the time. If you're assigned to a particular project, then you're the group leader for that project, because you know more about it than anyone else.

PETER So why do we need a head of marketing, or a head of any other department?

SARAH Because that's responsibility, not leadership. Whatever happens in marketing, I'm *ultimately responsible*. To Mike Vincey and to the shareholders. That doesn't mean I have to *chair* every meeting. I know – as part of your research, why don't you *sit in on* the management meeting this afternoon?

2.4
ultimately responsible Sarah means that, to Michael Vincey, she must take the blame or the credit for all the work done by any of her staff.
chair be the chairperson of; **chair** is also used for **chairman** or **chairwoman** if you don't know whether it is a man or a woman; you can also use **chairperson**.
sit in on be present at but not take part in.

2.5 Reading for key words

Find the words or phrases in 2.1 and 2.3 that tell you the following:

1 Peter has not worked for Keypoint for very long.
2 Irena is not sure how Peter will react to the task she has set him.

In the Keypoint organisation chart, which department heads are responsible for the following?

3 the company's accounts.
4 finding out what new products are needed to meet the clients' needs.
5 developing these products so that they are ready to be sold.

2.6 Directing the internal post

As part of his training, Peter spends some time in the post room. He is given a number of letters addressed simply to 'Keypoint Security Ltd'. The subjects of the letters are listed below. Write down the name of the department or the title of the person Peter should send each letter to.

SUBJECT:	SEND TO:
1 a request for information about the company's services.	
2 an application for a job as an electrical engineer.	
3 an invitation to send a representative to an official reception in the Town Hall.	
4 a copy of a scientific paper about infra-red security systems.	
5 a doctor's certificate: an employee will be absent from work for at least six months.	
6 an urgent request from the company representative in Edinburgh for 500 copies of the company's catalogue.	
7 the third reminder requesting payment of an invoice for £1340, six months overdue.	
8 a Christmas card, three months late, no signature, addressed to 'Jimmy'.	
9 a complaint that a client's alarm failed to operate when premises were burgled.	
10 a leaflet from a local garage, offering to service employees' cars at discount prices.	

Discussing the company's position

KEYPOINT SECURITY (UK) LTD

Industrial and domestic security specialists

Ordinary capital £1.25m (market value £6.1m)
25p ordinary share: market price 122p

Year to 30 April	Turnover £m	Pre-tax profit £m	Earnings per share p	Dividend p
1989	6.5	0.4	3.01	0.88
1990	18.2	2.7	9.36	4.82
1991	19.6	2.9	10.10	5.88
1992*	16.7	1.3	7.11	3.75

**estimated*

Keypoint's first-half performance was *extremely promising* but a downturn in sales in the second half of the year is likely *to hit profits*. The company could be *vulnerable* to a takeover bid if whole-year results lead to shares being undervalued.

INVESTMENT **GUIDE** 14 March 1992 | **15**

2.7 Speaking practice: talking figures

Read this extract from a weekly magazine called 'Investment Guide'. Write down the answers to the questions below. Then listen to the questions, and say your answers.

Note that in English a full stop is used for the decimals, not a comma. Figures after the decimal point must be read separately: 'five point eight eight'.

1. What was the dividend in 1991?
   The dividend in 1991 was 5.88p.
2. What was the turnover in 1989?
3. What was the pre-tax profit in 1990?
4. What were the earnings per share in 1989?
5. What's the estimated turnover for 1992?
6. Which was the best year for Keypoint?

2.8 Find the word

Read the text below on starting a business. Fill in the gaps with words from the box. If you're not sure of the meaning of any of the words, look them up in the glossary.

capital	dividend
earnings	profit
shares	turnover

To start a business, you need ___**a**___ – that is, money. You can borrow it; or you can sell parts of your company – equal parts, of course. These are called ___**b**___, and the people who buy them become shareholders. They expect to get something in return for their investment. If the company does well, it pays a ___**c**___ on each share. The value of the shares (of a public company) can rise, so that their market price is often much higher than the amount printed on the share certificate – though it may fall below it if the company does badly.

Serious investors read *the financial press*. They want to know not only the share prices but how much money a company has taken from its customers during the past year (its ___**d**___), how much of that money is left when all costs have been paid (the company's ___**e**___), and the result of dividing that amount by the number of shares (___**f**___ per share).

2.9 Listen and read

Michael Vincey is the Managing Director of Keypoint. The weekly management committee meeting is about to begin, around the table in his office. Listen to what they say. Who is chairing this meeting? How do you know?

MICHAEL Good afternoon, everyone. You've all got in front of you the *agenda* for this afternoon's meeting, but before we start discussing that, there's a piece about us in this week's 'Investment Guide'. Sarah pointed it out to me this morning – anyone else seen it?

BERT Yes, I did, but shouldn't we discuss this under *any other business*?

SARAH But it's important! We'll never *get round to it* under any other business!

MICHAEL OK, OK, I know it's not on the agenda, Bert, but Sarah's right, this is an important issue. I propose that we deal with it *under item five*, proposals for this month's board meeting.

SARAH Well, all right, as long as it's discussed sometime.

MICHAEL Right. Can we start, then, with item one, last month's sales figures?

2.7
extremely promising showing signs that it is likely to be very good.
to hit profits to reduce profits.
vulnerable weak, and unable to resist.

2.8
the financial press the newspapers and magazines that specialise in business and economics.

2.9
(an) agenda a list of things to be discussed at a meeting.
any other business on an agenda, usually the last item where additional things can be discussed if there is time.
get round to it have time to talk about it.
under item five things on an agenda are always called **items**; you talk about something **under** an **item**.

2.10 Structure practice: *each*, *every* and *all*

Read again the dialogues and documents in this unit. Look for examples of the words 'each', 'every' and 'all'.

'Each' and 'every' are used before singular nouns: 'each department', 'every meeting'. The difference between 'each' and 'every' is not very great. You can use 'each' when you are thinking about the separate members of the group, and 'every' when you are thinking more of the group as a whole:

Each department is trying to cut its costs.
The company is trying to cut costs in every department.

'All' is used before plural nouns, and before uncountable nouns: 'all the departments', 'all the information'. Its meaning is very similar to 'every':

They're trying to cut costs in all departments.

Fill in the gaps below with 'each', 'every' or 'all'. In some cases, there may be more than one possible answer; the one in the answer key is the one that most English speakers would probably use.

1 Did you give those reports to the directors?
Yes, I gave one to ______ director.
2 Did you check the copies to make sure they were complete?
Yes, I checked ______ the copies.
3 And did you send them the agenda?
Yes, I circulated the agenda to ______ the directors.
4 Have you got any more details about the takeover?
No, I've given you ______ the information I had.
5 ______ letter that is sent to Keypoint goes to the post room.
6 The letters for ______ department are put together in a box on the post-room trolley.
7 When ______ the letters have been sorted they are taken round the building and delivered.

2.11
rumours are going around people are talking about things that may or may not be true.
the image of the company the way the company appears, or would like to appear, to its staff, its customers and the public.
a hostile bid a takeover bid that the company does not welcome.
can I bring you in on this? Michael Vincey invites Peter to talk because, up until then, Peter has only been sitting in on the meeting, not taking part in it.

2.11 Listen and read

The management meeting at Keypoint continues. Listen to how Michael Vincey keeps the discussion moving forwards.

MICHAEL Good, that's agreed then. Can we press on? Item five, proposals for the next board meeting, which I would remind you is a week on Wednesday. Er – Sarah, I think there was something you wanted to . . .

SARAH Yes, Michael. As I think most of us are aware, *rumours are going around* about takeover bids. Now this may or may not be good news for the shareholders, but I can assure you, it's very damaging for *the image of the company*. What I would . . .

BERT With respect, Mr Chairman, I don't think we should waste time discussing rumours. There's always a risk of *a hostile bid*. It can happen to anyone at any time.

MICHAEL Let's not start arguing until we've got some facts to argue with. Peter, *can I bring you in on this*? You've been doing some research on takeovers. What was your reaction to the piece in the 'Investment Guide'?

PETER Er – well – I'm not quite sure what we're discussing at the moment. Are we talking about defending the company against a hostile bid? Or promoting its image?

Talking about incentives

2.12
I suppose I think you must have, but I don't know.
You're joking! Bert finds Peter's suggestion very difficult to believe.
hang on to keep.
get in touch with contact.
staff note that **staff** can be used with a singular or a plural verb.

2.13
I wouldn't mind I would like; Harry is using understatement here.
The thing is Harry is saying that he is now going to comment on what he has just said.
That's my idea of an incentive! that's what I think is a good incentive.
That's typical of Jane is criticising the company; she is saying that they have behaved as badly as they always do, in her opinion.

2.12 Listen and read

The management meeting continues. Again, listen to how Michael Vincey keeps the discussion moving forwards.

PETER Are we talking about defending the company against a hostile bid? Or promoting its image?

SARAH Well, both really.

PETER Hm. Well. I don't know. Er – you already have some kind of share bonus scheme, *I suppose*? Giving shares to employees if they achieve their objectives?

BERT *You're joking!* Another incentive scheme?

MICHAEL Not now, Bert. Go on, Peter.

PETER I know what Bert means, but this isn't just rewarding people for effort. This is making employees into shareholders – making them loyal to the company. They know if there's a takeover bid they can do something about it. They can *hang on to* their shares.

SARAH Well, why don't we propose it to the board?

MICHAEL Yes, I think perhaps we should do that. But before we do, I think I'll *get in touch with* the company's lawyers and accountants. Peter, perhaps you could find out what members of the *staff* think about a share bonus scheme.

2.13 Listen and read

Peter goes to ask people in Keypoint what they think about a share bonus scheme. Listen to what they say. How many people are in favour of the scheme?

HARRY DENT (storeman)
Yes, *I wouldn't mind* having a few shares. *The thing is*, of course, if you give them to one person, you've more or less got to give them to everyone, haven't you? Otherwise you get bad feeling among the staff.

ANDY SCUFF (salesman)
Shares? No thank you! If they want to give us incentives, why don't they charter an aeroplane and take us all for a week's holiday in Majorca? *That's my idea of an incentive!*

JANE PARGET (computer operator)
That's typical of this firm. No communication. I wrote a great long memo to Mike Vincey six weeks ago, explaining a brilliant scheme of mine. Never even had an acknowledgement!

MARY WILFORD (quality control)
Yes, I think it would be a good idea for us all to have shares, because if there's a takeover bid, the share price usually goes up, doesn't it, so we can sell our shares and make a bit of money that way.

2.14 Reading for key words

Find the words or phrases in 2.12 and 2.13 that tell you that:

1 Peter is 'playing for time' and trying to think what he should say.
2 the incentive schemes Keypoint has now do not work.
3 giving an unequal number of shares to employees may cause trouble.
4 a memo sent to Michael Vincey did not get a reply.

2.15 Document study: an agenda

The directors of Keypoint meet once a month. This is the list of matters that they will discuss at their next meeting. Which of these items will probably be on the agenda of every meeting? Why is Mrs Phillips asked to attend for only one item?

AGENDA

for the meeting of the Board of Directors
Wednesday 25 March 1992
at 3.00 p.m. in the boardroom

1 Apologies for absence.
2 *Minutes* of the meeting of 26 February 1992.
3 *Matters arising* from the Minutes.
4 Reports of Chairman, Marketing Director, Company Secretary and Technical Director.
5 Client services (Mrs Phillips to attend for this item).
6 Productivity bonuses and incentives.
7 Dates of meetings during 1993-94.
8 Arrangements for Directors' Annual Dinner (September).
9 Any other business.

Items of other business must be notified to the *Company Secretary* in writing before the start of the meeting.

The meeting will end not later than 6 p.m.

2.15
(the) Minutes the written record of a meeting.
Matters arising things that have happened since the last meeting concerning something that was discussed then.
(a) Company Secretary a company director who is responsible for calling the board meetings and officially recording the board's decisions; this is not the same person who takes the minutes of a meeting, and who may be the secretary of one of the directors.

2.17
Resolved agreed.

2.16 Writing practice: the company profile

Peter still has to write his company profile for Irena Phillips (see 2.1). These are his notes. Use them to write the first two paragraphs of his report.

Start with five sentences based directly on Peter's notes.

Then start a new paragraph: 'The company is organised as follows'.

Then write full-sentence answers to each of these questions (see 2.3). Remember that your sentences can be quite short – some of them may be only four or five words long:

How many directors are there? How many of them are non-executive?
Who holds the post of Chairman and Managing Director?
How many departments is the work of the company divided among?
Who is the Company Secretary?
Who are the other heads of departments?
Who do all the department heads report to?

This, of course, is only the beginning of Peter's report; but it is all we are concerned with here. Using this as a model, try to write a profile of the organisation you work for, or any other organisation you know.

KEYPOINT LTD

- Industrial and domestic security specialists: security equipment, burglar alarms etc; also security patrols, safe deposit facilities, deliveries of cash, wage packets, valuables.
- public company, established 1985
- head office and factory: Stevenage
- employees: about 350
- company organisation (see chart)

2.17 Listen and read

In Irena's office, a few days after the board meeting, she is reading from a copy of the minutes. Listen to what she says. The minutes are written in very formal language. Did the board agree that the share bonus scheme was a good idea?

IRENA Listen, this is from the minutes:
Resolved: That the company's lawyers be approached at once with a view to setting up a share bonus scheme within the company – target date for start of scheme: September 1993.

Study record	
2.1	
2.2	
2.3	
2.4	
2.5	
2.6	
2.7	
2.8	
2.9	
2.10	
2.11	
2.12	
2.13	
2.14	
2.15	
2.16	
2.17	

Answer key and commentary for unit 2

2.1 Listen and read

Irena gives Peter the following instructions: 'write a company profile'; 'visit all the department heads'; 'introduce yourself'; 'find out everything you can about how the company's organised'; 'write a short report'; 'make a start now'. Some of these instructions are phrased very politely.

2.3 Document study

a Marketing **b** reports **c** Chairman
d Factory **e** department **f** Managing

2.4 Listen and read

Peter questions Sarah by starting his response to her with 'But' and ending it with 'surely'.

2.5 Reading for key words

1 . . . you've only been with us a week or so
2 How would you like to . . .
3 Harold Young (Company Secretary)
4 Sarah Street (Marketing Director)
5 Hamish McTam (Technical Director)

2.6 Directing the internal post

1 The Client Services Manager
2 The Personnel Manager
3 The Managing Director
4 The Technical Director
5 Personnel Records
6 The Sales Manager
7 The Chief Accountant
8 The wastepaper basket!
9 The Client Services Manager
10 The Office Manager

2.7 Speaking practice

1 (Answer given in text.)
2 The turnover in nineteen eighty-nine was six point five million.
3 The pre-tax profit in nineteen ninety was two point seven million.
4 The earnings per share in nineteen eighty-nine were three point oh one pence.
5 The estimated turnover for nineteen ninety-two is sixteen point seven million.
6 The best year for Keypoint was nineteen ninety-one.

2.8 Find the word

a capital **b** shares **c** dividend
d turnover **e** profit **f** earnings

2.9 Listen and read

Michael Vincey is chairing the meeting. We know this because he greets everyone with 'Good afternoon, everyone', and because he says 'Can we start . . .'.

2.10 Structure practice

1 Yes, I gave one to **each** director.
2 Yes, I checked **all** the copies.
3 Yes, I circulated the agenda to **all** the directors.
4 No, I've given you **all** the information I had.
5 **Every** letter that is sent to Keypoint goes to the post room.
6 The letters for **each** department are put together in a box on the post-room trolley.
7 When **all** the letters have been sorted they are taken round the building and delivered.

2.11 Listen and read

Michael keeps the discussion moving forwards by saying 'Can we press on?', and then inviting people to speak: 'Sarah, I think there was something you wanted to . . .' and 'Peter, can I bring you in on this?'

2.12 Listen and read

Michael keeps the discussion moving forwards by saying 'Go on, Peter.'

2.13 Listen and read

Two of the people are in favour of the scheme: Harry Dent and Mary Wilford. Andy Scuff is against it, and we don't know about Jane Parget.

2.14 Reading for key words

1 Hm. Well. I don't know. Er – . . .
2 You're joking! Another incentive scheme?
3 you've more or less got to give them to everyone . . . Otherwise you get bad feeling among the staff.
4 I wrote a great long memo . . . Never even had an acknowledgement!

2.15 Document study

Items 1, 2, 3, 4 and 9 will probably be on the agenda for every meeting.

Mrs Phillips does not attend the whole meeting because she is not a director and member of the board. She is invited to attend for one item because it concerns her department.

2.16 Writing practice

This is a model answer.

> KEYPOINT LTD
> This is my report on the structure and organisation of Keypoint Limited. It sells security equipment, burglar alarms, etc. It also offers services, such as security patrols, safe deposit facilities and deliveries of cash, wage packets and valuables. It is a public company, and was established in 1985. Its head office and factory are located at Stevenage.
>
> The company is organised as follows: there are six directors. Two of them are non-executive. The post of Chairman and Managing Director is held by Michael Vincey. The work of the company is divided among five departments. The Company Secretary is Harold Young. The other heads of departments are Sarah Street (Marketing), Hamish McTam (Technical), Janet Brescott (Personnel) and Bert Field (Production). All the department heads report to the Managing Director.

2.17 Listen and read

Yes, the board did agree.

Unit 3: Appointments and applications

SITUATION

Industrias Montresor is a company based in Zaragoza, in northern Spain. It manufactures heavy machinery for the chemical industry. Every department in Montresor uses computers, and as the organisation grows, the computer systems grow with it. Montresor now decides that it needs a Divisional Software Engineering Manager. This unit is about finding the right person for this job.

CHARACTERS

Joe Andrews	is Staff Controller at Industrias Montresor, Zaragoza, Spain. He is American.
Pilar Soto	is Data Manager at Industrias Montresor. She is Spanish.
Carlos Vila	is Senior Software Development Engineer at Topdown Software, Consett, County Durham, England. He is Spanish.
Helen Tomlinson	is Manager of the Industrial Clients Department at Topdown Software. She is Carlos Vila's manager. She is British.

LANGUAGE

Vocabulary	Job descriptions; job advertisements.
Skills	Making a telephone call; writing a business letter; applying for a job; asking for and giving a reference.
Structures	Dates; in/from/for.
Documents	A job description; a job advertisement; a comparison chart; a c.v.; a letter of application; a reference request; a reference.

Describing the job – drafting the advertisement

3.1
I'm returning your call Joe had telephoned Pilar earlier, when she was not in her office. He left a message asking her to call him back.
have a chat about have an informal conversation about; this is not a formal meeting.
jotted down written a note by hand; Pilar expects to make changes before she shows them to Joe.

3.2
in good operational condition in good working order.
liaising with working with and exchanging information.
applications the word **application** is used in two different meanings in this unit. A **job application** is a form or letter you send when you want a job; a **computer application** is a particular task that a computer is used for.

3.3
take a seat, won't you? please sit down.
(a) draft an early version of something written, that you expect to change later.
That's more your line that's your area of responsibility and knowledge.
a postgraduate qualification a qualification you work for after you already have a degree.
they must be fluent/their first assignment both Joe and Pilar are using the plural forms **they** and **their**, even though they are talking about only one person, because they don't know if that person will be a man or a woman. This is quite common in speech, but not used in formal writing.

3.1 Speaking practice: returning a call

Joe Andrews is Staff Controller at Industrias Montresor in Spain. Pilar Soto calls him on the telephone. Listen to what they say. When you hear it the second time, there will be pauses. You speak the part of Pilar Soto.

JOE	Extension 7385: Joe Andrews speaking.
PILAR	Good morning, Joe. It's Pilar Soto. *I'm returning your call.*
JOE	Oh, hello, Pilar. That's right, there was something I wanted to ask you about. That new software engineering post.
PILAR	Yes, indeed. We need to appoint someone pretty soon.
JOE	Right. Do you want to come and *have a chat about* the job description?
PILAR	Well, I've *jotted down* a few ideas. I'll tidy them up and get them typed and you can have a look at them.

3.2 Document study

Pilar Soto is Data Manager at Industrias Montresor. This is what her notes looked like when they had been typed. Notice how careful she is to say exactly what the new employee will have to do.

Draft job description:
Divisional Software Engineering Manager (DSEM)

The DSEM is responsible to the Data Manager for:

1 ensuring that all software used by the Corporation is maintained *in good operational condition* at all times.
2 maintaining the strictest security with regard to computer programs.
3 *liaising with* manufacturers and consultants in keeping software up to date and in overcoming problems or errors in programs.
4 writing new programs, *applications*, etc. as required.

3.3 Listen and read

Joe Andrews and Pilar Soto meet to discuss the qualifications and experience they are looking for in the new software manager. Listen to what they say. Make notes of what they want, under the headings 'essential' and 'desirable'. You will need these notes for 3.7.

JOE	Come in, Pilar – *take a seat, won't you?* Thanks for your *draft* of the job description – it looks OK to me – what we need to do now is to draft the advertisement.
PILAR	Yes. *That's more your line,* of course. But I can tell you something about the qualifications we'll be looking for.
JOE	Previous experience?
PILAR	Well, to start with, a degree in computing – preferably *a postgraduate qualification* – plus at least three years' experience.
JOE	Mhm. Need that be in the chemical industry?
PILAR	We can't afford to be that specific. We just need a good software engineer.
JOE	Right. How old should he be?
PILAR	Joe, it needn't be a 'he'.
JOE	Sorry! What's the top age limit?
PILAR	Just say 'the successful applicant is likely to be under thirty-five'.
JOE	And *they must be fluent* in English, I suppose.
PILAR	Oh yes, that's essential, because whoever gets the job, *their first assignment* is going to be a training course in Japan.

3.4 Document study

This is the advertisement that appeared in several daily newspapers and specialist journals. Which of the items discussed by Joe Andrews and Pilar Soto (in 3.3) appear in the advertisement?

> # DIVISIONAL SOFTWARE ENGINEERING MANAGER . . .
>
> *. . . rapid career development for a high-flier . . .*
>
> INDUSTRIAS MONTRESOR is an expanding multinational corporation, active in chemical engineering and marketing its products and services to the petro-chemical industry. Our West European Division, located in Zaragoza, Spain, is urgently seeking an ambitious Software Engineer to build and take charge of an enthusiastic team.
>
> The successful applicant is likely to be under 35 and to have an outstanding *track record* in the field of software engineering (not necessarily relating to the chemical industry). *He or she* currently holds a post of responsibility at middle management level and is fluent in Spanish and English. A postgraduate qualification will be an advantage.
>
> *Salary negotiable.* Expense allowance, company car, generous fringe benefits.
>
> Apply with c.v. and names of two referees to:
> Dept. F, Industrias Montresor SA, Apdo 234, Zaragoza, Spain, before 17 January 1992.
>
> INDUSTRIAS MONTRESOR

3.4
(a) track record a list of the achievements, or failures, of a person or business.
He or she because this is a formal document, Joe has used **he or she**, and not **they**.
salary negotiable the salary is not fixed, but can be discussed with the applicant.

3.5 Reading for key words

Find the words or phrases in 3.1–3.4 that tell you the following:

1 Joe and Pilar have already discussed the software engineering post.
2 There is a risk of computer programs being stolen or deliberately damaged.
3 It may be difficult to find someone who is exactly suitable for the job.
4 Industrias Montresor operates in several countries, and is getting bigger.
5 The company needs a software engineer who is also a good leader.
6 Whoever gets this job can expect to be promoted quickly.

3.6 Find the word

Read the text below on recruitment. Fill the gaps with words from the box. If you're not sure of the meaning of any of the words, you will find them in the glossary.

Most companies recruit new staff by advertising in the press. Pages with job ___**a**___ are usually headed '___**b**___'. They contain descriptions or specifications of the sort of people the advertiser is looking for. ___**c**___ (degrees, diplomas, certificates) are obviously important, but ___**d**___ may count for much more. The aim is to attract a small number of well-qualified applicants, so that it is fairly easy to make a shortlist of the people you actually want to ___**e**___. If the advertisement is not specific enough, hundreds of people will send in their ___**f**___; but if it demands too much, they may be discouraged from applying at all.

advertisements applications appointments experience interview qualifications

3.7 Sorting out the applicants

Joe Andrews reads hundreds of applications each year. He has a printed form which he and Pilar use to help them choose who to interview. Write the qualifications and experience they are looking for, first the most important, then the less important. The notes you made for 3.3 will be useful here.

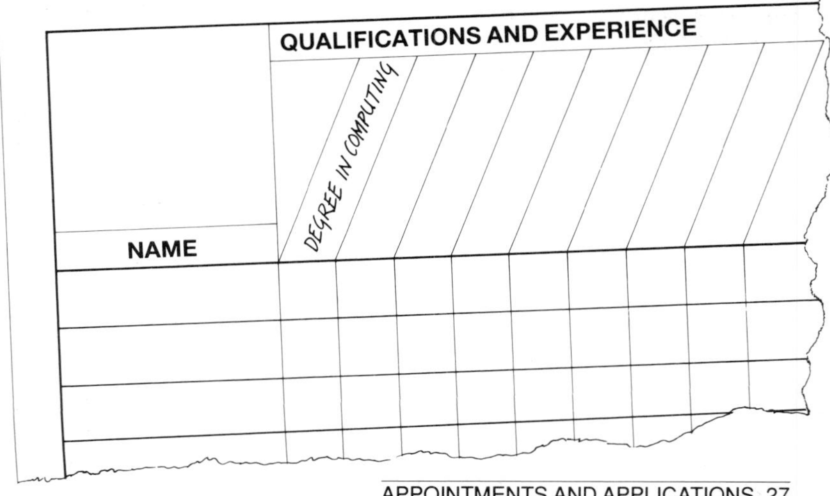

Putting in your application

3.9
(a) deadline the date by which all of the applications should have been received.

3.10
date of birth this is the exact day and year that someone was born; it is not their **birthday**, which they have each year.
As time is short as we do not have very much time.

3.8 Structure practice: writing and speaking dates

You will see and hear a lot of dates on these pages. Listen to the dates below being spoken and then practise saying them.

1 March 1988 'the first of March nineteen eighty-eight'
17 November 1990 'the seventeenth of November nineteen ninety'
2 June 1995 'the second of June nineteen ninety-five'

You could also say:

'March the first', 'November the seventeenth', 'June the second'

In America, and sometimes in Britain, dates are written like this, with the month first: November 17 1990; June 2 1995. Be careful! Dates are sometimes written in number form only: 3.7.90. In Britain this would mean 'the third of July nineteen ninety'; in America, and on many computers, it would mean 'the seventh of March nineteen ninety'.

3.9 Listen and read

Carlos Vila is a Spanish computer programmer working in Britain. He saw the Industrias Montresor advertisement after the closing date, but he thought he would telephone Joe Andrews anyway. Listen to what they say. Is Carlos too late?

JOE Joe Andrews speaking.
CARLOS Good morning. My name is Carlos Vila. I've just seen an advertisement in the 'International Herald Tribune'. It said you were looking for a Divisional Software Engineering Manager. I'm very interested, but I wonder if it's too late to apply.
JOE Well, the *deadline* was two days ago, but give me some details about yourself. What did you say your name was?
CARLOS Vila – Carlos Vila Monterde.
JOE Could you spell that, please – surname first.
CARLOS Vila, V-I-L-A. Monterde, M-O-N, T-E-R-D-E. First name, Carlos, C-A-R, L-O-S.

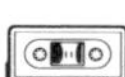

3.10 Speaking practice: talking about yourself

Joe and Carlos continue their conversation. Joe's part of the conversation is printed below. Listen to what they say, then listen again and speak the part of Carlos. To help you, the information that Carlos gives is printed on his c.v. in 3.11.

JOE OK, Mr Vila. Now, can we have your *date of birth*?
CARLOS ______**a**______
JOE And what about your education? – secondary education, I mean.
CARLOS ______**b**______
JOE Uh-huh. What qualification did you get when you finished school?
CARLOS ______**c**______
JOE I see. Where did you go then?
CARLOS ______**d**______
JOE Yes, I suppose everyone has to, don't they? What about further education?
CARLOS ______**e**______
JOE And that led to – a degree?
CARLOS ______**f**______
JOE And when you finished that, you started work?
CARLOS ______**g**______
JOE Oh, so it's Doctor Vila, is it? What year did you finish your PhD?
CARLOS ______**h**______
JOE What then?
CARLOS ______**i**______
JOE Did you? But then, I suppose, you started work. What company did you go to first?
CARLOS ______**j**______
JOE What post did you hold?
CARLOS ______**k**______
JOE OK. What other companies have you worked for?
CARLOS ______**l**______
JOE Mm, interesting. I think we'd certainly like to have your c.v., Dr Vila. *As time is short*, why don't you fax it to us today or tomorrow? I'll put your name on our list of applicants.

3.11 Document study: writing your c.v. – 1

This is the c.v. that Carlos sent to Joe Andrews. He also sent a handwritten covering letter.

There are many 'right' ways to write a c.v. Carlos has made his short and simple. He knows that all business documents must be easy to read and understand. That is why he has divided it into sections and tabulated it: the main headings are on the left of the page, the sub-headings a little further to the right. We can see at once where each section starts and ends.

You will find more about writing c.v.s in 4.11.

CURRICULUM VITAE

(A) PERSONAL INFORMATION

name: Carlos VILA Monterde
home address: Calle Sta Ana 47, Apt. 12a, Madrid, Spain
present address: Flat 7, 26 Newcastle Road, Consett, County Durham, DU4 3ME, England
date and place of birth: 13.5.61 in Santander, Spain
nationality: Spanish
sex: male
marital status: single

(B) EDUCATION

secondary education:
1976-79 Senior High School in Santander
High School Graduation Certificate
further education:
1979-80 military service
1980-85 University of Zaragoza:
BSc in Computer Studies
1985-87 University of Madrid:
PhD in Systems Engineering

(C) EMPLOYMENT

1990- Topdown Systems, UK: Client Consultant (promoted to Senior Software Development Engineer, July 1991)
1989-90 Imprimerie Ledoux, Paris: Control Systems Supervisor
1988-89 Franco-Italian Bank, Milan: Systems Analyst
1987-88 I took a year off and, with some friends, sailed round the world in a 12-metre sailing cruiser.

current salary: equivalent to $48,000 plus car and bonuses

(D) OTHER INFORMATION

languages: Spanish (native)
French, English (fluent, spoken/written)
Italian (fairly fluent)

(E) REFEREES

Mrs Helen Tomlinson
Manager, Industrial Clients Department
Topdown Systems Ltd
Unit 37, Medomsley Road
Consett, County Durham DU11 5AE,
England

[names of other referees will be supplied on request]

Flat 7, 26 Newcastle Road
Consett
Co Durham DU4 3ME
England

21 January 1992

Mr Andrews
Staff Controller
Industrias Montresor
Apdo 234
Zaragoza, Spain

Dear Mr Andrews

Application for the post of Divisional Software Engineering Manager.

Further to our telephone conversation this morning, I can confirm that I wish to apply for this post. I enclose a copy of my cv.

You will see that I have added the name of one of my referees, Mrs Helen Tomlinson. You may contact her at any time. If you require other referees, perhaps you will be so kind as to let me know.

I can come to Zaragoza for interview at almost any time, provided I have at least three days' notice.

Yours sincerely

Carlos Vila.

3.12 Structure practice: prepositions of time

The most common prepositions of time are 'in', 'from' and 'for':

in 1984 in March 1993
from 1976 from April to June from 14 December
for three years

Re-read the dialogues and documents in this unit, then answer the questions below, using 'in', 'from' or 'for'. Use the information from Carlos's c.v. in your answers. There are many possible answers; the answer key gives one typical answer for each question.

1 How long have you been working for Topdown Systems?
2 When were you in Italy?
3 I see that you did military service. When was that?
4 Have you travelled much?
5 You've lived in Zaragoza before, haven't you?
6 When did you live in Santander?
7 How long were you in Paris?
8 When were you at university?

Asking for and writing a reference

3.13
have a quick word have a short conversation.
officially Carlos does not want to tell the company that he might be leaving.
(a) referee someone who writes a letter about someone else, describing their work or personal qualities.
full particulars full information about the job.

3.15
(a) recipient the person who the letter is sent to; this is a formal word.
(a) logo a special design or symbol used by a company to identify itself and its products.

3.13 Listen and read

Before he wrote the letter to Industrias Montresor, Carlos wanted to speak to his manager at Topdown Systems, Helen Tomlinson. Listen to what they say. What words do they use to show that the conversation is private?

CARLOS	Helen, could I *have a quick word* with you?
HELEN	Sure! Come into my office. Have a seat.
CARLOS	There was something that I wanted to ask you about. I don't want to say anything about this *officially* yet – this is just between you and me – but . . .
HELEN	But you think it's time you moved on and you're applying for another job.
CARLOS	Well, yes. How did you know? Anyway, could I ask you a favour? Can I give your name as a *referee*?
HELEN	Of course you may. Are you applying for a particular job, or are you just looking generally?
CARLOS	Oh no! It's a chemical machinery corporation which operates in several countries, including Spain. They want a software engineering manager, someone to build up a new team. They're sending me *full particulars*. I'll photocopy them for you.
HELEN	There's no need. They'll send me a copy anyway if they ask for a reference. OK, Carlos, thanks for telling me. You'll let me know what happens, won't you?
CARLOS	If anything does! Actually, I've spoken to them on the phone. They sound quite interested.
HELEN	Well, I wish you luck. I promise I won't mention it to anyone else unless you're called for interview.

3.14 Reading for key words

Find the words or phrases in 3.13 that tell you the following:

1 Carlos doesn't want people to know that he is looking for another job.
2 Helen has already guessed that he is looking for another job.
3 She wants to end the conversation.
4 He thinks that he won't get the job.
5 But he also thinks that he might get the job.

3.15 Letter layout

Business letters are usually quite formal. The different parts of a business letter are listed below. Look again at Carlos's letter to Industrias Montresor, shown below. Which items has he not used?

Flat 7, 26 Newcastle Road
Consett
Co Durham DU4 3ME
England

21 January 1992

Mr Andrews
Staff Controller
Industrias Montresor SA
Apdo 234
Zaragoza, Spain

Dear Mr Andrews

Application for the post of Divisional Software Engineering Manager

Further to our telephone conversation this morning, I can confirm that I wish to apply for this post. I enclose a copy of my cv.

You will see that I have added the name of one of my referees, Mrs Helen Tomlinson. You may contact her at any time. If you require other referees, perhaps you will be so kind as to let me know.

I can come to Zaragoza for interview at almost any time, provided I have at least three days' notice.

Yours sincerely

Carlos Vila.

1 the writer's signature.
2 the subject of the letter.
3 the writer's name.
4 the company letterhead (that is, the company's name and address).
5 the signature block.
6 the farewell.
7 the date.
8 the greeting.
9 the name and address of the *recipient.*
10 the writer's job title.
11 the company *logo.*

3.16 Document study

A day or two later, Helen receives a reference request from the Staff Controller of Industrias Montresor. This is her reply. Each of the parts has a label. For each label (**a–k**) write the number of one of the parts of a business letter listed in 3.15.

3.16
attached to working for; Carlos has been 'loaned' to another department.
a support staff people who work for someone.
a natural aptitude an ability to do a job quickly and easily.

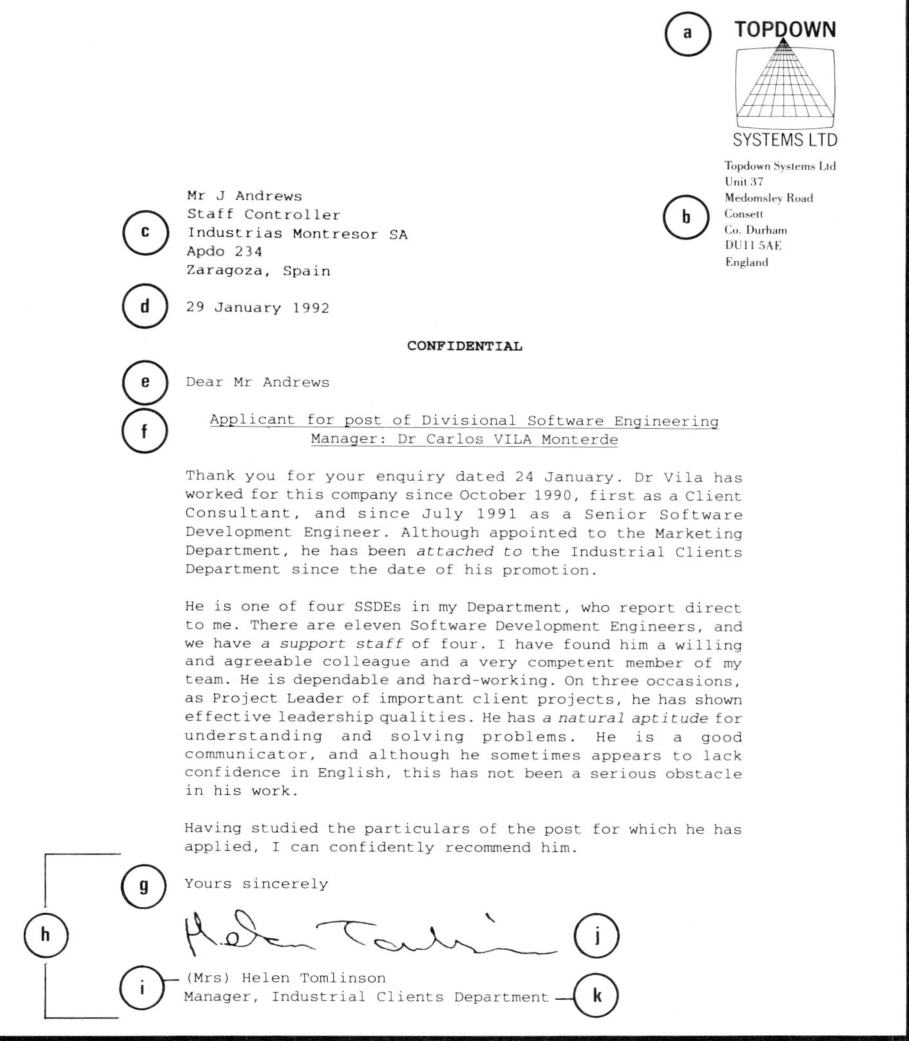

(a) TOPDOWN SYSTEMS LTD

(b) Topdown Systems Ltd
Unit 37
Medomsley Road
Consett
Co. Durham
DU11 5AE
England

(c) Mr J Andrews
Staff Controller
Industrias Montresor SA
Apdo 234
Zaragoza, Spain

(d) 29 January 1992

CONFIDENTIAL

(e) Dear Mr Andrews

(f) Applicant for post of Divisional Software Engineering Manager: Dr Carlos VILA Monterde

Thank you for your enquiry dated 24 January. Dr Vila has worked for this company since October 1990, first as a Client Consultant, and since July 1991 as a Senior Software Development Engineer. Although appointed to the Marketing Department, he has been *attached to* the Industrial Clients Department since the date of his promotion.

He is one of four SSDEs in my Department, who report direct to me. There are eleven Software Development Engineers, and we have *a support staff* of four. I have found him a willing and agreeable colleague and a very competent member of my team. He is dependable and hard-working. On three occasions, as Project Leader of important client projects, he has shown effective leadership qualities. He has *a natural aptitude* for understanding and solving problems. He is a good communicator, and although he sometimes appears to lack confidence in English, this has not been a serious obstacle in his work.

Having studied the particulars of the post for which he has applied, I can confidently recommend him.

(h)
(g) Yours sincerely

(j)

(i) (Mrs) Helen Tomlinson
Manager, Industrial Clients Department (k)

3.17 Writing practice: a formal letter

After reading Helen's letter carefully, you should be able to work out what Joe Andrews wrote in his letter to her. It was quite short, but it asked for all the information that Helen gave in her letter. Write Joe Andrews's letter. The beginning is shown below.

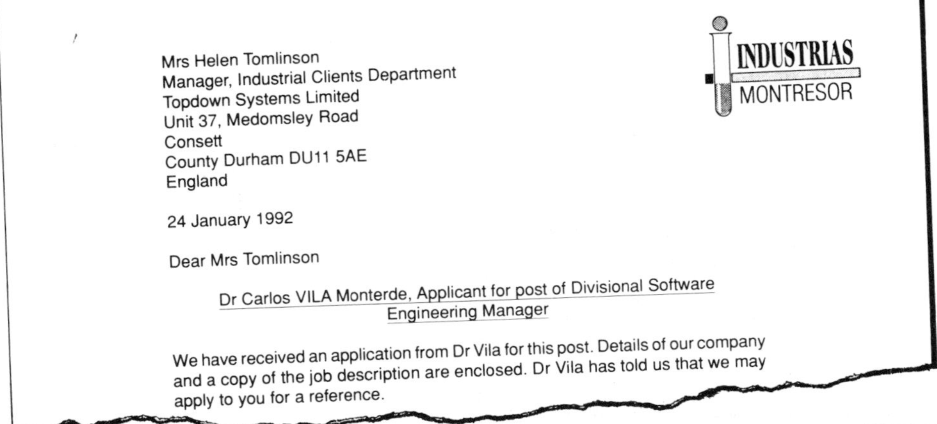

INDUSTRIAS MONTRESOR

Mrs Helen Tomlinson
Manager, Industrial Clients Department
Topdown Systems Limited
Unit 37, Medomsley Road
Consett
County Durham DU11 5AE
England

24 January 1992

Dear Mrs Tomlinson

Dr Carlos VILA Monterde, Applicant for post of Divisional Software Engineering Manager

We have received an application from Dr Vila for this post. Details of our company and a copy of the job description are enclosed. Dr Vila has told us that we may apply to you for a reference.

Study record	
3.1	
3.2	
3.3	
3.4	
3.5	
3.6	
3.7	
3.8	
3.9	
3.10	
3.11	
3.12	
3.13	
3.14	
3.15	
3.16	
3.17	

Answer key and commentary for unit 3

3.3 Listen and read
Essential: degree in computing; three years' experience; fluent in English.

Desirable: postgraduate qualification; experience in chemical industry; under 35.

3.4 Document study
'under thirty-five'; 'fluent in . . . English'; 'A postgraduate qualification will be an advantage'.

3.5 Reading for key words
1 Joe refers to it as 'That new software engineering post'.
2 The draft job description says the DSEM is responsible for 'maintaining the strictest security . . .'.
3 Pilar says 'We can't afford to be that specific.'
4 The advertisement says 'an expanding multinational corporation'.
5 The advertisement says 'to build and take charge of an enthusiastic team'.
6 The advertisement says 'rapid career development for a high-flier'.

3.6 Find the word
a advertisements **b** Appointments
c Qualifications **d** experience
e interview **f** applications

3.7 Sorting out the applicants
There is no one 'right' answer for this, but you should have something like this: degree in computing; three years' experience; middle management experience; fluent in Spanish; fluent in English; postgraduate qualification; experience in chemical industry; under 35.

3.9 Listen and read
Yes, Carlos is too late. The deadline was two days ago. But he may still be able to apply.

3.10 Speaking practice
a The thirteenth of May nineteen sixty-one.
b I attended the Senior High School in Santander from nineteen seventy-six to nineteen seventy-nine.
c I got the High School Graduation Certificate.
d I did military service for twelve months.
e I went to the University of Zaragoza.
f Yes, a BSc in Computer Studies.
g No, I went to the University of Madrid, where I got my PhD in Systems Engineering.
h Nineteen eighty-seven.
i I took a year off and, with some friends, I sailed round the world.
j I went to the Franco-Italian Bank in Milan. I worked there from nineteen eighty-eight to nineteen eighty-nine.
k I was a Systems Analyst.
l I worked for one year with a company in Paris called ILE as a Control Systems Supervisor. Then I came to England to work for Topdown Systems as a Client Consultant, but last July I was promoted to Senior Software Development Engineer.

3.12 Structure practice
1 For about two years, from 1990 until now.
2 From 1988 to 1989.
3 From 1979 to 1980.
4 Yes, in 1987 and 1988 when I sailed round the world.
5 Yes, for five years, from 1980 to 1985, when I was at university.
6 I was born in Santander and I went to school there, so from 1961 to 1979.
7 For about a year, in 1989 and 1990.
8 From 1980 to 1987.

3.13 Listen and read
Carlos says 'I don't want to say anything about this officially yet – this is just between you and me.'

Helen says 'I promise I won't mention it to anyone else.'

3.14 Reading for key words
1 I don't want to say anything about this officially yet – this is just between you and me.
2 you think it's time you moved on . . .
3 OK, Carlos, thanks for telling me.
4 If anything does!
5 Actually, . . . They sound quite interested.

3.15 Letter layout
The items that Carlos does not include in his letter are:

3 His name; he writes only his signature.
4, 11 The company letterhead and logo, because, as an individual, he is writing on plain paper.
10 His job title, because he is writing for himself, not as a representative of his company.

3.16 Document study
a 11 **b** 4 **c** 9 **d** 7 **e** 8 **f** 2
g 6 **h** 5 **i** 3 **j** 1 **k** 10

3.17 Writing practice
This is a model answer; there are many possible ways of writing this letter. Note that the sentences are short and simple:

Mrs Helen Tomlinson
Manager, Industrial Clients Department
Topdown Systems Ltd
Unit 37, Medomsley Road
Consett
County Durham DU11 5AE
England

24 January 1992

Dear Mrs Tomlinson

Dr Carlos VILA Monterde, Applicant for post of Divisional Software Engineering Manager

We have received an application from Dr Vila for this post. Details of our company and a copy of the job description are enclosed. Dr Vila has told us that we may apply to you for a reference.

We should be grateful if you can tell us how long Dr Vila has been employed by Topdown Systems, and what posts he has held.

We should like to have some information on his personal abilities. This post requires leadership qualities, ability to communicate and work in a team, and a good command of English.

Do you consider him to be a suitable person to hold a key management position in an expanding multinational corporation?

Thank you for your help.

Yours sincerely

J Andrews
Staff Controller

Unit 4: Selecting staff

SITUATION

This unit is about job interviews. Industrias Montresor have decided which of the applicants they would like to interview for the job of Divisional Software Engineering Manager. We look at what happens at Carlos Vila's interview, and also at what happens after the interview is over and the successful applicant is chosen.

CHARACTERS

Joe Andrews

Pilar Soto

Carlos Vila

LANGUAGE

Vocabulary	Careers and work experience; job titles and descriptions; money and the money market; computing.
Skills	Interviewing someone; being interviewed; comparing two things; writing a c.v.; writing a letter; accepting and rejecting an applicant for a job; accepting a job; resigning from a job.
Structures	rather/quite; comparing figures.
Documents	A c.v.; a job advertisement; letters.

Interviewing and being interviewed

4.1
quite good on paper Mr Schultz's qualifications and experience looked good on his c.v., but he was less impressive in the interview.
very sound, technically Mr Schultz knows the subject matter of his job thoroughly; **sound** is often followed by a criticism.

4.2
What's the set-up? what sort of equipment do you have?
IBM PCs and compatibles personal computers made by IBM, or any other personal computers that use the same programs.
access get data from.

4.3
More on the marketing side? you would prefer to move to marketing?
may well be this shows that Joe thinks that Carlos might seem to be clever, but that this isn't good enough.
global navigation sailing around the world.

4.1 Listen and read

Joe Andrews and Pilar Soto have just finished interviewing someone for the post c Divisional Software Engineering Manager. Listen to what they say. Do you think M Schultz is likely to get the job?

PILAR Well, thank you, Mr Schultz. Goodbye! Well?
JOE He looks *quite good on paper*.
PILAR I'm sure he's *very sound, technically*. The thing is, we must have someone who can communicate.
JOE But the Software Engineering Manager isn't going to be meeting customers.
PILAR You never know. Anyway, he's going to be talking to us every day! Schultz didn't sound very confident in either Spanish or English.
JOE Well, let's have the next one in, and see if he's any good!
PILAR Ask Dr Vila to come in, please.

4.2 Listen and read

Joe Andrews and Pilar Soto now interview Carlos Vila. Listen to what they say. D you think that this is a formal or an informal interview?

JOE Good afternoon, Dr Vila. Please sit down. My name is Andrews, I'm the Staff Controller, and my colleague here is Miss Soto, the Data Manager.
PILAR Good afternoon.
CARLOS Good afternoon.
JOE I think Miss Soto would like to discuss technical matters with you to begin with. Then I'll come in with some more general things. Pilar?
PILAR Thank you. Dr Vila, your c.v. doesn't go into details about the hardware you've been working with recently. Tell me about your present job. *What's the set-up?*
CARLOS Well, we have a network of *IBM PCs and compatibles*, which can operate as individual work stations or they can *access* a much more powerful minicomputer.

4.3 Listen and read

Later in the interview Pilar and Carlos are talking in Spanish and laughing. Then Jo takes over. Listen to what they say. Is Joe impressed by Carlos?

PILAR All right! Now I'll hand you back to Mr Andrews.
CARLOS Thank you.
JOE Yes, Dr Vila. While you've been talking to Miss Soto, I've been refreshing my memory of your c.v. It makes interesting reading. Rather a mixed career so far. Suppose you do join our company. Where do you expect to be in five years' time?
CARLOS Well, a head of department – assistant head, anyway – in technica sales, or overseas marketing.
JOE I see. *More on the marketing side?* You're quite sure about that? You think your track record will help you?
CARLOS Er, yes, I think it will.
JOE Hm. I'm glad you think so. You know what I think? I see a young man who *may well be* smart but who really doesn't know where he's going.
CARLOS Why do you say that?
JOE Well, you tell me, Dr Vila. Why did you move from banking to printing, to computer consultancy and now you want to move into heavy industry? And perhaps I ought to mention *global navigation*?

4.4 Reading for key words

Find the words or phrases in 4.1 and 4.3 that tell you the following:

1 Pilar has made her decision about Mr Schultz.
2 Pilar doesn't agree with Joe's comments on Mr Schultz.
3 Joe has been re-reading Carlos's c.v.
4 Joe disagrees with Carlos's view of his future.
5 Joe thinks Carlos is a bit too clever.
6 Joe is about to ask Carlos a question which he thinks will be hard to answer.

4.5 Listen and read

Carlos Vila is answering Joe Andrews's criticisms. Listen to what they say. Does Carlos succeed in changing Joe's view of his career?

JOE — And perhaps I ought to mention global navigation?

CARLOS — Because all those things are my career! In every position that I've had, I was developing my knowledge of computer systems. That knowledge I can apply equally well to banking, or machine automation, or image recognition – anything you like.

JOE — I see. Well, maybe you have a point. But taking a year off to go sailing, at the start of your career, when you've just got your PhD. Wasn't that a year wasted?

CARLOS — It depends on how you look at it. It was an adventure, of course, but we also carried out a research programme for computer-aided satellite navigation. So actually I think it was quite useful. Anyway, would you turn down a chance like that?

JOE — Hm! OK, Dr Vila. Are there any questions you want to ask us?

CARLOS — Well, yes. I'd like to know a little more about the group I would be working with.

. . . . . .

PILAR — It's been very interesting talking to you, Dr Vila. However, we still have one more person to interview.

4.6 Reading for key words

Find the words or phrases in 4.5 that tell you the following:

1 Joe agrees with what Carlos says about his frequent changes of job.
2 Carlos shows that he understands Joe's point of view.
3 Carlos refers to the scientific work that he and his friends did on their voyage.
4 Carlos is correcting Joe's wrong opinion.
5 Pilar wants the interview to end.

4.7 Speaking practice: at an interview

Listen to this conversation. It practises some of the structures and phrases you have heard in this unit. Then listen again, and speak the part of the man.

INTERVIEWER — Are there any questions you want to ask us?

APPLICANT — Yes. I'd like to know more about the people I'll be working with.

INTERVIEWER — Well, this is a new post. We're not quite sure which department it will be in – Marketing or Technical.

APPLICANT — The thing is, I see my career developing more towards marketing.

INTERVIEWER — Marketing's rather a big jump. After all, as an engineer, you won't be directly involved in selling.

APPLICANT — You never know! Anyway, I'm certainly going to be involved in product development.

INTERVIEWER — Well, maybe you have a point there. It depends on how you look at it.

APPLICANT — OK, let's say I'm going to be on the marketing side. Perhaps you can tell me who I'll be working with.

Matching and comparing

May 1984–July 1987
Assistant Data Services Manager, Globe Insurance Brokers (London) Ltd.

The Data Services Department had a staff of ten, out of a total staff in the London office of 150. The company had a turnover, in 1987, in the region of US$20m. I was responsible, under the Data Services Manager, for a staff of seven and for the functioning of all data processing services within the company and all data communication. In 1987 I also planned and supervised the installation of new equipment and software, and organised training courses for all employees.

Salary at time of leaving, approx. US$45,000 plus company mortgage, car, health insurance, pension scheme, etc.

August 1987– present
Computer Manager, del Conte Financial Services, Geneva.

Del Conte is a small, but successful, firm of financial and investment consultants. There are six partners and about seventy support staff, ten of whom report to me. We have clients in most European countries, North America and Japan. I am responsible for maintaining the firm's data processing system, which is in contact throughout the day and night with the world's major stock exchanges and money markets. I also maintain the software which processes portfolio values, clients' accounts, etc.

Current earnings, about $90,000 including bonuses, plus company accommodation and allowances.

4.8 Document study

Another applicant who is being interviewed is Angela Robbiani, from Italy. This is an extract from her c.v. When you have read this, start to fill in the form from 3.7 with details of Carlos and Angela. You will find more details about Angela in 4.12. Add these to the form.

4.9 Listen and read: making comparisons

Joe and Pilar have just finished interviewing Angela Robbiani. They now have to decide who to appoint. Listen to what they say. What words do they use to make their comments stronger?

JOE — It's been most interesting talking to you, Miss Robbiani, thank you very much!

PILAR — Well! Quite impressive. I could tell you were impressed.

JOE — Let's have another look at the job advertisement. How does she match up to that?

PILAR — Rather well, I think. And, Joe, she didn't waste time sailing around the world, like Carlos did.

4.10 Structure practice: *rather* and *quite*

Re-read the dialogues in this unit (4.1, 4.3, 4.5, 4.7 and 4.9) and notice how the words 'rather' and 'quite' are used. It might also help to listen to the dialogues again. 'Quite' has two meanings. Before some words, it means 'to some degree':

'What do you think of the new manager?' – 'Oh, I quite like him. He seems quite good.'

Before other words, 'quite' means 'completely' or 'exactly':

'Are you sure?' – 'Yes. I'm quite sure.'
'You're quite right. I had made a mistake.'

'Rather' also has two meanings. It can mean 'to a large degree':

'Can I have a word with you?' – 'Well, I am rather busy at the moment. Is it important?' – 'Yes, it is rather.' 'I thought she did rather well.'

'Rather' can also mean 'to a small degree':

'I'm rather surprised that he decided to sail around the world like that.'

4.11 Document study: writing your c.v. – 2

Look again at the extract from Angela Robbiani's c.v. in 4.8. These career details are important. Carlos could have put a lot more information in his c.v. than we showed in 3.11. This is what he might have written under 'Education'.

You should now write his descriptions of his three previous jobs yourself, from the information given below. You can use Angela's c.v. as a model.

```
1985-87    I carried out a research project in
           systems engineering. This related to the
           day-to-day handling of large financial
           databases. I also assessed existing
           data systems in use in various financial
           institutions. I attended a series of
           training courses in these institutions.
```

1 Carlos's first job was as a systems analyst with the Franco-Italian Bank in Milan. Use the table below to write sentences describing what he did there.

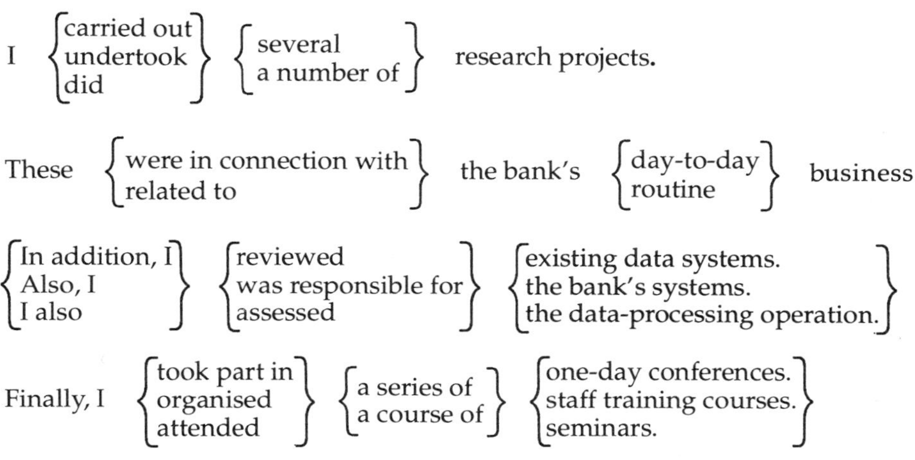

I	carried out / undertook / did	several / a number of	research projects.		
These	were in connection with / related to	the bank's	day-to-day / routine	business.	
In addition, I / Also, I / I also	reviewed / was responsible for / assessed	existing data systems. / the bank's systems. / the data-processing operation.			
Finally, I	took part in / organised / attended	a series of / a course of	one-day conferences. / staff training courses. / seminars.		

2 Next, the details of his job at Imprimerie Ledoux. This is what he said to Joe Andrews and Pilar Soto during his interview. His words here are informal, but you should be able to work out what he wrote:

CARLOS Yes, I was just a member of the team to start with – there were five of us, actually – we had to make sure that everything worked OK, not just the office computer but also the system that controlled the printing machines and the typesetting – it was all linked together – everything was automated, in fact my biggest job was actually to show the staff there how to use the machines properly, I think that was why they made me a supervisor.

3 Finally, his job with Topdown Software. This is the advertisement which led him to apply to Topdown, though he did not get this job straight away; he was promoted after working for nine months as a Client Consultant. The advertisement gives a good description of the job, but the language is not entirely suitable for a c.v. Rewrite it in the more formal style of a c.v.

We are the tops in software!

TOPDOWN SYSTEMS LTD needs TOP SOFTWARE ENGINEERS

Senior Software Development Engineer

We are seeking a dynamic individual to lead one of the brightest development teams in the country. He or she will be asked to –

- develop the systems of the future to meet our clients' specifications
- maintain our enviable reputation for customer service
- set up conferences and courses aimed at generating new business

TOPDOWN

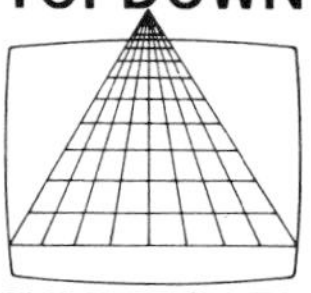

SYSTEMS LTD

Apply with full CV, to
The Personnel Controller
Topdown Systems Ltd
Unit 37
Medomsley Road
Consett
Co. Durham
DU11 5AE
England

Changing jobs

4.12
90K ninety thousand (dollars); **K** or **k** is now often used informally to mean 'thousand'.
the lack of Pilar means that Angela does not have enough industrial experience.
has the edge when it comes to is slightly better at.

4.12 Listen and read

In the interview room, Pilar and Joe must make a decision. Listen to what they say. Do they find it easy or difficult?

PILAR Under thirty-five. Currently holds a post of responsibility at middle management level, fluent in Spanish and English.

JOE Yes, but not as fluent as Vila.

PILAR She speaks English as well as he does, if not better.

JOE But, unlike Vila, she doesn't have a postgraduate qualification.

PILAR Look at their current salaries! He's making half what she is! I suppose we'd have to pay her twice as much as him!

JOE Considering the field she's in, *90K* isn't all that great. She was getting 45K in Britain five years ago. It's taken her five years to double her earnings. What really bothers me, though, is that her experience has been totally in the area of finance and banking.

PILAR Yes, *the lack of* industrial experience is rather a drawback. How about drive, ambition, motivation? How do you rate Robbiani on that – compared with Vila, I mean?

JOE Well, in spite of what I said to Vila, I really feel he *has the edge when it comes to* motivation. That appears to me to be the essential difference between them. He's much more ambitious than she is!

PILAR Yes. I think that, when we weigh them both up, we have to give it to Vila. His experience is more varied than Robbiani's. And, as you say, he's more highly motivated. And I get the impression that he's better at working with people.

JOE What makes you say that?

PILAR That boat trip. Can you imagine it? Living for months in a tiny boat with five other people? I'd go crazy. But when he talked about it, you could see that it was more important to him than anything else he'd ever done.

4.13 Figure practice: comparing salaries

The figures below give some details of Angela's and Carlos's earnings over the past five years (all in US dollars). Use the figures to help you answer the questions. Write a word from the box, or a figure, for each gap. Re-read dialogue 4.12 to help you.

doubled
half
more
twice

	Angela	Carlos
1987	45,000	–
1989	60,000	32,000
1991	–?	40,000
1992 (present job)	90,000	48,000
1992 (new job)	100,000+	55,000+

1 Angela and Carlos – how do their salaries compare at the moment?
Her salary is almost ___**a**___ as much as his.

2 How much does he earn, compared with her?
He earns just over ___**b**___ what she does.

3 Between 1987 and 1992, what did Angela's earnings do?
Her earnings ___**c**___ between 1987 and 1992.

4 Between 1989 and 1992, how much did Carlos's earnings rise?
Carlos's earnings rose by ___**d**___ per cent between 1989 and 1992.

5 How much did he earn in 1991, compared with 1989?
In 1991 he made about ___**e**___ per cent more than in 1989.

6 If Montresor appoint Angela, will they have to pay her more than they would pay Carlos?
Yes! They'll have to pay her about ___**f**___ what they would pay him.

7 Judging from these incomplete figures, has she always earned more than he has?
Yes, it looks as if she's always made ___**g**___. Her salary has always been about ___**h**___ his.

4.14 Document study

These are some of the letters that were written after the selection interviews. Are these formal or informal letters?

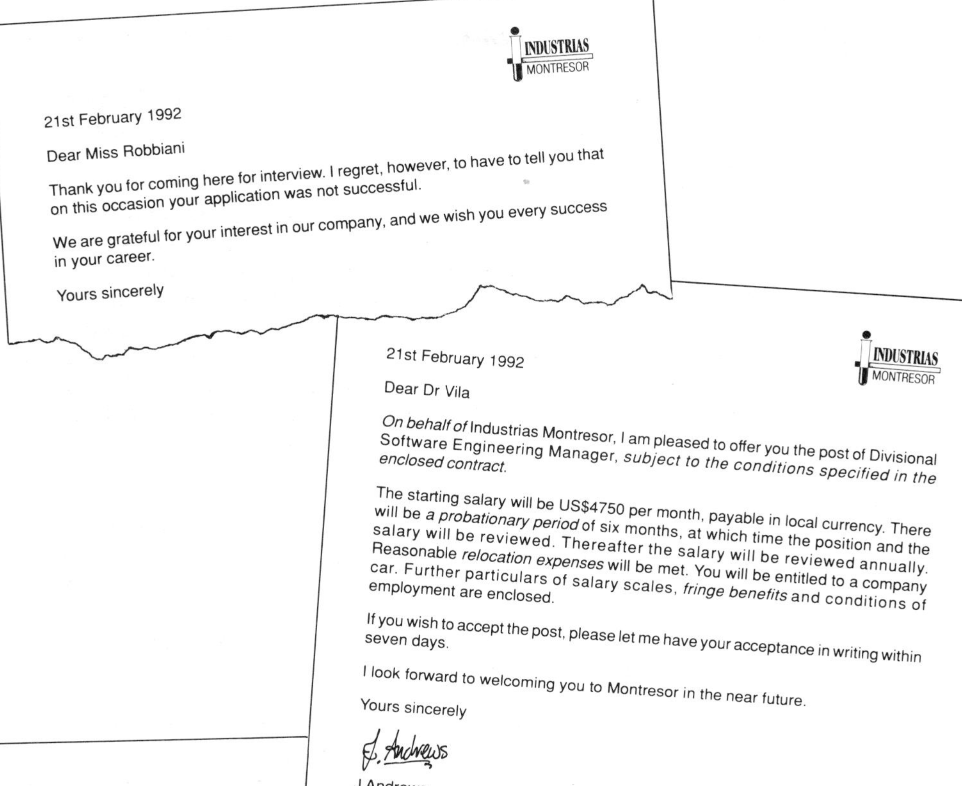

INDUSTRIAS MONTRESOR

21st February 1992

Dear Miss Robbiani

Thank you for coming here for interview. I regret, however, to have to tell you that on this occasion your application was not successful.

We are grateful for your interest in our company, and we wish you every success in your career.

Yours sincerely

INDUSTRIAS MONTRESOR

21st February 1992

Dear Dr Vila

On behalf of Industrias Montresor, I am pleased to offer you the post of Divisional Software Engineering Manager, *subject to the conditions specified in the enclosed contract.*

The starting salary will be US$4750 per month, payable in local currency. There will be *a probationary period* of six months, at which time the position and the salary will be reviewed. Thereafter the salary will be reviewed annually. Reasonable *relocation expenses* will be met. You will be entitled to a company car. Further particulars of salary scales, *fringe benefits* and conditions of employment are enclosed.

If you wish to accept the post, please let me have your acceptance in writing within seven days.

I look forward to welcoming you to Montresor in the near future.

Yours sincerely

J. Andrews

J Andrews
Staff Controller

Miss J F Matthews
Personnel Department

28th February 1992

Dear Miss Matthews

I am writing to tell you that I have decided to accept an offer of employment with another company. I am therefore giving you my notice in accordance with the terms of my contract.

Yours sincerely

Carlos Vila.

Carlos Vila Monterde
cc Mrs Tomlinson, Industrial Clients Department

TOPDOWN SYSTEMS LTD

2 March 1992

Dear Dr Vila

Thank you for your letter of 28 February. In accordance with company policy, you will be paid for one month from the date of handing in your notice, but I must ask you to *vacate* your office, remove your *personal effects*, and hand in all keys and *identity tags* before 1700 hrs today, 2 March. Security staff have been instructed not to admit you on site after check-out procedure has been completed.

On behalf of the company, I wish you success in your new post.

Yours sincerely

J. F. Matthews

(Miss) J F Matthews
Assistant Personnel Manager

4.14
On behalf of Joe is making the offer from the company, not from himself.
subject to the conditions specified in the enclosed contract Carlos must also agree to everything in the contract that was sent with the letter.
a probationary period the time during which you are assessed to see if you can do a job, before you are allowed to continue; at the end of the **probationary period** you may be dismissed.
relocation expenses money paid to help you change to a new job, usually to help you move, buy a house, etc.
fringe benefits extra things that you get with the job; often a car, travel tickets or luncheon vouchers, etc.
vacate leave completely and not come back.
personal effects things that belonged to Carlos; they might be photographs, plants, books, etc.
identity tags cards with a photograph showing who you are.

4.15 Writing practice: a letter of acceptance

Carlos telephones Joe Andrews at once to accept Montresor's offer, and confirms this with a letter to him. The letter is brief and formal, but Carlos should show that he is pleased to get the job. Write the letter for him.

4.16 Writing practice: explaining a decision

All the papers about the appointment of the new Divisional Software Engineering Manager are stored in a file in the Personnel Department. Before the file is put away, Joe Andrews writes a note, in the form of a memo, as a record of the selection board's decision. Write his note.

You should give your note a title, and say who the members of the selection board were. Explain that four applicants were shortlisted, but only two were seriously considered after the interviews had taken place; give their names. Give the reasons why Carlos was appointed. Re-read the dialogues in this unit for help with this exercise.

Study record	
4.1	
4.2	
4.3	
4.4	
4.5	
4.6	
4.7	
4.8	
4.9	
4.10	
4.11	
4.12	
4.13	
4.14	
4.15	
4.16	

Answer key and commentary for unit 4

4.1 Listen and read
Joe says 'He looks quite good on paper', and Pilar says 'he's very sound, technically'. Both of these comments show that they have some doubts. Pilar also says that he 'didn't sound very confident in either Spanish or English'. He is not likely to get the job.

4.2 Listen and read
Joe makes the interview a formal one by introducing everyone by their family name, title and job title for himself and Pilar, and by using the formal 'Good afternoon' as a greeting.

4.3 Listen and read
The way Joe handles the whole conversation shows that he is not too impressed, but, in particular, he says 'Rather a mixed career so far', 'I'm glad you think so', and 'I see a young man who may well be smart but . . . '.

4.4 Reading for key words
1 Pilar says 'we must have someone who can communicate', and 'Schultz didn't sound very confident in either Spanish or English'.
2 You never know.
3 I've been refreshing my memory of your c.v.
4 I'm glad you think so.
5 a young man who may well be smart . . .
6 Well, you tell me, Dr Vila.

4.5 Listen and read
Yes, he does succeed. Carlos explains how his career changes have helped to develop his computing skills. He also offers a different interpretation of his trip, starting with 'It depends on how you look at it'.

4.6 Reading for key words
1 maybe you have a point.
2 It was an adventure, of course.
3 we also carried out a research programme for computer-aided satellite navigation.
4 So actually I think it was quite useful. (We often use the word 'actually' to show that we are correcting the other speaker's mistake.)
5 It's been very interesting talking to you, Dr Vila.

4.8 Document study
Carlos and Angela have very similar qualifications: a degree in computing, at least three years' work experience, fluent in Spanish and English, under 35. Carlos doesn't have management experience, nor experience of the chemical industry, but he does have some industrial experience. Angela doesn't have a postgraduate qualification or any industrial experience, but she does have experience of middle management.

4.9 Listen and read
Joe says '**most** interesting', 'thank you **very much**'. Pilar says '**Quite** impressive', '**Rather** well'.

4.11 Document study
These are model answers; there are many possible ways of writing these sentences and paragraphs.
1 I undertook several research projects. These were in connection with the bank's routine business. I also assessed existing data systems. Finally, I organised a series of staff training courses.
2 This was a fully-automated typesetting and printing works. I joined the company as a member of a team of five people. We were responsible for making sure that all computer systems were in good working order at a times. My principal task was to train staff i the use of the equipment. I was promoted t supervisor.
3 This is a leading software developme company in the north of England. It develop computer systems to meet its client specifications. I was a Senior Softwar Development Engineer and was responsib for leading a team of software engineers. W worked closely with our clients and set u conferences and courses aimed at generatin new business.

4.12 Listen and read
Joe and Pilar find the decision difficult. They us lots of words and phrases comparing Carlos an Angela: 'not as fluent as Vila', 'as well as he doe if not better', 'unlike Vila', 'making half what sh is', 'compared with Vila', 'he has the edge 'essential difference between them', 'much mo ambitious', 'weigh them both up', 'more varied 'more highly motivated', 'better at working wi people'.

4.13 Figure practice
a twice **b** half **c** doubled **d** 50
e 25 **f** twice **g** more **h** twice

4.14 Document study
They are all formal letters.

4.15 Writing practice
This is a model answer.

> Dear Mr Andrews
>
> Post of Divisional Software Engineering Manager
>
> I am writing to confirm what I told you in our telephone conversation today. I am pleased to accept your company's offer of this post on the terms outlined in your letter of 21 February 1992. I look forward to joining Industrias Montresor and to contributing to the company's work.
>
> Yours sincerely
>
> Carlos Vila Monterde

4.16 Writing practice
This is a model answer.

> Memo from J Andrews (Staff Controller)
>
> 18 Feb 92
>
> Appointment of DSEM: selection interviews
>
> The members of the board were: J Andrews, P Soto (Data Manager)
>
> Four applicants were shortlisted, but after interview only two were seriously considered: Miss Angela Robbiani and Dr Carlos Vila.
>
> The board decided to offer the post to Dr Vila for the following reasons:
>
> 1 Miss Robbiani spoke less fluent Spanish.
> 2 She had no postgraduate qualification.
> 3 Although her current salary was almost double Dr Vila's, the board felt that it was not exceptional for the field she was in. It had taken her five years to double her salary.
> 4 Her experience was totally in the area of finance and banking.
> 5 Dr Vila seemed more highly motivated.
> 6 He appeared to be more used to working with people.

Unit 5: Going on a training course

SITUATION

In this unit Carlos Vila, the new Divisional Software Engineering Manager at Industrias Montresor, is being sent to Osaka, Japan, on a company training course. We look at how to make travel arrangements, and at meeting people in formal and informal situations.

CHARACTERS

Joe Andrews	
Pilar Soto	
Carlos Vila	
Akiko Ito	is a Software Course Organiser at the Sima Electronics Training Centre, Osaka, Japan. She is Japanese.
Bret Holman	is Head of Research and Development at Tahoe Data Systems in the USA. He is American.

LANGUAGE

Vocabulary	Training courses; air travel; computers.
Skills	Writing a telex; making travel arrangements; writing a letter; meeting people.
Structures	Possessive *'s;* formal and informal language; flight numbers and times.
Documents	A telex; a letter of acceptance; a letter of confirmation; a speculative letter; an advertising leaflet; an airline schedule.

Making arrangements

5.1
(a) familiarisation (course) a training course that helps you to start to understand something.
commencing starting; **commencing** is formal.
to take up to accept.
advise us tell us; in this use **advise** does not mean 'give advice'.
21 through 28 July from the 21 July up to and including the 28 July; American speakers use **through** in this way.

5.3
I take it I assume; Joe is checking that Pilar still wants to send Carlos.
get on to contact.
1700 hours local time Joe uses this long phrase to make absolutely sure that there is no confusion; it means five o'clock in the afternoon, in Japan in this case.

5.4
in due course when the time is right; in this case when Joe knows what the arrangements are.

5.1 Document study

Carlos Vila has now been with Industrias Montresor as Divisional Software Engineering Manager for three months. This telex arrives at the Zaragoza office about a training course for some new machinery that Industrias Montresor is buying from a Japanese company.

```
240692 SIMA JPN

CONS. NO. 7211   24.06.92   10:30

24.6.92

ATTN: MR ANDREWS
      INDUSTRIAS MONTRESOR

FROM: YAMASHITA
      SIMA CORPORATION

REGARDING YOUR REQUEST FOR SOFTWARE
FAMILIARISATION ON 9909 SERIES MACHINES WE HAVE A
VACANCY ON COURSE 37, COMMENCING 22 JULY AND
LASTING ONE WEEK, AT OUR CENTRE IN OSAKA. IF YOU
WISH TO TAKE UP THIS OFFER, PLEASE ADVISE US OF
THE DELEGATE'S NAME AND QUALIFICATIONS ASAP. WE
WILL ARRANGE TRANSPORT FROM AIRPORT, ACCOMMODATION
ETC IN OSAKA FROM 21 THROUGH 28 JULY. KINDLY MAKE
FLIGHT ARRANGEMENTS AND INFORM US OF THESE ALSO.

REGARDS
YAMASHITA
240692 SIMA JPN

/ENDS
```

5.2 Reading for key words

Find the words or phrases in the telex in 5.1 that tell you the following:

1 (four letters meaning) attention.
2 (four letters meaning) as soon as possible.
3 an empty place on a course.
4 say 'yes' to an offer.
5 give information about something (two answers).
6 until and including (a certain date).
7 'We ask you politely' (two answers).

5.3 Listen and read

Joe Andrews telephones Pilar Soto, Carlos's manager, about the training course. Listen to what they say. Joe then asks his secretary, Maria, to make the travel arrangements for Carlos's flight to Japan. Listen to what he says. Notice that this is a long instruction, and so he does not include any unnecessary words.

JOE Now, *I take it* that you want to send Carlos to Japan? You did say that it would be the new man's first assignment!

PILAR That's right, and he's been with us for three months now. Never mind. At least he's had a chance to settle in and get to know the place.

....

JOE Maria, would you please *get on to* the travel agents to make a flight reservation. Tell them we've got someone flying to Osaka in Japan, business class, arriving on 21 July, not later than *1700 hours local time*, departing Osaka on the morning of the twenty-ninth. The reservation is in the name of Dr Carlos Vila. Any queries, just contact me.

5.4 Find the word

This is another extract from Joe's telephone call to Pilar. Read the text, and fill the gaps with words from the box.

delegates	flight
to	training
travel	vacancy

JOE At last, Sima have contacted us to say there's a ___**a**___ on one of their ___**b**___ courses. I think we'll have to take it up, though the dates aren't very convenient: 22 ___**c**___ 28 July. Yes, July! All ___**d**___ have to arrive in Osaka on the afternoon of the twenty-first. Now, you want my department to make all the ___**e**___ arrangements, I suppose. I'll inform you *in due course* of Vila's ___**f**___ times and numbers.

5.5 Document study

A letter is faxed to Japan the same day, and a reply is received a few days later. The tone of both of these letters is rather formal, and most of the sentences contain standard business phrases. Which phrases might be useful in other business letters?

Mr M Yamashita
Vice-President, Customer Relations
Sima Machine Corporation
Osaka, Japan

24 June 1992

Dear Mr Yamashita

Thank you for your telex of today's date. We shall be pleased to take up your offer of a place for our Divisional Software Engineering Manager on your Software Familiarisation Course commencing on 22 July. He is Dr Carlos Vila, whose c.v. is enclosed.

Arrangements have been made for him to fly from Madrid to Osaka, arriving on Japan Air Lines flight JL456 at 1615 hours local time on 21 July, and returning via flight JL934 from Osaka at 0930 on 29 July.

We trust you will find these arrangements satisfactory.

Yours sincerely

J. Andrews

Joe Andrews
Staff Controller

Dr Carlos Vila
Systems Engineering Department
Industrias Montresor SA
Apdo 234
Zaragoza, Spain

Our ref.: AI/3267/trg/92
Your ref.:

26 June 1992

Dear Dr Vila

My colleagues and I look forward to welcoming you as a participant on our Course 37 (9909 Series Software Familiarisation) commencing at 8.30 a.m. on 22 July.

Our company car will meet you at the airport and take you to your hotel. Please be ready at 7.30 p.m. on 21 July to attend our welcome party and dinner. Our company coach will pick up delegates from the hotel at 8.00 a.m. next morning.

I enclose a brief summary of the course schedule, and wish you a pleasant journey from Zaragoza to Osaka. Please let me know at once if any problems arise.

Yours sincerely

Akiko Ito

(Miss) Akiko Ito
Course Organiser

5.6 Reading for key words

Find the words or phrases in Akiko Ito's letter in 5.5 that tell you the following:

1 the people who work with me in my company.
2 someone who takes part in something.
3 a car belonging to a company.
4 a timetable of activities for a course.
5 a short statement of the most important points.

5.7 Writing practice: telexes and letters

Telex messages are sent along ordinary telephone lines, and telephone calls cost money, so when you write a telex you don't use more words than are necessary.

Look again at the telex in 5.1. When you send a telex to an organisation, and you want it to go to a particular person, use 'ATTN' ('attention') or 'FTAO' ('for the attention of'), followed by the person's name or job title.

If you want to put your own name at the end, use 'REGARDS', followed by your name and/or job title, e.g. 'REGARDS ANDREWS, STAFF CONTROLLER'.

1 Rewrite Joe Andrews's letter to Mr Yamashita as a telex. It will be a little shorter, but not much.
2 Then rewrite Mr Yamashita's telex in 5.1 to Joe Andrews as a letter, laying it out correctly (see 3.16).

Meeting people

5.8
jet lag a feeling of tiredness and confusion after a long journey by plane; it usually happens when you travel into a different time zone.

5.10
the course is very intensive the course includes a lot of work in a very short time.
hands-on experience experience in actually using something, in this case computers, rather than just talking about them.
(a) course manual the book that contains the information used in the training course; the delegates will take it away with them to use when they get back to their own offices.

5.8 Listen and read

Carlos arrives at Osaka airport, and is greeted by Akiko Ito. Listen to how Carlos ar Akiko greet each other formally, and then relax a little.

AKIKO Hello! Dr Vila!
CARLOS Good afternoon. Miss – Ito? Do you say 'Ito'?
AKIKO That's quite right. I'm your Course Organiser. I hope you had a good flight?
CARLOS Yes, thanks. It was a bit long, but quite comfortable. I hope I won' suffer too much from *jet lag*.
AKIKO Oh, you mustn't have jet lag, because we have a party tonight an a very busy day for you tomorrow!
CARLOS Oh! I see. Well, I'll have to forget my jet lag until I get back to Spain, won't I?

5.9 Listening for meaning

Listen again carefully to the conversation in 5.8. There are many meanings carrie by the intonation of the speakers, by the way their voices rise and fall.

1 At the airport, Akiko says 'Dr Vila' and Carlos says 'Miss Ito'. One of them is question. Which one? And which of them is worried in case he/she has made mistake? How do we know this?
2 'I hope you had a good flight.' Akiko's words are in the form of a statement. Ho does she make it into a question?
3 Akiko says 'That's quite right.' Carlos says 'It was a bit long, but qui comfortable.' What does the word 'quite' mean in these two statements?

5.10 Listen and read

In a lecture theatre at the Sima Electronics Training Centre, Akiko Ito welcomes th members of Course 37. Listen to what she says. Notice that she is quite formal.

AKIKO Good morning, ladies and gentlemen. Welcome to Course 37: Software Familiarisation on our company's 9909 series machines. We have a full programme for you during the next seven days and *the course is very intensive*. This course has been developed especially for Industrias Montresor, and it's essential for all their Systems Engineers to have plenty of *hands-on experience* – that's why we can only take ten participants on each course.

On the table in front of you, you will each find a copy of the *course manual*. Please treat this as a confidential document. It contains detailed information about your company's computer installations – and I'm sure that your competitors would find it most interesting!

5.11 Listen and read

Later, in the training centre canteen, Carlos is having a cup of coffee when a strange comes and sits at his table. Listen to what they say. Notice how they start speakin to each other, without actually introducing themselves.

AMERICAN Hi there! Mind if I join you?
CARLOS Of course, please do. Are you studying here?
AMERICAN I'm on Course 35, Electronic Engineering. There's only six of us.
CARLOS Only six? On my course we have ten. Software Familiarisation. Today is our first day.
AMERICAN That's quite a book they've given you. May I see?
CARLOS Er – I'm sorry – we're not supposed to . . .
AMERICAN Oh, I understand. It's confidential, right? So, tell me about yourself. Who do you work for? Or is that confidential too?
CARLOS No. It's a large manufacturing corporation – in Spain. We make machines for the chemical industry.

5.12 Listen and read

Carlos is sitting talking to the American, Bret Holman, when he hears the bell that means he must return to his seminar. Read the dialogue and listen to how the two men now introduce themselves.

BRET — I'm sorry, I forgot to introduce myself. My name's Bret Holman. Here's my card.
CARLOS — Bret Holman. Head of Research and Development, Tahoe Data Systems. How do you do, Mr Holman. I'm Carlos Vila.
BRET — Good to meet you, Carlos. As it happens, Tahoe Data is very interested in Spain just now . . .
[Bell rings]
CARLOS — Oh, I'm sorry, that's for my group. Please excuse me.
BRET — Of course. Don't let me keep you.

. . . . . .

CARLOS — I am sorry, Mr Holman, I forgot to give you my card! Goodbye.
BRET — Gee, thanks. Ah! Industrias Montresor, Divisional Software Engineering Manager. Interesting!

5.13 Structure practice: possessive *'s*

Read again the dialogues and documents in this unit. Look for examples of *'s*. We usually use *'s* as a possessive form with nouns that refer to people or animals:

the new man's first assignment   Joe's telephone call

It is not normally used with nouns that refer to objects or things. For example, we don't say 'at the meeting's start' or 'a company's car'; we do say 'at the start of the meeting', 'a company car'.

But when the noun can be used to mean the group of people connected with something, then the *'s* form can be used:

our company's 9909 series machines
your company's computer installation

Read through the dialogue below, and decide whether each *'s* is right or wrong. The answer key shows you what a British speaker would probably say.

MAN — Hello! How was your conference?
WOMAN — Terrible! My company's car broke down, and I missed the conference's start.
MAN — Oh dear! That's not good for your company's image.
WOMAN — No. And it got worse! At lunch's end I got up to leave and my chair's leg broke!

5.14 Reading for key words: formal and informal language

Read and listen to 5.10 again. Find the more formal words and phrases in Akiko Ito's speech which mean the same as these informal ones:

1 you're going to have to study extremely hard.
2 to use computers a lot.
3 don't let other people read your manual.

Now listen to, and read, 5.11 and 5.12 again. Find the informal words in Bret Holman's comments which mean the same as these formal ones:

4 Good morning. May I sit here, please?
5 You've been given a large and impressive book.
6 Please don't apologise.
7 It's a pleasure to meet you.

The sentences that follow show a number of different ways of saying more or less the same thing. Mark them as F(ormal), I(nformal) or N(eutral).

8 I must inform you that this document is confidential.
9 Unfortunately, this is a confidential document.
10 You're joking! Do you want to get me into trouble?
11 May I, with great respect, point out that it is confidential.
12 Sorry, I'm afraid it's supposed to be confidential.

Which of these sentences would be most suitable for Carlos to use in 5.11?

Making an offer

5.15
was cut short was forced to stop before it was finished.
the front rank the best.
Without committing either of us in this case this means 'I am not saying that I will make you an offer, and you are not saying that you will accept an offer'.
Sincerely British speakers would use **Yours sincerely** here.

5.17
The hard facts facts that can be proved.
competition is stiffer business is more difficult.
budgets are tighter there is less money available for business.
ensure make certain of; do not confuse this word with **assure** and **insure**.
from the ground up from the very beginning.
integrate our equipment make our equipment work successfully with other equipment.

5.15 Document study

Carlos is now back in Spain, and he receives this letter from Bret Holman. It is informal, personal letter. Bret is trying to find out if Carlos would like to lea Industrias Montresor and take a job with Tahoe Data Systems. He makes this sou attractive, but does he actually make any offers?

Dr Carlos Vila
Industrias MontresorS
Apdo 234
Zaragoza

PRIVATE AND CONFIDENTIAL

Personal

TAHOE
DATA SYSTEMS

Dr Carlos Vila
Industrias Montresor SA
Apdo 234
Zaragoza

15 September 1992

Dear Dr Vila

You may possibly remember me. I am the American who introduced himself to you in the canteen at the Sima Machine Corporation a couple of months ago. Unfortunately our conversation *was cut short* when you had to return to your study group, but you were kind enough to give me your card.

As I may have indicated to you when we met, I have now transferred from the United States to Madrid, where my Corporation is establishing the head office of its European network. As Executive Vice-President (Operations), I have the responsibility of assembling a technical team that will put Tahoe Data straight into *the front rank* of data processing in the European Community.

Without committing either of us in any way, I think it might be useful and interesting for us to meet, in either Madrid or Zaragoza, in the near future. If you would like to discuss Tahoe Data's plans, and how they might influence your own, please contact me as soon as is convenient.

Sincerely

Bret Holman

Bret Holman

PS – we have not had time yet to get our sales literature translated into Spanish, but I enclose one or two leaflets in English that will give you some idea of what we do. – BH

5.16 Reading for key words

Read the letter from Bret Holman aga (5.15). Find the words or phrases th show you the following:

1 Bret Holman does not want Carlos employer or his colleagues to kno about the contents of the letter.
2 He wants to make it clear to Carl that he is not actually offering him job at this time.
3 He thinks Tahoe Data might be ab to offer Carlos an interesting job.

5.17 Document study

This is an extract from one of the leafle Bret sent to Carlos. The language is ve different from the language of a busine letter, though there is one sentence Bret's letter (5.15) that could have com from a leaflet or perhaps from a advertisement. Which one?

How many words can you find in th leaflet here that make a manager's wo sound very difficult?

The Hard Facts

Today's manufacturing managers face major challenges. *The hard facts* are that *competition is stiffer, budgets are tighter,* and technology is evolving more rapidly than ever before. How do you plan the best course for your company, the one that will *ensure* its continued success?

One solution is to implement a Computer-Integrated Manufacturing (CIM) strategy.

CIM covers the full range of computer use throughout a manufacturing company. It means that all the computers at every level of an organisation can communicate with one another, exchanging information as often as required.

It's often tough to commit capital when capital is tight. Few companies can afford to build a CIM factory *from the ground up.* Our approach to CIM lets you begin small and add to your system as your organisation's needs change and grow. You can see improvements in your operations in the short term while at the same time planning for the long-term success of your company.

The Good News

Once your organisation makes a commitment to CIM, come and talk to us. We offer customers a range of choices – hardware and software solutions that cover all manufacturing needs. Easy to learn and to use, these products improve the productivity and output of your staff almost as soon as they are installed.

In addition, you can easily *integrate our equipment* into your existing computer systems, prolonging the life of every piece of equipment you purchase . . .

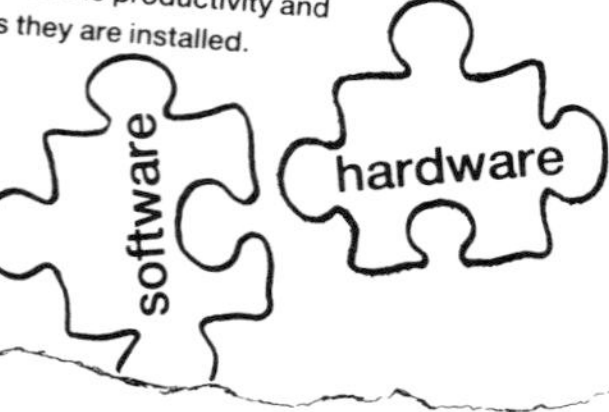

5.18 Reading for key words

Find the words or phrases in the leaflet (5.17) that show you the following:

1 three 'major challenges' in engineering.
2 it may be difficult to afford expensive computer systems.
3 two reasons why money spent on Tahoe Data products will enable you to get more value out of your computers.

5.19 Speaking practice: flight numbers and times

While he was in Osaka, Carlos decided to take a few days' holiday. He telephoned a travel agent to ask about changing the date of his flight from Osaka to Madrid. Read the dialogue, but don't listen to it yet! Part of the airline schedule is shown below. You must decide what flight numbers and times the agent gives Carlos. Listen to their conversation, and then listen again and speak the part of the travel agent.

> **5.19**
> **(a) direct flight** a flight between two places without stopping.
> **via Tokyo** stopping at Tokyo.
> **departing** leaving; **departing** is a formal word that is often used by travel agents; note that Carlos uses **leave** when he replies.
> **(a) stop-over in Tokyo** a short stay in Tokyo as part of a longer journey.

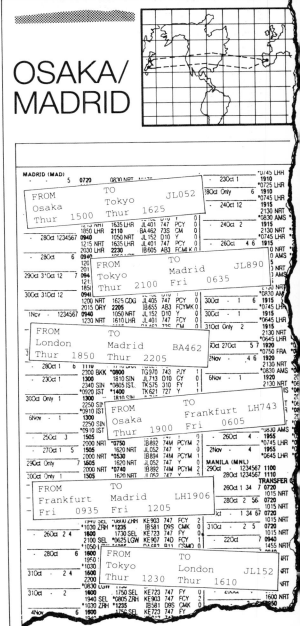

CARLOS I have to be in Madrid early in the morning on 31 July, that's a Friday.

AGENT Well, there's no *direct flight*. The best route is *via Tokyo*, or via Tokyo and London, which is a little quicker.

CARLOS What time do I have to leave Tokyo to get to Madrid before 0800 hours?

AGENT There's a Japan Airlines flight, JL890, *departing* Tokyo Narita on Thursday at 2100 hours, arriving Madrid on Friday at 0635.

CARLOS Suppose I take that, what time do I leave Osaka?

AGENT There's a Japan Airlines flight, JL052, departing Osaka on Thursday at ___**a**___ hours, arriving Tokyo Narita at ___**b**___.

CARLOS Oh! That's rather a long *stop-over in Tokyo* – four and a half hours!

AGENT Well, you could go via London. There's a Japan Airlines flight, JL___**c**___, departing Tokyo Narita on Thursday at 1230 hours, arriving London Heathrow at 1610.

CARLOS How long do I have in London?

AGENT There's a British Airways flight, BA462, departing London Heathrow at ___**d**___ hours, arriving Madrid at 2205.

CARLOS Hm. That means I have to leave Osaka early Thursday morning and change planes twice and I get to Madrid late on Thursday night.

AGENT Well, you could go via Frankfurt. There's a Lufthansa flight, LH743, departing Osaka on Thursday at 1900 hours, arriving Frankfurt on Friday at 0605.

CARLOS But that's even later than if I go Tokyo–Madrid! What time would I get to Madrid?

AGENT There's a Lufthansa flight, ___**e**___, departing Frankfurt on Friday at ___**f**___ hours, arriving Madrid at ___**g**___.

CARLOS My boss will kill me! On the other hand, it would give me a whole extra day in Osaka. Yes! That'll do fine, I'll take that one, if you can get my reservation transferred.

AIRLINE SCHEDULE 1992

OSAKA/ MADRID

FROM	TO	Flight
Osaka Thur 1500	Tokyo Thur 1625	JL052
Tokyo Thur 2100	Madrid Fri 0635	JL890
London Thur 1850	Madrid Thur 2205	BA462
Osaka Thur 1900	Frankfurt Fri 0605	LH743
Frankfurt Fri 0935	Madrid Fri 1205	LH1906
Tokyo Thur 1230	London Thur 1610	JL152

5.20 Writing practice: a memo

Write a memo for Carlos to send to Joe Andrews, telling him about the change in his return flight. Don't apologise to Andrews for returning late; just inform him politely.

Study record	
5.1	
5.2	
5.3	
5.4	
5.5	
5.6	
5.7	
5.8	
5.9	
5.10	
5.11	
5.12	
5.13	
5.14	
5.15	
5.16	
5.17	
5.18	
5.19	
5.20	

Answer key and commentary for unit 5

5.2 Reading for key words
1 ATTN **2** ASAP **3** a vacancy
4 take up this offer **5** advise us; inform us
6 through **7** please; kindly.

5.4 Find the word
a vacancy **b** training **c** to
d delegates **e** travel **f** flight

5.5 Document study
Some of the most useful phrases are: 'Thank you for . . . ', 'We shall be pleased . . . ', 'We trust you will find . . . '; 'My colleagues and I . . . ', 'I enclose . . . ', 'Please let me know . . . '.

5.6 Reading for key words
1 My colleagues **2** a participant
3 Our company car **4** the course schedule
5 a brief summary

5.7 Writing practice
These are model answers; there are many possible ways of writing the telex and letter.

1

ATTN MR YAMASHITA
THANK YOU FOR YOUR TELEX. WE ARE GLAD TO ACCEPT A PLACE FOR OUR CHIEF SOFTWARE ENGINEER, DR CARLOS VILA, ON COURSE 37 COMMENCING 22 JULY. HE WILL ARRIVE OSAKA AT 1615 LOCAL TIME ON 21 JULY ON FLIGHT JL456 AND DEPART AT 0930 ON 29 JULY ON FLIGHT JL934. C.V. AND LETTER FOLLOW.
REGARDS ANDREWS

2

SIMA MACHINE CORPORATION
Osaka, Japan

Mr Joe Andrews
Staff Controller
Industrias Montresor SA
Apdo 234
Zaragoza
Spain

24 June 1992

Dear Mr Andrews

Regarding your request for software familiarisation on 9909 series machines, I am pleased to tell you that we have a vacancy on Course 37, commencing on 22 July and lasting one week, at our Centre in Osaka.

If you wish to take up this offer, please advise us of the delegate's name and qualifications as soon as possible. We will arrange transport from the airport, accommodation, etc. in Osaka from 21 through 28 July. Kindly make flight arrangements for the participant, and inform us of these also.

Yours sincerely

5.9 Listening for meaning
1 Carlos thinks he may have made a mistake. Perhaps this isn't Miss Ito, or perhaps he has pronounced 'Ito' wrongly. His voice rises to show that this is really a question. Akiko's voice falls. She is making a statement: 'You are Dr Vila.'
2 Her voice rises quickly on the last word 'flight'.
3 'Quite right' means 'exactly right'. 'Quite comfortable' means 'a bit comfortable, but not very'.

5.13 Speaking practice
MAN: Hello! How was your conference?
WOMAN: Terrible! My **company car** broke down and I missed **the start of the conference**.
MAN: Oh dear! That's not good for your **company's image**.
WOMAN: No. And it got worse! At the end of lunch I got up to leave and **my chair leg** broke!

5.14 Reading for key words
1 We have a full programme for you . . . and the course is very intensive.
2 to have plenty of hands-on experience
3 Please treat this as a confidential document.
4 Hi there! Mind if I join you?
5 That's quite a book they've given you.
6 Oh, I understand.
7 Good to meet you
8 F **9** N **10** I **11** F **12** N
Carlos wouldn't use sentences 8 and 11; in this informal situation, he would sound self-important and a little ridiculous if he used too formal language. He probably wouldn't use 10 either because he doesn't know Bret Holman well enough to be so informal with him. He would probably use 9 or 12.

5.15 Document study
No, he does not.

5.16 Reading for key words
1 He marks the envelope 'Private and confidential', and the letter 'Personal'.
2 Without committing either of us in any way
3 to discuss Tahoe Data's plans, and how they might influence your own, . . .

5.17 Document study
'I have the responsibility of assembling a technical team that will put Tahoe Data straight into the front rank of data processing in the European Community.'

The words that make the manager's work sound difficult are: 'major challenges', 'competition is stiffer, budgets are tighter, and technology is evolving more rapidly than ever before', 'It's often tough . . . '.

5.18 Reading for key words
1 The major challenges are that 'competition is stiffer, budgets are tighter, and technology is evolving more rapidly than ever before'.
2 It's often tough to commit capital when capital is tight.
3 these products improve the productivity and output of your staff; you can easily integrate our equipment into your existing computer systems.

5.19 Speaking practice
a 1500 **b** 1625 **c** 152 **d** 1850
e LH1906 **f** 0935 **g** 1205

5.20 Writing practice
This is a model answer.

Memo to Joe Andrews
From Carlos Vila
Date 25 July 1992

I will be returning from Osaka on Thursday, Lufthansa flights LH743 and LH1906, arriving Madrid at 1205 Friday, via Frankfurt.

Unit 6: Office management

SITUATION

In this unit we look at what happens in the offices of Bookmart Publishing Services. We see how people work together and how they deal with the problems that arise, both within the office and with their customers.

CHARACTERS

Terry Cabe	is Personnel Manager at Bookmart.
Elsie Donnell	is Dispatch Room Supervisor at Bookmart.
Jane	works in the Dispatch Room at Bookmart.
Frank Penny	works in the Dispatch Room at Bookmart.
Gemma Tripp	is the Dispatch Room Manager at Bookmart.
Susan	works in the Order Processing department at Bookmart.
Mr Field	owns a bookshop in York.
Ben	is the office junior in the Order Processing department at Bookmart.
George Harvey	is Sales Manager at Bookmart.

All of these characters are British.

LANGUAGE

Vocabulary	Office management and routine; scheduling holidays; customer complaints; orders and invoices.
Skills	Managing people; arranging a holiday rota; dealing with a complaint; explaining to people.
Structure	Suppose.
Documents	A holiday chart; business letters; an order; an invoice.

Working with people

6.1
that the lot then? is that everything that you wanted to discuss?
a selection board a meeting where people decide who to appoint to a job.
He's put himself down . . . for he's written his name on a list for something, in this case on the holiday chart.
to delegate to give someone the power to make a decision that you usually make.

6.2
His phone's not answering he is not picking up his telephone when it rings.
I couldn't say I don't know; in this case Jane probably does know, but does not want to say so.
170 3762 many people answer the telephone by saying the number. They usually break it up into three or four numbers in a group.
on flexitime working on a system which allows you to start and stop work at times that you choose. You must still work a certain total number of hours per week, and you must be at work between certain times.
ten o'clock at the latest no later than ten o'clock.
half eleven half past eleven, eleven thirty; **half eleven** is an informal usage.

6.1 Listen and read

It's Thursday, 18 April 1991, at Bookmart Publishing Services. Terry Cabe, the Personnel Manager, is having his weekly meeting with Elsie Donnell, the Dispatch Room Supervisor. Listen to what they say. How do we know that Terry isn't really interested in the holiday arrangements?

TERRY Right, *that the lot then?* I've got *a selection board* at ten.
ELSIE Just one more thing. It's to do with the holiday arrangements. Frank Penny – you know who I mean, don't you?
TERRY What's he done now?
ELSIE *He's put himself down* on the chart *for* the first two weeks of August. He did exactly the same thing last year. He's the only one in the office with no children. He can go on holiday any time . . .
TERRY Elsie, whatever you say to Frank, I'll back you up, but I'm late for the selection board already, I'm afraid I simply have *to delegate* this one to you. Tell me tomorrow how you got on.

6.2 Listen and read

Elsie is looking for Frank Penny. She finds his colleague, Jane. Listen to what they say. What time should Frank start work? What time will he start today?

ELSIE Jane, where's Frank? *His phone's not answering*, isn't he in today?
JANE Mm, I don't think I've seen him today. *I couldn't say* where he is.
ELSIE I suppose I'll have to ring him at home.
[Phone rings]
FRANK *170 3762*.
ELSIE Frank, it's Elsie Donnell. Aren't you coming in today?
FRANK Of course I'm coming in. I am *on flexitime* now, remember.
ELSIE Frank, it's now 10.37. If you're on flexitime you're supposed to be here by *ten o'clock at the latest*.
FRANK Well, be fair, Elsie. I was working till half past eight last night on the papers for the selection board this morning. Don't worry. I'll be there by, oh, *half eleven*, OK?
ELSIE Well – I suppose so.

6.3 Structure practice: *suppose*

Elsie uses the word 'suppose' in three different ways:

a I suppose I'll have to ring him at home.
[I have to do it, but I'm not very pleased about it.]

b If you're on flexitime you're supposed to be here by ten o'clock at the latest.
[You should do it because that's the rule.]

c Well – I suppose so.
[I agree, but unwillingly.]

Now look at the sentences below. All of them include the word 'suppose'. Decide for each one whether 'suppose' is used like **a**, **b** or **c** above:

1 Can I borrow £10? – I suppose so!
2 You're supposed to take your holidays in June!
3 You're not supposed to use the office telephone to make personal calls.
4 I suppose I'll have to change my holidays!
5 I don't suppose we can afford a new car now? – I suppose not.
6 I suppose we'll have to wait and save up for it.

6.4 Listen and read

Elsie sees Frank when he comes to work. Listen to what they say. Why can't Frank change his holiday dates?

ELSIE Frank, can I have a word with you?

FRANK Look, *if it's about* me coming in late, I said I'm sorry.

ELSIE That's not what I wanted to see you about. It's your holiday dates. You've put down for the first two weeks in August. Now, we discussed all this last year, remember? You know everyone wants the first two weeks in August, and everyone else has young children. I really can't let you have those two weeks, *two years in a row*. Wouldn't you like to go in June instead?

FRANK *No way*. I can't. We've already booked our holiday. We're going on a cruise. And Chrissy's arranged with her employer to get those two weeks. *She didn't have any hassle.*

ELSIE Frank, I'm not hassling you. I just don't think it's fair, that's all.

> **6.4**
> **if it's about** if you want to speak to me about.
> **two years in a row** one year, and then again the next year.
> **No way** definitely not; **no way** is an informal usage.
> **She didn't have any hassle** she didn't have any problems or arguments, in this case with her employers; **hassle** is an informal word.

6.5 Document study: a holiday chart

This is part of the Dispatch Room holiday chart. In the left-hand column are the names of the staff. Study this chart. You will need to refer to it for 6.6.

WAL… 1991

DISPATCH ROOM-
HOLIDAY ROTA 1991
please DON'T WRITE ANYTHING on this chart until you have discussed your holiday requirements with the Supervisor

WEEK BEGINNING	JUNE				JULY					AUGUST				SEPTEMBER				
	3	10	17	24	1	8	15	22	29	5	12	19	26	2	9	16	23	30
Victor Azeri																		
ELSIE DONNELL																		
Sharon Gupta																		
Jacqui Jackson																		
RICHARD OGDEN																		
frank penny																		
Lola Phung																		
QUEENIE SMITH																		
Joe Smith																		

6.6 Speaking practice: sorting out the holidays

Gemma Tripp is Elsie's manager. She phones Elsie to discuss the holiday arrangements for the department. Read through the dialogue first, and write what you think Elsie says to Gemma (**a–g**). You will need to look at the holiday chart in 6.5. Then listen to the conversation. Don't worry if your answers are not exactly the same as the ones you hear. Listen again, and speak the part of Elsie.

GEMMA I've got to go away for a fortnight from 29 July. You'll be standing in for me, as usual. You've got the holiday chart there, haven't you? Let's see if we can sort it out so it's fair to everyone. When were you planning to take your holiday?

ELSIE ______**a**______

GEMMA Hm. We *overlap* by a week. Suppose you were to postpone your holiday till 12 August? How many people would be away from the office that week?

ELSIE ______**b**______

GEMMA And the following week, *the week of the nineteenth*?

ELSIE ______**c**______

GEMMA Mm. If you were away then, who could *deputise for you*?

ELSIE ______**d**______

GEMMA No, not Queenie, I think. Victor's too new, and so is Lola. That leaves Frank or Richard. How would you feel about Frank being in charge of the Dispatch Room?

ELSIE ______**e**______

GEMMA Yes, I thought you'd say that. I'll have a word with Richard Ogden. Why can't Frank take his fortnight off before the school holidays?

ELSIE ______**f**______

GEMMA Yes, but she hasn't got any children, has she? Go on, tell Frank to persuade her to go in June. Otherwise, I'm afraid you'll just have to change your dates.

ELSIE ______**g**______

> **6.6**
> **(to) overlap** to happen at the same time; in this case Elsie and Gemma are on holiday at the same time.
> **the week of the nineteenth** the week beginning the nineteenth, in this case 19 August.
> **deputise for you** manage the department when you are away.

Dealing with complaints

6.7
One two double-seven 1277; **double** is used to repeat the next number. When Mr Field says **one double-two seven** he means 1227.
dispatched sent; **dispatched** is a formal word often used in business.
Can you give it another couple of days? 'can you wait two more days?' This is an informal usage.

6.8
office junior a young person who is being trained in office work.
a remittance money sent by post; **remittance** is a formal word.
the statement the document which lists invoices and a total amount of money to be paid, usually sent to a company each month from a supplier.

6.9
a trade discount a deduction which is allowed only to members of 'the trade', in this case, booksellers or publishers.
Cheek! George Harvey is suggesting that Martinu are deliberately misinterpreting the discount terms to avoid payment.
play this by ear wait and see what happens, and decide what to do then.

6.7 Speaking practice: a complaint

Other staff at Bookmart deal with customers and suppliers. Listen to this telephone conversation, then listen again and speak the part of Mr Field, the bookseller.

SUSAN Hello, Order Processing, can I help you?
FIELD Good morning. My name's Field, I have a bookshop in York.
SUSAN Yes. What can I do for you, Mr Field?
FIELD I'm calling about an order that I've been waiting for since the end of March.
SUSAN The end of March! Can you give me the order number, please?
FIELD Yes, the order number was one two two seven.
SUSAN I'll just call it up on the computer. *One two double-seven*, did you say?
FIELD No, *one double-two seven*.
SUSAN Oh sorry, one double-two seven. Yes, I've got it. Well, it was *dispatched* to you on the twelfth of this month, so it should arrive any time now. *Can you give it another couple of days?*
FIELD Well, all right, as long as it has been sent. But if it doesn't arrive in the next forty-eight hours you'll be hearing from me again.
SUSAN Yes, do please contact me again if it hasn't arrived by then, Mr Field.
FIELD Who shall I ask for?
SUSAN Susan – I'm Susan. Thank you! Goodbye!
FIELD Goodbye.

6.8 Document study

Ben is the *office junior*. He is opening the morning post. Listen to what he says. What problem does he find?

BEN Susan? There's *a remittance* here, they've sent a cheque, but it's less than what it says on *the statement*.
SUSAN Really? Any explanation?
BEN Oh yes! There's this letter.
SUSAN Ben, get me the customer file on this, will you? I'll be back in ten minutes. Can you leave it on my desk so I don't forget to deal with it?

Bookmart Publishing Services Ltd
Unit 8
Ironbridge Way
Telford
Shropshire TF89 4RD

MARTINU BOOKS

15 April 1991

Dear Sirs

We enclose a cheque for £12,344.67 against your March statement (copy also enclosed). We are withholding payment on your invoice 8874503 for £1,340.03 because you have not yet given us a satisfactory reply to our letter of 22 January.

6.9 Document study

Susan is reading the file on Martinu Books. She finds a letter from Martinu. Read the letter and the handwritten comments from her manager, George Harvey, carefully. Should Martinu have the extra discount? Why/why not?

Bookmart Publishing Services Ltd
Unit 8
Ironbridge Way
Telford
Shropshire TF89 4RD

MARTINU BOOKS

22 January 1991

Dear Sirs

Invoice no. 8874503 dated 17 December 1990

We have to draw your attention to an error in this invoice. You have deducted *a trade discount* of 35 per cent. You will recall, however, that your sales representative agreed on 1 October that we should benefit under the terms of your 'Major Customer' plan. We are therefore deducting an additional 5 per cent from this invoice, and claim a similar deduction from invoices 8789820, 8791087 and 8849204.

We trust that you will find this in order, and remain

Yours faithfully

M. J. Martinu

M J Martinu
General Manager

SUSAN –

Cheek! – They're just trying it on because they think we're scared to lose their order. They know perfectly well that they only qualify for the extra 5% if their orders exceed £5,000 every month for six months. They totalled less than that in Jan and Feb – But we don't want a confrontation – we'll have to play this by ear. Ignore this letter and put the invoice into their next statement at the same figure. — GAH, 25-1-91

6.10 Listen and read: explaining discounts

Susan has explained about Martinu Books to George Harvey. He reads the file, and then telephones Susan. Listen to what he says, then do 6.11.

GEORGE — Susan, thanks for sending me the details about Martinu. I'd like you to write to them. Point out that we don't understand why they've *knocked off* five per cent, but say that we'll allow them a special *discount* of two point five per cent on everything since the beginning of December, OK? It'll be *deducted from* their April statement. No need to mention the invoice that they haven't paid; it'll just appear again on their next statement. Of course, *assuming* they go on ordering *five thousand plus* every month, they'll qualify for the full five per cent discount starting in August anyway. Is that OK?

SUSAN — OK, Mr Harvey. Thanks.

6.11 Writing practice: a letter to Martinu Books

Susan now has to write to Martinu Books explaining how the discount works. Write the letter for her. The letter should be formal, but polite. The aim is to persuade Martinu to pay, not to force them. Remember, you don't want to lose a customer.

Nearly all the phrases you need are shown in the text, but you will have to think carefully before starting to write. The following points must be covered:

a Start by saying that we (you are writing on behalf of your company, not of yourself) have received their letter and cheque.
b Say that we do not understand why they have deducted 5% from the four invoices mentioned in their letter of 22 January.
c Remind them that our representative explained the 'Major Customer' plan to them. They do not yet qualify.
d Offer them instead what Mr Harvey suggested – 2.5%. If their orders continue to total £5000 or more each month, they will qualify for the full 5% discount from 1 August.

6.12 Speaking practice: an angry customer

Susan has another telephone call from an angry Mr Field. Listen to what they say. Why is he angry? Listen again, and speak the part of Mr Field. Remember – you're supposed to be angry!

SUSAN — Hello, Order Processing, can I help you?

FIELD — Hello, this is Field Booksellers, in York. I'm calling about my order, number one two two seven . . .

SUSAN — Oh, good morning, Mr Field. Did the books reach you all right?

FIELD — They were finally delivered a few minutes ago.

SUSAN — Oh good!

FIELD — But most of them were damaged, and it's due to bad packaging.

SUSAN — Oh dear! Was the packaging damaged in any way?

FIELD — Yes. The boxes weren't *banded*, so they just split open.

SUSAN — I can't understand how that could've happened. Every parcel is supposed to be *machine-banded* before it leaves the warehouse. Look, can you return the books to us, *carriage forward* of course, and if you could possibly fax us a list of what's damaged, we'll get replacements sent off as soon as we can, provided of course we still have the titles in stock.

FIELD — And how long will that take?

SUSAN — Well, if you can send us the fax by, say, three o'clock this afternoon, I'll get back to you before you close tonight.

FIELD — Well if you could. You'll appreciate that I've got customers who've been waiting a long time for these books.

SUSAN — Yes, we do appreciate the inconvenience to your customers, and I assure you we'll do everything we possibly can to help. Thank you, Mr Field. Goodbye.

6.10
knocked off taken off, reduced the total by.
discount a reduction in price, usually because you buy a lot of something.
deducted from taken off, subtracted from the total.
assuming if it continues to be true that.
five thousand plus more than five thousand pounds' worth of goods; an informal usage.

6.12
banded when cartons of goods are dispatched, they are securely closed by a plastic or metal strip around the carton; **machine-banded** means that this is done by a machine.
carriage forward the person who receives the goods will pay for the cost of sending them; in this case Bookmart will pay because it was their mistake.

Placing an order

6.13
bulk packaging materials materials for wrapping goods, bought in large quantities.
what's-his-name George has forgotten the supplier's name.
to run low to have less than they would like.

6.14
Cat. an abbreviation for **Catalogue**.
Qty. an abbreviation for **Quantity**.
Unit price the price of one item or good.
cartons boxes, usually containing a number of items or goods.

6.15
raised the order in four copies written the order on a printed form that makes four copies.
to initial to write the first letters of your name to show that you approve something; George Harvey writes 'GAH'.
not valid will not be accepted as correct.

6.13 Listen and read

Susan rings George Harvey to remind him about an order for packaging materials. Listen to what they say. Susan thinks that George had forgotten about the order. How do we know this?

SUSAN — Mr Harvey, you remember we asked several office supply firms to quote us for *bulk packaging materials*.

GEORGE — Oh, when *what's-his-name* went out of business. I remember. Have we had the quotations?

SUSAN — Yes, and I think we should put in an order. The warehouse say they're starting *to run low* on most items, and we need stock for the office as well.

GEORGE — All right then. Perhaps I'd better have a look at the quotes. Meanwhile, if you'll make a list of what we want . . .

6.14 Document study

George Harvey decides that the order should go to Beloff Supplies. Susan makes out the order form below. Read through it carefully, and note how it is laid out. You will need to refer back to this order in 6.16.

ORDER

BOOKMART PUBLISHING SERVICES LTD

Order No. 00983

From: Bookmart Publishing Services Ltd
Unit 8
Ironbridge Way
Telford
Shropshire TF89 4RD

Date: 22 April 1991

To: Beloff Supplies Ltd
Oakengates Road
Telford
Shropshire TF13 8AE

PLEASE SUPPLY:

Cat. no.	DESCRIPTION	Qty.	Unit price
213	Corrugated paper, 100 cm	50 rolls	3.80
346	Plastic cell-wrap, 180 cm	20 rolls	10.45
471a	Parcel tape, brown	8 cartons	13.20
474	Clear adhesive tape, 2 cm	2 cartons	14.85

When acknowledging order please notify us of any alteration to the prices shown above.

SPECIAL INSTRUCTIONS:

Deliver by: 30.04.91
to: as above

6.15 Listen and read

Susan is teaching Ben about order forms. Listen to what they say. What mistake does Ben make? What would the correct figure be?

SUSAN — Now, Ben – remember what I told you? We've *raised the order in four copies*.

BEN — Top copy to the supplier. Pink to Warehouse. Blue to Accounts. Yellow, file copy. Right?

SUSAN — Right. But get Mr Harvey *to initial* them first, otherwise the order's *not valid*.

BEN — Oh, and there's something else you haven't done. You haven't put the total price. Let me see, it's, er, forty-two pounds thirty.

SUSAN — Ben, those are unit prices. You've got to multiply them by the quantities. The total will be several hundred pounds.

BEN — Then why don't you show it on the order form?

SUSAN — Because the prices may have changed, or Beloff may not have all the goods in stock. They'll show the total on their invoice. It's their job, not ours.

6.16 Document study

A delivery arrives from Beloff. Ben signs for the goods, and takes out the delivery note and invoice. Check the invoice against the order in 6.14. Is everything correct?

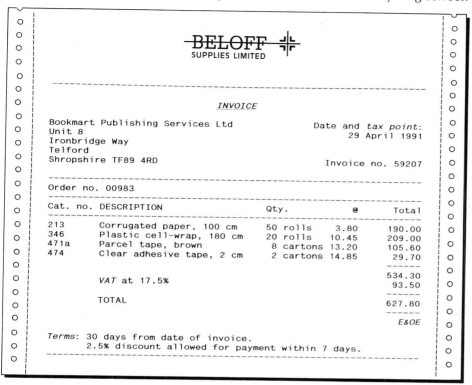

BELOFF
SUPPLIES LIMITED

INVOICE

Bookmart Publishing Services Ltd
Unit 8
Ironbridge Way
Telford
Shropshire TF89 4RD

Date and *tax point*: 29 April 1991

Invoice no. 59207

Order no. 00983

Cat. no.	DESCRIPTION	Qty.	@	Total
213	Corrugated paper, 100 cm	50 rolls	3.80	190.00
346	Plastic cell-wrap, 180 cm	20 rolls	10.45	209.00
471a	Parcel tape, brown	8 cartons	13.20	105.60
474	Clear adhesive tape, 2 cm	2 cartons	14.85	29.70
				534.30
	VAT at 17.5%			93.50
	TOTAL			627.80

E&OE

Terms: 30 days from date of invoice.
2.5% discount allowed for payment within 7 days.

6.17 Listen and read

Ben unpacks the goods, and ticks off each item against the invoice. Listen to his conversation with Susan. What does Ben have to do now?

SUSAN Have you checked that everything's there?

BEN It's all here. Only I think they've sent two and a half centimetre tape instead of two centimetre.

SUSAN Oh no! It'll have to go back. All our tape dispensers are two centimetres wide. Check it, will you, Ben? If it is the wrong *stuff, make out a returns slip* and ask them to replace the tape as soon as they can. And in the meantime we'll expect *a credit note* from them.

6.16
(an) invoice a document showing the cost of each item supplied, and the total price to be paid.
(the) tax point the date on which the transaction officially took place. This information may be required by the Customs and Excise authorities (who collect VAT).
VAT an abbreviation for 'Value Added Tax', a tax paid on most business transactions in the UK and most European countries.
E&OE an abbreviation for 'Errors and Omissions Excepted'. This means that a mistake in the invoice can be corrected later, and the correct payment demanded.
Terms terms of payment; the conditions under which the supplier agrees to do business with the customer.

6.17
stuff material, things; **stuff** is a very general and informal word that can be used to refer to something when you don't want or don't need to say what it is.
(to) make out a returns slip to write on a form details of goods that you are returning to the supplier, in this case because they are not what you wanted.
a credit note a document that shows that the supplier owes money to the customer, in this case because the wrong goods were sent and have been returned.

Study record	
6.1	
6.2	
6.3	
6.4	
6.5	
6.6	
6.7	
6.8	
6.9	
6.10	
6.11	
6.12	
6.13	
6.14	
6.15	
6.16	
6.17	

Answer key and commentary for unit 6

6.1 Listen and read
He tries to end the conversation by saying 'Right, that the lot, then?'; he tells her he has an appointment very soon; he refuses to offer any help in dealing with Frank.

6.2 Listen and read
Frank should start work before ten o'clock. He will start today at 11.30.

6.3 Structure practice
1 c **2** b **3** b **4** a **5** a, c **6** a

6.4 Listen and read
Frank can't change his holiday dates because he has already booked his cruise.

6.6 Speaking practice
a From the fifth to the sixteenth of August.
b One, two, three, four. Me, Sharon, Jacqui and Queenie. And Frank, of course.
c The same, except for Zoe Smith instead of Queenie.
d Well, there's Victor, and Richard, and Frank, and Lola. And Queenie, of course.
e No way!
f It's because of his girlfriend, Chrissy. Her holiday's then.
g Yes, I suppose I'll have to, won't I!

6.8 Document study
The problem is that Martinu have not paid £1340.03 for invoice 8874503.

6.9 Document study
Martinu should not have the extra discount of 5% because their orders have not exceeded £5000 per month for six months.

6.11 Writing practice
This is a model answer; there are many possible ways of writing this letter.

General Manager
Martinu Books

18 April 1991

Dear Mr Martinu

We have received your cheque for £12,344.67 and letter dated 15 April 1991. We do not understand, however, your deduction of an additional 5% from the four invoices mentioned in your letter of 22 January and from our March statement.

When our representative visited your office on 1 October, he explained that customers only qualify for the extra 5% discount under the terms of our 'Major Customer' plan if their orders exceed £5000 every month for six months. Your invoices from us totalled less than £5000 in January and February.

However, we are willing to allow a special 2.5% discount from 1 December last year. This will appear on your April statement.

Assuming your orders continue to total £5000 or more each month, you will, of course, qualify for the full 5% discount from 1 August.

We hope this arrangement will be satisfactory.

Yours sincerely

for G A Harvey
Sales Manager

6.12 Speaking practice
Mr Field is angry because when the books finally arrived, they were damaged.

6.13 Listen and read
She pretends he remembers by saying 'You remember . . . ', and at the same time tells him the important facts.

6.15 Listen and read
Ben adds up the unit prices but forgets to multiply them by the quantities. The correct figure is £534.30.

6.16 Document study
Yes. According to the invoice, everything on the order has been correctly supplied.

6.17 Listen and read
Ben has to make out a returns slip and ask for a credit note.

Unit 7: Paperwork

SITUATION

We are still at the offices of Bookmart Publishing Services. In this unit we see how to deal with the problems of credit control; how to conduct an employee assessment interview; and how to investigate and report an accident.

CHARACTERS

George Harvey

Terry Cabe

Frank Penny

Mr Harris	owns a bookshop in York.
Mr Martinu	is General Manager at Martinu Books.
Andy Brumshaw	is the warehouse foreman at Bookmart.
Alice Perkins	is an office cleaner at Bookmart.

All of these characters are British.

LANGUAGE

Vocabulary	Money transactions; records and record-keeping; employee assessment and relationships.
Skills	Simple negotiating; asking for credit terms; making conditions; chasing payment; basic report writing.
Documents	A statement; a formal letter; an Employee Assessment Record; an accident record book; an accident report form.

Collecting payments and settling accounts

7.1
pretty regularly often and repeatedly.
we do have some discretion we don't always have to follow the rules.
do me a favour do something to help me, even though you don't have to do it.
No, no here, George says 'No, no' to show that he agrees with Mr Harris. He means 'No, no, you don't . . .'
it's only a formality something that must be done, even though it won't affect what happens; George must have the references for the file.

7.1 Listen and read

George Harvey gets a phone call from Mr Harris, a bookshop owner. Listen to how they negotiate a change in their agreement.

GEORGE Sales.

HARRIS Good morning. Mr Harvey? My name is Harris, I have a bookshop in York.

GEORGE Oh, hello, Mr Harris, how are you? How can I help you?

HARRIS Well, I've been ordering books from you for eight or nine months now, *pretty regularly*. I thought it was about time I applied to open an account with you. I pay all my other suppliers monthly, but you still send me a pro forma invoice on every order.

GEORGE Ah, yes. There are reasons for that. Our new customers are supposed to pay cash with order for a year – but *we do have some discretion* in this matter, and I can well understand you'd prefer open account terms. That shouldn't be a problem. If you can let me have the names of a couple of referees, preferably firms you've had accounts with for at least twelve months . . .

HARRIS I can do that, of course, but I wonder if in this case you could *do me a favour* and open the account straight away? I'm just making up a rather large order, and I don't . . .

GEORGE *No, no*, I quite understand. Yes, I don't see why not. In that case could I ask you to write to your referees and let them know that I'll be writing to them, and would appreciate a quick response? I know *it's only a formality* but it could hold things up a bit.

7.2 Reading for key words

What words in 7.1 show us the following?

1 George Harvey is following the company rules.
2 He can sometimes change the rules.
3 Mr Harris wants special treatment.
4 George Harvey needs the references straight away.
5 He thinks that there won't be any problems.

7.3 Writing practice: a request for open account terms

Imagine that Mr Harris decided to write to George Harvey instead of telephoning him. Write the letter for him. Include the points he made in 7.1, and the names and addresses of two referees. They are: James Merridew, Publishers, 97 Henrietta Street, London WC2; The Fireside Press, PO Box 7591, Milton Keynes MK45 7ER.

7.4 Document study: a statement

This is Mr Harris's first statement from Bookmart. Someone at the bookshop didn't know that they now had an account. How do we know this?

Bookmart Publishing Services Ltd
Unit 8
Ironbridge Way
Telford
Shropshire TF89 4RD

STATEMENT

Harris's Bookshop
73a Longshipgate
York YK28 2CB

Account no. 2681651
Statement date: 31 May 1991

Date	Particulars	Ref.	Debit	Credit	Balance
	opening balance				00.00
01/05/91	Inv	4562	126.90		126.90
06/05/91	Inv	4701	360.91		487.81
06/05/91	Received			126.90	360.91
10/05/91	Inv	5002	1298.98		1659.89
15/05/91	Credit Note	782		62.23	1597.66
20/05/91	Inv	5238	438.02		2035.68
	closing balance				2035.68

current	1 month	2 months	3+ months	TOTAL BALANCE NOW DUE:
2035.68	0	0	0	2035.68

Please detach this portion and send with your remittance.

Account no: 2681651 Statement date: 31 May 1991 2035.68

7.5 Writing figures: a monthly statement

You are preparing Mr Harris's June statement for Bookmart. Draw up the statement using the following information: on 12 June Harris sends Bookmart a cheque for £438.02; on 10 June a consignment of books is invoiced to Harris; the invoice number is 5629 and the value is £759.

7.6 Document study: a formal letter

George Harvey has to write a letter to another bookshop, Martinu Books. They have not paid anything since the end of March. Read through the letter. Notice that it is very formal.

Mr G F Martinu
General Manager
Martinu Books
Eastgate
York YO1 1DX

13 June 1991

Dear Mr Martinu

Our statements dated 31 March, 30 April and 31 May 1991

As we have received no reply to our letters of 4 May and 30 May, *we are compelled* to draw your attention once more to your non-payment of the sums owed to us. The total amount outstanding is now £15,872.87.

We regret that we cannot continue to allow credit terms as long as this debt remains uncleared. Until further notice, therefore, goods will be supplied to you only on receipt of cash against a pro forma invoice.

I shall be obliged if you will contact me personally within the next seven days to discuss means by which the amount outstanding can be cleared. We are anxious to avoid any action which might *jeopardise* the good business relationship *we have enjoyed* in the past.

Yours sincerely

G.A. Harvey

G A Harvey
Sales Manager

7.6
we are compelled we must; this is a very formal letter.
jeopardise damage or destroy.
we have enjoyed we have had; **enjoy** here does not suggest fun, it is another slightly formal expression.

7.7
to be perfectly frank I am being very honest.
I can get that off to you I can send that to you.

7.7 Speaking practice: chasing payment

George Harvey did not get a reply to his letter, so he now telephones Mr Martinu. Listen to their conversation right through, then listen again and speak the part of George.

GEORGE — We don't appear to have had any payments from you for three months now.
MARTINU — Ah, yes! I thought you might be ringing about that.
GEORGE — Can you tell me what you propose to do about it?
MARTINU — Well, *to be perfectly frank* with you, we have had some cash-flow problems recently.
GEORGE — I see. What's the position at the moment?
MARTINU — Well, things are looking a lot better. Would you be willing to accept a sum of money on account?
GEORGE — Well, we don't usually accept part payment.
MARTINU — I could let you have three thousand pounds now, and the balance over three months.
GEORGE — Three thousand. Yes, that would be just about acceptable.
MARTINU — OK, *I can get that off to you* by the end of the week.
GEORGE — In the meantime, perhaps you won't mind paying cash with order until you've cleared your account?
MARTINU — Yes, of course.

Updating personnel records

7.8
I don't know what you're getting at I don't understand what you're suggesting.

7.9
to pick holes to criticise.
giving you a hard time causing you problems.
a place of your own a house or flat where you live by yourself.
a dead end something that doesn't lead on to anywhere else.

7.8 Listen and read

Terry Cabe, the Personnel Manager at Bookmart, is interviewing Frank Penny so tha he can complete Frank's annual Employee Assessment Report. Listen to what the say. Notice how Frank doesn't seem to trust any of his managers.

TERRY	Frank, come in. Sit down. Now, you've been with us very nearly two years, Frank, so this is your second annual assessment interview. I seem to remember there were one or two problems while you settled in. How've you been getting on this last year?
FRANK	Oh – all right.
TERRY	No problems?
FRANK	No.
TERRY	People treating you all right, are they?
FRANK	Look, *I don't know what you're getting at* here, but if there've been complaints about my work then I'd like to know what they are and who's making them!

7.9 Listen and read

Terry continues the interview. Listen to what they say. Notice how he works hard t reassure Frank, so that Frank feels able to talk about his job.

TERRY	Frank, believe me, I'm not trying *to pick holes*. It's just I know that last year you were still living with your parents, they were *giving you a hard time*, and there were some problems at work. Anyway, you've got *a place of your own* now, right? When was it you moved
FRANK	Last Christmas.
TERRY	How is it? Settled in OK, have you?
FRANK	Yeah. Yeah, it's nice, it's really good.
TERRY	Great. Great. And you don't have that terrible long journey to work any more.
FRANK	Right. It's only ten minutes on the bus.
TERRY	So, what do you reckon's the toughest part of your job here, Frank?
FRANK	To be honest, Mr Cabe, basically, the job's all right. I just feel it's not leading anywhere – it's *a dead end* – know what I mean?
TERRY	Uh-huh. 'Unsatisfactory prospects of promotion. Position lacks adequate career structure' – I'm quoting from a memo I wrote for the MD last week. That's what these annual assessments are all about, Frank. Now let's remind ourselves, shall we, of what I put on your form a year ago.

7.10 Reading for key words

Terry Cabe asks Frank Penny three questions that make Frank angry.

1. What are they?
2. Why does Terry ask these questions?
3. Why does Frank misunderstand them?
4. At the start of the interview, Terry asked a question that made Frank angry. Late he asked a very similar question, and Frank gave a friendly, direct answer. Wha words does Terry use this time?
5. Terry 'translated' some of Frank's words into very formal language. What word are they, and what is Terry's translation?

7.11 Document study: an Employee Assessment Record

Read Frank Penny's Employee Assessment Record below. Then write two short sentences describing his career with Bookmart. Frank is being considered for promotion to Senior Clerk. Make a list of points 'For' and 'Against' his promotion.

CONFIDENTIAL

EMPLOYEE ASSESSMENT RECORD

Name: PENNY, Frank
Joined: 16/08/89
Position: Messenger
Staff No: 3215
Dept/Section: General Office

TRANSFERS/PROMOTIONS

Date	Dept/Section	Position
12/02/90	Dispatch	Filing Clerk

DATE OF ASSESSMENT: 06/06/90
ASSESSED BY: Personnel Manager

1. Skills
Circle letter that best describes employee.
A = Exceptional;
B = Very good;
C = Satisfactory;
D = Below average;
E = Unsatisfactory

Knowledge of records system	A	**(B)**	C	D	E
Keyboarding: speed	A	**(B)**	C	D	E
accuracy	**(A)**	B	C	D	E
Neatness in maintaining records by hand	**(A)**	B	C	D	E
Telephone manner	A	B	C	**(D)**	E

2. Personal qualities (Please comment briefly)

Appearance, dress: Smart if he wants to be; generally careless.
Manner: At best, cheerful and friendly; at worst, impertinent and/or *abrasive*. Apt to be gloomy and unresponsive.
Ability to learn: Excellent.

3. Behaviour at work

Punctuality and attendance: Often late. Transferred to flexitime, November 1989, at his own request; some improvement.

Attitude to work: Varies greatly. Takes work seriously, sometimes conscientious.

Initiative: Has shown he can work well on his own, but tends to wait for instructions.

Relationships with colleagues and superiors: Relies on charm and good humour to deal with situations. However, he can also be *surly* (See above).

Further comments: Mr Penny has been faced with a number of problems during the year, not all of which were his own fault. Same of them arose from the fact that he was compelled by circumstances to live with his parents, and therefore had a 90-minute journey to his workplace. There was *a clash of personalities* with his first Supervisor. I consider that he has considerable potential, but he needs to achieve a more mature and balanced outlook if he is to realise it.

Signed	Position	Date	Employee's initials
T. Cabe	Personnel Manager	12 June '90	F.P.

7.11
Telephone manner the way he speaks on the telephone.
abrasive rude and unpleasant.
surly rude and bad-tempered.
a clash of personalities a situation where two people can't work together because they have different ideas or because they don't like each other.

7.12 Find the word

Read the text below on Frank's work. Write the word from the box for each gap.

Frank's Employee Assessment ___**a**___ shows how ___**b**___ Bookmart's career ___**c**___ is. Admittedly, Frank is not an ideal employee. He is not always punctual, and when he does get to work his behaviour is often ___**d**___. His telephone ___**e**___ can sometimes be surly and he rarely does anything on his own ___**f**___. His attitude to work will have to change if he wants ___**g**___. But he isn't stupid; he has some useful ___**h**___ and some of his personal ___**i**___ could be valuable; Terry Cabe even considers that he has the ___**j**___ to handle more responsibility.

inadequate initiative
manner potential
promotion
qualifications
qualities record
structure
unsatisfactory

7.13 Reading for key words

1 The Employee Assessment Record suggests two reasons why Frank Penny was promoted from the General Office to Dispatch. What are they?
2 In the Employee Assessment Record, what words suggest that some of Frank Penny's problems probably were his own fault?
3 In the interview, what words does Terry use to try to make these troubles seem small and temporary?

Reporting an accident

7.14
take a short cut follow a quicker way of getting somewhere.

7.15
negligible so small that it doesn't matter.

7.16
Third parties people who are not directly concerned with something; in this case people who are not employed by the company.

7.14 Listen and read

The Bookmart warehouse is always busy. Andy Brumshaw is the warehouse foreman on duty on the afternoon of 19 June. Alice Perkins is an office cleaner. Arthur Bell works in the warehouse. Listen to what they say.

ANDY Hey! Arthur! Get those cartons into the loading bay. The van's waiting.

ALICE [Pushing a large industrial vacuum cleaner] Hello, Mr Brumshaw. I've just vacuumed your office and the corridor.

ANDY Ah, thanks, Alice.

ALICE OK if I *take a short cut* through the warehouse?

ANDY Mind how you go, Alice – and watch out for the fork-lifts. You know you're not supposed to go through here during working hours.

ALICE That's all right. I've been through here hundreds of times.

ANDY Alice!

7.15 Document study

The Bookmart warehouse keeps an accident record book. This is what was written on 19 June. Read it carefully. You will need to refer to it later.

ACCIDENT RECORD BOOK

Date and time: Wednesday 19 June 1991, 3.45pm.
Place: Warehouse

Members of Staff involved: Alice Perkins, Arthur Bell.

Brief Particulars: Fork-lift truck struck vacuum cleaning machine. No injuries. Cleaning machine extensively damaged. Damage to truck negligible.

Action taken: Accident reported to Sales Manager and Safety Officer.

A. Brumshaw.

7.16 Document study

The next day, Bookmart's Safety Officer is investigating the warehouse accident. He must complete one of the company's standard accident report forms for the General Manager. Write down as many of the details as you can.

ACCIDENT REPORT FORM

Date of report: (1) Prepared by: (2)
for: (3)

Date of incident: (4) Time: (5)
Place: (6)

Members of staff involved:
Name: (7) Position: (8)
(9) (10)

Members of public involved:
Name: (11) Address:

Injury caused to:
A Staff: (12)
B Public: (13)

Witnesses *(at least two if possible)*:
Name: (14) Section and position: (15) Contact phone no: 491
(16)

Damage to: **Estimated value:**
1. **Company equipment:** (17) 1200.00
2. **Staff property:** (18)
3. **Third parties:** (19)

TOTAL 1200.00

7.17 Writing practice: the report's findings

The Safety Officer also has to write a description of what happened. Write this for him, using the questions below as a guide. Remember not to include any irrelevant information, and don't, at this stage, give any opinions.

1 What did Mr Brumshaw order Mr Bell to do at about 3.45?
2 What did Mrs Perkins do at about the same time? Where was she coming from? Why was she going through the warehouse? Is this allowed? Is it often done?
3 Why did Mrs Perkins not hear the truck coming? What happened? What damage was done?

7.18 Document study

The Safety Officer's findings lead to the conclusion that Mr Bell is most to blame for the accident, but that Mr Brumshaw and Mrs Perkins are also partly to blame. The report finally makes recommendations.

Damage to:		Estimated value:
1. Company equipment:	(17)	1200.00
2. Staff property:	(18)	
3. Third parties:	(19)	
	TOTAL	1200.00

RECOMMENDATIONS:

1. Safety regulations to be strictly enforced at all times and in all areas.
2. Foremen to be reminded of their responsibility for maintaining safety standards.
3. Mrs Perkins and Mr Brumshaw to be reprimanded. Mr Bell to be severely reprimanded. No deduction to be made from pay.
4. Manning levels in the warehouse to be investigated, with a view to lessening the workload on forklift truck drivers.

7.18
reprimanded officially told that he has done something wrong.
Manning levels the number of people who work somewhere; **manning** includes both men and women.

7.19
pallets wooden platforms on which goods can be stored, and which can be moved by a fork-lift truck.
gangways the passages between the piles of goods in the warehouse.
What's all the fuss about? the speaker doesn't understand why people are getting annoyed, because no real damage has been done.

7.19 Reading practice: separating fact from opinion

Here are eight statements that were made while the Safety Officer was collecting information. None of them was included in the report. Decide whether each statement is a fact or an opinion, and whether it is relevant or irrelevant. Tick two columns for each statement.

	Fact	Opinion	Relevant	Irrelevant
1 'Arthur was worried about one of the *pallets* on the rack. It came crashing down about twelve hours later.'				
2 'The noise that vacuum cleaner makes, you could hear it a mile off.'				
3 'Arthur's a menace in a fork-lift truck. He nearly killed me, about a year ago; I jumped out of his way just in time.'				
4 'The *gangways* between the racks in the stockroom aren't as wide as the Health and Safety Regulations say they should be.'				
5 'It was a miracle nobody was hurt.'				
6 'It's the management's responsibility to see this sort of thing doesn't happen.'				
7 '*What's all the fuss about?* The insurance will pay for a new vacuum cleaner.'				
8 'Do you know, those fork-lift trucks can do 50 kilometres an hour? They're terrifying!'				

Study record	
7.1	
7.2	
7.3	
7.4	
7.5	
7.6	
7.7	
7.8	
7.9	
7.10	
7.11	
7.12	
7.13	
7.14	
7.15	
7.16	
7.17	
7.18	
7.19	

Answer key and commentary for unit 7

7.2 Reading for key words

1 Our new customers are supposed to pay cash with order
2 we do have some discretion
3 I wonder if . . . you could do me a favour
4 I . . . would appreciate a quick response
5 it's only a formality

7.3 Writing practice

This is a model answer.

> 15 April 1991
>
> Dear Sir
>
> We have now been ordering fairly regularly from you from eight or nine months, and wish to apply for open account terms.
>
> Our trade references are: James Merridew, Publishers, 97 Henrietta Street, London WC2, and The Fireside Press, PO Box 7591, Milton Keynes MK45 7ER.
>
> We should be grateful if you could open the account immediately, as we shall be placing a large order with you shortly and we should prefer not to continue to pay cash with order.
>
> In return, we will ask our referees to reply as quickly as possible to your request for information.
>
> Yours faithfully
>
> E.J. Harris
> Manager

7.4 Document study

On 6 May £126.90 was paid to settle the invoice of 1 May, which was unnecessary because they now have an account.

7.5 Writing figures

See table at foot of page.

7.8 Listen and read

Frank gives very short answers to Terry's first questions: 'Oh – all right' and 'No'. He then says 'I don't know what you're getting at here', suggesting that he thinks that Terry is trying to accuse him of something.

7.9 Listen and read

Terry spends a lot of time asking Frank about his home life: about his problems with his parents, his new home and the journey to work. Then, when Frank has relaxed, he starts asking him about his work again.

7.10 Reading for key words

1 'How've you been getting on this last year?' 'No problems?' 'People treating you all right, are they?'
2 Because he knew that Frank had had problems at home.
3 Because he thinks that Terry is going to criticise him.
4 'So, what do you reckon's the toughest part o your job here, Frank?'
5 Frank said 'it's a dead end'; Terry sai 'Unsatisfactory prospects of promotio Position lacks adequate career structure'.

7.11 Document study

Frank Penny joined the company on 10 Augu 1989 as a messenger in the general office. He wa promoted to filing clerk in dispatch on 1 February 1990.

For: Good knowledge of records system; nea keyboard skills very good. Can dress smartly. Ca be cheerful and friendly. Learns quickly. Take work seriously; can work very hard; can wor well on his own. Recent changes in home life an flexible working hours have brought som improvement.

Against: Telephone manner poor. Is general careless. Is often gloomy, unresponsive sometimes rude. Appears to be difficult to wor with. Often late for work. Often unwilling to us his own initiative. Personality and outlook sti immature.

7.12 Find the word

a Record **b** inadequate **c** structure
d unsatisfactory **e** manner **f** initiative
g promotion **h** qualifications **i** qualities
j potential

7.13 Reading for key words

1 He writes very neatly, and learns quickly. Hi personality clashed with that of his fir Supervisor.
2 'at worst, impertinent and/or abrasive. Apt t be gloomy and unresponsive.' 'he can also b surly'
3 I seem to remember there were one or tw problems while you settled in.

7.16 Document study

1 20 June 1991 **2** Safety Officer
3 General Manager **4** 19 June 1991
5 3.45 p.m. **6** warehouse **7** Arthur Bell
8 fork-lift truck driver **9** Alice Perkins
10 cleaner **11** none **12** none
13 none **14** Andy Brumshaw
15 warehouse foreman **16** none
17 vacuum cleaner **18** none **19** none

7.17 Writing practice

This is a model answer.

At about 3.45 p.m., Mr Brumshaw, the forema on duty, ordered Mr Bell, driving one of th fork-lift trucks in the warehouse, to move som cartons of books to the loading bay, where a va was waiting to depart.

At about the same time, Mrs Perkins entere the warehouse, with the vacuum cleaner, from M Brumshaw's office. Mrs Perkins wanted to take short cut through the warehouse. This is agains safety regulations, but she states that cleanin staff often take short cuts through the warehous during working hours.

Mrs Perkins did not hear the truck because o the noise of the vacuum cleaner. Mr Bell did no see the machine until it was too late to stop. Th truck hit the machine, which was severel damaged. Nobody was injured.

7.19 Reading practice

This is a model answer. Do you agree?

1 Fact; Irrelevant **2** Opinion; Relevant
3 Opinion; Relevant **4** Fact; Irrelevant
5 Opinion; Irrelevant **6** Fact; Relevant
7 Fact; Irrelevant **8** Opinion; Relevant.

7.5

Date	Particulars	Ref.	Debit	Credit	Balance
	Opening balance				2035.68
10/06/91	Invoice	5629	759.00		2794.68
13/06/91	Received			438.02	2356.66
	Closing balance				2356.66

current	1 month	2 months	3+ months	TOTAL BALANCE NOW DUE:
2356.66	1597.66	0	0	2356.66

Unit 8: Data processing

SITUATION

Bookmart distribute books for Eckener Verlag, a publisher in Hamburg. To improve efficiency, the managers in both companies want to install the same data-processing systems, so they can share information. In this unit we find out how Bookmart's computer system works and look at ways of making data-processing systems compatible.

CHARACTERS

Frank Penny	
Terry Cabe	
George Harvey	
Trudi Hoffmann	works for Eckener Verlag. She is German.
Dieter Krauss	is Personnel Manager at Eckener Verlag. He is German.
Emmy Wolff	is a Sales Manager at Eckener Verlag. She is German.

LANGUAGE

Vocabulary	Computer applications; using a computer keyboard; networks.
Skills	Explaining how to do something; using a computer; formal and informal discussion and argument.
Structures	Emphasis; *-ing* forms; *have to* and *will have to.*
Documents	A personnel record; an advertisement; electronic messages.

Instructing a new operator

8.1
I'll just run through I'll tell you the whole thing quickly without too much detail.
the main menu the first list of choices on the computer.
a record one complete set of information that can be stored in a computer database.
do an update add new information to a record.
to input to tell the computer, usually by typing on a keyboard.
key in type on a keyboard.
hit 'Return' press the key marked 'Return'.

8.3
password-protected this means that you can't change the information in the computer unless you type in a secret word, the **password**.
dogsbody someone who does all of the boring and unpleasant jobs.

8.1 Listen and read

Frank Penny is now Assistant Supervisor in the Dispatch Department. He is bei visited by Trudi Hoffmann, from Eckener Verlag in Hamburg. Frank is demonstrati Bookmart's computer system. Listen to what they say. Notice that Frank is able to u technical terms without explaining them. Why?

FRANK Right. Let's get started then. Now, you've used a keyboard befor

TRUDI Oh yes! I've been using computers in my work for more than tw years.

FRANK OK. *I'll just run through* a typical job, the sort we do every day, an then I'll tell you a bit about the database and the hardware. Now, this is a menu-driven system, so – I'll just go back to *the main menu* and we can start from the beginning – there. See? Here's ou list of options – create *a record*, update a record, sort records, prin delete and so on. Let's *do an update*.

TRUDI Yeah – so now we get a message on the screen, it asks for the name.

FRANK It asks you *to input* a customer's name, yes. So if I *key in* the nam 'Martinu' – that's one of our biggest customers – M-A-R, T-I-N-U *hit 'Return'*, and there it is! All the details of the account – exactly as they appear on the monthly statement.

TRUDI Right. So now, if the customer orders some books, you key in the particulars . . .

FRANK And the system updates the file and prints out all the paperwork as well. Look, I'll show you.

8.2 Explaining how to do something

In 7.5 you recorded two items on the statement for Harris's bookshop. Imagine th you are Frank Penny and that you are using this example to demonstrate to Tru how to update the computer records. Write your explanation. Start like this:

> You go back to the main menu, and you select 'Update Customer Record'. It asks you to . . .

8.3 Listen and read

Frank now shows Trudi how the computer system handles confidential data. List to what they say. What does 'confidential' mean in this case?

TRUDI What about access to confidential data? I mean personal information about the staff. For example, can you find out how much your boss gets paid?

FRANK Huh! I know exactly what my boss's salary is, without needing t ask a machine. But I see what you're getting at. All records are *password-protected*, and there's three levels of protection. An offic *dogsbody* like me only knows the password for level one.

TRUDI And that means there are some records you can't read?

FRANK There are parts of each record I can't read, and there are parts I can read but I can't change. I'll show you. Er – now, whose . . .

TRUDI Let me. P-E-N-N-Y, 'Return'.

FRANK Oh no!

8.4 Document study

This is Frank Penny's record on the company database. Read it and answer the questions below.

1 How old is Frank?
2 In what subjects does he have the Certificate of Secondary Education?
3 What is his National Insurance number?

```
PERSONNEL RECORD [screen 1 of 3]            Record no. 266

Family name      PENNY                      Works no. 3215
First names      FRANK                      NI No.      Z/34/56/72/7

Address          123B, Brewhouse Lane       DOB            4.09.68
                 Market Drayton             Sex            M
                 MD14 7RE                   Status         S
Telephone        0630 1703762               Nationality    British
----------------------------------------------------------------------
Joined     10/08/89
- for transfers/promotions press F7 -

Current Dept./Section       Dispatch
Post/grade                  Assistant Supervisor
----------------------------------------------------------------------
Exam qualifications         CSE (English, Maths, Geography)
Skills (certified)          Keyboarding (Grade 2)
       (uncertified)        Filing
Courses etc. completed      Data processing (Stages 1 and 2)
Courses etc. in progress
```

8.5 Listen and read

Frank continues to demonstrate the personnel records on the computer system. Listen carefully to what he and Trudi say.

TRUDI This is just the first screen, isn't it? It says 'screen one of three'. How do you move to the next one?

FRANK *This'll do to be going on with.*

TRUDI How do you *amend* it, then?

FRANK Well – suppose I give myself some exam qualifications. You use the cursor control keys *to cursor down* to that line on the screen – when you get to *the field* that needs amending, you just key in the new data. So – er – like that. The thing is, of course, I can't write that to *the disk* – only Terry Cabe can do that, he's got a level-three password. Otherwise I could give myself all sorts of qualifications, couldn't I?

TRUDI Hm. 'BTEC Business Studies' – is that your secret ambition? What does BTEC stand for?

FRANK Oh, er – Business and Technical Education Council or some such thing! And then to delete it, you just hit the 'Delete' key and hold it down – it *auto-repeats*, of course.

TRUDI Of course!

8.5
This'll do to be going on with it's enough for us to deal with now.
amend change; a slightly formal word used in computing.
to cursor down to press the keys which move the **cursor** down the computer screen so that you can type there.
the field one part of a computer record, often a name or a date or part of an address.
the disk the part of the computer where data and programs are stored.
auto-repeats if you press the 'Delete' key and hold it down, it continues to delete characters on the screen.

8.6 Reading for key words

1 When Frank holds down the 'Delete' key, what words disappear from the screen?
2 Frank has just finished deleting his imaginary exam qualification. Now he wants to change his date of birth. What is the first thing he must do?
3 How do we know that there is more information about Frank that we haven't seen?

8.7 Speaking practice: using the computer

Trudi Hoffmann now tries the computer, with Frank's help. Listen to what they say. Then listen again, and speak the part of Frank.

FRANK Right, let's go back to the main menu and we can start from the beginning.

TRUDI So, now we get a list of options. Suppose I want to update a record?

FRANK I've already explained to you how to do that.

TRUDI I know – you cursor down to where it says 'Update record', and you hit 'Return'. It works! And now it's asking me to key in the person's name?

FRANK No it's not – it's asking for the password, and I'll tell you. It's 'Dogsbody', D-O-G-S, B-O-D-Y.

TRUDI Does that give us confidential data access?

FRANK Well, it'll do to be going on with.

Planning to expand the system

8.8
opposite number someone with a similar job in a different organisation.
That goes for me too I agree; that is true for me too.
spin-offs something useful that happens as a result of something else.
junk mail advertising material that you get through the post, and which you have not asked for.

8.9
to implement to actually do.
from scratch from the beginning; starting with nothing.
data formats the ways in which the data is organised and stored on the computer.
incompatible not able to work together because they are very different.
obsolete out of date and no longer useful because something newer is better.
the know-how the knowledge or ability; an informal usage.

8.8 Listen and read

Terry Cabe and George Harvey are visiting Eckener Verlag in Hamburg, to see ho their computer system works. They are there as members of a working party on da processing. Listen to how they introduce themselves and compliment their host and to how Terry Cabe corrects Emmy Wolff without making her feel silly.

GEORGE My name's George Harvey, I'm the Sales Manager, based at our distribution centre in Telford; and this is Terry Cabe, our Personnel Manager.

DIETER I'm Dieter Krauss, I'm really Terry's *opposite number* here in Hamburg, and Fraulein Emmy Wolff looks after our sales in Germany and now also in Central and Eastern Europe.

EMMY Hello, how do you do – welcome to Hamburg.

TERRY May I say how delighted we are to be here and how much we're enjoying your hospitality.

GEORGE *That goes for me too.*

DIETER Good. So let's get started. The purpose of this meeting, as I'm sur you are all aware, is to exchange information about our data-processing systems so that hopefully we can agree on organisation standards and, in effect, have a single databank which we can all have access to.

EMMY There would be other advantages too – off-spinners, I think you call them, Mr Harvey?

GEORGE Off-spinners? I don't think I'm quite with you . . .

TERRY I think you mean *spin-offs*, Fraulein Wolff. But you're quite right, and that's an important point. All Bookmart personnel – executives, anyway – would enjoy the benefits of an integrated electronic office system: electronic mail, electronic conferencing.

DIETER Electronic *junk mail*.

EMMY We all know what to do with junk mail, I'm sure.

8.9 Listen and read

The meeting continues. Listen to what they say, and to how the two sides politely b firmly express their opposing points of view.

EMMY I think we agree that a data-processing standard is desirable. But how are we going *to implement* this?

TERRY Oh, call in a reliable firm of consultants. We don't have the expertise to set up a new system *from scratch*.

DIETER But it's really not a question of starting from the beginning. We simply need to adapt our *data formats*, our procedures, so that they are compatible.

GEORGE If I may say so, Herr Krauss, I think there's more to it than that. Not only are our present systems *incompatible*, they're *obsolete* as well – which is much worse. With the huge expansion in the market, I mean with the end of trade barriers and so on, we've g to invest in technology. We're publishers and book distributors, we don't have *the know-how* to buy and install a computer system ourselves.

EMMY Oh, don't we? Our system was designed and installed by our ow engineers in 1985 and it's worked very well. Let me show you th

8.10 Reading for key words

What words in 8.9 show us the following?

1 a way of organising and arranging data (two answers)
2 advanced technical knowledge (two answers)
3 from the very beginning
4 able to work together; not able to work together
5 the problem is not as simple as y make it appear
6 regulations that make it harder import and export goods

8.11 Document study

Read the text below. Is it a magazine article about a new product, or is it an advertisement? Why is it not easy, at first, to be sure? What problem is NOBS intended to overcome?

NOBS NETWORK BREAKTHROUGH!

The PC Network

As the price of hard disks falls, any workgroup for PCs will almost certainly consist of more than one hard disk. The best network solution for PCs is the *distributed file server*, which combines distributed processing power, storage capabilities and file databases into a harmonious whole.

NOBS Network is the most *user-friendly* network for PCs. By allowing any computer to share its files with any other, it makes every computer both optionally a server and a network station. And by distributing the serving, it increases the speed and efficiency of the network. NOBS also saves money because you do not have to purchase expensive *dedicated* file-servers or hire a network administrator.

The Mixed Operating Systems Network

Many businesses with existing computer installations want to incorporate personal computers, so long as these can *integrate to* their mini or mainframe equipment. NOBS is a unique multi-operating system network, providing networking, *peripheral* sharing and file sharing between almost any hardware types and operating systems.

N O B S

12 *25 MARCH 1991*

8.11
distributed file server a computer with a very large disk which stores data and programs that can be used by other computers which are connected to it.
user-friendly easy to use.
dedicated able to perform only one specific task.
integrate to work together with.
peripheral something attached to a computer, e.g. a printer.

8.12 Making words

In English, you can use a number of nouns, or nouns and verbs, together, to form a group of words that behaves like a single noun. Some examples are:

a fact-finding visit
a cursor control key

These word groups still take a singular verb:

The fact-finding visit was a great success.
The cursor control key moves the cursor on the screen.

Look in the text of this unit for word groups which mean the following:

1 A key that moves the cursor on a computer screen.
2 A word that lets the user pass to the third level of security on a computer.
3 A system which processes data.
4 Data which passwords protect.
5 A computer system which menus drive.

8.13 Reading for key words

George Harvey and Emmy Wolff made a list of requirements for the new computer system. Look at the list (**1–6**) and read 8.11 again. If the NOBS network satisfies the requirement, tick the item. What words in 8.11 tell you this?

The new system must be:
1 as cheap as possible.
2 economical to run.
3 reliable.
4 easy to use.

It must work smoothly with:
5 existing hardware.
6 many operating systems (we have several).

Introducing new procedures

8.14
a non-starter something that has no chance of succeeding.

8.15
expense account an arrangement where you can spend money on business, e.g. for travel or meals, and the company will give you the money.
cooked up planned; invented; an informal usage.

8.14 Document study

Frank and Trudi can now send each other messages electronically. Read th messages below. Find words or phrases that mean:

1 as a result of
2 so much that
3 if . . . not

```
DATE    92/02/17        TIME 10:34
FROM    Trudi Hoffmann
TO      Frank Penny

SUBJECT Processing and payment of staff expense
        accounts

Mr Krauss has asked me to investigate the
possibility of putting all our management and
sales staff expense accounts onto the Personnel
Records system. With the setting-up of the
Education Publishing Division and our rapid
expansion into Central and Eastern Europe, the
number of accounts has increased to the point
where manual processing is no longer practical. I
believe Mr Cabe has talked to you about this as
well. Do you think there would be any technical
difficulties?
```

```
DATE    92/02/17        TIME 15:43
FROM    Frank Penny
TO      Trudi Hoffmann

SUBJECT Expense accounts

There are a lot of problems in putting expense
accounts on the DP system. To start with, expens
claims are not accepted unless supported by bil
which have to be originals. The management won't
even accept photocopies. I've told Terry Cabe I
think this scheme is a non-starter.
```

8.15 Listen and read

Frank telephones Trudi to talk about the changes to the system. Listen to what the say. What phrase does he use to try to 'bully' Trudi into agreeing with him?

TRUDI	Trudi Hoffmann.
FRANK	Trudi? This is Frank, in Telford. Hi, how are you?
TRUDI	Fine, thank you.
FRANK	Listen, I'm ringing about this crazy *expense account* idea that your boss has *cooked up* with my boss. I mean, you do agree, don't you – that it is crazy?
TRUDI	Well – no, I thought it made sense. I mean, the software we're using now can handle all the calculations – it'll even print the cheques.
FRANK	That's no good. Only Accounts can issue cheques!
TRUDI	Yes, but we're all on the same network, we can authorise the cheques and Accounts can issue them. The people who put in the claims still give us their bills and their credit-card receipts, so what's the problem?

8.16 Structure practice: emphasis

When Frank is trying to persuade Trudi to agree with him, he uses the emphatic

You do agree, don't you?

You can use 'do' and 'did' with the base form of many verbs for emphasis:

You do know that he's already gone?
They did know because I told them.

Note that you do not use the past tense form of the main verb with 'did'. Now rewri these sentences, adding 'do', 'does' or 'did' for emphasis:

1 You know that the meeting has been cancelled?
2 He understands how important this is?
3 She left before the meeting was finished.
4 I hope you'll make sure that people don't leave early.

8.17 Listen and read

George Harvey calls Frank in to give him some good news. Listen to what they say. How does Frank show that he doesn't want to seem to be too eager to agree?

GEORGE Frank. Thanks for coming in. Do sit down. I've – er – got something to say that I'd like you *to keep to yourself* for a few days. You've been Assistant Supervisor now in Dispatch for – what, six months? Anyway, you seem to be doing a good job. Sadly, Elsie Donnell is retiring shortly, for health reasons. I was wondering whether you'd be interested in taking over.

FRANK Well . . .

GEORGE *We've had our difficulties in the past*, I know, but I've got complete confidence in you.

FRANK I'd need to think it over.

GEORGE Quite right! I ought to mention that the board have decided to upgrade the post from Supervisor to Assistant Dispatch Manager. The only thing is, you will have to do a two-year part-time stock-control course.

FRANK I wouldn't mind doing that.

GEORGE Good! I'll get the paperwork started.

8.17
to keep to yourself to not tell anyone else.
We've had our difficulties in the past we used to have problems, but they are finished now.

8.18 Structure practice: *-ing* forms

If you want to refer to an action, activity or process, you can use a noun based on the '-ing' form of the verb:

She studied computing at university.
Writing is important in all business activity.

Some verbs have a related noun which is not like an '-ing' form of the verb, for example:

We waited for the arrival of the train.

English speakers prefer to use the related form (like 'preference'), rather than the '-ing' form (like 'preferring').

In the text below, change the verbs in brackets into noun forms. Use your dictionary to check if the verb has a related noun form. The first two have been done as an example.

Somebody has to be responsible for the efficient (**a**) processing [process] and (**b**) payment [pay] of expenses claims. With the (**c**) [set up] of new departments and the company's (**d**) [expand] into Central and Eastern Europe, Trudi finds the present (**e**) [proceed] too slow, and she is pressing for its (**f**) [computerise]. Frank's (**g**) [reject] of this (**h**) [propose] will no doubt be dropped when he realises that (**i**) [promote] to (**j**) [manage] status could mean (**k**) [have] an expense account of his own, and (**l**) [pay] for the (**m**) [entertain] of customers in expensive restaurants just by (**n**) [write] his (**o**) [sign] on a slip of paper.

8.19 Structure practice: *have to* and *will have to*

We use 'have to' when we talk about something that is always necessary: 'Anyone who wants to travel abroad has to have a passport.' We use 'will have to' when we talk about a particular occasion in the future: 'If you want to come abroad with us next month, you will have to get a passport.' Both of these mean 'must'.

In the following sentences, change 'must' to 'have to' or 'will have to':

1 I'm going abroad next month, and I've lost my passport. – You must get a new one.
2 What happens if you lose your birth certificate? – You must get a new one.
3 I'm going to rent a car in Britain this summer. – You must drive on the left.
4 I'm going to take tomorrow off. – You must get your manager's permission.
5 The computer system in this place is obsolete. – It must be replaced.
6 I'm putting in my expenses claim, and here are photocopies of all the bills to support it. – That's no good. You must submit the originals.

Study record	
8.1	
8.2	
8.3	
8.4	
8.5	
8.6	
8.7	
8.8	
8.9	
8.10	
8.11	
8.12	
8.13	
8.14	
8.15	
8.16	
8.17	
8.18	
8.19	

Answer key and commentary for unit 8

8.1 Listen and read
Because Trudi has been using computers in her work for more than two years.

8.2 Explaining how to do something
This is a model answer.
You go back to the main menu, and you select 'Update Customer Record.' It asks you to key in the customer's name, like this – H-A-R, R-I-S, and you press 'Return'. The record comes up on the screen. You cursor down to 'Date', and you key in the date, 10 June. Then you move the cursor to the Debit column and you key in the invoice number, 5629, and the amount, £759. Hit 'Return' and go on to the next item. Key in the date, 13 June, then cursor across to the Credit column and key in the amount that he's paid, £438.02. Hit 'Return' again, and there you are – all done!

8.3 Listen and read
'Confidential' here means personal information that other people should not see.

8.4 Document study
1 Frank is 24 in September 1992.
2 His CSE subjects are English, Maths and Geography.
3 His National Insurance (NI) number is Z/34/56/72/7.

8.6 Reading for key words
1 BTEC Business Studies.
2 Move the cursor to the date-of-birth (DOB) field.
3 Because on the screen it says 'Screen 1 of 3'.

8.10 Reading for key words
1 a data-processing standard; our data formats
2 expertise; know-how
3 from scratch
4 compatible; incompatible
5 If I may say so . . ., I think there's more to it than that.
6 trade barriers

8.11 Document study
It is an advertisement. It is not easy to be sure at first because it has a headline and a page number, like a magazine article, and it seems to provide information about a new product. NOBS is an attempt to solve the problem of making data easily available to all the computers and other machines in a network.

8.12 Making words
1 a cursor control key
2 a level-three password
3 a data-processing system
4 password-protected data
5 a menu-driven system

8.13 Reading for key words
The new system must be:
1 as cheap as possible – Yes, 'saves money . you do not have to purchase . . . '
2 economical to run – No, the ad doesn't say.
3 reliable – No, the ad doesn't say.
4 easy to use – Yes, 'user-friendly'.
It must work smoothly with:
5 existing hardware – Yes, 'providir networking . . . between almost any hardwa types'.
6 many operating systems – Yes, 'a uniqu multi-operating system network'.

8.14 Document study
1 With
2 to the point where
3 unless

8.15 Listen and read
Frank tries to bully Trudi into agreeing with hi by saying 'You do agree, don't you – that it crazy?'

8.16 Structure practice
1 You do know that the meeting has bee cancelled?
2 He does understand how important this is?
3 She did leave before the meeting was finishe
4 I do hope you'll make sure that people do leave early.

8.17 Listen and read
Frank says 'I'd need to think it over.'

8.18 Structure practice
c setting-up
d expansion
e procedure
f computerisation
g rejection
h proposal
i promotion
j management
k having
l paying
m entertainment
n writing
o signature

8.19 Structure practice
1 You will have to get a new one.
2 You have to get a new one.
3 You will have to drive on the left.
4 You will have to get your manager permission.
5 It will have to be replaced.
6 You will have to submit the originals. *or* Yo have to submit the originals.

Unit 9: Organising a one-day conference

SITUATION

The Department of Trading is organising a one-day conference for the manufacturers of weighing and measuring machines. In this unit we look at the work of the committee who are in charge of arranging the conference and see how they make their decisions. We find out how to choose and book hotel facilities and how to keep to a budget. We also look at planning a schedule and at contacting exhibitors and delegates.

CHARACTERS

Graham Flinston	is Assistant Secretary in the Department of Trading. He is British.
Maria Barbero	is on an exchange training scheme from the Ministry of Economic Affairs in Italy. She is Italian.

Valerie Tipstock, Peter and Mark work for the Department of Trading. They are all British.

LANGUAGE

Vocabulary	Conference organisation; hotels and conference facilities; calculating estimates.
Skills	Taking part in meetings; acting as chairperson; making decisions based on evidence.
Structures	Adverbials; modifying nouns; linking clauses.
Documents	Hotel brochures; a booking letter; a conference schedule; a formal letter.

Booking conference facilities

9.1
I've got a little job for you Graham is suggesting that the job is not very important.
things like that similar things.
three of our people three people who work for me.
There's no time to lose we don't have very much time.
lay on supply; provide.

9.1 Listen and read

Graham Flinston is an Assistant Secretary in the Department of Trading. Maria Barbero works for the Ministry of Economic Affairs in Italy. She is spending a year in Britain on an exchange training scheme. Listen to what they say.

GRAHAM Come in, Miss Barbero. Do sit down. Now, *I've got a little job for you* this week. I see from your file that you've organised various events in the past – sales conferences, exhibitions, *things like that*?

MARIA Yes. I've organised conferences and exhibitions quite often.

GRAHAM Good. Good. Now, we run short conferences each year for companies who wish to exhibit at overseas trade fairs. For next year we've got to pick the exhibitors for the British stand at the Leipzig Trade Fair in the spring. One of the areas we'll be promoting next year is instruments of calibration – machines for measuring and weighing things – so I'd like you to make the arrangements for the conference of the machine manufacturers. Can you do that?

MARIA Well, yes, of course. I'd be very pleased to do it, but I'm not sure that I could manage it all by myself.

GRAHAM No, no! Of course not! Naturally, I'll give you all the assistance I can. And I've already asked *three of our people* to work with you on this. Here's a list of their names. I'd like the four of you to act as a steering committee, with you as the chair.

MARIA Thank you. Oh! I see that the first meeting is today!

GRAHAM This afternoon, 2.30 in room 513. *There's no time to lose*. The conference will take place on 2 November. Now, I must also give you some other information straight away. The budget: you must not exceed six and a half thousand pounds for hotel expenses. Five people will be going from the division: they'll want dinner, bed and breakfast for two nights. There'll be up to five hundred delegates. They pay for themselves, except that we *lay on* a buffet lunch, and morning coffee and afternoon tea. You may also find these useful. They're the files on the last three one-day conferences.

9.2 Structure practice: adverbials

An adverbial is a word or a group of words which you can add to a clause or sentence when you want to say something more about it, for example how, where or when the activity occurred.

Adverbials are usually placed at the end of the clause or sentence, or after the object if there is one. We do not normally put anything between a verb and its direct object. For example:

You've organised various events in the past.
I'd like you to make the arrangements for the conference.

You can use more than one adverbial in a sentence:

We've got to pick the exhibitors for the British stand at the Leipzig Trade Fair in the spring.

These examples are all from the dialogue in 9.1. Read through the dialogue in 9.1 again, and see what other examples you can find. Then answer the questions below making sure that you put the adverbials in the right place.

1 When has he got a little job for her? – this week.
He's got a little job for her this week.
2 What do they do every year? – hold short conferences.
3 When has she organised various events? – in the past.
4 How often has she organised such things? – quite often.
5 What must he also give her straight away? – some other information.
6 What must she not exceed for hotel expenses? – six and a half thousand pounds.

9.3 Document study: hotel brochures

Maria has received brochures from two hotels that the committee chose for the conference venue. Read through them carefully. Make a list of things the committee might look for in a hotel. For each item on your list, say which hotel seems to be better. You can add to your list as you work through the unit.

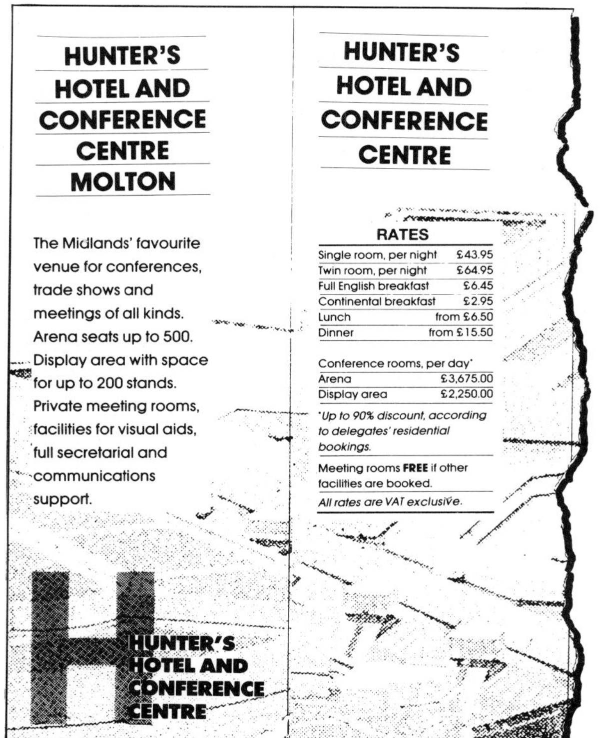

HUNTER'S HOTEL AND CONFERENCE CENTRE MOLTON

The Midlands' favourite venue for conferences, trade shows and meetings of all kinds. Arena seats up to 500. Display area with space for up to 200 stands. Private meeting rooms, facilities for visual aids, full secretarial and communications support.

HUNTER'S HOTEL AND CONFERENCE CENTRE

RATES

Single room, per night	£43.95
Twin room, per night	£64.95
Full English breakfast	£6.45
Continental breakfast	£2.95
Lunch	from £6.50
Dinner	from £15.50
Conference rooms, per day*	
Arena	£3,675.00
Display area	£2,250.00

**Up to 90% discount, according to delegates' residential bookings.*

Meeting rooms **FREE** if other facilities are booked.

All rates are VAT exclusive.

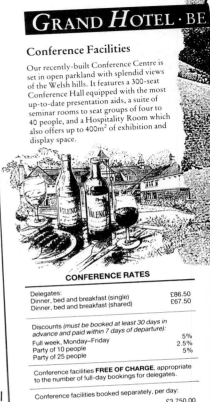

GRAND HOTEL · BE

Conference Facilities

Our recently-built Conference Centre is set in open parkland with splendid views of the Welsh hills. It features a 300-seat Conference Hall equipped with the most up-to-date presentation aids, a suite of seminar rooms to seat groups of four to 40 people, and a Hospitality Room which also offers up to 400m² of exhibition and display space.

CONFERENCE RATES

Delegates:	
Dinner, bed and breakfast (single)	£86.50
Dinner, bed and breakfast (shared)	£67.50
Discounts *(must be booked at least 30 days in advance and paid within 7 days of departure)*:	
Full week, Monday–Friday	5%
Party of 10 people	2.5%
Party of 25 people	5%

Conference facilities **FREE OF CHARGE**, appropriate to the number of full-day bookings for delegates.

Conference facilities booked separately, per day:	
Conference Hall	£3,750.00
Seminar Rooms	£24.00 to £210.00
Hospitality Room/Display Area	£1,450.00

All rates exclude VAT.

9.4 Listen and read

Valerie is explaining the hotel charges to Maria. She has to do some mental arithmetic, because the hotels present the information in different ways. Listen carefully to how she says the figures. Note how the word 'pounds' is sometimes not said.

MARIA: How much is a room in the Grand, per night?

VALERIE: £86.50 for a single room, £67.50 for a shared room.

MARIA: That's for dinner, bed and breakfast. What about Hunter's?

VALERIE: I'll have to add their charges for a room, breakfast and dinner. That's £43.95, call it £44; plus £2.95, say £3; plus £15.50. £44 plus £3 is £47, plus £15.50 makes £62.50.

MARIA: So Hunter's is a bit cheaper. What about a shared room?

VALERIE: Hunter's only gives the cost of the room, whereas the Grand gives the cost per person. I'll have to divide Hunter's figure by two. £64.95, £65, near enough; divided by two is £32.50. And then we've got to add breakfast and dinner. £32.50 plus £3 for breakfast is £35.50, and £15.50 for dinner makes £50, £51.

MARIA: Right. I think all our people will want single rooms. If we go to the Grand, they should give us a 5% discount.

VALERIE: Right. Five per cent off £86.50 is – well, 10% would be £8.65, so 5% is half of that, which comes to just over £4.30. £4.30 from £86.50 is – it must be £82-something – £82.20.

MARIA: So even with the discount, Hunter's is still how much cheaper, per person?

VALERIE: £82.20 for the Grand, minus £62.50 for Hunter's, that's nearly £20.

MARIA: That's what I thought. That's quite a small saving, isn't it?

VALERIE: Well, £20 is almost a quarter of £82.20, getting on for 25%. If five of our staff are going, we save five times £20, £100 a day. And we can't risk going over budget.

Chairing a meeting

9.5
produce food that is grown to be sold; the Grand grows the vegetables it uses.
we'll come to that in a moment we'll deal with that later.
On the face of it Peter is suggesting that although it doesn't look good straight away, there are good things about it which he will say later.

9.7
there's not a lot to choose between them they are very similar.
a keynote speech the most important speech, one which includes all the main points.

9.5 Listen and read

Maria and the rest of the committee are meeting to decide on the conference venue. Maria is rather a strict chairwoman for such a small committee. Listen to how she tries to make sure that the speakers keep to the point.

MARIA Right, everybody, if we can make a start. Thank you. Now, the most important thing we have to do today is to decide where the conference is to take place – the Grand Hotel or Hunter's. Peter, you've been looking at them from the point of view of access. How easy are they to get to?

PETER Yes. As you know, the Grand advertises the fact that it's convenient for British Rail, it's half an hour's journey from the airport and only ten miles from the M5. It's even got its own helicopter pad.

VALERIE I'd also like to point out that it's got a fifty-hectare dairy farm and its own vegetable garden, supplying its kitchens with fresh *produce*.

MARIA Valerie, I know you want to talk about the catering, but *we'll come to that in a moment*. Peter, how does Hunter's compare with the Grand for transport?

PETER *On the face of it*, not very well. It's a forty-minute drive through heavy traffic to the nearest railway station, and Birmingham Airport is even harder to get to. But it's less than a mile from the nearest motorway junction. Now, I went through last year's list of delegates, and every single one arrived by car.

9.6 Structure practice: nouns

In English, you can use a noun in front of another noun, to give more information about it:

She shut the door. – She shut the car door.

If you use a countable noun in this way, you usually use it in the singular form and add a hyphen:

The conference centre has 300 seats. – A 300-seat conference centre.

Rewrite the phrases below, moving the underlined words in front of the first noun. Remember to use hyphens.

1 An arena with 500 seats
2 A conference lasting two days
3 A building fifteen storeys high
4 A committee of four people
5 A job with a salary of £20,000 a year
6 A child who is three years old

9.7 Listen and read

Maria and the committee are still discussing the two hotels. Listen to how Maria tries to keep control. Which hotel do you think they will choose?

MARIA Mark, what was your impression of the actual conference facilities?

MARK Well, *there's not a lot to choose between them*. I think everything depends on whether we have to put all the delegates together to talk to them all at once. If we get four hundred and fifty people this year, as we did last year, then the Conference Hall at the Grand is too small.

VALERIE Why should we want to talk to all of them at once?

MARK Flinston may want to give *a keynote speech*.

PETER That's right. At all the conferences I've been to, he did just that.

VALERIE But that's completely unnecessary!

PETER It's hardly unnecessary! It's absolutely crucial!

VALERIE You weren't even at last year's conference!

MARIA Everybody, please! We do have a conference to organise. Mark, perhaps you could find out if Mr Flinston intends to make a speech at this year's conference?

9.8 Listen and read

The steering committee is now discussing food. Listen to what they say. Notice how Maria starts guiding the committee towards a decision. Which hotel do you think they will choose now? Why? Why does Valerie still prefer the Grand?

VALERIE So, *as far as food is concerned*, in my experience the Grand at Beecham is certainly superior to Hunter's. And may I add, *by the way*, that I know Mr Flinston thinks so too.

MARIA Hm. Thank you. OK then, we've looked at these two places from the point of view of transport, and facilities, and food. We seem to agree on one thing: the Grand's Conference Hall isn't big enough.

MARK But we ought to bear in mind that we may not attract as many delegates this year.

PETER Mark *has a point* there. *On the other hand*, it is our job to try to attract as many as possible.

MARIA I quite agree. The fact that Hunter's is *so handy for* the motorway and it's got this big arena – don't you think that rather points to Hunter's this year?

MARK May I point out another thing? A lot of the firms that send delegates will want to set up stands to display their products. Hunter's say they can accommodate up to two hundred. The Grand only has four hundred square metres of floor space – you couldn't possibly get two hundred stands on that.

9.8
as far as food is concerned what I say is only true of the food, not necessarily of other things.
by the way Valerie is using **by the way** here to show that what she is saying is very important.
has a point Peter is suggesting that Mark might be right.
On the other hand Peter is using this to introduce an argument against what he has just said.
so handy for convenient for.

9.10
That came across very strongly many people said that.
Fair enough Valerie is saying that she accepts what Maria has said.

9.9 Structure practice: linking

In 9.5, 9.7 and 9.8 the speakers use a number of words and phrases to link two statements together, either to add to them or to provide a contrast:

. . . it's half an hour's journey from the airport <u>and</u> only ten miles from the M5.
I know you want to talk about the catering, <u>but</u> we'll come to that in a moment.

Read through the dialogues again, and look for these phrases. Then match the sentence parts below.

1 It's a half-hour journey by rail,
2 He may not like it,
3 There may not be so many;
4 I have to admit that it is bigger.
5 The rooms are better furnished.

a And another thing, they grow their own food.
b on the other hand it's our job to attract more.
c May I add that it's also cheaper.
d but it's not his decision.
e and it's only ten miles from the M5.

9.10 Listen and read

Maria now brings the committee meeting to a close. Listen to how she sums up, and how she persuades Valerie to accept the committee's decision.

MARIA Valerie, you have seen both these places, and you were at last year's conference – any comment?

VALERIE Well, I have to admit, I suppose, that the Grand was rather cramped last year.

PETER *That came across very strongly*, I thought, from reading the correspondence in the file.

VALERIE But if this committee recommends Hunter's, I think you'll find that Mr Flinston is not going to be very happy.

MARIA Nevertheless, the feeling of the meeting seems to be that Hunter's is the right place. Valerie, all we can do is make a recommendation on the information we have available. And I'm sure you'd agree that we're bound to recommend what we think is right – in the light of that information.

VALERIE *Fair enough*. I've said what I wanted to say.

MARIA Right. Hunter's it is, then. At our next meeting, we ought to be able to produce a draft schedule for the conference.

Booking the hotel; announcing the schedule

9.11 Document study: booking the hotel

Maria writes a letter to the manager at Hunter's Hotel to book it for the conferenc Read through it carefully. Then make a note of all of the costs of the conference, fill in Valerie's pencil notes below. You will need these notes for 9.12.

The Manager
Hunter's Hotel
Molton M06 5RT

d.o.t
the department of trading

4 January 1991

Dear Sir

Calibration Machine Manufacturers' One-Day Conference 1991

We write to confirm our telephone conversation of this morning. Please book the following accommodation on behalf of the Department:

20-21 March 1991
5 single rooms, for two nights, with dinner and continental breakfast. Use of Arena and Display Area from 6 p.m. on 20 March to 6 a.m. on 22 March.

21 March 1991
Use of Meeting Rooms nos. 1-8.
Coffee and biscuits for 480 people in the Display Area at 9.30 a.m. (cost, £1.20 per person).
Buffet lunch for 420, in the Huntersmoon Banqueting Room at 12.45 p.m. (cost, £7.50 per person).
Tea and biscuits for 300, in the Display Area at 3.30 p.m. (cost, £1 per person).

Our estimates of the numbers requiring lunch etc. are based on previous years' experience. We will inform you of the actual numbers expected one week before the conference.

We understand that you will give the Department a discount of 60 per cent on the hire of the Arena and Display Area. In addition, a discount of 7.5 per cent may be deducted from your invoice, provided the account is settled within 30 days.

We look forward to receiving your confirmation of these arrangements in writing. If you have any queries, please contact Miss Maria Barbero on ext. 3171.

Yours faithfully

Maria Barbero

Maria Barbero
for Assistant Secretary

Accommodation:	(1)	
5 single rooms × 2 nights × £43.95	(2)	
5 dinners × 2 × £15.50	(3)	(4)
5 breakfasts × 2 × £2.95		
Facilities:	(5)	
Conf. Room (1 day) £3675 × 40%	(6)	(7)
Display Area (1 day) £2250 × 40%		
Catering:	(8)	
Coffee: 480 × £1.20	(9)	
Lunch: 420 × £7.50	(10)	(11)
Tea: 300 × £1.00		
		(12)
less 7.5% for payment within 30 days		(13)
	TOTAL	(14)

9.12 Listening practice: calculating the final estimate

Maria has to tell Graham Flinston what the total costs for the conference will b Before she does this, she checks the figures again with Valerie, who uses her penc notes above. Listen to what they say, and check your figures from 9.11. Note th Valerie tells Maria not only the figures, but also how she calculated them.

MARIA Can we just go through the figures again before I report to Mr Flinston?

VALERIE I've got the figures here. First accommodation:

......

Next, the facilities:

......

Now for the catering:

......

Adding up the three totals gives us seven thousand and twenty pounds. Less seven and a half per cent for payment within thirty days is five hundred and twenty-six fifty. That leaves six thousand four hundred and ninety-three pounds fifty pence.

MARIA Hm, that is more than we paid last year. The bill then was just on six thousand pounds. I thought Hunter's was going to be cheaper?

VALERIE Well, if you allow for seven point seven per cent inflation, six thousand times seven point seven per cent gives six thousand four hundred and sixty two, so in real terms this year's total is within about fifty pounds of last year's.

9.13 Listening practice: the conference schedule

Peter is telephoning Maria with the provisional conference schedule. Listen to him, and write the schedule in three columns, showing the time of each event, the event itself, and where it will take place. Use the form below as a model.

PROVISIONAL CONFERENCE SCHEDULE

TIME	EVENT	PLACE

> **9.14**
> **We are obliged to** we must; this is part of a very formal letter.
> **in strict rotation** in the order in which we receive them.
> **all traces of occupation** Maria is saying that they must take everything away with them.

9.14 Document study

This is Maria's letter to firms which enquired about the conference. Read through it carefully, and then answer the questions in 9.15.

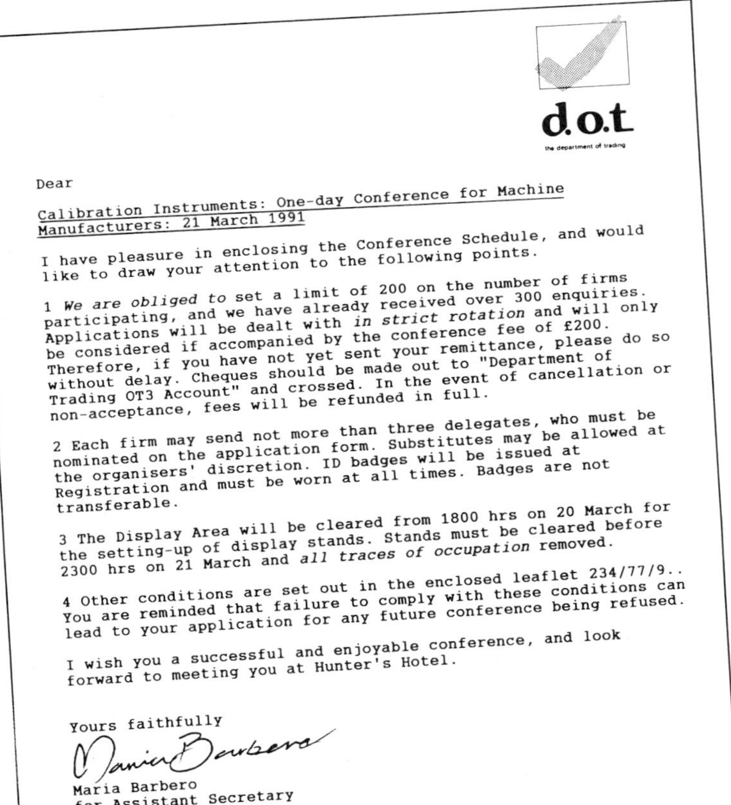

Dear

Calibration Instruments: One-day Conference for Machine Manufacturers: 21 March 1991

I have pleasure in enclosing the Conference Schedule, and would like to draw your attention to the following points.

1 *We are obliged to* set a limit of 200 on the number of firms participating, and we have already received over 300 enquiries. Applications will be dealt with *in strict rotation* and will only be considered if accompanied by the conference fee of £200. Therefore, if you have not yet sent your remittance, please do so without delay. Cheques should be made out to "Department of Trading OT3 Account" and crossed. In the event of cancellation or non-acceptance, fees will be refunded in full.

2 Each firm may send not more than three delegates, who must be nominated on the application form. Substitutes may be allowed at the organisers' discretion. ID badges will be issued at Registration and must be worn at all times. Badges are not transferable.

3 The Display Area will be cleared from 1800 hrs on 20 March for the setting-up of display stands. Stands must be cleared before 2300 hrs on 21 March and *all traces of occupation* removed.

4 Other conditions are set out in the enclosed leaflet 234/77/9.. You are reminded that failure to comply with these conditions can lead to your application for any future conference being refused.

I wish you a successful and enjoyable conference, and look forward to meeting you at Hunter's Hotel.

Yours faithfully

Maria Barbero

Maria Barbero
for Assistant Secretary

9.15 Reading for key words

What words in 9.14 indicate the following?

1 Applications are not likely to be accepted unless cheques are enclosed with them.
2 Some applications may be refused even if cheques are enclosed – the conference might even be cancelled.
3 You cannot give or lend your identity card to anyone else.
4 People who take the place of people named previously.
5 If the organisers agree.
6 If you do not obey the rules, you may not be allowed to come to next year's conference.

Study record	
9.1	
9.2	
9.3	
9.4	
9.5	
9.6	
9.7	
9.8	
9.9	
9.10	
9.11	
9.12	
9.13	
9.14	
9.15	

Answer key and commentary for unit 9

9.2 Structure practice

1 (Answer given in text.)
2 They hold short conferences every year.
3 She has organised various events in the past.
4 She has organised such things quite often.
5 He must also give her some other information straight away.
6 She must not exceed six and a half thousand pounds for hotel expenses.

9.3 Document study

See table at foot of page for a model answer.

9.6 Structure practice

1 A 500-seat arena
2 A two-day conference
3 A fifteen-storey building
4 A four-person committee [note 'person' here, not 'people']
5 A £20,000-a-year job
6 A three-year-old child

9.7 Listen and read

We still don't know which hotel they will choose. As Mark says, 'There's not a lot to choose between them'.

9.8 Listen and read

The committee seem to prefer Hunter's: 'don't you think that rather points to Hunter's this year?' Valerie prefers the Grand because the food is better and because Graham Flinston prefers it.

9.9 Structure practice

1 e **2** d **3** b **4** c **5** a

9.11 Document study

1 £439.50
2 £155
3 £29.50
4 £624
5 £1470
6 £900
7 £2370
8 £576
9 £3150
10 £300
11 £4026
12 £7020
13 £526.50
14 £6493.50

9.13 Listening practice

See table at foot of page.

9.15 Reading for key words

1 Applications . . . will only be considered accompanied by the conference fee
2 In the event of cancellation o non-acceptance
3 [ID] badges are not transferable.
4 Substitutes
5 at the organisers' discretion
6 failure to comply with these conditions ca lead to your application for any futur conference being refused.

9.3

Requirement	Grand	Hunter's
Comfortable accommodation	?	?
Good food	yes	?
Easy access from all parts of UK	yes	yes, by road
Modern conference facilities	yes	fairly
Large meeting hall	300 seats	500 seats
Large exhibition area	400 m^2	200 stands
Smaller rooms for presentations	yes	yes
Reasonable cost	fairly	about 25% less

9.13

TIME	EVENT	PLACE
9.30–10.00	Registration and coffee	Exhibition area
10.00	Flinston's keynote speech	Arena
10.30	Briefing sessions	Seminar rooms and arena
12.30–2.00	Lunch	Huntersmoon banqueting room
2.00–3.30	Product presentations	Seminar rooms and arena
3.30	Tea	Exhibition area
4.00–5.30	Product presentations	Seminar rooms and arena
5.30	Finish	

Unit 10: Making a product presentation

SITUATION

Mikan Electronics is one of the companies attending the one-day conference organised by the Department of Trading. It has selected two representatives to attend the conference, and one of them is giving a presentation on the company's electronic postal weighing machine. This unit looks at how to prepare for and give an effective presentation, and how to deal with follow-up questions from an audience.

CHARACTERS

Valerie Tipstock	
Tetsuo Endo	is a technician at Mikan Electronics. He is Japanese.
Jenny Price	works for Mikan Electronics. She is British.

LANGUAGE

Vocabulary	Simple machines and their operation; public speaking; visual aids.
Skills	Reassuring someone; giving help and advice; making a presentation to a small audience; asking and answering questions in a small group; making notes.
Structures	Parallel structures; imaginary time, *suppose* and *would*.
Documents	Notes; a series of slide pictures to compare.

Preparing the presentation – advice

10.1
How are we doing for time? do we have enough time?

10.3
You're not your usual happy self you seem a bit unhappy.
a big hit a success.

10.1 Listen and read

Tetsuo Endo and Jenny Price are driving along the motorway from South Wales t get to the conference at Hunter's Hotel. Listen to what they say. Why is Tetsu anxious?

TETSUO	*How are we doing for time?* There's such a lot of traffic.
JENNY	There's plenty of time, no problem. When we get over the bridge, we just follow the signs for the M5, then another hour and we're there.
TETSUO	What are those warning lights, why are they flashing?
JENNY	Oh-oh – twenty miles an hour speed limit. There must be a hold-up on the bridge.
TETSUO	A hold-up? You mean a robbery?
JENNY	No, much worse! Either there's been an accident, or they're repairing the road.
TETSUO	You think that's worse than a robbery?
JENNY	It is from our point of view.
TETSUO	You're right. Look at this queue!
JENNY	Oh, it's not really so bad. Relax. We're less than a mile from the bridge.

10.2 Reading for key words

In what words does Tetsuo express:

1 anxiety about the traffic?
2 great surprise at what Jenny has just said?
3 alarm at what he sees in front of them?

In what words does Jenny:

4 assure Tetsuo that they won't be late?
5 suggest that finding the way will be easy?
6 express alarm at the 20 m.p.h. speed limit?

10.3 Listen and read

Tetsuo and Jenny continue their journey. Listen to what they say. Why does Tetsu really feel anxious? What does he have to do at the conference?

JENNY	*You're not your usual happy self* this morning, are you?
TETSUO	To tell you the truth, I'm a little bit anxious about this presentation I'm doing at the conference. Mr Takahama only briefed me last night, after he got that message calling him back t Tokyo. I've never done a presentation before.
JENNY	You don't need to worry, your English is excellent! You'll be *a big hit*.
TETSUO	Oh I can handle the language all right. But I've never done a sales presentation, even in Japanese! I'm a technician, not a communicator.
JENNY	Tetsuo, everyone in the company is a communicator!
TETSUO	Yeah, that's what Mr Takahama said. But I've listened to lots of presentations by sales reps – I've seen how many things can go wrong.
JENNY	Look, don't be nervous. I tell you what – I've got my notes from the marketing course. Perhaps we could take some time and go through them together.
TETSUO	That would be great!

10.4 Reading for key words

How does Jenny:

1 express concern about Tetsuo's state of mind?
2 show that she has misunderstood the reason for Tetsuo's nervousness?

In what words does Tetsuo:

3 show that he doesn't like to admit to a lack of confidence?
4 express confidence in his English?
5 say that he's seen some very bad sales presentations?

Jenny says something which probably expresses Mikan's company policy.
6 What does she say?

10.5 Speaking practice: reassuring someone

Listen to this conversation. Then listen to it again, and speak the part of the woman.

WOMAN	Is everything all right? How are things going?
MAN	Fine, thanks! Actually, to be honest, I'm a bit worried about this aptitude test tomorrow.
WOMAN	You don't need to worry. I'm sure it'll go well. I mean, the first part is just recognising shapes.
MAN	Yes, I think I can handle that all right.
WOMAN	I'm sure you can.
MAN	It's the second part of the test that worries me. My problem is I'm not very good with figures.
WOMAN	Part two isn't really so difficult, you know. It's just applied common sense. Relax! Stop worrying.
MAN	Yes, perhaps you're right.
WOMAN	I know I am. Look – I tell you what. I've got some old test papers here. We can go through them together if you like.

10.6 Document study

These are Jenny's notes for Tetsuo. Imagine that tomorrow you are going to talk to a group of six or eight foreign business people or students. You can only communicate with them in English. You want them either to come to your country as tourists, or to learn your language, or to buy a product from your country or your company. Make notes about what you will say to them, based on the suggestions given in part 1 (Preparation), sections a, b and c.

1. Preparation
a. Think about:
- principal objective – what you are trying to do: inform? convince? encourage?
- audience – who will be there? – job titles, responsibilities, needs.
- audience reaction – what will they think / feel / do as you speak: will they be impressed? bored? friendly? hostile?

b. Select:
- what you will talk about: topics, subject areas.
- the benefits your product offers – these should match and satisfy the needs of your audience.

c. Plan:
- what you will say: one general benefit statement; 3 or 4 specific benefit statements; closing statement.

d. Prepare / rehearse:
- language aids: examples, comparisons, stories, jokes...
- visual aids: flipcharts, OHP transparencies, chalk / whiteboards, handouts, slides, video.

2. Delivery
- body language: dress, posture, gesture, eye contact, facial expression. Be relaxed, avoid nervous habits.
- voice: vary volume, tempo, pitch, rhythm.

3. Handling audience questions
- keep till end as far as possible.
- anticipate likely questions – especially hostile ones.

Making the presentation

10.7
standing in line queuing; an American usage.
to cash a cheque to present a cheque at a bank in exchange for cash.

10.7 Listen and read

Tetsuo is making his presentation at the conference. Listen to what he says here and in 10.10. As you listen, try to write Tetsuo's notes. Use the following headings Audience, Needs, Benefits, Delivery.

TETSUO Good afternoon, ladies and gentlemen. My name is Tetsuo Endo; I represent the Mikan Electronics Corporation and I am going to talk to you for a few minutes about my company's products – in particular, about our post office weighing machines.

I came to Britain for the first time a few months ago and of course I was very interested to see how people here live. I had heard lots of stories, but this was my first opportunity to see for myself. The British are well known in other countries for *standing in line* – for queuing. Ah, you know that? I discovered this was true when I waited for a bus, when I entered a bank *to cash a cheque*, and when I sent a parcel to my mother in Tokyo. And I discovered it again this morning when we had to queue on the motorway to cross the Severn Bridge. The reason that you are so good at queuing is that you have so much practice. Now, Mikan Electronics is going to change that, because one place where you won't have to queue for nearly as long in future as you have done in the past is a British post office. That is, if you adopt our Eagle range of electronic postal weighing machines.

10.8 Document study

Tetsuo shows a series of colour slides, showing what happens in a post office wit conventional weighing machines.

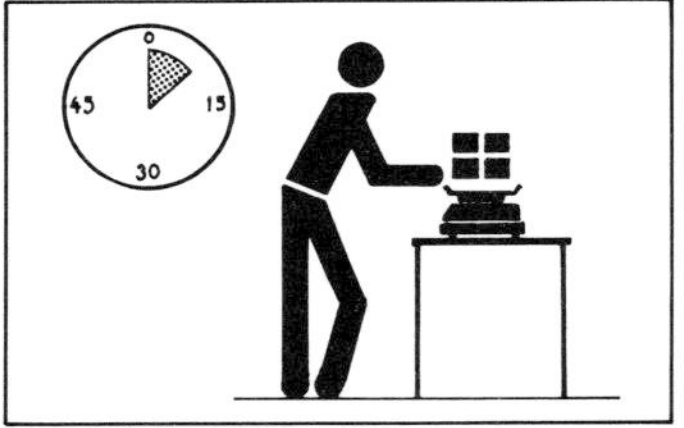

Put parcel on scale

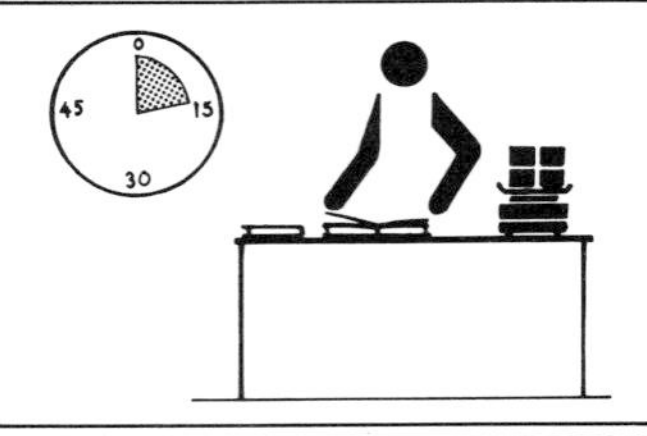

Look up postage rates in manual

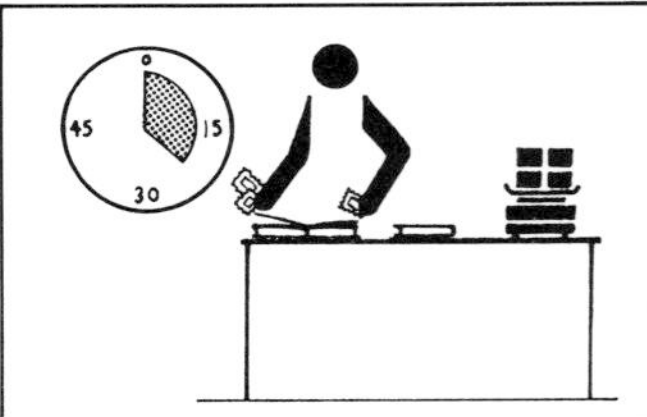

Find stamps to total value

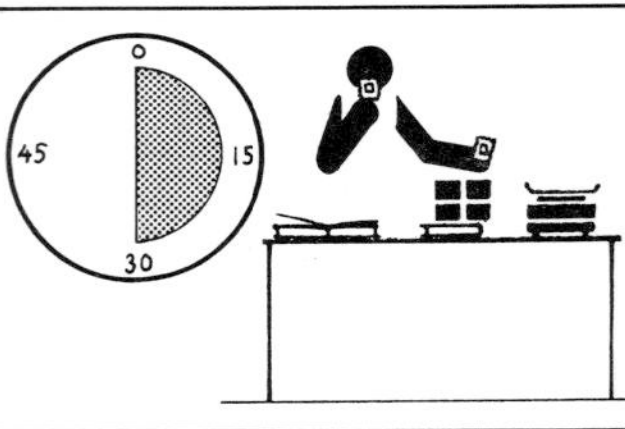

Stick stamps on parcel

Then he shows another series of pictures, demonstrating the new weighin machine:

Put parcel on scale

Press button for type of postage and destination

Machine prints post-paid label

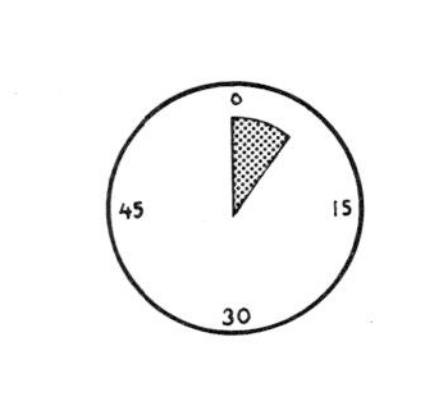

Ready for next customer!

10.9 Writing practice: describing a process

As Tetsuo shows his sequence of pictures, he describes what happens at each stag

TETSUO First, the clerk puts the parcel on the weighing machine . . .

Write the rest of his commentary for him, using the pictures from 10.8. Note th when we describe a process like this we normally use the simple present form of th verb.

10.10 Listen and read

Tetsuo continues his presentation. Listen to what he says. What benefits does he claim for the Eagle weighing machine? At the end he tells a joke. What is it? What does he mean?

TETSUO Of course we don't claim that this is *new technology*. *On the contrary* – this is technology that has been developed and tested over a long period in supermarkets everywhere. We are all familiar with it at *the supermarket check-out*, so why not at the post office counter also?

The benefits of our Eagle weighing machine are not limited to the rapid printing of postage labels. Changes in postal rates can quickly be programmed into the machine. The machine is so sensitive that it can weigh a single gram, so the post office clerk doesn't need a special balance any more for weighing air letters. And it is easily modified to accept any credit or debit card. The clerk *swipes* the card through the machine and the customer's account is automatically debited. In the future that could mean less cash passing across the counter – less incentive for the criminal to threaten the clerk with a gun. So, with one machine we eliminate two kinds of post office hold-up!

10.10
new technology electronic machines, especially computers.
On the contrary the opposite is true.
the supermarket check-out the place in the supermarket where you pay for your goods.
swipes moves a magnetic card through a machine.

10.11 Structure practice: parallel structures

Tetsuo speaks fluently, but his sentences are quite simple in construction. Even his long sentences are just simple groups of words joined together, like items in a list. Look at the example below, from 10.7. When he introduces himself, he says what his job is and then what he is going to do:

I am going to talk to you for a few minutes about my company's products –
in particular, about our post office weighing machines.

He repeats the word 'about' so that his audience, and he himself, can easily see how the sentence is put together. Here is another example, a list of three word-groups, all starting with 'when'.

I discovered this was true
when I waited for a bus,
when I entered a bank to cash a cheque and
when I sent a parcel to my mother in Tokyo.

If you listen to 10.7 again, you will hear how he repeats not only the structure, but also the rhythm in these sentences. Here are two more examples from Tetsuo's presentation:

The reason that you are so good at queuing is
that you have so much practice.

We are all familiar with it
at the supermarket check-out, so why not
at the post office counter also?

Now practise writing some 'parallel structures' like Tetsuo's:

1 Introduce Tetsuo to the audience, using the words from 10.7. Say what company he represents, and what he is going to do, in general and in particular.

2 Tetsuo said 'I discovered this was true . . . ' Continue his sentence using the examples below:

. . . waited in line to cross the Severn Bridge
. . . tried to get in to see the Wimbledon men's tennis final
. . . wanted to get money from a cash machine on a Saturday night

3 Write a sentence explaining why the Eagle is so quick, using the information below.

One reason that . . . is that . . . (displays postage rates),
another is that . . . (prints the postage label) and
a third is that . . . (accepts credit cards).

Dealing with questions

10.12
The unit price the price for one item.
magnetic card reader a machine which 'reads' the magnetic cards.
makes the names of the companies which make a particular product.

10.14
touched briefly on said a little bit about.
the question of reliability how reliable the machines are.
goes down fails; stops working. **Go down** is used only about computers and computer-controlled machines.

10.12 Listen and read

Valerie Tipstock from the Department of Trade is attending the conference. She asks Tetsuo about costs. Listen to what they say.

TETSUO	I've told you something about our product – now does anyone have any questions?
VALERIE	Could you give us some indication of cost?
TETSUO	*The unit price*, for the basic machine without *magnetic card reader*, is £1470. The card reader costs £195 extra, plus of course the connection charge by the telephone company.
VALERIE	But at the Leipzig Fair we'll be getting enquiries from foreign postal services who'll be seeking to place contracts to purchase hundreds of machines – over a period of perhaps five years. What do you say to them?
TETSUO	Yes, I appreciate that, of course, and my company is always willing to discuss generous discount and finance terms. But I gave you the unit price because often that is the fairest basis for comparison between competing *makes*.

10.13 Reading for key words

What words do the speakers use to express these ideas?

1 Roughly, what's the price?
2 I know that already.
3 The cost of connecting the machine to the telephone network.
4 The price of a single machine.
5 [They] will want to make agreements with suppliers.
6 [It] is the most accurate way to compare them.

10.14 Listen and read

Valerie is again questioning Tetsuo about the Eagle weighing machine. Listen to what they say. Listen to how Valerie tries to get Tetsuo to say more about the reliability of the machines, and then tries to make him be more and more specific.

VALERIE	Mr Endo, you *touched briefly on the question of reliability*. I wonder if you'd like to say a bit more. The mechanical weighing machines we have in use are some of the finest in the world, and they virtually never go wrong. What happens when one of your machines *goes down*?
TETSUO	Well – that's an extremely rare event.
VALERIE	OK, so it never happens, but suppose it did happen, what would you do about it?
TETSUO	We would supply a replacement within . . . six hours.
VALERIE	You don't sound very confident. Suppose it was in Eastern Europe or somewhere?
TETSUO	I was going to say, six hours on the UK mainland. It could take twenty-four hours to somewhere more remote. But in most areas of the EC, we can deliver a new machine within six hours.

10.15 Reading for key words

What words or phrases in 10.14 show these ideas?

1 You mentioned it.
2 Hardly ever. (two answers)
3 [It] stops working.
4 You didn't let me finish what I was saying.

10.16 Listen and read

Valerie's third question to Tetsuo concerns maintenance contracts. Listen to what they say. What two problems does Valerie raise?

VALERIE All right then, that brings me to my next point. Do I assume that your customers are obliged, or advised, to take out *annual maintenance contracts*? And if so, is your company in a position *to honour these contracts* abroad?

TETSUO I would like to suggest that it would be better if my company trained post office staff in the various countries to do the servicing themselves.

VALERIE Well, would it? I mean, to start with you've got the language barrier. And what about spare parts, who's going to handle *that side of it*?

TETSUO Remember, our parent company, Mikan International, already runs a world-wide sales and maintenance network. That will take care of spare parts. And our experience is that staff from different countries are very pleased to come to one of our training courses. In this case, I think they would see that their new skills would improve their ratings in *the job market*.

10.16
annual maintenance contracts an agreement where you pay a sum of money each year, so that any repairs or maintenance on a machine will be paid for by the manufacturer.
to honour these contracts to be able to carry out any work.
that side of it that part of the contract, i.e. the spare parts.
the job market the group of people who are looking for work.

10.17 Structure practice: imaginary time

In English, we have many ways of talking about events which do not actually happen. This allows us to talk about and solve problems before they become real. For example, Valerie says, in 10.14:

suppose it did happen

What she means is 'imagine that it happens'. Notice that even though she is talking about the future, she uses the past tense 'did happen'. She goes on to say:

what would you do about it?

Here she uses 'would', because she is still talking about something that is not real; she is talking about something imagined. When Tetsuo answers, he also uses 'would':

We would supply a replacement within . . . six hours.

Valerie goes on to say:

Suppose it was in Eastern Europe or somewhere?

This time, Tetsuo answers with 'could'; he is still talking about an imaginary event:

It could take twenty-four hours . . .

but when he talks about the EC he uses 'can':

we can deliver a new machine within six hours

This is because now he is talking about real events. He knows he can deliver in Europe because he has already done it; he is not talking about possibility, but reality.

Now write answers to these questions for Tetsuo. You have to decide whether Tetsuo knows the answer, or whether he has to imagine a solution to the problem:

1 Suppose I wanted to order ten machines. What would the price be?
2 Suppose a machine broke down in Tokyo. How long would it take to supply a replacement?
3 Suppose I wanted to buy the card reader later. Would I be able to do that?
4 Suppose the machine broke down in a month. Who would pay for that?

Study record	
10.1	
10.2	
10.3	
10.4	
10.5	
10.6	
10.7	
10.8	
10.9	
10.10	
10.11	
10.12	
10.13	
10.14	
10.15	
10.16	
10.17	

Answer key and commentary for unit 10

10.1 Listen and read
Tetsuo is anxious because he thinks they may be late.

10.2 Reading for key words
1 There's such a lot of traffic.
2 You think that's worse than a robbery?
3 Look at this queue!
4 There's plenty of time, no problem.
5 we just follow the signs
6 Oh-oh . . . There must be a hold-up on the bridge.

10.3 Listen and read
Tetsuo is anxious about the presentation he has to make at the conference. He has to make a sales presentation.

10.4 Reading for key words
1 You're not your usual happy self this morning
2 You don't need to worry, your English is excellent!
3 To tell you the truth
4 I can handle the language all right.
5 I've seen how many things can go wrong.
6 everyone in the company is a communicator!

10.6 Document study
No model answers are provided for this. The object of this exercise is not to test your English but to make you think about what you need to do when you give a presentation.

10.7 Listen and read
This is a model answer.
Audience: civil servants, responsible for selecting products to be shown on UK stand at Leipzig; other exhibitors; intelligent, professional, critical; may or may not be trained technologists; don't talk down to them.
Needs: to select best products.
Benefits: avoids hold-ups in post offices; simple and quick operation; displays weight and postal charges; prints postage labels; reprogrammable; can weigh air letters; can take credit and debit cards; reliable.
Delivery: get audience interested and relaxed; general benefits – hold-ups; specific benefits – show slides; closing statement; questions.

10.9 Writing practice
This is a model answer.
First, the clerk puts the parcel on the weighing machine and reads the weight. Then he looks up the postage rates in the manual. Next he finds stamps of different values and tears them off. Finally he sticks the stamps on the parcel. It takes up to thirty seconds.

Now we see the Eagle weighing machine. The clerk puts the parcel on the scale, and pushes one button to show the class or the type of postage, and another for the destination. The machine prints a post-paid label, and the clerk sticks it on the parcel. It's all done in about five seconds.

10.10 Listen and read
Tetsuo's joke is 'So, with one machine w eliminate two kinds of post-office hold-up!' Th joke rests on the two meanings of 'hold-up' customers shouldn't have to wait for so long because there will be less cash, criminals won try to rob the post office.

10.11 Structure practice
These are model answers.
1 I would like to introduce Mr Tetsuo Endo, wh represents the Mikan Electronics Corporatio He is going to talk about his company products, and in particular about their po office weighing machines.

2 I discovered this was true when I waited in lin to cross the Severn Bridge, when I tried to ge in to see the Wimbledon men's tennis final an when I wanted to get money from a cas machine on a Saturday night.

3 One reason that the Eagle is so quick is that displays postage rates, another is that it prin the postage label and a third is that it accep credit cards.

10.13 Reading for key words
1 Could you give us some indication of cost?
2 I appreciate that
3 the connection charge
4 The unit price
5 [They will] be seeking to place contracts
6 [It] is the fairest basis for comparison

10.15 Reading for key words
1 you touched briefly on
2 virtually never / that's an extremely rare eve
3 [It] goes down
4 I was going to say

10.16 Listen and read
Valerie raises two problems of maintenance. Sh is not sure that Mikan can maintain machine abroad, and she's not sure that they could trai post office staff to do their own maintenance.

10.17 Structure practice
These are model answers.
1 The price would depend on the discount an finance terms. [Tetsuo does not know wh they will be.]
2 We can supply a replacement in two hour [Tetsuo knows this because Mikan is based i Japan.]
3 You will be able to buy a card reader at an time. [Tetsuo knows that they will always b available.]
4 That would be covered by the servic contract. [Tetsuo doesn't know if the compan will actually have a service contract.]

Unit 11: Discovering a new market

SITUATION

Tortuga Toys is a Spanish toy manufacturer which would like to expand into South-East Asia. The owner has travelled to the area to assess the market for his company's latest product. This unit examines finance, investment, business forecasting, the stock markets and market research. It also looks at how to make travel arrangements.

CHARACTERS

Ramon Figueras	is the owner of Tortuga Toys. He is Spanish.
Jack Lytton	is a teacher at UCLA. He is American.
Receptionist	at Thaipro Consultants. She is Thai.
Supa	is a marketing consultant at Thaipro Consultants. She is Thai.
Travel agent	works for Executive Travel. He is British.
Fred Hagendahl	is Director of Marketing at Tumblehome Inc. He is American.

LANGUAGE

Vocabulary	Stock markets; business forecasting; market research; air travel.
Skills	Getting information from press cuttings and reports; making travel arrangements.
Documents	Press cuttings; a market analysis report; a booking form; a credit card.

Doing some desk research

(11.1)

Bangkok catches cold, Tokyo sneezes

Dealers on the Tokyo Stock Exchange yesterday were cautious *in the face of* rumours that Thai share prices might be threatened by inflation, now running at over 8% and expected *to top* 9% by the end of this year.

The *Nikkei* continued its slow upward trend, closing at 35,289 (up 37 on the day), but the market was *bearish* and expects a downturn. The growing strength of the Thai economy is shown by the fact that its short-term problems can affect the market in Tokyo. This may not, however, be much comfort to Thai finance managers, who struggle to cope with high interest rates, the shortage of skilled labour, and the *migration* of venture capital to neighbouring countries.

19 11 January 1991 (11.1)

TUMBLEHOME ROLL ON TO THAILAND

Thailand may soon become Toyland if leading US toy retailers Tumblehome *follow through* their recent announcement that they will set up their first South-East Asian subsidiary in Bangkok.

'Continued expansion is built into our company policy,' a *spokesperson* for the company said at a press conference in San Francisco yesterday. 'The Pacific Rim is the *flywheel* of tomorrow's world economy, and South-East Asia is going to be the motor that turns it.'

11.1 Document study

Ramon Figueras works for Tortuga, in Madrid. Tortuga makes toys, and Ramon is looking at the possibility of expanding into South-East Asia. He finds some press cuttings. Read through them, and make a list of 'Good news' and 'Bad news'.

11.2 Reading for key words

Find the words or phrases in 11.1 that tell you the following:

1. Prices will soon rise more quickly.
2. Share prices are expected to fall.
3. Highly-trained workers are difficult to find.
4. People with money to invest in new business tend to invest it abroad.
5. This company intends to go on growing.
6. The countries around the edge of this ocean will soon be the most productive in the world.

11.3 Document study

Ramon finds another article. Read through it. You will need it for 11.4.

(11.3) News in Brief

Question mark over Spanish toy firm

Rumours that Spanish toymakers Tortuga of Madrid may be going into liquidation were dismissed as 'utter nonsense' by the firm's founder and chairman, Juan Figueras, last week.

'We *struck a bad patch* a year ago,' he admitted, 'when we failed to keep up with changes in taste and lagged behind on design and marketing. Since then we've invested heavily in new equipment and we've got *new blood* in the design and management teams. Repayments on the new loans aren't due to start for another nine months – by that time I'm confident we'll be paying our way and back in profit.'

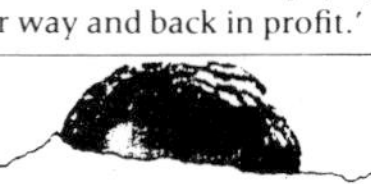

11.1
in the face of against.
to top to exceed.
Nikkei the Japanese stock exchange index.
bearish expecting falling share prices.
migration movement from one place to another, especially to another country.
follow through complete; do the next thing.
spokesperson someone who makes a statement on behalf of a company or organisation.
flywheel a part of a machine that stores energy and keeps the machine working at a steady rate; here the suggestion is that South-East Asia may provide the economic 'energy', but it is the Pacific Rim countries that will actually keep the world economy going.

11.3
struck a bad patch had a period with a lot of problems.
new blood new, usually young, people who join a company and whose ideas are likely to make it better.

11.4
UCLA the University of California, Los Angeles.
marketing seminars a discussion class on marketing in a college or university.

11.4 Listen and read

A month after the article in 11.3 appeared, Ramon's father died and Ramon took over the company. Ramon receives a telephone call from Jack Lytton. Listen to what they say. Who is Jack Lytton? Why has he phoned?

RAMON Ramon Figueras.
JACK Ramon? Jack Lytton here – from *UCLA*.
RAMON Jack! Hi, how are you? Are you in Spain?
JACK No, but I'll get around to it sooner or later, don't you worry. The reason I'm calling is I keep picking up rumours about Tortuga. How are things over there in Madrid?
RAMON Well – it's what in your *marketing seminars* you used to call 'a very interesting situation'.
JACK Oh boy! As bad as that, is it?
RAMON No, it's not all bad. In fact I did this fantastic deal last time I was in California. Let me tell you about it . . .

11.5 Listen and read

Ramon continues his telephone conversation with Jack Lytton. Listen to what they say. What arrangements does Ramon already have with countries in South-East Asia?

RAMON So, anyway, I'm planning to go to Bangkok in about three weeks to start investigating the market for the Dolphin Commando merchandise in Asia.

JACK Good thinking. I'm glad you learnt something in my classes. Dolphin Commando looks set *to take off* here. Those toy whales look like being the big *craze* for *kids* this fall.

RAMON Yes, I know. We're going flat out here to meet the orders from the big retailers. We've *contracted out* a lot of the manufacturing work to firms in Taiwan and the Philippines, and all the packaging and distribution is being done in Cleveland, Ohio. But when the Asian countries get the programmes *beamed* to them by satellite in the new year, the market's likely to explode overnight.

JACK In that case I'd better get off the line and let you get on with it! I have one or two contacts in Bangkok you might find useful, by the way – I'll dig out their addresses for you.

RAMON Thanks, I'd really appreciate it if you could do that. Well, it's been good talking to you, Jack. I'll speak to you again soon.

JACK Surely. Take care now. Goodbye!

11.5
to take off to become very successful and popular.
(a) craze something that is very popular, but usually only for a short time.
kids children; **kids** is an informal word.
contracted out employed another company to do the work, rather than do it ourselves.
beamed sent by radio waves.

11.6
lagging behind progressing more slowly than others.

11.6 Document study: an interview

Read this interview about the economy, and then answer the questions that follow.

INTERVIEWER It seems that the economy has struck a bad patch. How do you see the situation developing?

MAN Well, the most serious threat is that of high interest rates plus rising inflation.

INTERVIEWER How do you think companies will cope with this, if they can't afford to borrow?

MAN They simply won't invest. They'll go on using old machinery and equipment. They won't train new labour.

INTERVIEWER But a lot of companies are already *lagging behind* on capital investment, and the venture capital is going abroad.

MAN In that case, when the upturn in the economy does come, they won't be ready for it. They won't be able to meet the increased demand for goods.

INTERVIEWER And if they're not competitive?

MAN The companies will simply go into liquidation.

1 Why can't companies afford to borrow?
2 Why won't companies be able to meet the increased demand for goods?
3 Why will companies go into liquidation?

11.7 Writing practice: making notes

Ramon makes brief notes of things he has read and things he has heard in his conversations which might be useful to him. Read the articles in 11.1 and 11.3 again, and listen to 11.5. Now write notes for Ramon. Start with your list from 11.1.

Commissioning a market study

11.8
commissioning asking someone, usually a professional person, to do some work for you.

11.9
a bit nearer the time when you are about to come.
we're quite central the company has an office in the centre of the city.
If by any chance if for any reason.

11.10
infrastructure the roads, railways, power, communications etc., of a country or city.
is set for looks likely to experience.
joint ventures new business operations that involve more than one company.
entrepreneurs people who put money into new businesses to make a profit.
Interim findings the information that you have at a point before a project is finished.
windows of opportunity times at which something is possible.

11.8 Listen and read

Ramon telephones a firm of market consultants in Bangkok. Listen to the way that Ramon says only enough to make sure that he is talking to the right person. Notice also how the people in the firm explain exactly what they can do to help him.

RECEPTIONIST Good afternoon, Thaipro Consultants, can I help you?
RAMON Ah! Hello. I'm thinking of *commissioning* your company to do some market research for me in Thailand. I shall be coming to Bangkok in a week or so, but I wonder if there's someone I could have a word with now?
RECEPTIONIST Yes, I think so. We have several departments here which specialise in different market sectors. Can you give me some idea of what type of business you're in?
RAMON Yes, we manufacture and distribute toys. All kinds of toys!
RECEPTIONIST Oh yes. Hold on, I'll put you through to someone who can help you. Oh! What name shall I say?
RAMON Figueras – Ramon Figueras.
. . . . . .
WOMAN Good afternoon, Mr Figrash? How can I help you?
RAMON Oh, good afternoon! My name is Ramon Figueras, I am chairman of . . .

11.9 Listen and read

The telephone conversation continues. Notice how the woman and Ramon show that they have finished the conversation.

WOMAN Right, Mr Figueras, I look forward to meeting you when you come to Bangkok. If you telephone me *a bit nearer the time*, we'll make an appointment to meet at my office; *we're quite central*.
RAMON Good. And meanwhile I'm looking forward to getting that investment fact-sheet you mentioned. Thank you for your help. Oh! I don't think I have your name.
WOMAN Just ask for Supa – S-U-P-A. *If by any chance* I'm not in the office, my colleague will make the appointment.
RAMON Right, thank you very much indeed, Supa.

11.10 Document study

Opposite is part of the leaflet on the economy and investment prospects that the consultant, Supa, sent to Ramon. Read through it carefully. Make a list of things that Ramon might think are 'Good', and a list of things he might think are 'Bad', for his company.

11.11 Reading for key words: formal and informal language

In her written report, Supa uses more formal language than when she talks to Ramon on the telephone. The phrases below are taken from the report. Write what Supa might say to Ramon to express the same meanings.

1 rapidly-expanding young urban population
2 This strong demand-led growth is projected to continue
3 [it] offers outstanding medium-term market prospects
4 Interim findings . . . suggest that large-scale investment will be required

The Foreign Investment Outlook in Thailand, 1992–96

INTRODUCTION

Thailand, with its modern *infrastructure* and services, rapidly-expanding young urban population and educated workforce, *is set for* spectacular economic and industrial growth. This is particularly true of textiles, electrical goods and light industrial products such as toys.

Targets and Forecasts for the Sixth and Seventh Plans

(based on official figures and Thaipro research)

	Fifth Plan (actual) (1982–86)	Sixth Plan (targets) (1987–91)	Seventh Plan (forecast) (1992–96)
Trade deficit*			
Average per year**	57,300	35,900	24,700
As percentage of GDP	5.9	2.7	1.8
Exports: goods			
Value (%)	7.6	10.7	11.0
Quantity (%)	8.0	8.1	6.5
Average annual value**	176,100	290,700	402,600
Earnings from tourism*			
Value (%)	12.2	7.4	7.0
Imports: goods			
Value (%)	2.9	9.5	14.6
Quantity (%)	3.3	4.6	5.8
Average annual value**	233,300	324,900	417,400
Economic growth***			
Agriculture	2.9	2.9	2.5
Industry	5.6	6.6	8.2
Mining	6.5	6.4	4.5
Total production	4.9	5.0	5.8
Expenditure growth***			
Private consumption	4.6	3.7	3.8
Private investment	0.6	8.1	10.7
Government consumption	3.6	5.3	6.0
Government investment	2.4	1.0	0.7
Tax revenue and other income as % of GDP	14.6	15.3	16.9
Population growth (%)	2.1	1.7	1.1
Inflation (%)	2.7	2.3	4.9

* 1987 prices
** Million baht
*** % annual increase; 1987 prices

Source (1986–91 figures): Thai Government Board of Investment

This strong demand-led growth is projected to continue at least throughout the 1990s and offers outstanding medium-term market prospects to overseas suppliers and investors.

On the manufacturing side, we are conducting a research programme to assess the long-term outlook for overseas companies willing to set up *joint ventures* under Thai business law with local *entrepreneurs*, as well as 100% foreign-owned businesses. A crucial factor will be the speed with which Thai manufacturers can meet the increasing demand for good design and durability as well as volume of goods. *Interim findings* of this project suggest that large-scale investment will be required and that overseas companies may need to be prepared to take risks and to move fast to exploit *windows of opportunity*.

Making a business trip

11.13
Splendid! very good!
dialling code the telephone code for a country or area.

11.14
expiry date the date after which something is no longer usable or valid.

11.12 Listen and read

Ramon is now in London, booking his flight on to Bangkok. Listen to what he sa to the travel agent.

AGENT Right, Mr Figueras – if I can just check the details again: that's a single ticket for one person, club class, from Heathrow to Bangkok, Thai Airways flight TG917, departing Friday 22 May at 1000 hours, reporting at Terminal 3 not later than 0830. And in Bangkok we've made a reservation for you at the Oriental Hotel. This is the total amount payable.
RAMON Right. You take Visa?
AGENT Yes, no problem. It will just take a moment for the machine to check the details. While we're waiting, can I ask you if you need to take out any travel insurance?
RAMON Thanks, I took out a policy before I came to Britain.
AGENT Covering the whole world?
RAMON Yes, world-wide.
AGENT Ah! Right. If you'd just like to sign here.

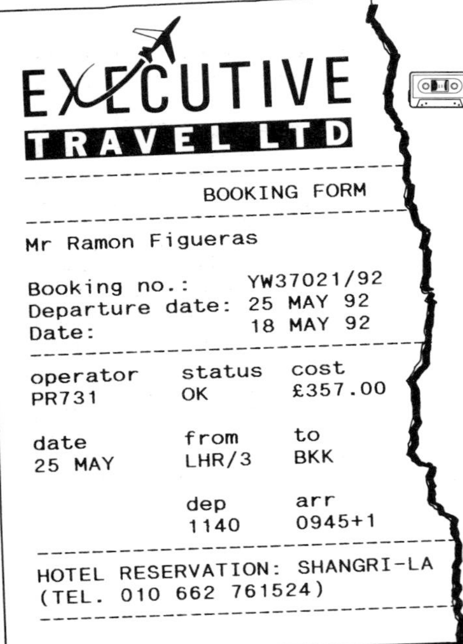

EXECUTIVE TRAVEL LTD

BOOKING FORM

Mr Ramon Figueras

Booking no.: YW37021/92
Departure date: 25 MAY 92
Date: 18 MAY 92

operator	status	cost
PR731	OK	£357.00
date	**from**	**to**
25 MAY	LHR/3	BKK
	dep	**arr**
	1140	0945+1

HOTEL RESERVATION: SHANGRI-LA
(TEL. 010 662 761524)

11.13 Listen and read

Ramon has to change his plans and postpone his flight to Bangkok. The travel age telephones Ramon to tell him the new details. First read through the dialogue belo and write what you think the travel agent will say, using the details from the bookir form. Then listen to what they say, and check your answers.

RAMON *Splendid!* What's the airline and the flight number?
AGENT Philippine Airways, ___**a**___.
RAMON Leaving Heathrow what time?
AGENT ___**b**___.
RAMON From Terminal 4?
AGENT No. ___**c**___.
RAMON When does it arrive in Bangkok?
AGENT ___**d**___ next morning, local time.
RAMON I see. Am I still in the same hotel?
AGENT No, the Oriental was full, so I booked you into the ___**e**___.
RAMON Oh, right. I may need to ring them. Do you have the phone number? With the *dialling code*, please.
AGENT ___**f**___.
RAMON Thanks. Now, suppose I need to call you again. Is there a booking number I should quote?
AGENT Your booking number is ___**g**___.

11.14 Speaking practice: checking the details

Ramon continues his conversation with the travel agent. First read through th dialogue below, and write what Ramon says, using the details from the credit car Then listen to what they say. Listen again, and speak the part of Ramon.

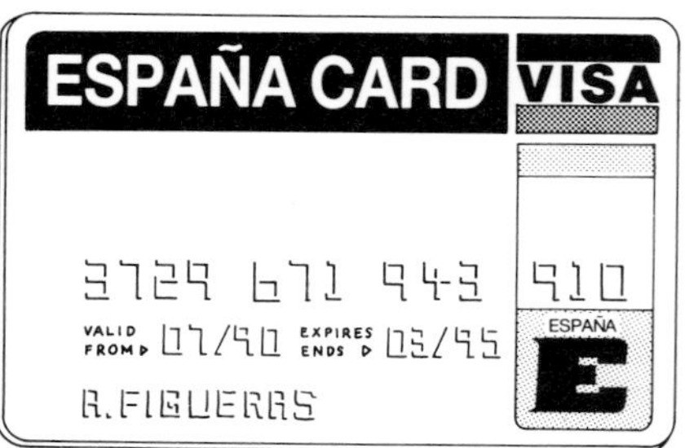

AGENT Is that all right, Mr Figueras?
RAMON Fine, thank you. One other thing. I gave you my personal credit card yesterday, and I should have given you my business Visa card.
AGENT Right, that's easy. I can charge that to your business card if you will give me, first, your card number.
RAMON ___**a**___ .
AGENT Right. And the *expiry date*.
RAMON ___**b**___ .
AGENT Also I need to know the exact name on the card, please.
RAMON ___**c**___ .
AGENT Right, that's it then. Your ticket will be ready for collection tomorrow. Thank you, Mr Figueras! Goodbye!

11.15 Listen and read

Ramon is now on his journey from London to Bangkok. Listen to these statements and conversations. Where do you think Ramon is when each voice speaks?

VOICE 1 Your attention please – passengers for flight PR731 to Bangkok, please *proceed at once* to the Departure Lounge. PR731 passengers, boarding now at Gate 4. Please have your boarding cards ready.

. . . . . .

VOICE 2 We shall be cruising at thirty-five thousand feet at a speed of four hundred and thirty miles an hour. On behalf of Philippine Airways, may I wish you a pleasant flight.

. . . . . .

VOICE 3 Good morning, sir. Would you like a newspaper?
RAMON Er, yes. If you've got a 'Financial Times', I'll take that.

. . . . . .

VOICE 4 Ladies and gentlemen, we are now approaching Bangkok and we shall *touch down* in approximately ten minutes. Please fasten your seatbelts and extinguish all cigarettes. The weather on the ground is cloudy and wet, air temperature twenty-nine degrees. We may *encounter a little turbulence on our approach*, but nothing to worry about.

. . . . . .

VOICE 5 Good morning, sir. You are travelling from London?
RAMON Yes, that's right.
VOICE 5 Do you have *anything to declare*?
RAMON No.
VOICE 5 Go straight through to passport control and *immigration*, please.

11.16 Listen and read

While he is waiting for a taxi, Ramon is approached by someone. Listen carefully to what they say. Listen to how Ramon cannot at first remember the other person.

MAN Excuse me – aren't you Ramon Figueras?
RAMON Yes, but I'm afraid . . .
MAN I knew it. I remember you from college – we were at UCLA together.
RAMON Well yes. I was at UCLA but . . .
MAN Hagendahl. Fred Hagendahl. I was reading Management Science – you were on the *MBA*.
RAMON Ah, right! Didn't you *have something to do with that IBM thing*?
FRED No, that was Johnson. I was the one who tried to organise the monkeys.
RAMON Of course, I remember. *You wanted them to write Shakespeare.*
FRED That's me. You do remember! *You staying in Bangkok?*
RAMON Yes. At the Shangri-la.
FRED Great. I'm at the Oriental. They're real close to each other. *You want to share a taxi?*

11.17 Writing practice

Ramon decides to add to the notes he made in 11.7, by writing details of what has happened to him since them. Write the details for him in note form.

11.15
proceed at once go immediately; this is an example of the formal language of announcements.
touch down land.
encounter a little turbulence on our approach meet some violent weather as we approach the airport.
anything to declare you declare something which you may not take into a country, or something on which you may have to pay a tax.
immigration the officials who check passports at airports, ports, etc.

11.16
MBA Master of Business Administration degree.
have something to do with be connected with; be involved in.
that IBM thing something to do with IBM, which I can't remember.
You wanted them to write Shakespeare this is a reference to an old saying, or joke, that if you put enough monkeys with enough typewriters into a room for enough time, one of them will eventually write the plays of Shakespeare. Fred had tried to set this up when he was at UCLA.
You staying in Bangkok? are you staying in Bangkok? Note how Fred omits the 'are' in this question. Also in **You want to share a taxi?** he omits the 'do'. This is possible in speech, especially in American English.

Study record	
11.1	
11.2	
11.3	
11.4	
11.5	
11.6	
11.7	
11.8	
11.9	
11.10	
11.11	
11.12	
11.13	
11.14	
11.15	
11.16	
11.17	

Answer key and commentary for unit 11

11.1 Document study

Good news: the growing strength of the Thai economy; importance of Pacific Rim countries; leading US toy retailer to set up subsidiary in Bangkok.

Bad news: rising inflation; short-term economic problems; high interest rates; shortage of skilled labour; migration of venture capital to neighbouring countries.

11.2 Reading for key words

1. inflation, now running at over 8% and expected to top 9% by the end of this year.
2. the market was bearish and expects a downturn.
3. the shortage of skilled labour
4. the migration of venture capital to neighbouring countries.
5. Continued expansion is built into our company policy
6. The Pacific Rim is the flywheel of tomorrow's world economy

11.4 Listen and read

Jack Lytton is probably a teacher at UCLA. Ramon refers to 'your marketing seminars'. Jack is calling Ramon because he has heard that Tortuga is in financial difficulties. He says 'I keep picking up rumours about Tortuga'. He has probably read the article in 11.3.

11.5 Listen and read

Some of Ramon's production of the Dolphin Commando goods is done in South-East Asia. He says 'We've contracted out a lot of the manufacturing work to firms in Taiwan and the Philippines'.

11.6 Document study

1. Companies can't afford to borrow because of high interest rates plus rising inflation.
2. Companies won't be able to meet the increased demand for goods because they won't invest in new machinery and labour training.
3. Companies will go into liquidation because they are not competitive.

11.7 Writing practice

Tortuga not too strong financially – needs to make Dolphin Commando a success – South-East Asia promising market – growing strength of the Thai economy – importance of Pacific Rim countries – other toy retailers going there – would need to set up meetings in Bangkok – must move quickly.

11.8 Listen and read

The receptionist explains that Thaipro is organised into departments which deal with different market sectors. She asks Ramon 'what type of business' he's in. She knows he wants market research in Thailand, and when she learns he makes toys, she is able to connect him to the right person.

11.9 Listen and read

The woman, Supa, says 'Right, Mr Figueras' and then gives him directions. Ramon says 'Good' and then goes on to thank her. This use of 'Rig or 'Good' often signals that a conversation is at, coming to, an end.

11.10 Document study

Good: Everything in the 'Introduction', b Thaipro want to attract overseas clients so th are very positive.

Trade deficit is expected to fall; value exports will grow; rate of industrial growth w increase.

Bad: private consumption will grow le rapidly; population growth will slow dow therefore fewer small children wanting to conditions may be more competitive than Ram had expected – the final paragraph mentio 'large-scale investment', and the need f overseas companies to take risks and sei opportunities quickly.

11.11 Reading for key words

These are model answers.

1. The towns are growing very quickly, mos with young people.
2. This growth of the economy is going continue, and it's caused by people wanti to buy things.
3. The market in Thailand during the next five ten years will be very good.
4. From what we've found out so far, it looks if firms are going to have to put a lot of mon into whatever they do in Thailand.

11.13 Listen and read

a PR731.
b 1140.
c From Terminal 3.
d 0945
e Shangri-La.
f 010 662 761524.
g YW37021/92.

11.14 Speaking practice

a Yes. It's 3729 671 943 910.
b 03/95.
c Yes, it's R. Figueras.

11.15 Listen and read

VOICE 1: In Terminal 3, Heathrow Airport, Londo
VOICE 2: In the aircraft, soon after take-off. It is t voice of the pilot or co-pilot.
VOICE 3: In the aircraft. It is the voice of stewardess.
VOICE 4: In the aircraft, just before landing. It is t voice of the pilot or co-pilot.
VOICE 5: In the customs area at Bangkok airpor

11.17 Writing practice

Report from consultants in Bangkok very positi – economy looks good and will expand – tra will grow. But – the returns on investment m take a long time – and the investment will be lar – need to move quickly. Don't know if Tortu can manage this at the moment. – What is Fr Hagendahl doing?

Unit 12: Researching the market

SITUATION

Ramon is investigating the market for his products in South-East Asia. He studies a market research report, and has a very interesting offer from Songthai Enterprises.

CHARACTERS

Fred Hagendahl

Ramon Figueras

Supa

Mrs Sombat	is the owner of Songthai Enterprises. She is Thai.
Waiter	in a Bangkok restaurant. He is Thai.

LANGUAGE

Vocabulary	Restaurants and social skills; analysing data.
Skills	Being a guest; offering, accepting and delaying or refusing; getting information from graphs and diagrams; playing 'power games'.
Documents	Data files; a map; bar and pie charts; a draft agency agreement; a letter.

Talking business over dinner – in a restaurant

12.1
log onto to connect one computer to another, using a telephone line.
college alumni former students of a college or university; used in American English.
Inc. Incorporated; used of public limited liability companies in the United States.
plc public limited company; used of public limited liability companies in Britain.

12.3
coincidence when two things happen at the same time by chance.
Extraordinary very surprising.
I needn't ask I don't need to ask because it is obvious.
a set menu in a restaurant, a menu for a complete meal at a fixed price.
à la carte in a restaurant, a menu where you choose a meal from a number of separate dishes, each with its own price; this is always more expensive than the set menu.

12.1 Document study

Ramon decides to find out about Fred Hagendahl. He uses his portable compute *log onto* the UCLA data network, and searches the public data files on *coll alumni*. This is what he finds. Read it carefully. You will need it for 12.2 and otl exercises in this unit.

```
HAGENDAHL, Frederick Gamlin
b. 30 April 1962; son of James Hagendahl III,
financier, and Melanie Gamlin. Educ. Choate,
Harvard and UCLA. Grad. BSc Economics, 1983; MSc
Business Science, 1986. Joined Universal Data Inc.,
Austin, Texas, as Divisional Sales Representative,
1986; promoted Area Sales Manager 1987; trans-
ferred to European subsidiary Universal Euro-Data
plc, London, England, 1988. Joined Tumblehome Inc.
1990 as Deputy Vice-President, Marketing; Director
of Marketing since June 1991.
```

12.2 Writing practice: personal details

You are a publisher. Fred Hagendahl has just written a book on internatio marketing which you are going to publish. Write a short paragraph about Fr which will be printed on the cover of the book. You can get all the facts you ne from the UCLA alumni record in 12.1.

12.3 Listen and read

Ramon meets Fred for dinner at a large restaurant in the centre of Bangkok. Lis to what they say. How does Ramon try to start talking about business?

FRED: Well, it was a real *coincidence*, running into you at the airport like that.
RAMON: Yes. *Extraordinary*. But *I needn't ask* you why you're here . . .
FRED: Now. How are you with the Thai food? Been here before?
RAMON: No, never. But I expect there's *a set menu*.
FRED: Not for me. Set menus are strictly for tourists. I always go for th *la carte*. Now then – which is our waiter?
WAITER: Are you ready to order now, sir?
FRED: Yes, please. I'd like numbers four, thirty and sixty-two.
WAITER: Four, thirty and sixty-two. Thank you. And you, sir?
RAMON: Well, I'm not sure. Perhaps you can advise me . . .

. . . . . .

RAMON: Mm, I enjoyed that seafood. I hope I can remember what it was called. Your spicy duck seemed to be a bit too spicy for you.
FRED: No! Not at all. I was raised in New Mexico. We invented chilli peppers. Er, waiter, can you bring me another beer, please?

12.4 Listen and read

Ramon continues his conversation with Fred in the restaurant. Listen to what they say. Does Fred think that Ramon is going to be successful?

RAMON So, Fred, how are you getting on at Tumblehome? *I hear* you're Director of Marketing now.

FRED How did you know about Tumblehome?

RAMON I dialled up the UCLA alumni public data file from the hotel this afternoon. So you're in the toy business too? How's it going?

FRED Great! Great! Of course, it'd be even greater if we'd got the *merchandising concession* for Dolphin Commando. That's a very interesting piece of property.

RAMON That's right. It's the *chance of a lifetime* for us. We'll never get another one like this.

FRED Well, Ramon, don't waste it. Now that I know you're here, I'll be *keeping an eye on* you, and if it looks like you're going to *blow it* . . .

RAMON Well, when I've worked out what I'm doing, I'm sure you'll be the first to know.

FRED You mean you don't have any idea what you're going to do with it yet?

RAMON I know what I'm going to do right now. Waiter! Could I have the bill, please?

12.4
I hear I have been told.
merchandising concession permission to make and sell, from the people who own copyright of the goods.
chance of a lifetime an opportunity that you don't get very often.
keeping an eye on watch with interest.
blow it ruin it.

12.5
pick up the tab pay the bill; used in informal American English.
a clear head to be able to think clearly.

12.5 Listen and read

Ramon continues his conversation with Fred in the restaurant. Listen to what they say. Who pays the bill?

WAITER Your bill, sir.

FRED No, no. I insist. I asked you here, let me *pick up the tab*.

RAMON Oh! Well, in that case.

FRED You do take credit cards?

WAITER Thank you, sir.

RAMON An excellent dinner. Thank you very much, Fred.

FRED You're welcome. Hey, let's go on to a night club.

RAMON I'd like to, but I've got an early appointment tomorrow morning. I'm afraid you must excuse me.

FRED Of course. You're going to need *a clear head*.

12.6 Listening practice: the games people play

Ramon and Fred are both working for toy companies, and they could be in competition with one another. Listen again to their conversations in 12.3, 12.4 and 12.5, and this time listen carefully to how they say things, as well as to what they say. What things does Fred say to make Ramon feel bad? What does Ramon do and say to show Fred that he is a capable business manager? For the rest of this unit, listen out for other examples of these two playing 'power games'.

Talking to a marketing consultant

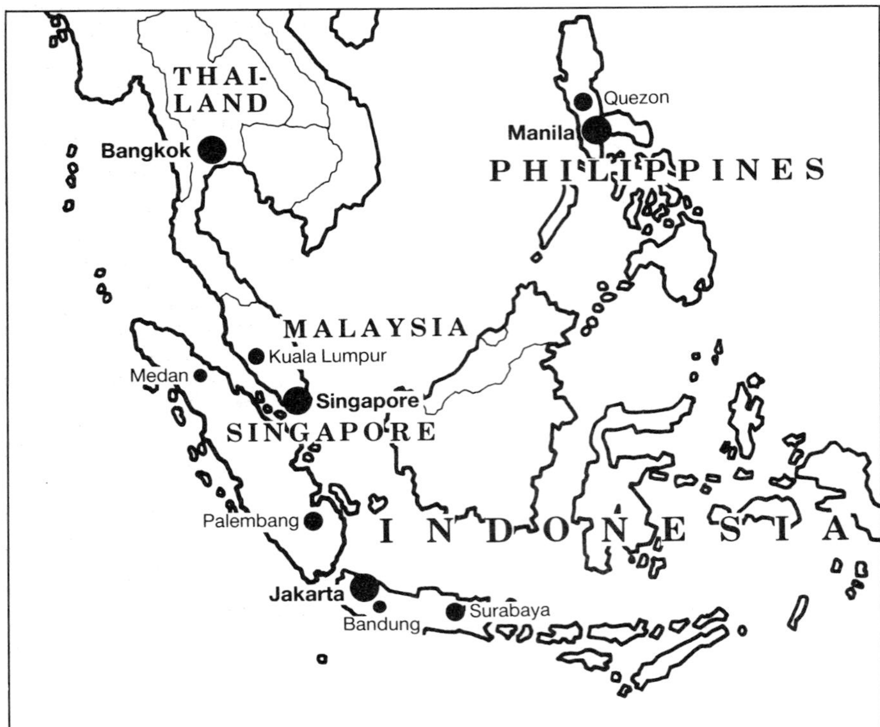

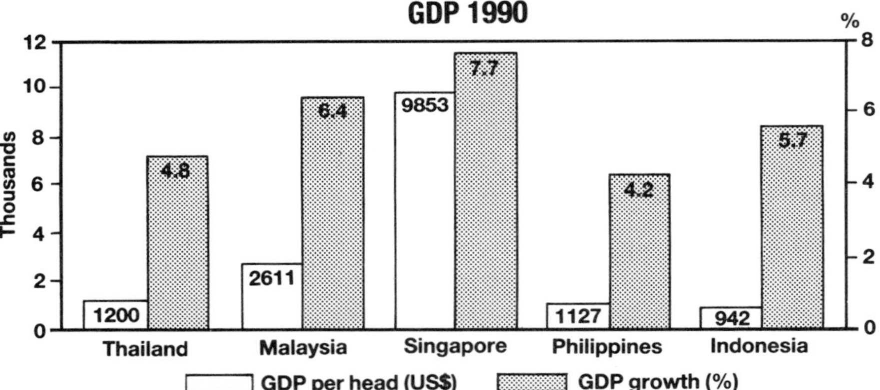

12.7 Document study: looking at a map

Ramon is now at the offices of Thaip Consultants. Supa is showing him a m and some diagrams that she h prepared for him. Listen to what th say.

SUPA Right, this is a map of South-East Asia, so that w can see the position of Thailand relative to neighbouring countries. The circles show the majo urban centres of population, and there's a bar chart showing gross domestic product for each country, and pie charts showing the percentage of the population living in cities and large towns . . . Indonesia is the largest country in South-East Asia

RAMON Yes, and I see that Malaysia's the second largest.

SUPA Yes. Singapore is the smallest in area.

12.8 Writing practice: makin comparisons

Read 12.7 again. Then study t diagrams and write sentences maki comparisons about the biggest, t second biggest and the smallest, each of the topics below.

1 population
2 percentage of population living cities
3 GDP per head
4 rate of GDP growth

Total population (1990) (M)

Philippines 58.7
Malaysia 17
Thailand 54.5
Singapore 2.6
Indonesia 166

Population in rural and urban areas (1990)

Indonesia
Rural 74%
Urban 26%

Malaysia
Rural 63%
Urban 37%

Philippines
Rural 58%
Urban 42%

Singapore
Urban 100%

Thailand
Rural 80%
Urban 20%

12.9 Listen and read

Ramon continues his meeting with Supa. Listen to what they say. Why does Ramon want more figures? Why is Supa cautious about the figures for the future?

RAMON But I thought that this survey was supposed to cover Thailand, not the whole of South-East Asia.

SUPA That's right! This is just *to set* the country *in* its market *context*. However, we believe that a broader view of the market may be needed – I'll have some more to say about that later . . .
Here we see the population of Thailand analysed by age – you notice the very high proportion of young people – and on the right by social classification – basically that means by occupation and *disposable income*, per head.

RAMON These are very interesting, but we would need to compare them with similar *breakdowns* for, say, Spain or the United States, and if we're to spot any trends we'd also need disposable *per-capita* incomes for Thailand in previous years.

SUPA Yes, of course! All that information is available in the rest of the report. What I would ask you to remember is although we've *extrapolated* the figures over the next five years, under conditions of high inflation, reliable forecasting isn't easy.

RAMON No. It doesn't make my decisions very easy, either!

SUPA Obviously you want to consider all this data *at your leisure*. All the statistics and diagrams – together with some supplementary data – are in our report. In addition, we've prepared a series of appendices on this floppy disk – it's really a series of spreadsheet files which you can *interrogate* or *browse* through. You can *amend* the figures and re-calculate, whatever you want.

RAMON Great! That should keep me busy. I'd like to talk to you again when I've *digested* this lot. How about Thursday?

12.9
to set . . . in . . . context to put something together with all of the other factors which affect it, and thus make it easier to understand.
disposable income money that you can spend on what you want, after you have paid tax, etc.
breakdowns analyses.
per-capita per head; for each member of a population.
extrapolated looked at the existing figures, and made calculations about what we think will happen.
at your leisure taking as much time as you need.
interrogate to ask questions; in this case to look at a database and get lots of information from it.
browse to look through something, without looking for a particular thing, so that you get a general idea about it.
digested thought about.

12.10 Reading for key words

Find the words or phrases in 12.7 and 12.9 that show you the following:

1 The only purpose of this is to show how Thailand fits into the present-day market.
2 The amount of money each person is able to spend for themselves. [Two expressions]
3 Large towns and cities.
4 Made a forecast by assuming that past trends will continue into the future.
5 When prices are rising quickly.

12.11 Find the word: marketing jargon

Read the text below on marketing. Write a word from the box to fill each of the gaps.

Any company that enters a new overseas market needs to know as much about that market as it can. It looks first at the country as a whole, the location of the major ___**a**___ centres and the ___**b**___ of the population that lives in them. The country's economic situation is important: its GDP, or ___**c**___ ___**d**___ product, and the ___**e**___ of GDP over a period of time, expressed as a percentage and measured in real terms – that is, allowing for ___**f**___ . But the product is going to be bought by individual ___**g**___ , so the company also needs a ___**h**___ of the population by age, sex, income and occupation. Most countries have a system of ___**i**___ classification. Marketing people usually want to know, not gross income, but ___**j**___ income per head. They also want the figures for several years; if they can identify ___**k**___ , they can ___**l**___ these into the future and ___**m**___ what people will be earning and spending a year or five years from now.

breakdown
consumers
disposable
domestic
extrapolate
forecast gross
growth inflation
proportion social
trends urban

Conversation at a private function

12.12
I understand I believe; I think.
a soft drink a drink without alcohol.
ticking over working smoothly, but rather slowly and not progressing.
diversified increased the variety of the company's activities.

12.13
marketing strategy a plan for promoting and selling things.
you're going to have your work cut out you're going to have to work very hard.
tricky difficult.
hospitality friendly and welcoming behaviour.
think it over to take some time to think about something.

12.12 Listen and read

Ramon goes to meet Mrs Sombat. She is one of the contacts that Jack Lytton ga Ramon, and she has asked him to her house for dinner. Listen to what they say. H do we know that Mrs Sombat is a successful business manager?

RAMON How do you do, Mrs Sombat. It's very kind of you to invite me t your house.

MRS SOMBAT You are very welcome, Mr Figueras. I am always glad to mee a former student of Professor Lytton. *I understand* this is your firs visit to Bangkok? I hope you are enjoying yourself and finding i interesting.

RAMON Yes, it's fascinating. And I'm also learning a great deal – which o course is what I came here for.

MRS SOMBAT Yes, we must discuss that. First let me offer you a drink. Champagne?

RAMON I'd rather have *a soft drink*, if I may. Some fruit juice perhaps, or iced tea – or is there a popular local drink?

MRS SOMBAT Ah, I know! I'll get you some passion-fruit juice. This used to be my husband's favourite drink when he came back from the office. Very refreshing.

RAMON Is that your husband's portrait?

MRS SOMBAT Yes. He died five years ago. I took over the business – Songth Enterprises – then, and I have been able to keep it *ticking over* since.

RAMON Jack Lytton told me you've doubled the turnover and *diversified* into three other industries.

MRS SOMBAT Well, you have to keep busy, don't you? Jack Lytton told me that you occupy yourself with making toys, on quite a large scal

12.13 Listen and read

Ramon continues his conversation with Mrs Sombat. Listen to what they say. D Mrs Sombat think that Ramon will find things easy or difficult?

RAMON I must say, that was the most delicious curry I've ever tasted.

MRS SOMBAT Good! I'm glad you enjoyed it. Now tell me more about your *marketing strategy* for Thailand. It all sounds very exciting. My grandchildren in Wisconsin are Dolphin Commando fans, and I think the show is going to have terrific impact here. But *you're going to have your work cut out* to exploit it.

RAMON Yes, it's a tremendous challenge, I just hope I don't blow it.

MRS SOMBAT You won't blow it, but you've got some hard times ahead of you – and some *tricky* decisions.

RAMON Well, thank you for a very pleasant evening. I'm most grateful fo your *hospitality*.

MRS SOMBAT It's a great pleasure. Before you go, I'd like to suggest something to you. You needn't give me an answer straight away

RAMON This sounds very interesting – what's the suggestion?

MRS SOMBAT How would you feel about my company acting as your agen in this country?

RAMON That certainly is interesting! I'd like to *think it over*, if I may?

12.14 Reading for key words

Find the words or phrases in 12.12 and 12.13 that show you the following:

1 Mrs Sombat wishes to appear very modest about her business success.
2 Ramon wishes to compliment her on it by listing what she has achieved.
3 Ramon wants to give emphasis to what he is about to say.
4 The plans you are making to mar your goods.
5 The show will be very popular.
6 You're going to have to work v hard indeed.

12.15 Speaking practice: offering, accepting, refusing

Listen to this conversation. Then listen again and speak the part of the man.

WOMAN Hello. Do come in.
MAN It's very kind of you to invite me to your house.
WOMAN You're most welcome. I hope you're enjoying your visit to this country. Now, let me get you a drink.
MAN Thank you, I'd like one.
WOMAN How about a glass of champagne?
MAN I'd rather have a soft drink, if I may.

12.16 Speaking practice: thanking and leaving

Listen to this conversation. Then listen again, and speak the part of the man.

WOMAN Do you have to leave so soon?
MAN Yes, I'm afraid so. But thank you for a very pleasant evening. I'm most grateful for your hospitality.
WOMAN It was a great pleasure. Before you go, I'd like to make a suggestion. You don't need to answer me now.
MAN That sounds interesting. What is it?
WOMAN I would like my company to be your agent in this country.
MAN Well, that is interesting. I'll think it over, and let you know tomorrow.

12.17 Document study

When Ramon returns to his hotel room the next day, he finds some documents from Mrs Sombat. Read through them carefully. Make a list of what Songthai are offering to do. Make another list of what Tortuga would have to do.

12.17
The parties the people involved.
commission a sum of money, usually paid to someone for each item they sell.
meet all reasonable expenses to pay for all the things we need to spend money on in order to do the job.
reimburse to give someone money to replace money they have already spent while doing something for you.
incurred that we have to pay.
chase ask for payment from.
factor a company that 'buys' a debt from another company, and then tries to collect the money from the debtor.
f.o.b. free on board; up to the point when the goods are on board the ship.
in the first instance as a first step.
to put you in the picture to tell you the information you need to understand something; an informal use.
the formalities the things that have to be done to make the document legal.

DRAFT AGENCY AGREEMENT

The parties: Juguetes Tortuga SA (the principal); Songthai Enterprises (the agent).
Territory: Thailand initially, and subsequently whatever other areas may be agreed between the parties.
Terms:
3.1 It is a sole and exclusive agency, i.e. Songthai is not to represent any other toy company, Tortuga is not to deal with any other agent in the territory. If you deal direct with any customer in the territory, you will be liable to pay the normal agent's *commission* - see below.
3.2 Songthai will actively promote your business, supply you with market information, and undertake advertising campaigns, product launches, etc.
3.3 You will provide us with samples, etc. as required and will *meet all reasonable expenses* for advertising and promotion and will *reimburse* us for travelling and other expenses necessarily *incurred*.
3.4 We will provide copies of all orders, invoices and correspondence, and will send details of orders, sales and payments at the end of each month.
3.5 We will collect payments on your behalf and make a settlement with you at the end of each month through our bank.
3.6 We will *chase* late payers and may, at your expense, use the services of a *factor* or debt collector.
3.7 Our commission will be at the rate of 10 per cent, to be calculated on prices *f.o.b.* Santander or other Spanish port. Commission will be deducted from our monthly payments to you.
The agreement shall run for two years *in the first instance*, and may be renewed. It can be terminated by either party giving 3 months' notice in writing.
The agreement shall be interpreted in accordance with the laws of Thailand.

Dear Mr Figueras

I enjoyed talking to you at dinner last night. I've been thinking about your situation and I'd like to make a proposal to you - that I, or rather my company, should become your agent in Thailand. At the moment we are in the motor trade, building construction, warehousing and distribution, and scientific instruments - so toys, at least, wouldn't clash with our other interests. I've tried to draft an agency agreement (enclosed) but this is just *to put you in the picture*; we would of course get a lawyer to look after *the formalities*. I look forward to hearing what you think of the idea.

Yours
Mrs Sombat

Study record	
12.1	
12.2	
12.3	
12.4	
12.5	
12.6	
12.7	
12.8	
12.9	
12.10	
12.11	
12.12	
12.13	
12.14	
12.15	
12.16	
12.17	

Answer key and commentary for unit 12

12.2 Writing practice

This is a model answer.

Frederick Gamlin Hagendahl comes from a distinguished business background. He was educated at Choate, Harvard and UCLA, and has degrees in Economics and Business Science. He started his career in computers, working for Universal Data in Texas and its London subsidiary, Universal Euro-Data. He subsequently transferred to retailing, and is now, at the age of 29, Director of Marketing for Tumblehome Inc., the world-famous US toy corporation.

12.3 Listen and read

Ramon says 'But I needn't ask you why you're here'. Fred either doesn't hear him, or he simply ignores him.

12.4 Listen and read

Fred does not think that Ramon is going to be successful. He says to Ramon 'don't waste it', 'I'll be keeping an eye on you', 'if it looks like you're going to blow it', and 'You mean you don't have any idea of what you're going to do with it yet?' All of these suggest that Ramon doesn't know what he is doing, and that Fred thinks he would be more successful.

12.5 Listen and read

Ramon asked for the bill, but Fred pays it. Ramon agrees when he says 'Well, in that case.' He means that he accepts that, as Fred asked him to the restaurant, then Fred should pay.

12.6 Listening practice

Fred tries to make Ramon feel bad in a number of different ways: he laughs at Ramon for wanting to eat from the tourist menu, while Fred can order à la carte; he suggests that Ramon might 'waste' his opportunity with Dolphin Commando; he says that he will 'keep an eye on him', as though Ramon is not capable of doing the job properly; he laughs at Ramon because he doesn't know what he is going to do; he says that Ramon will need 'a clear head', or he will make mistakes. What Fred is suggesting is that he could do all of these things better.

Ramon is not as rude as Fred. He is amused when Fred's dinner is obviously too spicy for him – Fred obviously doesn't know Thai food very well after all; he surprises Fred by knowing that he is Director of Marketing at Tumblehome – Fred is impressed that Ramon knows this.

12.8 Writing practice

1 Indonesia had the biggest population in 1990; the Philippines had the second biggest; and Singapore had the smallest.
2 Singapore had the highest percentage of the population living in cities; the Philippines had the second highest; and Thailand had the lowest.
3 Singapore had the highest GDP per head in 1990; Malaysia had the second highest; and Indonesia had the lowest.
4 Singapore had the highest rate of GDP growth in 1990; Malaysia had the second highest; and the Philippines had the lowest.

12.9 Listen and read

Ramon wants more figures so that he can compare the market in Thailand with that in the United States and Spain, and so that he ca identify any trends in Thailand.

Supa is cautious because inflation in Thailan makes it difficult to predict figures for the future She says 'under conditions of high inflatior reliable forecasting isn't easy'.

12.10 Reading for key words

1 This is just to set the country in its mark context.
2 disposable income, per head; disposabl per-capita incomes
3 major urban centres of population
4 extrapolated the figures
5 under conditions of high inflation

12.11 Find the word

a urban
b proportion
c gross
d domestic
e growth
f inflation
g consumers
h breakdown
i social
j disposable
k trends
l extrapolate
m forecast

12.12 Listen and read

Mrs Sombat has been running Songth Enterprises for five years. In that time she h doubled the company's turnover and diversifi into three other industries.

12.13 Listen and read

Mrs Sombat thinks that Ramon will find it difficu She says 'you're going to have your work cut o to exploit it', and 'you've got some hard tim ahead of you – and some tricky decisions'.

12.14 Reading for key words

1 I took over the business . . . then, and I ha been able to keep it ticking over since.
2 Jack Lytton told me you've doubled t turnover and diversified into three oth industries.
3 I must say
4 your marketing strategy
5 the show is going to have terrific impact he
6 you're going to have your work cut out exploit it.

12.17 Document study

Songthai are offering to act as agent for Tortuga Thailand. They will promote the Dolph Commando merchandise, carry out advertisi campaigns and product launches, and provi market information to Tortuga. They will a collect all payments, and provide copies of documents. They will do this on an exclusi basis for two years.

Tortuga would be required to provide sampl and to pay for advertising and promotion, a travelling and other expenses. They would a have to pay for a factor or debt collector if th are necessary. They would also have to p Songthai commission on sales.

Unit 13: Seizing an opportunity

SITUATION

Ramon still hasn't decided what to do. The marketing consultants have advised him to think bigger, and Mrs Sombat of Songthai Enterprises has proposed that she should become his agent. But Ramon has to think about his company's long-term future in South-East Asia and this may mean setting up a manufacturing base in Thailand.

CHARACTERS

Fred Hagendahl	
Ramon Figueras	
Supa	
Mrs Sombat	
Coach driver	on a trip to Pattaya. He is Thai.
Secretary	at Songthai Enterprises. She is Thai.

LANGUAGE

Vocabulary	Time off.
Skills	Telephoning – a bad line; reasoning with somebody; bidding and negotiating.
Structures	Putting an argument; interested and interesting; participles; the past perfect tense.
Documents	A company annual report; a letter of thanks; an informal letter.

Taking a trip out of town

13.1
time off time at which you do not work.

13.3
souvenirs things that you buy to remind you of a place.
take you for a ride cheat you; Fred is making a joke here, as 'ride' is being used both literally and idiomatically.
quite a while a long time.

13.1 Listen and read

Ramon still has to make a decision about production, as well as marketing ar distribution. He is about to leave the hotel when Fred arrives. Listen to how Ramc builds up a list of reasons for doing what he wants to do.

FRED Hi, Ramon! Buenos días! So, how are things, how's business?

RAMON Oh, hello, Fred. Well, I've had some interesting meetings with various people – learned quite a lot about local conditions.

FRED Uh-huh. Why don't you take some *time off*? We could go rent a car, go out of town for the day. I'd like to go to the beach at Pattaya.

RAMON I was thinking of doing just that – but if you're going to Pattaya, you can take a tourist bus. They sell tickets at the hotel reception desk.

FRED Ramon, you don't want to ride on a bus with a lot of tourists.

RAMON OK, please yourself. You go and rent a car. You do realise that it'll cost you about five times as much, and, of course, you'll be responsible for the car – and for parking it. I'll take the coach, anc I'll see much more, because I'll be sitting high up instead of dowr near the road.

13.2 Structure practice: putting an argument

If you know you are going to have to persuade someone, it helps to have a few goc arguments ready to use. But you also need to link them together, to make the stronger. Listen again to how Ramon links his arguments in 13.1.

You are going on holiday with a friend. Your friend wants to take a lot of cas you want to take traveller's cheques. Write the arguments you would use persuade your friend to take traveller's cheques. Use the information below, ar remember to link the arguments together.

a You can change traveller's cheques into any currency.
b If you lose them, or if they are stolen, you can get them replaced.
c You need your passport for identification, so only you can use them.
d You don't need to take your cheque book and cheque card with you.

13.3 Listen and read

Ramon and Fred agree to take a coach trip to Pattaya. Listen to what they say. Wh do you think Ramon is interested in the deserted factory?

COACH DRIVER Now, ladies and gentlemen, if you look over to your left-hand side you can see Muang Boran, the Ancient City. That is a big model of the whole of Thailand with many old buildings, palaces temples, half as big as the real ones. It was built by a Thai businessman, and cost ten million baht.

FRED Look at that! Amazing! Hey, Ramon, it's on the other side. On the left.

RAMON What? I'm sorry – I was interested in that factory over there – I thought I recognised the logo.

DRIVER We stop here for twenty minutes! So you can take photographs, buy *souvenirs*, eat, drink.

FRED What did I tell you! You take a tourist bus, they *take you for a ride*. No thank you, I do not want any ice cream; I do not want any fried rice; I do not require a woodcarving of an elephant. Can we get out of this place?

RAMON Yes, let's just walk over to the other side of the road. Just as I thought – this is, or was, one of Songthai's factories. They must have built it out of town to keep the costs down.

FRED You're sure it wasn't located here as a tourist attraction?

RAMON Doesn't seem to have attracted anything much. It's certainly been empty for *quite a while*. Interesting! Well, come on, we'd better not miss the coach.

13.4 Structure practice: *interested* and *interesting*

Ramon says 'I was interested in that factory over there', and later 'Interesting!' ('That is interesting'). You must be careful not to confuse the two forms ending in '-ing' and '-ed'. It is helpful to think of the '-ing' form as 'active', and the '-ed' form as 'passive'. For example, if something interests you, then that something is 'interesting', and you are 'interested'. Practise using both '-ing' and '-ed' forms by answering these questions. The first one has been done for you.

1 Does Thai culture interest you?
I'm sure many people find it interesting, but I'm not very interested.
2 Does the prospect of a takeover bid excite you?
3 Or does it alarm you?
4 Do the Dolphin Commando TV programmes amuse you?
5 Do the company's interim results disappoint you?
6 Does travelling by bus bore you?

13.5
ultra-modern very modern.
proximity nearness.

13.5 Document study

Ramon goes to the Bangkok Business Library, and finds a complete series of Songthai Enterprises' annual reports, in English and Thai, going back to 1953, the year the company was founded. He starts with the most recent one, and works back year by year until he finds what he is looking for. Why is he interested?

ANNUAL report

MUANG BORAN SITE NEARING COMPLETION

Songthai's Scientific Instrument Division will shortly move into its new premises at this magnificent *ultra-modern* factory about 30 km outside Bangkok. Carefully chosen for its *proximity* to major transport networks, Muang Boran will meet our production requirements for at least the next five years.

13.6 Structure practice: participles

The annual report in 13.5 says 'Carefully chosen for its proximity . . . , Muang Boran will meet our production requirements'. This means that Muang Boran was carefully chosen, and that Muang Boran will meet the production requirements. When you write sentences like this, you must make sure that the 'subject' of both parts is the same. In 13.5 we could have written, 'Starting with the most recent one, he works back . . . ', because it was Ramon who started, and Ramon who is working back. Read through the four sentences below carefully. Which ones are not right? Why?

1 After spending several hours in the library, Ramon found what he wanted.
2 After reading the article, Songthai may be able to sell the factory to Ramon.
3 By locating the factory outside the town, Ramon may be able to buy it cheaply.
4 By locating the factory outside the town, Songthai saved on labour costs.

13.7 Writing practice

It is time for Ramon to add to the notes he made in 11.7 and 11.17. Write notes for him about what has happened during and after his trip to Pattaya.

Chasing up your enquiries

13.8
I might be getting somewhere I am making progress.
I didn't quite catch that I didn't hear what you said.
a bad line a poor telephone line, so I can't hear what you say.
morale the feelings of confidence, pride, etc. that people have toward something; in this case to the company.
to turn the company round to make a poor company profitable and successful again.
under-capitalised not having enough money to work properly or to expand.

13.9
playing a hunch working on an idea I have.
hang up end a telephone call.

13.8 Listen and read

Ramon telephones Supa to ask her about Songthai Enterprises. Listen to what they say. It is a poor telephone line. Notice how Supa has to ask Ramon to repeat things.

SUPA — Good morning, Ramon! How are things?

RAMON — Good morning! Things are not so bad. In fact, I've got an idea *I might be getting somewhere* at last.

SUPA — I'm sorry? *I didn't quite catch that.*

RAMON — I said, I think I'm making progress at last. I may need to come and see you again very soon – but first of all, does the name Songthai mean anything to you?

SUPA — You mean Songthai Enterprises? Yes. The founder died a few years ago, but his widow is keeping up the business, and it continues to grow.

RAMON — Mm. I met Mrs Sombat a day or two ago, and I must say I was rather impressed. I wondered how you rated the organisation.

SUPA — I beg your pardon? This must be *a bad line*. Could you repeat that?

RAMON — I wonder how you rate the Songthai organisation? What's your professional opinion of it?

SUPA — We rate it highly. Well, it depends on what you are trying to do. It's well run – well equipped. I'm told *morale* is high. If you're thinking of buying shares in it, I can only say that financially it has been through rather a difficult time. Mr Sombat left many debts when he died. He had borrowed heavily to finance the growth of his company. I believe these debts are mostly paid off now. Mrs Sombat managed *to turn the company round*, but it's still *under-capitalised*.

13.9 Speaking practice: a bad telephone line

Listen to this conversation. Then listen again and speak the parts, first of the man and then of the woman.

WOMAN — I'm just *playing a hunch*. Is there a business library anywhere in town?

MAN — I'm sorry, I didn't quite catch that. Could you repeat it, please?

WOMAN — Sorry – I'm looking for the business library. I think they may be able to help me.

MAN — Oh, the business library! It's in New Road, near the post office.

WOMAN — It's a dreadful line, this – do you mind saying that again?

MAN — New Road, near the post office. What are you hoping to find in the business library?

WOMAN — I'm interested in some annual reports.

MAN — I beg your pardon? I can hardly hear a word you say!

WOMAN — Look, I'll *hang up* and call you again – maybe we'll get a better connection.

13.10 Structure practice: the past perfect tense

Supa says to Ramon 'Mr Sombat left many debts when he died. He had borrowed heavily . . . ' She uses the simple past 'left' to show that she is talking about a particular time in the past, and then the past perfect 'had borrowed' to show that something else happened before that time.

Here are some pairs of sentences, describing two separate events. Make each pair into a single sentence, using the past perfect.

1 Mrs Sombat heard about Dolphin Commando. She invited Ramon to dinner.
Mrs Sombat had heard about Dolphin Commando when she invited Ramon to dinner. OR
When she invited Ramon to dinner, Mrs Sombat had heard about Dolphin Commando.
2 Ramon spent five hours in the library. He found what he wanted.
3 He returned to the hotel. He telephoned Madrid.
4 He left his briefcase in a taxi. He realised this when he got back to the hotel.

13.11
returning your hospitality asking you to be my guest, after I have been your guest.
call on you visit you.

13.11 Document study: writing a letter of thanks

Ramon writes to Mrs Sombat to thank her for the dinner. He decides to ask her for another meeting. Read the letter below.

Dear Mrs Sombat

First, I should like to thank you for the enjoyable evening that I spent at your house and the excellent dinner you gave me. I shall remember your kindness for a long time, and I hope very much to have the opportunity of returning your hospitality if you should visit Madrid.

Thank you, too, for your letter, which I received on my return to my hotel from a trip to Pattaya yesterday. Your suggestion that you should act as our sales agent in Bangkok certainly deserves very careful consideration. I should like to call on you again, if I may, and discuss it further. I will telephone you tomorrow morning in the hope that we can make an appointment to meet.

Yours sincerely

13.12 Listen and read

Ramon telephones Mrs Sombat's house the next day. Listen to how he makes an appointment to see her, and sends a message via her secretary.

SECRETARY Ah, Mr Figueras. Mrs Sombat has gone out but she told me that you might ring and she asked me to give you a message: she will be very pleased to see you in her office any time this afternoon between two and four thirty.

RAMON Two to four thirty this afternoon – right. Will you be seeing her before then?

SECRETARY No, but I shall probably speak to her on the telephone. Can I give her a message?

RAMON Could you say that I will call at about three o'clock?

SECRETARY Three o'clock, certainly. You have the address of the office?

RAMON Yes, thanks – she gave me her card. Thank you for your help. Goodbye.

13.13 Writing practice: making notes

Ramon now has to decide what he wants to do. Read through the notes you made for him in units 11, 12 and 13. Make a list of options for him. What are the advantages and disadvantages of each option?

Being in the right place at the right time

13.14
address the real problems try to understand and deal with the real problems.
Broadly speaking that's more or less what I mean, but I also mean something more specific.
On the contrary the opposite is true.

13.15
bidding for offering money for.
a feasibility study work done to see if a plan of action is practical.
You have been doing your homework! you have done some research and found a solution.
putting our cards on the table saying what you mean, after you have been keeping it secret for a time.

13.14 Listen and read

Ramon goes to see Mrs Sombat in her office. Listen to what they say. Notice ho they each begin by stating their positions.

MRS SOMBAT Let me see if I've got this right. You say you can't accept an agency agreement on the lines I've drafted because it doesn't *address the real problems* you're faced with – which are production and development problems.

RAMON *Broadly speaking*, yes.

MRS SOMBAT Which implies that Songthai Enterprises has nothing to offer except warehousing and distribution.

RAMON *On the contrary*, I think Songthai has a lot to offer. I have a counter-proposal . . .

MRS SOMBAT Just a moment, please! [To intercom] Arineeka, ask Mr Hagendahl to come in, will you?

13.15 Listen and read

Ramon is surprised to find Fred at the meeting, but he makes his offer to Mrs Somba Listen to what they say. What is Ramon's counter-proposal? Notice how Mrs Somb very carefully considers both of her options before she makes a decision.

MRS SOMBAT Hello, Mr Hagendahl! Come back in and sit down.

FRED Thank you. Hello, Ramon.

RAMON Fred! I didn't know you knew Mrs Sombat!

FRED Why should I tell you everything? You're supposed to be on a fact-finding mission. It seems that I'm one of the facts.

MRS SOMBAT Please, don't be upset, Mr Figueras! The reason I've asked you both in here together is that you seem to be *bidding for* the same thing.

FRED But any deal we make must be exclusive.

RAMON Mrs Sombat, I'm now in a position to make you an offer. When I came to Bangkok, I was thinking in terms of a distributor or perhaps an agent for Tortuga. What I've learnt here has made me aim higher. I'm going to commission *a feasibility study*, and, if the results are favourable, as I'm confident they will be, I intend to se up a manufacturing base in Thailand.

FRED Ah! *You have been doing your homework!*

RAMON My company has no experience of the Far East, so we shall need a Thai partner. Will Songthai Enterprises consider a joint venture with Tortuga?

MRS SOMBAT Well, well – we all seem to be *putting our cards on the table* now, don't we? I must say, I'm faced with rather a difficult choice here. Most people would say that Tumblehome have more to offer – simply as major retailers. On the other hand, Tortuga has a good reputation and a valuable TV merchandising agreement – and I like the idea of getting involved on the manufacturing side.

13.16 Speaking practice: bidding for a contract

Listen to this conversation. Then listen again and speak the part of the man.

WOMAN Let me see if I've got this right. You say you won't consider our offer.

MAN We couldn't accept an agreement on the lines you drafted. It doesn't address our real problems.

WOMAN That seems to imply that we've nothing more to offer.

MAN On the contrary. I should like to make a counter-proposal which I'm sure you'll find attractive.

WOMAN Well, any deal must be exclusive.

MAN Of course! And I'm now in a position to make you an offer on the basis of a joint venture as manufacturer and distributor.

WOMAN Hm. I must admit I like the idea of getting involved on the manufacturing side.

13.17 Listen and read

Mrs Sombat has told Ramon and Fred what her decision is. Listen to what they say. Who will she work with? Why are Ramon and Fred both taken by surprise?

FRED Well, good luck, Ramon. You're going to need it!

RAMON Thanks. I hope you get something sorted out.

FRED Oh, we'll find an agent, no problem. As a matter of fact, I'm flying to Jakarta tomorrow.

RAMON It still seems like a coincidence, both of us wanting to work with Songthai.

MRS SOMBAT It's no coincidence at all. I spoke to Jack Lytton. He told me you were both coming out here, so . . .

13.18 Listening practice: some idioms

When Ramon, Fred and Mrs Sombat speak to each other, they use many idiomatic expressions. Listen to their conversations in this unit again, and then answer the questions below, using expressions from their conversations.

1 When the coach stops at Muang Boran, what does Fred complain of?
2 When Ramon telephones Supa, why does he sound rather pleased?
3 Why does Fred think that he needn't explain everything to Ramon?
4 How does Mrs Sombat react when Ramon reveals his new business proposal?
5 Why does Mrs Sombat seem more likely to reach agreement with Tortuga than with Tumblehome?

13.19 Writing practice: a message to Jack Lytton

Ramon is pleased to have got a contract with Mrs Sombat. He decides to write to Jack Lytton and tell him all about it. Write the letter for him, using the notes you have made, and any other details you think might help. Jack is a friend, so the letter does not need to be too formal. The beginning of the letter is shown below.

Jack,

You don't change do you? You might have told me you were sending Fred Hagendahl and me to Mrs Sombat on approval! Anyway, I think I have persuaded her that Songthai and Tortuga ought to set up a joint venture in Thailand. What clinched it was my proposal that

Study record	
13.1	
13.2	
13.3	
13.4	
13.5	
13.6	
13.7	
13.8	
13.9	
13.10	
13.11	
13.12	
13.13	
13.14	
13.15	
13.16	
13.17	
13.18	
13.19	

Answer key and commentary for unit 13

13.2 Structure practice
This is a model answer.
You can take cash, but I'm going to take traveller's cheques. I can change them into any currency. You do realise that if you lose your cash, it's gone. I can get my traveller's cheques replaced if they are lost or stolen. And they're safer because only I can use them, and I don't need to carry my cheque book and cheque card. It's a much better idea!

13.3 Listen and read
Ramon is interested in the deserted factory because it belongs to Songthai, and because he is now thinking of production opportunities in Thailand.

13.4 Structure practice
These are model answers.

2 I'm sure many people find it exciting, but I'm not very excited.
3 I expect many people find it alarming, but I'm not really alarmed.
4 A lot of people may find them amusing, but I'm not specially amused.
5 I suppose some people may find them disappointing, but I'm not disappointed myself.
6 I know people do find it boring, but I'm never bored.

13.5 Document study
Ramon is interested because the factory is a modern one, in a good position for transport.

13.6 Structure practice
1 This sentence is correct. It was Ramon who found what he wanted, and Ramon who spent several hours in the library.
2 This sentence is not correct. It is Songthai who are selling the factory, but Ramon who read the article.
3 This sentence is not correct. It is Ramon who may be able to buy the factory, but it was Songthai who located it outside the town.
4 This sentence is correct. It was Songthai who located the factory outside the town, and Songthai who saved on labour costs.

13.7 Writing practice
This is a model answer.
Must think about production as well as marketing and distribution – interesting coach trip to Pattaya – stopped at Muang Boran, where there is an empty Songthai factory – annual reports say it is ultra-modern and well located – interesting?

13.8 Listen and read
Supa has to ask Ramon to repeat things several times. She says 'I'm sorry? I didn't quite catch that', 'I beg your pardon?', and 'Could you repeat that?'

13.10 Structure practice
These are model answers.

2 After Ramon had spent five hours in the library, he found what he wanted.
3 When he had returned to the hotel, he telephoned Madrid.
4 When he got back to the hotel, he realised that he had left his briefcase in a taxi.

13.13 Writing practice
This is a model answer.
Options for Tortuga Toys in South-East Asia: appoint an agent (e.g. Songthai) – advantages are knowledge of market and existing facilities and capacity – disadvantages are where to produce, short term only?

If we set up our own distribution company in Thailand – advantages are more control, closer contact with market, respond quickly to changes in demand – disadvantages are very expensive, perhaps slow, we could risk failure in exploiting demand for Dolphin Commando products, return might be long term.

Third option needed?

13.14 Listen and read
Mrs Sombat begins the statement of her position with 'You say . . . '. Ramon begins his with 'On the contrary, I think . . . '.

13.15 Listen and read
Ramon's counter-proposal is that Tortuga and Songthai should set up a joint venture in Thailand, to handle production and distribution.

Mrs Sombat considers her options very carefully. She says that it is a difficult choice; that most people would favour Tumblehome; that on the other hand Tortuga has a good reputation; that she likes the idea of manufacturing.

13.17 Listen and read
Mrs Sombat has decided to work with Ramon. We know that because Fred says that Ramon is going to need good luck.

Ramon and Fred are both taken by surprise because they both thought that they were in control of the negotiations with Mrs Sombat. It turns out that Mrs Sombat had really been in control all the time.

13.18 Listening practice
These are model answers.

1 He complains of being taken for a ride.
2 He's got an idea he might be getting somewhere.
3 Because Ramon is supposed to be on a fact-finding mission, and Fred is one of the facts.
4 She's glad that they seem to be putting their cards on the table.
5 She likes the idea of getting involved on the manufacturing side.

13.19 Writing practice
This is a model answer.
Jack, You don't change do you? You might have told me you were sending Fred Hagendahl and me to Mrs Sombat on approval! Anyway, I think I have persuaded her that Songthai and Tortuga ought to set up a joint venture in Thailand. What clinched it was my proposal that we should not just import and distribute toys but have a factory, design team, everything, right where the market is. Songthai actually have a large modern factory about 30km outside Bangkok which has been sitting there, empty, since Mr Sombat died – but I'm sure you know all about this. The person who persuaded me to think big was a young woman in the marketing consultants' office here, who was very impressive and positive about prospects in Thailand. As for Fred, he was obviously disappointed to miss out with Songthai – we all agreed the deal had to be exclusive – but, as he said, Tumblehome, as retailers, just need a good agent, and there are plenty of those. He flew to Jakarta this morning. All the best, and, should you be in Madrid any time . . . Goodbye for now, Ramon.

Unit 14: Bookkeeping

SITUATION

Metro-Polo Office Cleaning is a franchise organisation. Its founder is Arturo Foscatelli, whose head office is in Rome. The small businesses which join his franchise are given training, allowed to use the Metro-Polo brand name and benefit from Metro-Polo's advertising. In return, each franchisee pays a quarterly subscription to the franchisor. In this unit we see if Metro-Polo's newest franchisee can manage to run the business and cope with all the financial paperwork involved.

CHARACTERS

Arturo Foscatelli	is president of Metro-Polo Office Cleaning. He is Italian.
Patrick Flynn	runs a Metro-Polo office cleaning franchise. He is British.

LANGUAGE

Vocabulary	Bookkeeping; overheads; cash flow.
Skills	Understanding and explaining accounts; explaining what the figures mean.
Structures	Figures; present tense and future time.
Documents	A trial balance; a postage ledger; a profit and loss account; a balance sheet.

Looking at the trial balance

14.1
getting on for nearly.
That's well on target that's what you were supposed to do.
outgoings money that you spend.
overheads the regular costs of a business, like rent, wages, electricity, etc.
transactions anything that involves spending or receiving money.
the first quarter the first three months of the financial year.

14.2
Wages and salaries in Britain, wages are usually paid weekly to manual workers; salaries are usually paid monthly to office workers.
leasing a form of renting.
Drawings money that you take from the business for personal use.
in hand available for use.

14.1 Listen and read

Patrick Flynn runs a Metro-Polo office cleaning franchise. He gets a visit from Arturo Foscatelli, the company's president. Listen to what they say. Why is Arturo visiting Patrick?

ARTURO Mr Flynn? Good morning. I'm Arturo Foscatelli.

PATRICK Hello, Mr Foscatelli. Come on in – do sit down.

ARTURO Thank you. As I explained on the phone, I make a point of visiting new members of our organisation at least once during their first year of operation. In your case, it seems that things are going well: lots of contracts, and morale is high.

PATRICK Well, yes, as long as you don't mind working sixteen hours a day!

ARTURO Yes, indeed! Now, I wonder if we can put some figures on the performance so far. You've completed your first three months' trading. Do you have any idea what your turnover was, roughly?

PATRICK Er – yes – *getting on for* thirteen thousand pounds.

ARTURO Mm. *That's well on target*. Now, how about the *outgoings*, especially the *overheads*? That's always something we have to watch in a new business.

PATRICK I must say, Mr Foscatelli, I think this is where I probably need your advice. I've been recording all my *transactions* very carefully on the computer, and everything seems to be OK. But I don't really understand this idea of 'double entry'.

ARTURO Don't the figures balance?

PATRICK Oh, yes, they balance, but I don't understand what they mean. Look. This is the trial balance I printed out for *the first quarter*.

METRO-POLO
OFFICE CLEANING

TRIAL BALANCE
as at 31/10/91

Purchases	2406.00	
Sales		12874.00
Stock at 1/8/91	1050.00	
Wages and salaries	3995.00	
Advertising	2860.00	
Postage	118.00	
Petrol	263.00	
Telephone	142.00	
Premises (rent)	900.00	
Gas and electricity	230.00	
Vans (*leasing*)	840.00	
Equipment (leasing)	390.00	
Bank	3682.00	
Cash	371.00	
Midland Furniture	98.00	
Goodies Ltd	205.00	
Wonder-Bar Security	36.00	
Q Smith & Sons	582.00	
Capital		7260.00
Drawings	3872.00	
Metro-Polo		1500.00
All-Clean Supplies		406.00
	22040.00	22040.00

Stock *in hand* 31/10/91 2079.00

14.2 Document study

This is the trial balance that Patrick prepared. Read through it carefully. Which of the names here are probably those of Patrick's customers? Why does the name Metro-Polo appear here?

14.3 Writing practice: figures

Look again at the trial balance in 14.2. Then answer the questions below.

1 What are the total sales for the period?
2 How much cash has Patrick Flynn got in the bank?
3 How much money did he draw out of the business?
4 How much stock did he have at the start of the period?
5 How much does he owe the franchisor?
6 These figures are for one quarter. What's his wages bill going to be for a year, at this rate?
7 Roughly how much money do people owe him?

14.4 Listen and read

Arturo explains the trial balance to Patrick. Listen to what they say. Is Metro-Polo a creditor or a debtor of Patrick Flynn?

ARTURO Yes, that seems reasonable. What's the problem?

PATRICK I know I did a training course on this, but I never really *got the hang of* it. Which side is which?

ARTURO Well, briefly, the left-hand column shows you the debits – that's where the money went to. The right-hand column is the credits – where the money came from. Or we can say that the right-hand side represents the sources of *funds*, and the left-hand side the uses of funds.

PATRICK But I thought debit meant that you owed money to somebody?

ARTURO It depends who 'you' are, doesn't it? Look at these four people here – Midland Furniture, Goodies, Wonder-Bar and Smith and Sons. They owe you money, right? They are your debtors. Metro-Polo and All-Clean Supplies, on the other hand, are your creditors – you owe money to them.

PATRICK But that's money going out, so why is it on the right-hand side, with sales, which is money coming in?

ARTURO Because creditors are people you haven't paid yet! As long as you don't pay them, All-Clean and the others are lending money to your business. In effect, they are giving you free use of their money. So you benefit, just as you do from sales.

PATRICK Ah! So Midland Furniture and Goodies and the other debtors – they're doing business with my money?

ARTURO Well, until they pay you, yes.

PATRICK I'll *get on to them* right away!

14.4
got the hang of understood.
funds money available for use.
get on to them contact them.

14.5 Find the right word: bookkeeping

Read the text below on bookkeeping. Write a word from the box to fill each of the gaps.

___**a**___-___**b**___ bookkeeping is a system which enables the business manager to record all money coming in (___**c**___) and all money going out (___**d**___), and to work out the company's progress and present position. For every ___**e**___, there are two ___**f**___ in the ledgers. In one ledger, it is shown on the ___**g**___ side, and in the other, as a ___**h**___. Each ledger records transactions of a particular type. By adding the transactions for a period of time, you find the amount needed to ___**i**___ the account. All the balances from the different ledgers are added together in the trial balance. If everything has been entered correctly, their totals must ___**j**___ – that is, they must be equal. The bookkeeper can then go on to prepare the profit and loss account and finally the balance sheet, which shows the state of the business on the date it was drawn up. You can see at a glance the ___**k**___ and uses of funds.

balance balance
credit debit
double entries
entry income
outgoings sources
transaction

14.6 Structure practice: present tense and future time

When Arturo says in 14.4 'Well, until they pay you, yes', he is referring to some time in the future, but note that he uses the present tense form of 'pay', not 'will pay'.

You use the present tense to refer to the future in clauses beginning with 'until', 'when', 'after', 'before', 'as soon as', 'while', 'if', 'in case', 'as long as', etc. Often the verb in the main clause is a future verb, with 'will'.

Write answers to the questions below. In each answer use a clause with one of the words above.

1 Really, we're doing business with our creditors' money – is that right?
Yes, that's right, until you pay them.
2 As this is our first order, will the suppliers want cash on delivery? – Yes, . . .
3 Our suppliers won't refuse to go on supplying us, will they? – No, . . .
4 They'll go on giving us credit, won't they? – Yes, . . .

Entering a transaction in the ledger

14.7
quite a bit a lot.
direct mail advertising posted to particular people.
(a) mailing list a list of people or companies that you think may be interested in your company's products; the people you send direct mail advertising to.
(a) ledger an accounts 'book' in which you enter credits and debits for a company, or part of the activities of a company.

14.7 Listen and read

Arturo asks Patrick how he finds his customers. Listen to what they say. What is Patrick's most successful method?

ARTURO Judging from your trial balance, most of your customers are quite small. How do you attract them? Just by advertising?

PATRICK I spend *quite a bit* on advertising, as you can see. I think I've done better, though, with *direct mail.* I keep adding to the *mailing list.* That reminds me, I bought another fifty pounds' worth of stamps today; I must put them on the computer. Er – now . . .

ARTURO 'New transaction.' Right, now it's asking you in which *ledger* you want to enter the transaction.

PATRICK 'Purchases'. No! 'Postage'.

ARTURO That's better!

14.8 Document study

The print-out below shows the entries in Patrick's postage ledger. Read through it carefully. You will need it for 14.9.

POSTAGE

01/08	*Cash*	50.00	01/08	Opening balance	0
15/08	Bank	50.00			
30/09	Cash	11.04			
15/10	Cash	6.57	31/10	To P&L a/c	117.61
		117.61			117.61
01/11	Balance *b/d*	117.61			
05/11	Cash	50.00			

14.8
Cash any form of money, including cheques, that is paid immediately.
b/d brought down; from the previous date in the opposite column.

14.9
incidentally I add this bit of information because it is interesting, even though it is not crucial to the point I am making.
the induction course the training course when someone first joins a company, which tells them about the company and how it works.

14.9 Listen and read

Patrick asks Arturo about the postage ledger. Listen to what they say. Why does Patrick keep a separate ledger for postage?

PATRICK Suppose I had put postage stamps in the 'Purchases' ledger – what would happen?

ARTURO Nothing. The computer won't know that you made a mistake. The figures will still balance, but you won't know how much you've spent on stamps.

PATRICK Right, fifty pounds. Now, why does it ask me how I paid for them?

ARTURO Because every transaction has to be entered twice. You've debited the postage account, so another ledger has to be credited, and then they balance. How did you pay?

PATRICK Cash.

ARTURO Right, so hit 'C' for 'Cash' – then the computer credits the cash ledger. And there you have the principle of double-entry bookkeeping. Invented by Italian merchants in the twelfth century, *incidentally.*

PATRICK Ah! It seems so simple when you explain it. If only I'd paid more attention on *the induction course.*

ARTURO Speaking of induction courses, did you make up a profit and loss account at the end of your first quarter?

PATRICK No! Should I have done?

ARTURO Well, it is a condition of the franchise agreement, but don't worry, you can still do it. Watch! If you select 'Profit and Loss' from the menu, and key in the date for the last day of the quarter, the computer will do the rest for you.

14.10 Find the right word

Read the text below on bookkeeping. Write a word or phrase from the box to fill each of the gaps.

In Britain, the ___**a**___-___**b**___ side of the ledger is the debit side, the ___**c**___-___**d**___ side is the credit side. Suppose you sell something for £20, and you allow your customer, Mr Smith, credit. He says he will pay at the end of the month. You enter this in the ___**e**___ ledger, as a credit – after all, it's money ___**f**___. To make your books ___**g**___, you must also record it on the ___**h**___ side of a ledger that has Mr Smith's name at the top of the page. You ___**i**___ his account £20, because that is the amount he ___**j**___ you. At the end of the month, Mr Smith pays his debt of £20. You write this on the ___**k**___ side of his ledger, so that it ___**l**___. But what about the ___**m**___ ledger? That £20 must now be recorded somewhere else – but where? It depends how Mr Smith paid. If he gave you a cheque, you ___**n**___ the bank ledger; if he gave you a £20 note, it is recorded as ___**o**___.

balance	balances	
cash	coming in	
credit	debit	
debit	debit	hand
hand	left	owes
right	sales	sales

14.11 Document study

This is an example of what Patrick Flynn's profit and loss account might look like. Read through it carefully.

METRO-POLO
OFFICE CLEANING

METRO-POLO OFFICE CLEANING (KINGSTON)
Profit and Loss Account
for the quarter ending 31/10/91

Opening stock	1050.00	Sales	12874.00
Add purchases	2406.00		
	3456.00		
Less closing stock	(2079.00)		
Cost of sales	1377.00		
Gross profit	11497.00		
	12874.00		12874.00
Wages	3995.00	Gross profit	11497.00
Advertising	2860.00		
Postage	118.00		
Petrol	263.00		
Telephone	142.00		
Rent	900.00		
Gas and electricity	230.00		
Vans (leasing)	840.00		
Equipment (leasing)	390.00		
	9738.00		
Net profit	1759.00		
	11497.00		11497.00

Reading the balance sheet

14.12
assets anything of value which a company uses to carry on its business; **fixed assets** are buildings, machines, vehicles and other items which may be used for many years; **current assets** are stocks, cash and money owed to the company.
liabilities anything that costs, or will cost, money: taxes, bills, debts.

14.13
a nice profit quite a large profit.
indicators figures that are especially important in telling you how the company is doing.

14.14
on a shoestring with very little money.
an overdraft money that you have spent from your bank account, even though you didn't have it; a form of loan.
what with inflation and all that when you take inflation and everything else into account.

14.12 Document study

This is Patrick Flynn's balance sheet. It is very unusual for fixed assets to be shown on a balance sheet as 'nil'. Why? Is this a problem for Patrick?

```
METRO-POLO OFFICE CLEANING (KINGSTON)
Balance Sheet as at 31/10/91
-----------------------------------------------------
SOURCE OF FUNDS
Capital                 7260.00
Net profit              1759.00            9019.00
                      ---------
less drawings                             (3872.00)
                                          ---------
                                           5147.00
                                          =========
USE OF FUNDS
Fixed assets                  0

Current assets
  Stock                 2079.00
  Debtors                921.00
  Bank                  3682.00
  Cash                   371.00            7053.00
                      ---------
less current liabilities                  (1906.00)
                                          ---------
                                           5147.00
                                          =========
```

14.13 Listen and read

Arturo starts to comment on Patrick's balance sheet. Listen to what they say. Why does Patrick sound pleased?

PATRICK Why do you say we ought to do the balance sheet now? I thought the accountants only looked at the balance sheet once a year.

ARTURO For a small business it can be very useful to look at your balance sheet every quarter, or even every month, especially when you have a computer to do the work for you.

PATRICK Well – how am I doing?

ARTURO Considering you've only been in business three months, not badly.

PATRICK Sales are way over target – we've even made *a nice profit*!

ARTURO Yes, that's good, and that's one reason for keeping accounts, to see how well you've done in the past. But another reason is to see your present position, and to get some idea of where you're going. There are one or two *indicators* here that you may need to watch.

14.14 Listen and read

Arturo continues to comment on Patrick's balance sheet. Listen to what they say. What problems does Arturo see?

ARTURO You're running this business of yours *on a shoestring*; I suppose you realise that. You're under-capitalised, and with no fixed assets you'll find it difficult to get a bank loan or *an overdraft*. You've very little to fall back on.

PATRICK Well, it was you who approved my application for the franchise! You knew how I stood – what my situation was.

ARTURO Yes, yes! And I've every confidence in you. All I'm saying is, don't relax. For example, you drew more out of the business in the last quarter than you put in by way of profit.

PATRICK Well! Living expenses – you know – *what with inflation and all that* . . .

ARTURO Don't look so miserable! You're going to do all right! In fact, there are some very good figures here, but you've got to learn to recognise which they are.

14.15 Listen and read

Arturo continues to comment on Patrick's balance sheet. He sees two further problems. What are they? Does Patrick agree?

ARTURO Do you remember, on the course, what they told you about accounting ratios?

PATRICK Er – oh – current assets *over* current liabilities, that was one of them.

ARTURO That's the current ratio. It's a test of whether a company can meet its liabilities – whether it can pay its bills.

PATRICK Well, all my assets are current assets, so my ratio is about three and a half to one! That ought to be high enough.

ARTURO On the contrary, it's much too high. More than half your capital is just sitting in the bank. I hope at least it's in an interest-bearing account. You've also got a lot of *working capital tied up* in stock.

PATRICK Well, those are all cleaning materials, chemicals – you know – what d'you call them – *consumables*! It's much cheaper to buy in bulk.

ARTURO On the other hand, your stocks are tying up capital you may need somewhere else, and they cost money to store, and they are liable to depreciate in storage.

PATRICK No, Mr Foscatelli, I can tell you, I went into all that very thoroughly. I know I've got that bit right.

ARTURO Now that's what I like to hear. It suggests you're keeping an eye on the cash flow, and that's a key factor in financial management. By the way, perhaps you can let me have a cheque for your franchise subscription. Then you won't have so much surplus cash *floating about* in the bank!

14.15
over divided by.
working capital money which is available immediately for running a business; money which is not used to pay for fixed assets.
tied up not available for use.
consumables things that you buy and use regularly.
floating about there, but not doing anything useful.

14.16 Find the right word: cash flow

Read the text below on cash flow. Write a word or phrase from the box to fill each of the gaps.

The movement of money through a firm is called ___**a**___ ___**b**___ . The company may be successful and ___**c**___ and may own valuable fixed ___**d**___ , but if, at the end of a month, there are ___**e**___ to be paid and no cheques have come in, its financial position may be weak. On the other hand, if the accountant allows a large amount of ___**f**___ to stay in the bank, when it should be invested and earning ___**g**___ , the board of directors will not be pleased. Control of cash flow is, as Arturo says, a key ___**h**___ in financial management.

Managers complain that ___**i**___ are slow to pay and ___**j**___ want to be paid at once. New firms are often short of ___**k**___ . Early success can be dangerous. If Patrick Flynn gets a lot of office-cleaning contracts, he will have to buy stock and take on staff. This will cost money, so his ___**l**___ capital will increase, and it will be ___**m**___ in things like vacuum cleaners which will not show a return for several weeks or even months.

assets bills
capital cash cash
creditors debtors
factor flow
interest profitable
tied up working

14.17 Writing practice

Arturo Foscatelli likes to write a report whenever he visits a franchisee. Write the report on Patrick Flynn for him. Make notes on all the good things and the bad things he discovered, and quote figures to support what you say.

Study record	
14.1	
14.2	
14.3	
14.4	
14.5	
14.6	
14.7	
14.8	
14.9	
14.10	
14.11	
14.12	
14.13	
14.14	
14.15	
14.16	
14.17	

Answer key and commentary for unit 14

14.1 Listen and read
Arturo is visiting Patrick because he visits all new franchisees in their first year. He says 'I make a point of visiting new members of our organisation at least once during their first year of operation.'

14.2 Document study
Patrick's customers are Midland Furniture, Goodies Ltd, Wonder-Bar Security and Q Smith & Sons. Metro-Polo is the franchisor; Patrick has to pay a quarterly subscription in return for the use of the name, and the training and help that Metro-Polo has given him.

14.3 Writing practice
1 Twelve thousand, eight hundred and seventy-four pounds.
2 Three thousand, six hundred and eighty-two pounds.
3 Three thousand, eight hundred and seventy-two pounds.
4 One thousand and fifty pounds' worth.
5 Fifteen hundred pounds.
6 About sixteen thousand pounds.
7 A little over nine hundred pounds.

14.4 Listen and read
Metro-Polo is a creditor of Patrick Flynn. Patrick owes Metro-Polo money.

14.5 Find the right word
a Double
b entry
c income
d outgoings
e transaction
f entries
g credit (or debit)
h debit (or credit)
i balance
j balance
k sources

14.6 Structure practice
These are model answers.
2 Yes, they will, in case you don't pay them.
3 No, they won't, not if you pay them.
4 Yes, they will, as long as you pay them.

14.7 Listen and read
Patrick's most successful method of finding customers is by posting advertising to particular people. He says 'I've think I've done better, though, with direct mail.'

14.9 Listen and read
To attract new business, he sends a lot of letters to firms on his mailing list. To find out if this method is effective, he must know how much it costs him. Arturo says that if Patrick didn't keep a separate postage ledger 'you won't know how much you've spent on stamps.'

14.10 Find the right word
a left
b hand
c right
d hand
e sales
f coming in
g balance
h debit
i debit
j owes
k credit
l balances
m sales
n debit
o cash

14.12 Document study
It is very unusual for a business to have no fixed assets: no property, no machinery or equipment, no vehicle.

This is not a problem for Patrick at the moment. He leases the equipment he needs. But if he wants a bank loan he may find it hard to get one because he has nothing to offer as security.

14.13 Listen and read
Patrick sounds pleased because his company has 'made a nice profit' in his first quarter.

14.14 Listen and read
Arturo sees problems in that Patrick's business has too little capital; he has no fixed assets to support a bank loan or overdraft if that becomes necessary; Patrick has drawn out more money than the net profit.

14.15 Listen and read
Arturo thinks that Patrick has too much capital sitting in the bank, and that he has too much working capital tied up in stock.

Patrick does not agree. He says he knows he has got his stock levels right.

14.16 Find the right word
a cash
b flow
c profitable
d assets
e bills
f cash
g interest
h factor
i debtors
j creditors
k capital
l working
m tied up

14.17 Writing practice
This is a model answer.
The Patrick Flynn franchise has made a good start. He has lots of contracts and morale seems to be high. Turnover, at £12,874, is on target for the first quarter.

Patrick is still uncertain about his bookkeeping. We will have to watch this carefully.

He has built up quite a good base of customers, and seems to handle his mailing list and advertising well.

His first quarter profit and loss account was not too bad. We need to watch his capital and his assets. I suspect he carries too much stock (£2079), but he is confident that he has the level about right. He may have difficulties with expanding in the future.

Patrick is very keen and should make a good franchisee. But I will visit him again in three months.

Unit 15: Budgeting

SITUATION

At Metro-Polo's UK head office the staff are preparing for their annual budget meeting. In this unit we look at Metro-Polo UK's financial performance and see how individual departments present their figures as they fight for their individual budget allocations for the coming year.

CHARACTERS

Arturo Foscatelli

Dee	works in the advertising department. She is British.
Nigel	works in the advertising department. He is British.
Ida	is Advertising Department Manager. She is British.
Alan Scott	is Managing Director. He is British.
Glyn	is the Company Accountant. He is British.
Vikki Denson	is responsible for Franchise Development. She is American.
Sarah	works in Glyn's department. She is British.

All of these characters apart from Arturo work at Metro-Polo UK.

LANGUAGE

Vocabulary	Financial performance; forecasting and budgeting.
Skills	Taking part in meetings; defending a position in discussion; using figures and percentages in discussion.
Documents	A summary of business objectives; a sales chart.

Small-group discussion: preparing a budget

15.1 Document study

It is September 1991. In the UK head office of Metro-Polo, the Chief Accountant has circulated these figures. Are the 1991 figures better or worse than the figures for 1990?

METRO-POLO UK: Summary of business objectives 1990-94
(all figures in millions of pounds or percentages)

	1988/89 target	actual	1989/90 target	actual	1990/91 target	actual	1991/92 target	forecast	1992/93 target
Capital employed	2.00	2.20	2.50	2.80	3.00	3.10	3.50	3.40	3.75
Revenue	0.35	0.50	1.35	1.15	2.65	1.90	3.95	2.75	4.50
Profit	0	0.09	0.25	0.24	0.45	0.28	0.70	0.45	0.75
Profit margin	0	22%	22.7%	26.4%	20.4%	17.3%	21.5%	19.6%	20%
ROCE	0	4%	10%	8.6%	15%	9%	20%	13.2%	20%

15.2 Listen and read

Nigel and Dee work in the advertising department. They are discussing the figures in 15.1. Listen to what they say. Why are people worried by the figures?

DEE Why are people so upset by these figures?

NIGEL Well, 1990 was pretty good. 1991 was disappointing. It's the 1992 figures that are worrying.

DEE They look OK to me.

NIGEL Well, starting at the top – capital employed looks like being a hundred thousand pounds below target. But there's going to be over a million *shortfall* on revenue.

DEE Well, does that matter?

NIGEL It is over twenty-five per cent!

DEE But profits are up over 1991 – almost double, in fact.

NIGEL It's true the profit margin is quite healthy. But I'm afraid what counts is the return on capital, and the forecast for that is still way down, six point eight per cent below what it should be.

15.3 Listen and read

Nigel and Dee are joined by Ida, the Advertising Department Manager. They are preparing for the budget meeting. Listen to what they say. What is their main concern for the meeting?

IDA *What gets me* is that revenue forecast for 1992. Why is it so low?

NIGEL *I've been on to* Accounts, and I've also talked to Franchise Development. They say it's because of very uneven performances by franchisees. Some are doing well, others are struggling.

IDA I suppose the *lame ducks* are falling behind on their payments.

DEE Yes, and some of the ones that are doing well aren't paying anything extra to us, because a lot of the franchise agreements have a clause in them freezing *royalties* for the first three years.

IDA For heaven's sake! I thought royalties were *performance-linked* – a percentage of turnover?

DEE They are, but this was *a gimmick* that Metro-Polo used when they started up in the UK. You know – the first fifty applicants get special *concessions*.

NIGEL Look, we can't waste time talking about *the finer points of* franchise agreements. We have to increase *our spend* – particularly in *local news media*.

DEE I thought we agreed, Nigel, *office environment decision-makers* don't listen to local radio stations?

IDA Just a minute! Hold on, will you? We can argue about our budget allocations later. I agree that we have a strong case for more money, but let's work out how we should present it – bearing in mind, of course, that they're going to try *to cut us back*.

15.1
ROCE return on capital employed; the rate of income received from capital.

15.2
shortfall less than expected.

15.3
What gets me what annoys me.
I've been on to I have been in contact with.
lame ducks people or companies that perform badly.
royalties money paid to a company on the basis of sales or profits.
performance-linked related to how well the company performs.
a gimmick something that is not usual, but is used to attract interest or attention to something.
concessions things that you allow a company to do in special circumstances.
the finer points of the details of.
our spend the amount of money we spend.
local news media local newspapers, magazines, radio and television.
office environment decision-makers people who work in offices and make decisions; this is an example of marketing jargon.
to cut us back reduce the amount of money we have to spend.

15.4 Listen and read

The meeting to discuss the next year's budgets is about to start. It may be a difficult meeting. Alan Scott is the Managing Director. Listen to him describe how the meeting will proceed.

ALAN Ladies and gentlemen – if I may have your attention – thank you. We have to examine this afternoon our departmental budgets for the coming financial year, in the light of recent information on the company's performance in 1991/92. I'm going to ask each department head to make a brief statement of the projected figures and the reasoning behind them. Then I shall open up the meeting to a general discussion. First of all, though, Glyn, I'd like you to take us through the performance projection in a little more detail.

GLYN Thank you, Alan. As you know, there's been *a bit of a hiccup* in the first-half results for this year, and we don't foresee this shortfall being made good in the second half, unfortunately, so . . .

. . . . . .

ALAN Well, only time will tell. Right! Let's go round the departments now. Vikki – Franchise Development?

VIKKI I think everyone has a copy of our paper – anyone without? No? Right, I'll start by explaining how we see our place in the corporate plan, and come back to the figures later. As you know, the plan *envisages* a fairly rapid growth rate, with a return on capital of twenty per cent from year four onwards. This implies that expansion is going to be financed from retained profits, at any rate *for the foreseeable future.*

15.4
a bit of a hiccup a small problem, usually one that you think will go away in time.
envisages assumes to be true; a formal word.
for the foreseeable future for as far into the future as we can think.

15.6
a slight shift in emphasis a small change in what we do.
a key strategy something that has been thought about and is important to the longer-term interests of the company.
a tactical response something that has been suggested as a short-term solution to a particular problem.
sidetracked moved on to something I did not want to do.

15.5 Reading for key words

Find the words or phrases in 15.3 and 15.4 that mean the following:

1 Not paying at the proper time.
2 Holding payments at a fixed amount.
3 Low payments, as an incentive to join or to buy.
4 The divisions of money that have been allocated.
5 Being careful not to forget.
6 Please listen to me.
7 The twelve-month accounting period that is about to begin.
8 The income and expenditure that each person expects.
9 Explain to us what each part of the document means.
10 The rest of the year is not likely to bring results that will make up for the first half.

15.6 Listen and read

The meeting continues. Listen to what they say. Notice how Ida makes her points quite forcefully, and how Alan keeps the meeting on course.

VIKKI And so finally, I'd like to re-affirm my department's commitment to achieving the company's objectives. We believe it can be done – only *a slight shift in emphasis* is necessary.

ALAN Thank you, Vikki. Now . . .

IDA Mr Chairman, forgive me for interrupting, but may I ask how we're supposed to see this 'slight shift of emphasis'? Is this *a key strategy*, or just *a tactical response* to a problem?

VIKKI Does it make any difference what we call it? It's still the same thing.

IDA It makes a great deal of difference. What you're proposing could lead the company down a totally different road in its development.

ALAN I'm sorry, I'd rather not get *sidetracked* into discussion at this stage – you'll all have plenty of opportunity for questions later. Now, may we proceed? Ida, how do you see advertising over the next twelve months?

Putting your case in a formal meeting – 1

15.7
we're kidding ourselves we are lying to ourselves, wanting to believe something that we know isn't true.
Yellow Pages a telephone directory which lists businesses.
mail shots sending advertising material to people on a mailing list; this is an example of direct mail.
an across-the-board expenditure increase an increase in spending on everything.
to come back on to reply to.
to put their heads together to get together and think about something.
adjourn pause for a while before continuing a meeting.

15.8
Let's face it we have to admit this, whether we like it or not.
the bottom line the net profit or loss.

15.7 Listen and read

The meeting continues. Listen to what they say. Listen to how Ida gives a very positive image of the advertising department. Why does she speak in this way?

IDA — I think *we're kidding ourselves* if we talk about these results as a hiccup in the company's strategy. Well, let's face it, as far as the UK is concerned we're just another start-up franchise organisation. Nobody owes us a living. We've got to promote our brand image to office managers and site managers. Now, the figures before you show how accurately we can target our advertising, using a mix of trade journals, trade directories, *Yellow Pages*, local news media to a limited extent, and a co-ordinated programme of *mail shots*.

ALAN — Just a moment, please, Ida. It all sounds very exciting, but could we get to your actual budget figures?

IDA — Yeah, of course. Well, in brief, the advertising department is looking for *an across-the-board expenditure increase* in 1992/93 of eighty-five per cent. I know it sounds like a lot of money. But bearing in mind inflation, and the increase in media rates, in real terms it's a much smaller increase than we asked for, and got, last year. We all agree that we must grow. I don't think we can afford anything less.

ALAN — I can see some of you want *to come back on* what Ida has just said, but I think it's only fair to give the working groups a chance *to put their heads together*. We'll *adjourn* for twenty minutes. Back at four o'clock, please.

15.8 Speaking practice: defending a position

Listen to this conversation. Then listen again and speak the part of the woman.

MAN — It's results that count, and, quite frankly, your department isn't delivering.

WOMAN — I think I ought to remind you that our results last year were thirty per cent over target.

MAN — Some of us were sixty per cent over target.

WOMAN — And a hundred per cent over budget.

MAN — *Let's face it*, if we're to increase our market share, we've got to spend money. We have to have five hundred new franchises this year – never mind what it costs.

WOMAN — So budget overruns don't matter?

MAN — Provided *the bottom line* looks good.

WOMAN — We'll see!

15.9 Listen and read

Vikki has gone to the canteen to get some coffee. She bumps into Arturo Foscatelli. Listen to what they say. Will Vikki support Ida's budget?

VIKKI — Black coffee, please, no sugar – thank you. Oh! I'm sorry, I didn't see you. Mr Foscatelli!

ARTURO — My fault, my fault. Ah! Miss Denson. You're just the person I wanted to see. Are you in a hurry?

VIKKI — No, the budget meeting is adjourned for a while, so I thought I'd grab a coffee.

ARTURO — How's it going in there?

VIKKI — Well, obviously you've seen the expected performance figures for this year. Advertising are making a case for a huge increase in budget, and I'm about to go back in and tell Alan why I think they shouldn't get it.

15.10 Reading for key words

Find the words or phrases in 15.7 and 15.9 that show the following:

1 Make people recognise our products and approve of them.
2 A bit, but not too much.
3 The cost of buying advertising space in newspapers, time on TV, etc.
4 Allowing for inflation and the fall in the value of money.
5 Drink a cup of coffee in a hurry.
6 The results that are forecast.
7 Putting forward reasons for doing something.

15.11 Listen and read

The meeting resumes, and Arturo joins the others. Does Alan Scott agree with Arturo's assessment of Metro-Polo's performance?

ALAN Ladies and gentlemen! Right, I'd like to welcome Signor Arturo Foscatelli, our founder and president.

ARTURO Thank you! I have just completed a tour of our franchisees in the United Kingdom and I must say I am very much encouraged by what I've seen.

ALAN That's good news, Mr Foscatelli, but I think I ought to tell you that some of us here are not very happy about *the way things are going*.

ARTURO Perhaps that's because you have been looking at figures while I have been talking to people. But I don't want to take up your time; please carry on.

ALAN Thank you. I'd now like to open up the meeting to questions and discussion. Vikki, I think you had something you wanted to say?

15.12 Writing practice: making notes

As chairman of the meeting, Alan Scott makes informal notes of what happens and of what is said. These are brief and not at all detailed, but they will remind him later of the points he will make in his report.

Listen again to all the extracts from the meeting that you have heard so far, and write these notes for him. Write a few words about each point, just enough to help you to remember later. As you listen to further extracts in this unit, continue making notes.

15.13 Listen and read

The meeting continues. Listen to what they say. Is Nigel friendly or hostile to Vikki? What about Alan?

VIKKI Yes. I'd like to have a second look at the sales chart that was distributed at the start of this meeting.

IDA Sales chart?

VIKKI The sales gap analysis. Ida and her team used it to show that we ought to spend more on advertising. Now, on this chart, I'd like *to plot* the money that's been spent already. The scale on the *y-axis* will be different, of course; we can read it in hundreds of thousands instead of millions. It's the shape of the curve that I'm interested in.

NIGEL With respect, may I ask just what this exercise is supposed to achieve?

ALAN *All in good time*. Vikki?

15.11
the way things are going what is happening.

15.13
to plot to draw a line on a graph, etc. by marking a series of points from a set of figures.
y-axis the vertical side of a graph; the horizontal side is the x-axis.
All in good time wait a minute; we'll deal with that when we're ready; be patient, we will deal with that later.

Putting your case in a formal meeting – 2

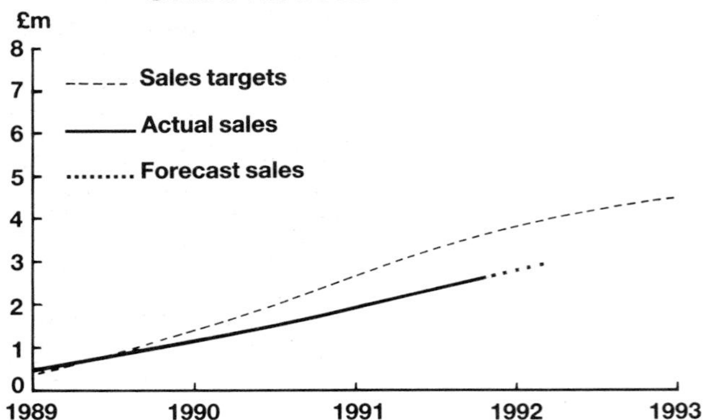

15.14 Document study: a sales chart

This is the chart that the advertising department used to present their figures. Vikki is going to use it to make her case against advertising. As you listen to 15.15, mark the points on the chart, and then join them into a curve.

15.15
Hang on wait.
is anybody's guess we don't know; we can't be certain.

15.16
An eight-fold increase an increase of eight times.

15.15 Listen and read

Vikki dictates figures so that the others can mark them on their copies of the chart. Listen to what they say. Why does Ida protest?

VIKKI The advertising expenditure in 1989 was negligible, because the franchise wasn't fully operational. In 1990 it was fifty thousand; 1991 – a hundred and seventy thousand; 1992 – four hundred and ten thousand pounds.

NIGEL *Hang on*, what was 1992 again?

VIKKI Four-ten. Right. We can only get a whole-year figure for 1993 based on the advertising department's proposals: their budget will amount to – four hundred and ten thousand times one point eight five – nearly seven hundred and sixty thousand. What happens after that, in 1994 and '95, *is anybody's guess*. But let's join the dots and see what the curve looks like.

IDA Mr Chairman, and Mr Foscatelli, I really must protest. We didn't come here today to play party games.

ARTURO Oh, I rather enjoy party games. Look at this line. It goes up even more steeply than the sales forecast.

15.16 Listen and read

The meeting continues. Listen to how Vikki and Ida use the figures to present their own analyses of the chart. Does Ida think that 20% is high or low? What about Vikki?

VIKKI Thank you! That's precisely my point. *An eight-fold increase* in advertising over two years has produced less than two and a half times the revenue.

IDA And how do you suppose we got the extra revenue? An extra three hundred and sixty thousand in advertising to bring in an increase in turnover of one point six million! Or to put it another way, in 1991 our advertising budget was ten point five per cent of total outgoings. In 1992 it rose to eighteen per cent.

VIKKI Exactly!

IDA But – but, according to our 1993 figures, even with my proposed eighty-five per cent increase, advertising will still only account for twenty per cent of outgoings. Twenty per cent!

ALAN Ladies, ladies, please! Mr Foscatelli?

ARTURO All I wanted to say was that these 1993 figures are simply targets, and the way we're going I'm afraid we're going to fall short of them. Figures are valuable, statistics are valuable, but statistics, especially percentages, can hide as much as they reveal. What matters to me is the bottom line.

NIGEL I'm very glad to hear you say that, sir. I was afraid we were going to lose sight of it altogether.

VIKKI Oh please!

15.17 Listen and read

The meeting continues. Listen to what they say. Why does Ida ask her question about 'no confidence'? Why, at the end, is Ida so angry?

ARTURO A franchise network is only as good as its franchisees. I've just seen *a cross-section* of our people and I am impressed. Our selection procedures are obviously working well. It does seem to me, however, that on the training side *we are falling down somewhat*.

IDA Forgive me for interrupting. Are we to take this as *a motion of no confidence* in Franchise Development?

ALAN Hold on, Ida – *don't jump the gun.*

ARTURO All the advertising in the world will not help our brand image if our franchisees are not running their own businesses efficiently. The budget that I would like to see rise sharply next year is that for education and training.

NIGEL How do you think the money should be spent?

VIKKI I really don't think the president should be expected to answer a question like that *off the top of his head*. I would like to point out, however, that my remarks at the beginning of this meeting echo what Mr Foscatelli has just said.

IDA It can't be easy echoing something that hasn't been said yet!

15.17
a cross-section a number of people from different parts and levels of the company.
we are falling down somewhat we are failing.
a motion of no confidence saying that you don't believe that someone is able to do their job properly.
don't jump the gun we might come to believe that, but not yet; don't come to that conclusion yet, it's too soon.
off the top of his head without having time to think about it properly.

15.18 Listen and read: figure practice

Glyn is explaining to Sarah, one of his staff, how Ida prepared her figures. First, read through the dialogue, and try to work out what the missing figures are by re-reading the documents in this unit. Then check your figures by listening to what they say.

SARAH I must admit I didn't quite follow Ida's figures at the meeting yesterday. Where did she get them from?

GLYN You mean things like ___**a**___ more spent on advertising, bringing in a ___**b**___ increase in turnover? She was comparing the figures for 1990 and '92. In 1990 we spent ___**c**___ on advertising. In '92 it was up to ___**d**___ – right? That's an increase of three hundred and sixty thousand pounds. But turnover rose from one point one five million to ___**e**___ – that's a ___**f**___ increase.

SARAH But she tried to show that advertising had got wonderful results. The percentages she was using – were they correct? Where did she get them from?

GLYN She was talking about advertising as a percentage of all expenditure. In 1991, revenue was ___ **g** ___ and profits were ___**h**___ , so outgoings must have been roughly one point six two million. Advertising was ___**i**___ , which is about ten per cent of outgoings.

SARAH But in 1993 she said advertising would still be only twenty per cent of outgoings. Why was the figure so low?

GLYN Ah, that was where she went wrong. She assumed that the target figures would be the real ones. The target figures for '93 are actually quite high, with revenue at ___ **j** ___ , and profit at ___**k**___. That means outgoings would be about three and three quarter million pounds. So her big advertising target would be quite small in comparison – about twenty per cent, in fact.

Study record	
15.1	
15.2	
15.3	
15.4	
15.5	
15.6	
15.7	
15.8	
15.9	
15.10	
15.11	
15.12	
15.13	
15.14	
15.15	
15.16	
15.17	
15.18	

Answer key and commentary for unit 15

15.1 Document study
Generally, the figures are below target (for revenue, profits) and above target (for capital employed). In other words, results are worse than they should be, especially for 1991; 1990's results were better.

15.2 Listen and read
People are worried because the return on capital employed is too low.

15.3 Listen and read
The advertising department's main aim is to get an increase in their budget for the next year.

15.5 Reading for key words
1 falling behind on their payments
2 freezing royalties
3 special concessions
4 budget allocations
5 bearing in mind
6 if I may have your attention
7 the coming financial year
8 the projected figures
9 take us through (the performance projection)
10 we don't foresee this shortfall being made good in the second half

15.7 Listen and read
Ida wants to give a very positive image of the advertising department because she is going to ask for a very large increase in her budget.

15.9 Listen and read
No. She's going to say why she thinks that Ida should not get her budget increase.

15.10 Reading for key words
1 promote our brand image
2 to a limited extent
3 media rates
4 in real terms
5 grab a coffee
6 the expected performance figures
7 making a case for

15.11 Listen and read
Alan does not agree with Arturo. He says 'some of us here are not very happy about the way things are going.'

15.12 Writing practice
This is a model answer.
Glyn: explained performance projection - problems continue into second half of year.
Vikki: Franchise Development – can suppor corporate plan – shift in emphasis.
Ida: – FD 'shift in emphasis' or new strategy – Advertising – queried Glyn's analysis – '92/'9 85% budget increase! – much interest! – meetin adjourned for working groups to talk together.
Meeting resumes – Foscatelli joins – happ with franchisees.

15.13 Listen and read
Nigel is hostile. He says 'With respect, . . . ', bu he is in fact being rude. Listen to how he says it Alan, as chairman, is careful not to take sides, a least not yet. He says 'All in good time', an invites Vikki to continue.

15.14 Document study
See diagram at the bottom of the page.

15.15 Listen and read
Ida protests because Vikki is using her figures t make a case against the advertising department.

15.16 Listen and read
Ida thinks that 20% is low. She says 'only accoun for twenty per cent', and then repeats 'Twenty pe cent!' with emphasis.
Vikki thinks that 18% is high. She say 'Exactly!' to show that she thinks that th advertising budget is already too high.

15.17 Listen and read
Ida asks her question about 'no confidence because she wants to criticize Franchis Development. She is angry when she says 'It can' be easy echoing something that hasn't been sai yet!', because she feels that she is not going to ge her budget increase after all.

15.18 Listen and read
a 360,000
b 1.6 million
c 50,000
d 410,000
e 2.75 million
f 1.6 million pound
g 1.9 million
h 280,000
i 170,000
j 4.5 million pounds
k three quarters of a million

15.14

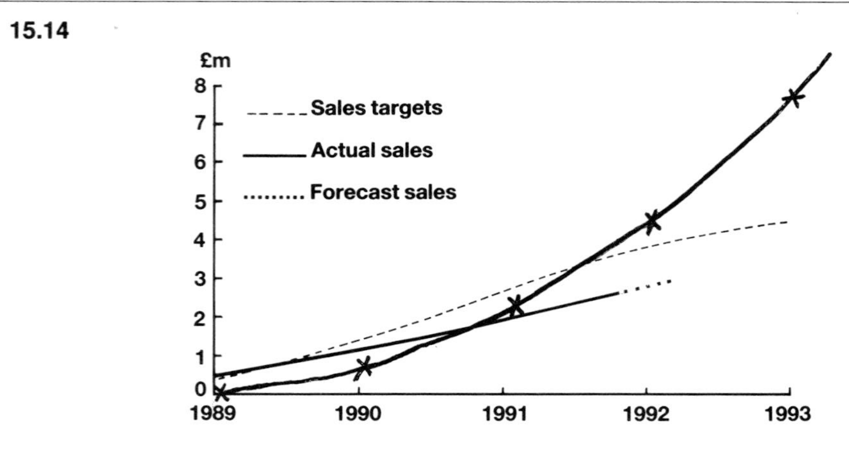

Unit 16: Management techniques

SITUATION

Tibor Horvath, a businessman from Budapest, wants to set up a company to recycle waste paper in Hungary. He has discovered that Melina Karavatis, daughter of a Greek shipowner, has inherited a paper mill in Thessaloniki which she wants to redevelop. Most of the equipment will be scrapped, and Tibor is interested in acquiring it for his new venture. He has the backing of Arturo Foscatelli, and Alan Scott has been called in to arrange the finance. They meet in Rome to try to sort out the problems of setting up this new business.

CHARACTERS

Alan Scott	
Arturo Foscatelli	
Receptionist	at the Hotel Palestrina. She is Italian.
Tibor Horvath	is a businessman. He is Hungarian.

LANGUAGE

Vocabulary	Company finance; negotiation and agreement.
Skills	Checking into a hotel; making contact with someone you know only by name; looking at a problem from different points of view.
Structures	If and the conditional; quantity.
Documents	A telex; a letter; a critical path analysis (CPA) diagram; a spreadsheet.

Information for a management decision

```
487290 METRO ITL

CONS NO. 9422 11.09.91 12.15

11.9.91

ATTN: TIBOR HORVATH
URBAN PROJECT
ATTN: ALAN SCOTT
METRO-POLO UK

FROM: FOSCATELLI

RE PROPOSED RECYCLING PLANT AND PAPER MILL
I AM HAPPY TO INFORM YOU THAT AGREEMENT ON TRANS-
FER OF MACHINERY FROM THESSALONIKI TO BUDAPEST HAS
BEEN REACHED IN PRINCIPLE. A BANK LOAN HAS ALSO
BEEN AGREED BUT NO DECISION HAS BEEN MADE AS TO
TIMING. MISS KARAVATIS HAS GIVEN US 3 WEEKS TO
SETTLE DETAILS OF FINANCE AND TRANSPORT. I SHOULD
LIKE TO HAVE YOUR ADVICE ON MATTERS IN WHICH YOU
ARE EXPERT AND THEREFORE REQUEST YOU BOTH TO MEET
ME IN ROME ON 17 SEPTEMBER. I HAVE RESERVED ROOMS
FOR YOU AT THE HOTEL PALESTRINA FOR THE NIGHTS OF
THE 17 AND 18. PLEASE INFORM ME AT ONCE IF THIS
ARRANGEMENT IS NOT CONVENIENT FOR YOU. I PROPOSE
WE HAVE LUNCH AT THE HOTEL AT 1 PM.

REGARDS
FOSCATELLI
487290 METRO ITL

/ENDS
```

16.1 Document study

Arturo Foscatelli has set up a ne project with Tibor Horvath, businessman from Hungary. He senc Alan Scott and Tibor Horvath a tele about the project. Read through carefully. What raw material will Tib Horvath's factory require, and what wi its main product be?

16.1
recycling plant a factory where used goods or materials are processed so that they can be used again.
paper mill a factory where paper is made.
in principle an agreement has been made, but the details and practice still have to be decided.

16.2
a Mr Horvath a man called Mr Horvath.
page him call him over a public address system.
to freshen up to have a quick wash and make yourself look tidy again.

16.3
very big in very important and powerful in.
a container terminal a port where ships can load and unload only large containers of goods.

16.2 Listen and read

Alan Scott checks into the Hotel Palestrina. Listen to what he and the desk clerk sa Is Tibor Horvath in the hotel?

DESK	Buon giorno, signor.
ALAN	Good morning. My name's Scott. I have a reservation.
DESK	Mr Scott – yes, that's right. For two nights. You are in room 735. Would you like to sign the register, please?
ALAN	Yes, certainly. By the way, do you have *a Mr Horvath* staying here? From Hungary. I'm supposed to be meeting him for lunch.
DESK	Mr Horvath? – Yes, we do. I think he's in the bar. Shall I *page him* for you?
ALAN	In a few minutes, perhaps. I'd like *to freshen up* a bit first.
DESK	Certainly, sir. I'll get the porter to show you to your room. Gino!

16.3 Document study

This is the letter that Tibor Horvath sent to Arturo Foscatelli several weeks befor Read through it carefully. Why do you think that Tibor wants Arturo to becom involved in his new project?

Dear Arturo,

How are you, my old friend? I hope you are keeping busy cleaning your offices! I am writing to tell you about something you might be interested in.

Karavatis – you remember him, he was *very big in* shipping – has died, and left everything to his daughter, the delightful Melina. She wants to concentrate on the shipping side of things, and has a site in Thessaloniki she wants to develop as *a container terminal*.

Now, this is where it gets interesting. At the moment there is a paper mill on the site. Most of the machinery will be scrapped, but some of it may be useful in my new venture in Budapest – paper recycling!

How would you like to get involved? Perhaps you could talk to Melina about financing the sale and transfer of the machinery?

16.4 Listen and read

Alan and Tibor are discussing the plans in the hotel coffee shop. Listen to what they say. What is the problem?

ALAN — Now, let me get this right. You're setting up a company to recycle waste paper in Hungary, and Metro-Polo is backing you.

TIBOR — That's correct. We shall in fact become *a wholly-owned subsidiary* of Metro-Polo when all the formalities have been completed. Everything would have been settled a fortnight ago, if it had gone according to plan.

ALAN — Yes, I gathered there'd been some kind of legal problem. I can't say I'm surprised. There usually is with deals like this.

TIBOR — Lawyers! Well, anyway, I am right in thinking, aren't I, that you are here to help sort out the financing?

ALAN — Well, I presume that's what Foscatelli wants to talk about. There seems to be a problem in the timing. The bank loan has been agreed, the question is when *to draw down the money*.

TIBOR — That's it in a nutshell. I'm so pleased we have this opportunity to talk before Foscatelli comes, because . . .

ALAN — Ah! Here he comes now. Buon giorno, Signor Foscatelli!

ARTURO — Tibor! Alan! Welcome to Rome! How are you both? I see you have already introduced yourselves. Now, we have a lot to discuss . . .

16.4
a wholly-owned subsidiary a company which is completely owned by another company.
to draw down the money to take the money from the bank and start using it.

16.5 Reading for key words

Find the words or phrases in 16.1 and 16.4 that show the following:

1 We agree on the main points, but the details have not been settled.
2 We have not yet decided exactly when these things will be done.
3 I want to confirm or correct my knowledge. (Two ways of saying this.)
4 To manufacture paper from paper that has been used and thrown away.
5 In very few words.

16.6 Structure practice: *if* and the conditional

In 16.4, Tibor Horvath says:

Everything would have been settled a fortnight ago . . .

He means that everything wasn't settled a fortnight ago. He continues:

. . . if it had gone according to plan.

He means that it didn't go according to plan.

To describe something in the past that didn't happen, and so is in a sense 'imaginary', we use 'would have' with the '-ed' form of the verb. To explain why it didn't happen, we use an 'if'-clause and 'had' with the '-ed' form of the verb. For example:

I would have stayed longer if I had saved more money.

This means 'I didn't stay longer because I didn't save more money.'

We would have walked to the station if it hadn't rained.

This means 'We didn't walk to the station because it rained.'

Join these sentences together, using 'would have' and an 'if'-clause, to show the reason why something didn't happen.

1 The contract wasn't signed. The formalities weren't completed.
2 The formalities weren't completed. There was a legal problem.
3 We didn't start work on the factory. We didn't get the bank loan.
4 We didn't talk about the financing. Foscatelli arrived.

Discussing resource limitations

16.7
the archives a collection of papers that are no longer in use, but which cannot be thrown away, and so they are stored.
shredded torn into very small pieces by a machine, so that they cannot be read by anyone.

16.7 Listen and read

Alan and Tibor are discussing the recycling project. Listen to what they say. I shredded paper easier or more difficult to recycle?

TIBOR Another coffee? Or would you prefer a cognac?
ALAN No, thanks! But I will have an espresso, thank you.
TIBOR Waiter!
ALAN Tell me, Tibor, how did you become interested in recycled paper?
TIBOR Ah, well! I realised that my country, like most such bureaucracies, doesn't just consume huge amounts of paper, it also produces a great deal of waste paper. These offices do everything not just in duplicate or triplicate, they do it in twelve, fifteen, twenty copies.
ALAN Yes, but the vast majority of government documents are confidential, surely?
TIBOR A few of them go into *the archives* – maybe five per cent of the total. A lot of official papers get *shredded*.
ALAN That's good. Shredded paper is much easier to recycle.
TIBOR Yes and no. It is easier to recycle, but it's much more expensive to transport. Still, they've done part of our work for us. But most of the stuff goes into departmental filing cabinets. Sooner or later, al the filing cabinets are full; boxes of old papers in all the corridors; piles of paper on the desks; paper everywhere; that's what we're after.

16.8 Structure practice: quantity

In 16.7 there are many words used to describe quantities. Look for examples o 'another', 'most', 'one', 'all' and 'few'. There are also phrases describing quantitie Look for 'huge amounts of', 'a great deal of', 'the vast majority of', 'a lot of' and 'part of

The questions below are based on the dialogue. Write answers using the words an phrases listed above.

1 What does Tibor say his country consumes?
2 What does it produce?
3 What does he compare his country to?
4 What does Alan say about government documents?
5 What happens to them, according to Tibor?
6 What gets shredded?
7 What does Tibor say happens to most government paper?
8 So what happens sooner or later?

16.9 Listen and read

Alan and Tibor continue their discussion. Listen to what they say. Why must Tibor make the new business grow so quickly?

ALAN — Yes. You'd think waste paper would be cheap, wouldn't you? In fact, I was amazed when I found out how expensive it was.

TIBOR — Recycling only starts to pay when you achieve economies of scale. That's why we've got to move fast on this project. The plant's got *to come on stream* within two months of the contract being signed. We want sales to hit five hundred thousand US dollars a month within one year.

ALAN — Hm. Don't you think that's *rather a tall order*?

TIBOR — Look, I'll draw you *a critical path analysis diagram* for the installation of the recycling plant.

> **16.9**
> **to come on stream** to start production.
> **rather a tall order** a difficult thing to do.
> **a critical path analysis diagram** a diagram which shows a sequence of actions, and therefore shows which is the most important, or most critical, for a job to be successfully completed.

16.10 Reading for key words

Find the words or phrases in 16.7 and 16.9 that show the following:

1 In three copies.
2 Provides a profit.
3 Reductions in unit cost as a result of large-scale operation.
4 We must put this plan into operation quickly.
5 Difficult to achieve.

16.11 Document study

This is what Tibor draws. Study it carefully. You will need it for 16.12.

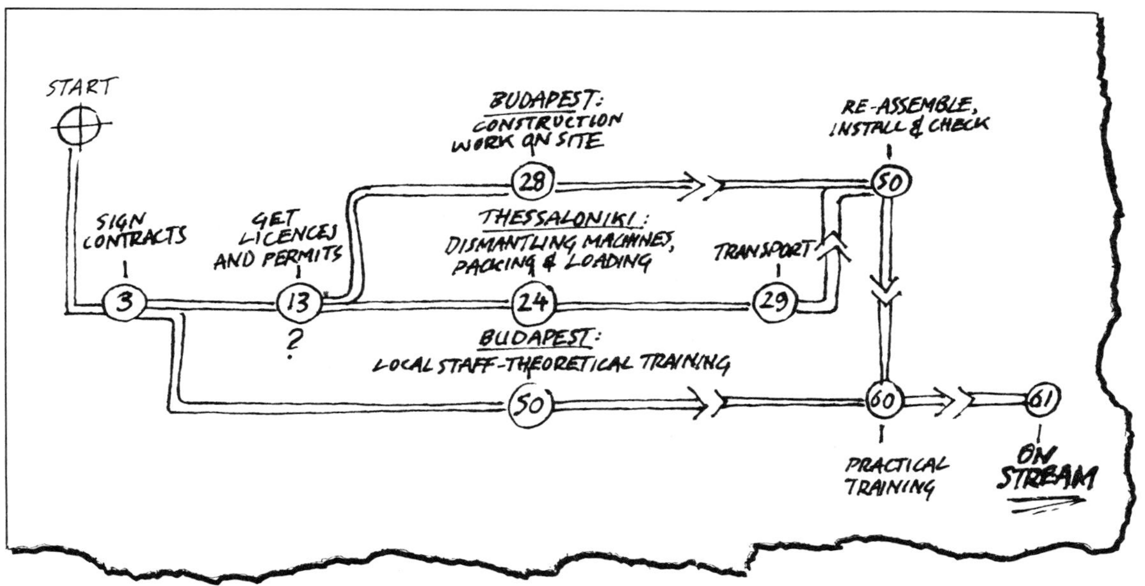

16.12 Listen and read

Alan and Tibor discuss the diagram. Listen to what they say and study the diagram in 16.11. Which is the critical path? What will happen if one stage of it is completed five days late?

ALAN — So this is your network analysis, is it?

TIBOR — That's my CPA diagram, yes.

ALAN — I see. We read it from left to right; each stage on each path has to be completed before the next stage can begin. The numbers in the circles show the total number of days from the start until each stage is complete. And which is the critical path?

TIBOR — Believe me, anything that has to do with getting licences, permits – anything that has to go through a government office – that's critical!

Using a spreadsheet

> **16.13**
> **A spreadsheet** a computer program that holds figures, and that can perform different calculations on them.
> **a cash-flow forecast** a statement of the expected income and expenditure of a company.

16.13 Listen and read

Alan is working on some figures the next day when Tibor arrives. Listen to what th say. Are Alan's figures likely to be very accurate?

TIBOR	Good morning, Alan!
ALAN	Oh, Tibor, good morning. How are you this morning?
TIBOR	Fine, thank you. Tell me, do you always share your breakfast tabl with a computer?
ALAN	Ah! Well, no, but as we're going to meet Foscatelli in a few minutes I thought I'd show you what I was working on last night after we got back from the cafe. Look!
TIBOR	Aha! *A spreadsheet.*
ALAN	Yes. I tried to sketch out *a cash-flow forecast* for the first year's operation of your paper recycling plant. I didn't have very much to go on, of course – just some estimates you and Foscatelli had mentioned – but, er, I'd like to see your reaction to it.

16.14 Reading for key words

Find the words or phrases in 16.13 that show the following:

1 To make a rough draft of a proposal.
2 I had to work with very few facts, very little evidence.
3 I wonder what you will think of this.

16.15 Document study: the spreadsheet

This is the spreadsheet that Alan has prepared. Study it carefully. You will need it f the rest of this unit.

INCOME (U$000)	OCT	NOV	DEC	JAN	FEB	MAR	APR	MAY	JUN	JUL	AUG	SEP	TOT
start-up capital	500.00												500.
bank loan		200.00	200.00	100.00									500.
sales			100.00	200.00	200.00	250.00	250.00	400.00	500.00	500.00	500.00	600.00	3500.
TOTAL	500.00	200.00	300.00	300.00	200.00	250.00	250.00	400.00	500.00	500.00	500.00	600.00	4500.
EXPENDITURE													
materials	50.00	50.00	80.00	100.00	100.00	100.00	150.00	250.00	250.00	250.00	250.00	300.00	1930
labour	40.00	40.00	50.00	50.00	60.00	60.00	60.00	80.00	80.00	80.00	80.00	90.00	770.
rent, etc.	10.00	10.00	10.00	10.00	10.00	10.00	10.00	10.00	10.00	10.00	10.00	10.00	120.
equipment	240.00	200.00	180.00										620.
loan repayments								45.00	45.00	45.00	45.00	45.00	225.
energy	1.00	10.00	10.00	15.00	20.00	20.00	20.00	20.00	20.00	20.00	20.00	25.00	201.
marketing	8.00	10.00	30.00	30.00	20.00	10.00	10.00	10.00	20.00	25.00	10.00	10.00	193
distribution			10.00	20.00	20.00	30.00	30.00	50.00	50.00	80.00	80.00	100.00	470.
TOTAL	349.00	320.00	370.00	225.00	230.00	230.00	280.00	465.00	475.00	510.00	495.00	580.00	4529.
PROFIT/LOSS	151.00	-120.00	-70.00	75.00	-30.00	20.00	-30.00	-65.00	25.00	-10.00	5.00	20.00	
BALANCE	151.00	31.00	-39.00	36.00	6.00	26.00	-4.00	-69.00	-44.00	-54.00	-49.00	-29.00	

16.16 Document study

Tibor is looking at the figures, trying to work out what they mean. He asks Alan a number of questions. Answer the questions for Alan, using the figures from the spreadsheet in 16.15.

1. In October, the balance is $151,000 – that's good! Why is it so high?
   Because you've got your start-up capital – that's $500,000 – and expenditure is low, except for a payment of $240,000 for equipment.
2. But by December we're $39,000 *in the red*. Why?
3. And then a month later, we're *in the black* again, $36,000. How come?
4. Then it goes down, then up in March. Why up in March?
5. The worst month is May. How can it be so bad?
6. Then after that it gets better, but why so slowly?

16.16
in the red in debit.
in the black in credit.

16.17
getting cold feet becoming afraid of doing something.

16.17 Listen and read

Alan and Tibor are discussing the figures on the spreadsheet. Listen to what they say. What is Alan's solution? Why does Tibor think that it won't work?

TIBOR This is why I wanted to talk to you yesterday before Foscatelli arrived. Isn't there some way we can delay repaying the bank loan? I don't want him to think I'm *getting cold feet*. If he gets cold feet as well, then it will all be – pouf!

ALAN Hm. Well, there's that figure for equipment. What's that? Six hundred and twenty thousand dollars altogether. If Melina would agree to postpone the start of repayments for a few months, that way you'd have a chance to build up some capital reserves.

TIBOR If we start to pay for the machinery in April – and spread the payments over six months instead of three. But won't she need the cash to build her new container terminal?

ALAN Not straight away. They have to clear the site first. She won't really need it till next year, when they're ready to start rebuilding.

TIBOR We'll pay her interest on what we owe her, of course. What if we make that a hundred and ten thousand dollars a month for six months, starting in April? Aagh! What's happened? The screen's gone blank.

ALAN It's all right, you've pressed the wrong key, that's all.

16.18 Find the right word

Read the text below on financing the recycling plant. Write a word from the box to fill each of the gaps.

Tibor Horvath plans to set up a ___**a**___ ___**b**___ which will ___**c**___ waste paper. He has got the support of Arturo Foscatelli, and when the ___**d**___ are complete, Horvath Paper will be a ___**e**___ of Metro-Polo. A bank loan has been approved in ___**f**___, with ___**g**___ spread over several years. Horvath intends to buy used machinery from a site in Greece which is to be redeveloped as a ___**h**___ ___**i**___. According to Alan Scott's ___**j**___ calculations, the company will still be deep in the red at the end of the first year. The ___**k**___ reason seems to be that Melina Karavatis is demanding immediate payment. If this can be ___**l**___ until the factory comes on stream, things will be easier. But Horvath appreciates the importance of economies of ___**m**___ in operating a business like this. The company won't start to make a profit until it is producing at least 500,000 dollars' worth of paper every month.

container formalities
mill paper
postponed principal
principle recycle
repayments scale
spreadsheet
subsidiary terminal

Study record	
16.1	
16.2	
16.3	
16.4	
16.5	
16.6	
16.7	
16.8	
16.9	
16.10	
16.11	
16.12	
16.13	
16.14	
16.15	
16.16	
16.17	
16.18	

Answer key and commentary for unit 16

16.1 Document study
Tibor Horvath's factory will need waste paper. Its main product will be recycled paper.

16.2 Listen and read
The desk clerk thinks that Tibor is probably in the hotel bar.

16.3 Document study
Tibor probably needs Arturo because he doesn't have enough money to finance his new project himself. He also wants Arturo to talk to Melina Karavatis about finance.

16.4 Listen and read
The problem is probably that the company's lawyers are still working on the details of the contract.

16.5 Reading for key words
1 agreement . . . has been reached in principle
2 no decision has been made as to timing
3 let me get this right; I am right in thinking, aren't I
4 to recycle waste paper
5 in a nutshell

16.6 Structure practice
1 The contract would have been signed if the formalities had been completed.
2 The formalities would have been completed if there hadn't been a legal problem.
3 We would have started work on the factory if the bank loan had been agreed.
4 We would have talked about the financing if Foscatelli hadn't arrived.

16.7 Listen and read
Shredded paper is easier to recycle, but it is also more expensive to transport.

16.8 Structure practice
These are model answers.
1 His country consumes huge amounts of paper.
2 It produces a great deal of waste paper.
3 He says his country is like most such bureaucracies.
4 The vast majority of government documents are confidential.
5 A few of them go into the archives.
6 A lot of official papers get shredded.
7 Most of the stuff goes into departmental filing cabinets.
8 Sooner or later all the filing cabinets are full.

16.9 Listen and read
Because it doesn't become profitable until it reaches a high level of production and sales. Tibor says 'Recycling only starts to pay when you achieve economies of scale.'

16.10 Reading for key words
1 in . . . triplicate
2 starts to pay
3 economies of scale
4 we've got to move fast on this project
5 a tall order

16.12 Listen and read
All of the paths are critical, because if one stage i completed five days late, the final completio date of the project will be at least five days late

Tibor's remark about government offices is joke.

16.13 Listen and read
Alan's figures are not likely to be very accurat He says he 'tried to sketch out' a cash-flo forecast, and that he 'didn't have very much to g on'. He thinks that they are accurate enough fo the purpose, however.

16.14 Reading for key words
1 to sketch out
2 I didn't have very much to go on
3 I'd like to see your reaction to it

16.16 Document study
These are model answers.
2 Because we've paid the full cost of th equipment – $620,000.
3 There are no more payments for machiner and sales are up to $200,000 a month, s there's a profit for the month of $75,000.
4 That's because sales have increased again, b costs haven't.
5 Well, a big increase in the cost of material and labour; and in May you start to pay bac the bank loan, that's $45,000 a month.
6 Mainly because sales don't rise at all for thre months; they're stuck at $500,000 a mon from June to the end of August.

16.17 Listen and read
Alan suggests postponing the payments to Melin Karavatis. Tibor thinks Melina will not agree t postpone payment for the machinery because sh will need the money to help to finance her ow project.

16.18 Find the right word
a paper
b mill
c recycle
d formalities
e subsidiary
f principle
g repayments
h container
i terminal
j spreadsheet
k principal
l postponed
m scale

Unit 17: Negotiating a deal

SITUATION

Nicole Vernay is a French dress designer who also runs a chain of small boutiques in Paris. She has come to Seoul, in South Korea, to negotiate two deals with Park Kyu Hun, who runs a clothing factory called Fashionpark. Nicole wants to buy his factory's ready-made clothes for resale in France and Park wants to buy the exclusive manufacturing rights to her dress designs. They have a lot of negotiating to do!

CHARACTERS

Nicole Vernay	is a dress designer. She is French.
Park Kyu Hun	is the owner of Fashionpark Corporation. He is Korean.

LANGUAGE

Vocabulary	Terms of business; licensing agreements; contracts and legal documents.
Skills	Negotiating the terms of a deal; countering an unacceptable suggestion; being firm, but flexible; understanding legal language.
Documents	A draft licensing agreement; letters; a spreadsheet.

Opening negotiations

17.1
I can save you the trouble I can make it unnecessary for you; in this case it means that Park has already done it.
You certainly don't waste any time here, Nicole is saying that Park has acted very quickly; she is surprised and annoyed.
Clause 14 a clause is a numbered section or paragraph in a legal document.

17.2
licensee a person who has been given a licence to do something.
be entitled to have the right to.
(a) garment an item of clothing; **garment** is a slightly formal word, used by people who work in the clothing business.
licensor a person who gives a licence to another person; a **licensor** usually agrees to allow a **licensee** to use or sell the **licensor's** products.
whatsoever at all; **whatsoever** is used to make a point very strongly.
the term of this agreement the time when the agreement is in force; notice that **the terms of this agreement** means the conditions of this agreement.

17.3
In consideration of in return for; in payment for. A contract is not normally valid unless there is a **consideration**, a payment of some kind.
aforesaid already mentioned; **aforesaid** is a very formal word, usually used only in legal documents.
in advance before; here the payment must be made before any goods are sold.
the equivalent thereof other money of the same value; this is a very formal phrase.
in arrears after; here the payment must be made after any goods have been sold.
a royalty a payment made for the use of someone's goods or property; here Park is paying for the use of Nicole Vernay's name on the clothes.
In the event of if; this is a very formal phrase.

17.1 Listen and read

Park Kyu Hun and Nicole Vernay are negotiating two deals: he wants to manufacture the dresses that she designs, and she wants to buy the made-up dresses from him for sale in her shops. They are travelling in a car from her hotel to the Fashionpark offices, to start their second session of talks. Listen to what they say. Why is Nicole surprised?

NICOLE I thought we should begin today by going over again the main points we agreed yesterday. Then this afternoon I can telephone my lawyer in Paris.

PARK *I can save you the trouble*, Miss Vernay. I talked to my lawyers last night, and we drafted the agreement. It was faxed to Paris immediately.

NICOLE Ah! *You certainly don't waste any time.* Did you include what we said about exclusive rights to the Nicole Vernay label?

PARK I've got the document here. There. *Clause 14.*

17.2 Document study – 1

The agreement is a very formal document. Clause 14 is shown below. Listen to Nicole read it. Notice how she breaks up the long sentences into short word groups to help her understand and check the document. Put a slash / to mark where each word group begins and ends.

Clause 14
The *licensee* shall *be entitled to* attach to each *garment* manufactured under the terms of this agreement a label supplied by the *licensor* and bearing the name and trade mark of the licensor. The licensor shall not use nor permit any other individual or company to use a similar label or to attach a similar label to any garment *whatsoever* during *the term of this agreement.*

17.3 Document study – 2

Nicole reads Clauses 17 and 18 of the agreement. Listen to her, and put a slash / to mark where she breaks up the document.

Clause 17
In consideration of the *aforesaid* licence, the licensee shall make the following payments to the licensor:
(a) *in advance* on the first day of each month a licence fee of US$100,000 or *the equivalent thereof* in French francs at the current rate of exchange.
(b) at the end of each quarter and *in arrears a royalty* of 5% (five per cent) calculated in US dollars on the f.o.b. value of all goods invoiced under the terms of this agreement during the quarter.

Clause 18
In the event of any payment being due from the licensor to the licensee, the licensee shall be entitled to deduct from the licence fee a sum of money in full or partial payment of the amount owed by the licensor to the licensee.

17.4 Listen and read

Park and Nicole continue their journey. Listen to what they say. Why does Park think that Nicole would accept Clause 18? Why does Nicole object to Clause 18?

NICOLE Er – *what's going on here?* Mr Park, I think you are trying *to get one jump ahead* of me here.

PARK Oh, you are looking at Clause 18 – *setting off* your debts *against* our fee payments. I mentioned it in my letter.

NICOLE I'm sorry, Mr Park, this point is just *not negotiable*. There is no way I could *consent* to linking the two agreements together like this. They are two quite separate deals.

PARK I think we would find my proposal well worth considering. We'd save time and bank charges. Not so many *transfers* and *letters of credit* – a simple entry each month in the account books. Then we *settle up* at the end of the period. What's wrong with that?

NICOLE *Nice try*, Mr Park, but you know very well what's wrong with it – you're asking me to give you a big slice of free credit. You don't even allow me the *normal terms of trade, payment at ninety days*. Just when I need cash – for advertising, *trade shows* – I get nothing! I must have more money *up front*.

PARK I'm sure we can find a way round this. Look – we have already found a way through the traffic. Let's go up to my office and talk there.

17.4
what's going on here? 'what's happening here?' Nicole is surprised and annoyed.
to get one jump ahead to do something to gain an advantage over somebody else; an informal phrase.
setting off (x) against (y) subtracting x from y; arranging for a debit to cancel out a credit.
not negotiable here, Nicole means that what Park wants is not possible; her position is fixed and she will not negotiate.
consent agree.
transfers payments of money from one person to another.
letters of credit letters sent from one bank to another bank, saying that a person should be given some money.
settle up pay what is due.
Nice try Nicole is saying to Park that she knows he is trying to trick her.
normal terms of trade usual rules for doing business together, in this case for paying bills.
payment at ninety days payment ninety days after the date shown on the invoice.
trade shows events at which a designer shows the new season's dresses to other people in the fashion business, fashion journalists, buyers for shops and stores, etc.
up front as a payment in advance; an informal phrase.

17.5 Find the word: licensing agreements

Read the text below on licensing agreements. Write a word from the box to fill each of the gaps.

advance	arrears
clauses	exclusive
fee	licence
licensee	licensor
period	royalty
term	terms
trade	

A company may want to use another company's ideas, designs, or just its name. Every country has laws protecting these things through the registration of patents or copyrights. A ___**a**___ to use another company's ___**b**___ mark can be bought just as its products can be bought, and the price is negotiable, though the process is often complicated; each side is anxious to protect its rights. Business people and their lawyers spend much time and care in negotiating and drafting the ___**c**___ of licensing agreements; even a simple agreement may contain many ___**d**___ . The owner of the idea or design is the ___**e**___ ; the company that wants to use it is the ___**f**___.

Mr Park will be entitled to use Nicole Vernay's designs only for a limited ___**g**___ – the ___**h**___ of the agreement – and under certain conditions. For example, the licensee must pay 'consideration'; without this, no contract is valid. This will be in the form of a fixed amount, a license ___**i**___ , payable in ___**j**___ at the beginning of each quarter, and a ___**k**___, payable in ___**l**___, based on the quantity of Nicole Vernay clothes he has sold during the quarter. The agreement is ___**m**___ ; Nicole cannot allow any other manufacturer to produce clothes to her designs while the contract is in force.

17.6 Writing practice: dictation

Listen again to Nicole reading the clauses from the contract in 17.2 and 17.3. As you listen, write what she says. When you have finished, compare what you have written with the printed clauses in 17.2 and 17.3. You might like to cover up 17.2 and 17.3 while you do this exercise.

Being firm

17.7
I appreciate I understand.
To compensate to pay for something that has been lost; here, Park is offering Nicole a discount because she may have to pay more for her overdraft.
exchange rates the rates for changing money from one currency into another.
It's the thin end of the wedge it's something which seems all right now, but which may be the beginning of something bad.
come on don't ask me to believe things that are obviously not true.

17.8
playing for time trying to make something happen at a later date, so that you gain an advantage.
obstacles problems.
on the same wavelength sharing the same view of things; Nicole is saying that she and Park have such different ideas that they will never agree.

17.7 Listen and read

Nicole and Park are now in the Fashionpark office. Listen to what they say. What arguments does Park use to try to persuade Nicole to accept Clause 18?

PARK Surely the way to fix this is for me to give you a discount on the shipments that I send you. *I appreciate* that if I don't pay you cash on the first of the month, that may increase your overdraft. *To compensate* you for that, I'll give you a discount on the price of the clothes. Your accountant will tell you it's the same in the end, either way.

NICOLE In theory, maybe, but it's too complicated. This is the real reason why I don't want the two agreements to be linked. Both of us will spend time and energy worrying about *exchange rates* and discounts when we should be selling clothes.

PARK I'm sure you have an accountant, and your accountant has a computer – they will do the work for you!

NICOLE *It's the thin end of the wedge.* We shall end up, each of us, convinced that the other is cheating. Neither of us will be happy.

PARK Oh, really, Miss Vernay – I think you exaggerate the difficulties. As I told you, in order to pay you, I have to purchase foreign currency through my bank, and I must do this when the exchange rate is favourable.

NICOLE Oh *come on*, Mr Park! You're not trying to tell me that your company doesn't have a US bank account?

PARK Ah! But we must also consider Korean tax laws, which are very strict.

17.8 Listen and read

Nicole and Park continue their discussion. Listen to what they say. What words and phrases does Nicole use here and in 17.7 to show that she thinks Park is simply trying to trick or mislead her?

PARK There are many problems in doing foreign currency deals overseas if one is importing.

NICOLE But you're not importing, you're paying a licence fee!

PARK I would have to discuss the matter in detail with my financial advisers.

NICOLE Now you're just *playing for time.*

PARK I assure you . . .

NICOLE Mr Park, I simply do not understand why you are creating *obstacles* to a perfectly simple agreement. I'm very sorry, but we don't appear to be *on the same wavelength* here at all. I'm going to have lunch. No, thank you – I will take a taxi and have lunch by myself. I'll come back at three o'clock and I hope that we can sort it all out then.

17.9 Speaking practice: being firm

Listen to this conversation. Then listen again, and speak the part of the man.

WOMAN This deal's too complicated. We shall each end up thinking that the other is cheating.

MAN Oh really! I think you exaggerate the difficulties. As I told you, I have to purchase foreign currency.

WOMAN Oh come on! You're not trying to tell me that your company doesn't have a US bank account?

MAN Well, I would have to discuss the matter with my financial advisers.

WOMAN Now you're just playing for time! I'm sorry, but we don't appear to be on the same wavelength here at all. I'm going to have lunch. I'll come back at three o'clock and I hope we can sort it all out then.

17.10 Document study

Park decides to read through the file of his correspondence with Nicole. Read the letters. How did Nicole first contact Park?

Nicole Vernay
PARIS

11th February 1991

Dear Mr Park

Your name has been given to me by the Commercial Attaché of the Korean Embassy in Paris. I am a dress designer and I am also building up a chain of *in-store boutiques* selling Nicole Vernay-branded ready-made dresses.

Fashionpark
CORPORATION

04/03/91

Dear Miss Vernay

Thank you for your telephone call confirming our appointment to meet at your salon on the occasion of the presentation of your *autumn collection*. I look forward to seeing you in Paris.

Nicole Vernay
PARIS

24th August 1991

Dear Mr Park

I am glad to be able to tell you that the first *consignment* of Fashionpark suits and *accessories* arrived safely on Tuesday, and the reaction to samples rushed to our boutiques has been extremely favourable. Our *pilot scheme* seems to have been entirely successful. I look forward to visiting you in Seoul to negotiate the licensing and purchase agreements for the spring collection.

31/08/91

Dear Miss Vernay

Thank you for your letter of 24 August. My colleagues and I will be very pleased to welcome you on your first visit to Seoul and to our company. Before we meet, you may like to consider the possibility of payments between us being set off against each other so that we reduce the actual transfer of cash to a minimum. This would reduce bank charges and simplify accounting for both parties. I am aware that it may *have implications* with regard to discounts and credit, but I am confident we can reach agreement on such matters during your visit.

I intend to meet you at the airport myself, provided no urgent business arises at short notice, and to escort you to your hotel. I trust your stay in Seoul will be a pleasant and productive one.

Yours sincerely

17.10
in-store boutiques small shops selling a particular type of goods inside a large department store.
autumn collection a range of clothes for wearing in the autumn.
consignment load.
accessories things you wear with clothes; hats, belts, scarves, jewellery, etc.
(a) pilot scheme a small scheme to test whether a much larger operation would be successful.
have implications here, have an effect on other matters.

17.11 Writing practice

Suppose that, instead of speaking to Park in Seoul, Nicole had to write to him in reply to his letter of 31 August. Write the letter for her, using her arguments from 17.4, 17.7 and 17.8.

Drawing closer to an agreement

17.12
an irrevocable letter of credit a letter of credit that cannot be cancelled or changed.
(a) sight bill a bill of exchange which must be paid when it is presented; it doesn't matter what date is on it, it must be paid immediately or 'on sight'.
a one-off payment a payment which is made only once; not a regular payment.
to call in my overdraft to force me to pay in enough money to end my overdraft at very short notice. A bank normally has the right to do this at any time, either because it is short of funds or because it suspects the borrower is about to go bankrupt.
stretch a point allow a rule to be broken in a small way on a special occasion; Park is saying that he may be a little more generous than the agreement says.

17.13
shortfall the amount needed to make up the full amount; here, the difference in Nicole's balance if she accepts Park's proposals.

17.12 Listen and read

Nicole and Park meet again after lunch. What is Park's latest offer? How does he 'extend' his offer?

PARK — Hello again, Miss Vernay. I hope you had a good lunch. I've been thinking about things, and I believe I have come up with a solution.

NICOLE — That is good news!

PARK — This is what I suggest. On the day the agreement comes into force, I will open *an irrevocable letter of credit* at your bank in Paris and I will accept your *sight bill* for an advance payment against royalties.

NICOLE — How large an advance?

PARK — A hundred thousand dollars.

NICOLE — I'm sorry – a hundred thousand is no use to me as *a one-off payment*. I must have a decent cash flow every month, in case the bank decides *to call in my overdraft* – which will be more like half a million!

PARK — Well, in case of emergency, I'm sure we could *stretch a point*.

NICOLE — Mr Park, over lunch, I've been looking again at the cash-flow figures I worked out before I came here. These figures are for the six months of the agreement and then three months afterwards. The printed figures show how I want to do it. On the right of each column I've put in the figures for what you want to do – setting off my debts against yours each month.

17.13 Figure practice

When Nicole is back in Paris, one of her colleagues questions her about the figures. Read the spreadsheet carefully, and then answer these questions for Nicole.

All amounts are in US$ x 1000

	OCT	NOV	DEC	JAN	FEB	MAR	APR	MAY	JUN
NV orders	150.00	150.00	150.00	150.00	150.00	150.00			
NV's INCOME									
fee	100.00 (0)	100.00 (0)	100.00 (0)	100.00 (0)	100.00 (0)	100.00 (0)			
royalty				500.00			500.00		
NV sales				200.00	200.00	200.00	200.00	200.00	200.00
LESS									
NV pays				-150.00 (-50)	-150.00 (-50)	-150.00 (-50)	-150.00 (-50)	-150.00 (-50)	-150.00 (-50)
total for month	100.00 (0)	100.00 (0)	100.00 (0)	650.00 (650)	150.00 (150)	150.00 (150)	550.00 (650)	50.00 (150)	50.00 (150)
balance	100.00 (0)	200.00 (0)	300.00 (0)	950.00 (650)	1100.00 (800)	1250.00 (950)	1800.00 (1600)	1850.00 (1750)	1900.00 (1900)
NV's shortfall	100	200	300	300	300	300	200	100	0
Interest @ 18% p.a.	1.5	3	4.5	4.5	4.5	4.5	3	1.5	

1. These amounts look very small. Is he really only going to pay a hundred dollars a month?
2. Why has somebody written different figures on the spreadsheet?
3. Why didn't he want to pay you anything as a fee?
4. If you stop ordering goods in March, why do you go on paying until June?
5. What percentage profit do you make on the clothes you import from Park to sell in France?
6. If Fashionpark pays you a 5% royalty, what's their total annual turnover expected to be?

17.14 Document study

Look at the spreadsheet again. What is the result of Park's proposal to Nicole's figures? How much would it cost Nicole in interest payments?

17.15 Listen and read

Nicole and Park are about to finish their discussion. Listen to what they say. How did Nicole calculate her interest payments? Why does Park think that the new figures don't make any difference?

PARK — But this is *hypothetical* – you are guessing what the royalty will be, and how big your orders will be.

NICOLE — Oh? I thought we agreed on these figures as the basis for discussion a month ago?

PARK — Well, there you are, then! You see – the result is the same either way, just as I said! *You may clear two million dollars.*

NICOLE — I need two million dollars! But look at the differences between the balances, month by month, and then the interest I have to pay each month on my overdraft. I'm just reckoning eighteen per cent annually, that's one point five per cent a month at simple interest. If you total those interest payments, they come to twenty-seven thousand dollars! If anyone's going to pay that much interest, it should be Fashionpark, not Nicole Vernay.

PARK — Can't you pass it on to your customers?

NICOLE — Why should my customers pay you twenty-seven thousand dollars? Look, I'll tell you what. You make me an interest-free loan of three hundred thousand dollars for a period of three months, starting on the date the contract starts . . .

PARK — I'd be better off paying you a hundred thousand a month. Hm. I wonder, though. Perhaps I could arrange some sort of *guarantee* with my bank. Would you excuse me while I make a phone call?

17.15
hypothetical based on what is imagined rather than what is true; Park is suggesting that Nicole has simply made up the figures as an example.
You may clear two million dollars you may make a net profit of two million dollars.
(a) guarantee a promise by a bank to a creditor to pay a sum of money if a debtor fails to pay.

17.16
go along with agree to; an informal phrase.
the small print the part of a legal document that contains all of the details; it is often written in smaller print than the rest of the document.

17.16 Listen and read

Nicole and Park have now reached agreement. What has Park agreed to pay Nicole? What has Nicole agreed in return?

PARK — So, as part of our contract, Fashionpark will include a clause guaranteeing a minimum royalty payment of three hundred thousand dollars on 1 December, three months into the contract period.

NICOLE — Yes, I think my bank will *go along with* that – it'll enable me to get my overdraft extended if I have to. And on my side I agree to any money I owe you being offset against the monthly licence fee. In return you will give an additional two point five per cent discount on all invoices.

PARK — Yes – on the f.o.b. price, that is.

NICOLE — Well, I'm very encouraged by the conversations we've had.

PARK — I'm confident we're going to have a very big success this spring.

NICOLE — I'll have to go through *the small print* with my lawyer and my accountant. But I don't think there will be any problems. Thank you for everything you've done, Mr Park. I've enjoyed my visit and I look forward to seeing you in Paris in the New Year. Au revoir!

PARK — Au revoir, mademoiselle. You'll be hearing from me soon. Have a good flight!

17.17 Reading for key words

Find the words or phrases in 17.15 and 17.16 that tell you the following:

1. This may happen, but it is not certain.
2. I don't think they ought to pay.
3. I've got a suggestion to make.
4. Lend me some money, with no interest.
5. It would be more profitable for me.
6. The contract will compel Fashionpark to pay a minimum royalty.
7. Three months after the contract comes into force.
8. Agree to that course of action.
9. Make it possible for me to.
10. Discuss every detail of the agreement.

Study record	
17.1	
17.2	
17.3	
17.4	
17.5	
17.6	
17.7	
17.8	
17.9	
17.10	
17.11	
17.12	
17.13	
17.14	
17.15	
17.16	
17.17	

Answer key and commentary for unit 17

17.1 Listen and read
Nicole is surprised that Park has already faxed the agreement to Paris. She thought she should have seen it first.

17.2 Document study
The licensee / shall be entitled to attach to each garment / manufactured under the terms of this agreement / a label supplied by the licensor / and bearing the name and trade mark of the licensor. / The licensor shall not use / nor permit any other individual or company to use / a similar label / or to attach a similar label to any garment whatsoever / during the term of this agreement.

17.3 Document study
17. / In consideration of the aforesaid licence, / the licensee shall make the following payments / to the licensor: / (a) / in advance / on the first day of each month / a licence fee of US$100,000 / or the equivalent thereof / in French francs / at the current rate of exchange. / (b) / at the end of each quarter / and in arrears /a royalty of 5% (five per cent) / calculated in US dollars / on the f.o.b. value of all goods invoiced under the terms of this agreement / during the quarter.

18. / In the event of any payment being due / from the licensor / to the licensee, / the licensee shall be entitled / to deduct from the licence fee / a sum of money / in full or partial payment / of the amount owed by the licensor to the licensee.

17.4 Listen and read
Park thinks that Nicole would accept Clause 18 because it makes the paperwork simpler. Nicole objects to it because it means that she will get part of her money from him several months late.

17.5 Find the word
a licence **b** trade **c** terms **d** clauses
e licensor **f** licensee **g** period
h term **i** fee **j** advance **k** royalty
l arrears **m** exclusive

17.7 Listen and read
Park offers Nicole a discount to compensate her for her extra costs.

17.8 Listen and read
In 17.7 Nicole says 'Oh come on, Mr Park'. In 17.8 she says 'Now you're just playing for time'.

17.10 Document study
Nicole was given Park's name by the Commercial Attaché of the Korean Embassy in Paris.

17.11 Writing practice
This is a model answer; there are many possible ways of writing this letter.

17.12 Listen and read
Park offers Nicole an advance payment of $100,000. He 'extends' his offer by saying that, in an emergency, he could 'stretch a point' and offer her some more money.

17.13 Figure practice
These are model answers.
1 Look, it says at the top – these figures are in thousands of dollars.
2 I wrote those figures in to show what would happen if I agreed to Park's proposal.
3 Oh, he was going to pay eventually. He wanted to deduct from each month's fee the cost of the goods I ordered during that month.
4 Because I pay for the goods ninety days after the date of the invoice. I start ordering in October, but I don't start paying until January.
5 As you see, I reckon I order a hundred thousand dollars' worth each month, and I sell two hundred thousand dollars' worth. So the profit is one hundred per cent – on paper.
6 They pay five hundred thousand dollars a quarter. That's two million dollars a year, so their turnover must be forty million dollars.

17.14 Document study
The result of Park's suggestion is that Nicole's monthly balances are lower. This would cost Nicole $27,000 in interest charges.

17.15 Listen and read
Nicole calculated her interest payments at 1.5 per cent a month at simple interest. Park thinks that the figures don't make any difference because Nicole will still make $2 million.

17.16 Listen and read
Park has agreed to pay Nicole $300,000 on 1 December, and to allow her an additional 2.5% discount on all invoices. Nicole has agreed that money she owes Park can be offset against the licence fee.

17.17 Reading for key words
1 this is hypothetical
2 Why should my customers pay
3 I'll tell you what
4 make me an interest-free loan
5 I'd be better off
6 a clause guaranteeing a minimum royalty payment
7 three months into the contract period
8 go along with that
9 enable me to
10 go through the small print

Dear Mr Park,

Thank you for your letter dated 31 August. I read your suggestion that my debts should be set off against your fee payments, and I think there are some problems with this idea. First, the two deals are quite separate and should not be linked like this. We would spend time and money working out exchange rates when we should be working at selling more clothes. Second, the arrangement would involve me in giving you free credit. This is a problem for me when I need cash most, for advertising and trade shows. Third, I don't agree that the present arrangements are a problem. Both of our companies have lawyers and accountants who are used to dealing internationally.

So, I'm afraid that I cannot consent to your suggestion.

I look forward to meeting you in Seoul to discuss this further.

An overseas contract

Unit 18: Buying from an overseas supplier

SITUATION

Nicole Vernay also sells her clothes in the United States. Karen Shersteen is a fashion buyer for Skopje's, a big department store in Los Angeles. She wants to order the new clothes from Nicole's spring collection, but because Fashionpark has the exclusive rights to manufacture Nicole Vernay designs, Karen must order from Korea. We look at how the supplier organises the goods to be shipped from the factory to California and how they are paid for by the customer.

CHARACTERS

Nicole Vernay

Park Kyu Hun

Karen Shersteen — is the fashion buyer for Skopje's Department Store, Los Angeles. She is American.

LANGUAGE

Vocabulary — International trade; finance and documents.

Skills — Offering and receiving congratulations and commiserations.

Documents — Covering letters; documentary credits; letters of agreement; bill of lading; bill of exchange.

Placing an order

18.1
fashion correspondents people who write about fashion for newspapers and magazines.
to file their stories to send their articles to newspaper editors.
the sweatshops the small factories or workshops, where people work in poor conditions for low pay.
turning out producing at high speed.
exclusives clothes with the Nicole Vernay label, which are supposed to be produced only by Nicole Vernay's licensee.
to ship to send to the customer.
they'll have you all stitched up here, they will make money from your work, and you won't be able to stop them.
pirates people who copy and sell goods when they have no right to do so.

18.1 Listen and read

Karen Shersteen is in Paris, where she has just been watching the showing of Nicole Vernay's spring collection. What is Karen worried about? Why is Nicole not worried?

KAREN	Nicole, the dresses are wonderful, and my customers on the West Coast are going to love them.
NICOLE	Thank you. There were one or two tricky moments, but I think it all worked out in the end.
KAREN	One thing in the show did bother me, though.
NICOLE	Really? What was that?
KAREN	All those so-called *fashion correspondents* with their sketch books, sketching everything that came through the door. I don't see them here at the reception.
NICOLE	Oh, they've gone off *to file their stories* for tomorrow's newspapers.
KAREN	Some of them, maybe, but a lot of them are busy faxing those sketches back home to *the sweatshops*. By tomorrow they'll be *turning out* Nicole Vernay *exclusives* ready *to ship* – and *they'll have you all stitched up*.
NICOLE	Well, I've signed a deal with a very respectable firm in South Korea. They already have my designs, so I hope that the *pirates* won't be able to compete.
KAREN	Great idea! Does that mean I have to order from Korea as well?
NICOLE	Yes, I'm sorry, Karen – Skopje's will have to place its orders with Fashionpark just like everyone else. Even I have to get my stock from them – for my own little boutiques here in Paris.

18.2 Speaking practice: congratulations

Listen to this conversation. Then listen again and speak the part of the man.

WOMAN	Congratulations on the presentation you gave this morning. I must say, I thought it was really excellent.
MAN	Oh! Well, it's very kind of you to say so. I hope it achieves something.
WOMAN	I particularly liked the way you handled the questions at the end.
MAN	Thank you. Some of them were a bit tricky, but I think it all worked out OK.

18.3 Find the word: documentary credits – 1

Read the text below on documentary credits. Write a word from the box to fill each of the gaps.

charges charges
cost credit
credit
documentary
forwarders insured
irrevocable letter
place premium
pro-forma shipped

Selling your goods overseas is never as simple as selling them at home. But the exporter has plenty of professional help to call on. The business of transporting the goods is usually entrusted to a firm of freight ___**a**___ . They will arrange for the goods to be ___**b**___ by sea or by air and for all freight ___**c**___to be paid. They handle all the necessary documentation and arrange for the shipment to be ___**d**___ against all risks.

Banks also offer many services which make life easier and more secure for exporters and importers. Among these are ___**e**___ credits, which facilitate payment. Suppose your overseas customer says that he wishes to ___**f**___ an order with you. You calculate the total ___ **g** ___ of the goods, add on the insurance ___**h**___ (fixed by the insurance company) and freight ___**i**___ (fixed by the freight forwarder), and send him a ___ **j** ___ invoice. He instructs his bank to open a ___**k**___ in your favour for the amount of the invoice and to inform your bank, who in turn will advise you of the details. The ___**l**___ of ___**m**___ (L/C for short) is normally ___**n**___ : that is, the customer cannot recall or cancel it.

18.4 Listen and read

Karen Shersteen contacts Park on the telephone. Listen to what they say. Do you think Fashionpark is an efficient business? Why?

KAREN Oh hello – is that Mr Park?
PARK Speaking.
KAREN Hello, Mr Park. My name is Karen Shersteen and I'm interested in your products. I'm the buyer for Skopje's, that's a big store over here in LA.
PARK Yes, of course. I know Skopje's well.
KAREN You've heard of it, good. Now, Mr Park, I was in Paris last week and I saw some dresses by Nicole Vernay and I was just swept off my feet.
PARK They are good, aren't they? I'm very pleased to have the exclusive rights to manufacture Mademoiselle Vernay's spring collection.
KAREN Yes, that's what she told me. That's why I'm calling you now, Mr Park.
PARK I expect that you would like to see our catalogue and price list?
KAREN A catalogue and price list, that's precisely what I want.
PARK In fact, we have already sent them to you by air mail – you should receive them in a day or two.
KAREN Oh, have you? Oh well, in that case I guess all I have to do is sit back and wait.

18.5 Document study

When Karen faxed her order to Fashionpark, she sent the covering letter below. What do Fashionpark have to do? They acknowledged Karen's letter. What does Karen have to do?

18.5
promotions publicity campaigns.
documents against acceptance the customer needs the shipping documents so that the goods can be released from customs. These documents will be handed over by the bank as soon as the customer signs, or accepts, the supplier's bill of exchange.
documentary credit an arrangement between an exporter, an importer and their banks. The importer's bank will make credit available when it receives the correct documents from the exporter.
freight forwarders a company that prepares the documents and arranges for the transport of goods for a fee.
c.i.f. 'cost, insurance, freight'; the supplier has already paid the insurance premium and the freight charges, so these are shown on the invoice and repaid by the customer.

1001 Pacific Boulevard
Los Angeles

Overseas Sales Manager
Fashionpark Corporation
PO Box 12236
Seoul

18 December 1991

Dear Sir

Following my recent telephone conversation with Mr Park, I enclose our order no. 5529. Please inform me immediately if any items in it are not available, as I have to plan our spring *promotions* and fashion display within the next three weeks. It would be greatly appreciated if you could airfreight a sample of each garment at once, so that we can model them for our own photographs.

We understand that your terms are payment at 90 days, *documents against acceptance*, and that you require *documentary credit* to be opened with the Korean Trading Bank. Our bankers are First California Commercial, Albuquerque Plaza, Los Angeles. Please also ask your *freight forwarders* to advise us of their expected delivery date.

Yours faithfully

Karen Shersteen
Chief Buyer

PO Box 12236
Seoul

Miss Karen Shersteen
Chief Buyer
Skopje's Department Store
Los Angeles

19 December 1991

Dear Miss Shersteen

Thank you for your message of 18 December and order no. 5529. I am happy to say that we can supply every item that you require. A parcel has been dispatched to you via Delivery Express, and will reach you within three days. I hope very much that you will find everything in it completely to your satisfaction; your comments will be welcomed.

We enclose our pro-forma invoice for the complete shipment, which you will see totals US$117,000, *c.i.f.* San Francisco. Please make arrangements for an irrevocable credit to be opened in our favour with the Korean Trading Bank for this amount. As soon as we are advised by the bank that this has been done, the consignment will be shipped.

We are pleased to have this opportunity of doing business with you, and we hope that there will be many more.

Sincerely

for Fashionpark

Arranging credit

18.6
certificate of origin a document that shows in what country goods were made, and usually what country the raw materials and/or components come from.
authenticated the chamber of commerce stamps the certificate to show that the information it gives is correct.
chamber of commerce an association of local business people.
bills of lading documents showing that goods have been safely loaded onto a ship. There are several copies, so the bank requires a full set.
to buyer's warehouse until the goods have reached the buyer's warehouse safely.
plus 10% the goods must be insured for 10% more than the value shown on the invoice.

18.7
endorsed here, stamped and signed by the exporter's bank as an additional guarantee that the goods have been sent and payment can therefore be made.
as per instructions in the way that the instructions say.

18.6 Document study

These two documents are part of the arrangements between Skopje's and Fashionpark. For each document: who sends it, and to whom? What action will be taken by the company that receives it?

DOCUMENTARY CREDIT

TO **FIRST CALIFORNIA** Commercial Bank

Request to open ▲ Documentary Credit

BRANCH Los Angeles

DATE 01/20/92

Please open for our Account a Documentary Credit in accordance with the undermentioned particulars.

SIGNED A.W. Macaulay

Method of Advice	AIRMAIL (TELEX) CABLE
Type of credit	(IRREVOCABLE) REVOCABLE
Date of expiry	ENTER DATE 02/28/92

853921 SKOPJE'S CAL

CONS. NO. 2324 01.20.92

1.20.92

FASHIONPARK CORPORATION
FTAO: OVERSEAS SALES

FROM: SHERSTEEN
SKOPJE'S DEPT STORE

WE INFORM YOU THAT WE HAVE TODAY OPENED AN IRREVOCABLE LETTER OF CREDIT IN YOUR FAVOUR WITH THE FIRST CALIFORNIA COMMERCIAL BANK.
THE CREDIT IS ON THE ACCOUNT OF SKOPJE'S DEPARTMENT STORE AND IS TO THE AMOUNT OF US$117,000 (ONE HUNDRED AND SEVENTEEN THOUSAND UNITED STATES DOLLARS), VALID UNTIL FEBRUARY 28 1992. YOUR DRAFT FOR THE ABOVE AMOUNT WILL BE ACCEPTED IF ACCOMPANIED BY:
1. INVOICE (4 COPIES, SIGNED)
2. *CERTIFICATE OF ORIGIN AUTHENTICATED* BY *CHAMBER OF COMMERCE*
3. FULL SET OF CLEAN ON-BOARD SHIPPING COMPANY'S *BILLS OF LADING* MARKED 'FREIGHT PAID' AND 'NOTIFY SKOPJE'S LOS ANGELES' (3 COPIES).
4. INSURANCE CERTIFICATE (2 COPIES) COVERING MARINE AND WAR RISKS *TO BUYER'S WAREHOUSE*, FOR INVOICED VALUE *PLUS 10%*.

REGARDS
KAREN SHERSTEEN
853921 SKOPJE'S CAL

18.7 Document study

The freight forwarder writes to Skopje's to say that the goods have been shipped. Read the letter carefully, and check the details against the bill of lading in 18.8. Are the details correct?

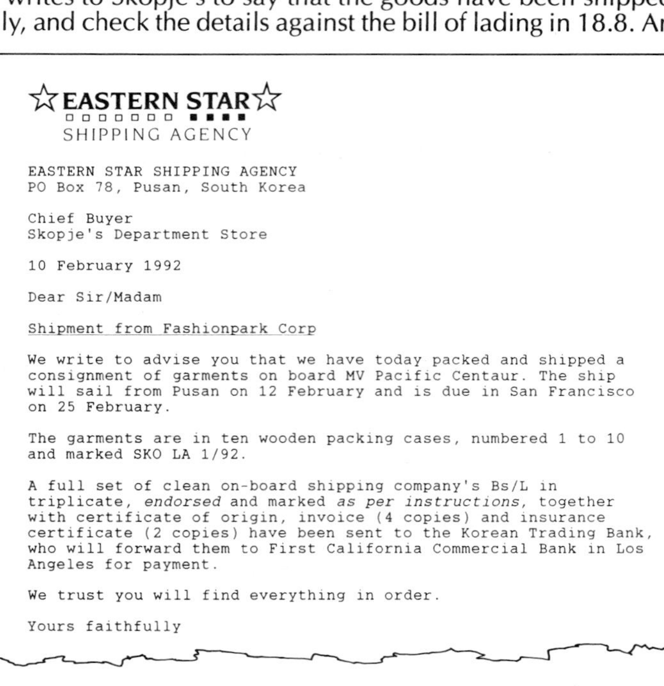

☆EASTERN STAR☆
SHIPPING AGENCY

EASTERN STAR SHIPPING AGENCY
PO Box 78, Pusan, South Korea

Chief Buyer
Skopje's Department Store

10 February 1992

Dear Sir/Madam

Shipment from Fashionpark Corp

We write to advise you that we have today packed and shipped a consignment of garments on board MV Pacific Centaur. The ship will sail from Pusan on 12 February and is due in San Francisco on 25 February.

The garments are in ten wooden packing cases, numbered 1 to 10 and marked SKO LA 1/92.

A full set of clean on-board shipping company's Bs/L in triplicate, *endorsed* and marked *as per instructions*, together with certificate of origin, invoice (4 copies) and insurance certificate (2 copies) have been sent to the Korean Trading Bank, who will forward them to First California Commercial Bank in Los Angeles for payment.

We trust you will find everything in order.

Yours faithfully

18.8 Document study

You work as a clerk in the buying department of Skopje's. A customs official rings, asking for particulars of the bill of lading. Read the official's part of the conversation, and write down the clerk's replies using the details from the bill of lading below and the letter in 18.7. Then listen to the conversation and check what you wrote.

OFFICIAL OK. What's the serial number?
CLERK ___a___
OFFICIAL And is there a reference number for the forwarding agent?
CLERK ___b___
OFFICIAL OK. Consignee's name and address, please.
CLERK ___c___
OFFICIAL And the name of the ship?
CLERK ___d___
OFFICIAL Loading Inchon, is that right?
CLERK ___e___
OFFICIAL And where's she discharging?
CLERK ___f___
OFFICIAL Now, I need the details of marks and numbers on the cases.
CLERK ___g___
OFFICIAL Right, now the number and description of the packages.
CLERK ___h___
OFFICIAL Gross weight?
CLERK ___i___
OFFICIAL Any measurements?
CLERK ___j___
OFFICIAL Now give me the place and date of issue of the bill of lading.
CLERK ___k___
OFFICIAL And the number of bills in the set.
CLERK ___l___
OFFICIAL OK, thank you.
CLERK You're welcome. Have a nice day!

BILL OF LADING

© GCBS 1979

Shipper: Fashionpark Corporation

Shipper's Reference: 34/92

F/Agent's Reference: 05/92

Serial No. 175

Consignee (if "Order" state Notify Party and Address):
Skopje's Department Store
1001 Pacific Boulevard
Los Angeles
California 96034

Name of Carrier: Eastern Star Shipping Agency

Notify Party and Address (leave blank if stated above):

Pre-carriage by*	Place of Receipt by Pre-Carrier*
Vessel	**Port of Loading**
MV PACIFIC CENTAUR	PUSAN
Port of Discharge	**Place of Delivery by On-Carrier***
SAN FRANCISCO	

*Applicable only when document used as a Through Bill of Lading

Particulars declared by Shipper

Marks and Nos: Container No.	Number and kind of packages: Description of Goods	Gross Weight	Measurement
SKO LA 1/92 1 – 10	10 Packing cases: clothes	9736 kgs	1.75 x 2.9 x 0.95m = 48.3m³

Freight Details: Charges etc.

Ocean Freight Payable at	Place and Date of Issue
Prepaid	Seoul 9.2 1992
Number of Original Bs/L	**Signature for Carrier: Carrier's Principal Place of Business**
Three	Eastern Star Shipping Agency

18.9 Find the word: documentary credits – 2

Read the text below on documentary credits. Write a word from the box to fill each of the gaps.

Your customer has opened an irrevocable credit on his account and in your favour. You can now go ahead and ___a___ the goods. You must not delay too long; the credit is only valid until its ___b___ date. As soon as the goods are on board ship, the bill of ___c___ is signed and sent to your freight forwarder. You can now send it to your bank with the other documents which will enable ___d___ to be made. The first is the ___e___, showing the total cost 'c.i.f.' - cost of goods, plus ___f___, plus ___g___. This must be accompanied by the insurance ___h___, and often by a certificate of ___i___, to show where the goods, and the raw materials in them, originated. This often has to be authenticated by your local ___j___ of commerce. If the goods are going by sea, you must also enclose the ___k___ set of clean ___l___ of lading.

bills	certificate
chamber	expiry
freight	full
insurance	invoice
lading	origin
payment	ship

Collecting the money

PO Box 12236, Seoul

The Chief Buyer
Skopje's Department Store
1001 Pacific Boulevard
Los Angeles

13 February 1992

Your ref.: Order no. 5529
dated 18 December 1991

Dear Miss Shersteen

The goods which you ordered have been dispatched to you via our freight forwarders, the Eastern Star Shipping Agency. They will notify you that shipping documents have been sent to your bank in accordance with instructions.

We now enclose our *bill of exchange*, drawn in US dollars at 90 days, which we ask you to accept and return to us as soon as possible so that the documents may be released to you.

We are confident that the goods will reach you in perfect condition, and we trust that you have found our service satisfactory.

Sincerely

Nam-Hoon Chun
for Fashionpark Corp

18.10 Document study

Fashionpark start the process of collecting their money from Skopje's letter of credit. First, Skopje's must 'accept', or sign, a bill of exchange. The text of this standard covering letter is stored on a word processor and the secretary only needs to key in a few words and figures. Which ones?

18.11 Document study: a bill of exchange

Bills of exchange originated nearly 300 years ago, and their wording is still rather old-fashioned. Read the example below. Are the details correct?

17th February 1992 $117,000
Place and date of issue

At: 90 days date pay against this only Bill of exchange

To the order of: Fashionpark Corporation

The sum of: one hundred and seventeen thousand dollars only

Drawee: Skopje's Department Store, L.A.

The New York City Bank
New York; NY 10016 USA

Signature of Drawer
For Fashionpark Corporation

18.12 Listen and read

Park, Nicole and Karen meet, months later, in Paris. Listen to what they say. Why does Karen complain about delivery times? What solution does Park have?

KAREN *One thing strikes me* about *the rag trade* nowadays: delivery times are too long, and that's one area where we can still make significant savings. Next time I order from you, Mr Park, I want at least thirty per cent of the shipment sent by air freight.

PARK Fine. If you want, I'll *charter a jumbo* and send the whole lot by air.

KAREN Two other stores in LA were selling Nicole Vernay dresses before I was – and that can't happen again.

NICOLE I am surprised that Fashionpark doesn't start up a North American subsidiary to handle its distribution.

PARK Well, this is *off the record*, you understand, but I think we may do that quite soon. Also in Europe.

KAREN Well, now, Mr Park, if you're looking for someone who knows the fashion business on the West Coast *inside out* . . .

PARK Oh, I shall know where to come!

NICOLE It will certainly be a great help to have your warehouse somewhere close to Paris. The ordering will be so much more flexible – we can respond more quickly to the market.

KAREN And we can just write a dollar check instead of all those letters of credit and banker's drafts.

18.10
bill of exchange this is like a cheque, except that it is written by the supplier and then signed (accepted) by the customer. Once it is accepted, payment is certain and the bill can therefore be bought and sold.

18.12
One thing strikes me one thing comes into my mind.
the rag trade the business of making and selling clothes; an informal use.
charter a jumbo hire a large aeroplane (a jumbo jet).
off the record confidential – do not repeat this to anyone else.
inside out very well.

18.13 Listen and read

Park, Nicole and Karen continue their discussion. Listen to what they say. Are Park and Nicole enthusiastic about Karen's proposed 'vertical integration'?

KAREN What do you do with those bills of exchange, Park? Wait for ninety days and then change the dollars into Korean won?

PARK It depends on the state of the currency market. Once the bill has been accepted, it's negotiable – I can sell it for cash anywhere I like, *at a discount* of course. Right now I'd probably get it discounted in Tokyo.

NICOLE Aren't you going to have problems, setting up inside the European Community?

KAREN Yeah, and in the United States – we're very protectionist, you know.

PARK Well, there are ways to overcome problems like that.

NICOLE Something like a joint venture, perhaps?

KAREN Hey, how about that? The three of us. An international marketing *consortium*! *Vertical integration* – designer, manufacturer, distributor, all under one umbrella.

NICOLE No thank you!

PARK Three companies under one umbrella – all get wet.

18.13
at a discount here, the bill is not due for payment for another 90 days, so if the bank pays cash for it today they are in effect lending the money and will deduct 90 days' interest.
(a) consortium a group of companies who have agreed to work together.
Vertical integration the bringing of different stages of production or distribution into the same organisation. If Fashionpark merged with another clothing manufacturer, this would be **horizontal integration**.

18.14 Reading for key words

Find the words or phrases in 18.12 and in 18.13 that tell you the following:

1 I'll hire a Boeing 747 to make a special trip.
2 To look after the sale of your corporation's products.
3 Please don't tell anyone I told you this.
4 Someone who knows everything about this business.
5 When there's a sudden demand, we shall be able to meet it.
6 The relative values of different currencies.
7 I would probably exchange the bill for cash.
8 We don't encourage foreign goods or businesses to enter our country.
9 I think that's a very good idea.
10 A group of companies which act together, though they may not be formally linked.

18.15 Find the word: documentary credits – 3

Read the text below on documentary credits. Write a word from the box to fill each of the gaps.

Once the shipment is safely on its way, the ___**a**___ documents are sent to your customer's bank, while your own bank notifies you that everything has been done in accordance with your instructions. The documents will only be ___**b**___ to the customer '___**c**___ payment'. The customer, however, doesn't want to hand over the money yet, because it will be several days or weeks before the goods are delivered to his ___**d**___ . You, the supplier, therefore send him a bill of ___**e**___ and ask him to accept it by ___**f**___ it.

Some bills are payable as soon as the bank sees them – these are called ___**g**___ bills. Most are payable at 30, 60 or 90 days; this gives the customer time to receive and use or re-sell the goods before the money is transferred from his letter of ___**h**___ . But an accepted bill is a guarantee of payment, and it is therefore ___**i**___ ; it can be bought and sold. In fact, it is almost as good as ___**j**___ , except for the delay in payment. As the supplier, you will probably sell it to a bank, which will ___**k**___ it – that is, deduct interest from the total amount.

against cash
credit discount
exchange
negotiable
released shipping
sight signing
warehouse

Study record	
18.1	
18.2	
18.3	
18.4	
18.5	
18.6	
18.7	
18.8	
18.9	
18.10	
18.11	
18.12	
18.13	
18.14	
18.15	

Answer key and commentary for unit 18

18.1 Listen and read
Karen is worried that Nicole's designs will be copied by other garment manufacturers without permission or payment. Nicole believes her agreement with Fashionpark will protect her because unlicensed manufacturers will not be able to compete.

18.3 Find the word
a forwarders
b shipped
c charges
d insured
e documentary
f place
g cost
h premium
i charges
j pro-forma
k credit
l letter
m credit
n irrevocable

18.4 Listen and read
Fashionpark is an efficient business because it has already sent catalogues and price lists to Nicole Vernay's customers.

18.5 Document study
Fashionpark have to tell Karen if any items in the catalogue are not available; airfreight a sample of each garment to Los Angeles; tell her the expected delivery date. Karen has to open an irrevocable letter of credit with the Korean Trading Bank for $117,000.

18.6 Document study
The request for documentary credit is sent by Skopje's to the First California Commercial Bank. They will open an irrevocable letter of credit in Fashionpark's favour. The telex is sent by Skopje's to Fashionpark. They will prepare an invoice, a certificate of origin, a full set of bills of lading and an insurance certificate to go with their banker's draft for the money.

18.7 Document study
The details are correct.

18.8 Document study
a 175
b 05/92
c Skopje's Department Store, 1001 Pacific Boulevard, Los Angeles, California 96034
d MV Pacific Centaur
e No, loading Pusan
f San Francisco
g SKO LA 1/92, 1 to 10
h Ten packing cases
i 9,736 kilograms
j 1.75 by 2.9 by 0.95 metres – total 48.3 cubic metres
k Seoul, 9 February 1992
l Three

18.9 Find the word
a ship
b expiry
c lading
d payment
e invoice
f insurance
g freight
h certificate
i origin
j chamber
k full
l bills

18.10 Document study
The customer's name and address, the date, the order number, the date of the order, the number of days on the bill of exchange.

18.11 Document study
Yes, the details are correct.

18.12 Listen and read
Karen complains because delivery times are too long; two other shops in Los Angeles had Nicole Vernay clothes on sale before Skopje's. Park says that he hopes to set up a distribution company in North America.

18.13 Listen and read
Park and Nicole are not enthusiastic. Nicole says 'No thank you!', and Park makes a joke about umbrellas.

18.14 Reading for key words
1 I'll charter a jumbo
2 to handle its distribution
3 this is off the record
4 someone who knows the . . . business . . . inside out
5 we can respond more quickly to the market
6 the state of the currency market
7 I'd probably get it discounted
8 we're very protectionist
9 Hey, how about that?
10 (a) consortium

18.15 Find the word
a shipping
b released
c against
d warehouse
e exchange
f signing
g sight
h credit
i negotiable
j cash
k discount

Unit 19: Setting up a business

SITUATION

Hans Gast wants to set up his own road haulage business, based in Cardiff. He draws up a business plan and approaches his bank for start-up funding. Later, business is going well, and he and his partner, Andreas Tsoulas, decide that the time is right to expand – but first they have to persuade the bank to lend them the additional funding.

CHARACTERS

Hans Gast	is studying business in South Wales. He is German.
Richard Price	is a bank manager. He is Welsh.
Andreas Tsoulas	is a businessman. He is Greek.

LANGUAGE

Vocabulary	Small businesses; start-up finance; banking services; business expansion.
Skills	Presenting and discussing a business plan; looking for a way round a problem; reacting to a proposal or announcement.
Documents	A business plan; a letter.

Presenting a business plan

19.3
(a) sole proprietor a person who owns a business completely; there are no partners or shareholders.
chilled food food which is very cold, but not frozen. It must therefore be delivered to retailers as quickly as possible.
security something of value which a borrower promises to give to a lender, if the borrower is not able to repay a loan or debt.
the break-even point the time when income from sales equals the costs of production; it is neither a profit nor a loss.

19.1 Listen and read

Hans Gast is studying business in South Wales. He telephones his bank manager, Richard Price. Listen to what they say. What does Hans want to do?

HANS: Good morning – is that the manager?
RICHARD: Speaking.
HANS: Hello. My name is Gast, Hans Gast. I'm from Germany, but I am living in Cardiff and I'm a customer of your bank. Why I'm calling, I've been taking a business course at Cardiff Polytechnic, and I would like to set up a small business of my own here in South Wales.
RICHARD: Oh yes. And what sort of business do you have in mind?
HANS: Well, I'd like to tell you about it personally, if I can come and see you.
RICHARD: Of course. You're most welcome to come in here and have a talk, Mr . . . Gast did you say?
HANS: Yes, Gast, that's right.
RICHARD: Do you have a business plan? It can save a lot of time if . . .
HANS: A business plan? Of course, I have already prepared one.
RICHARD: Splendid. Let me have a look in my diary. How about Monday morning, the seventeenth, at ten o'clock?
HANS: Yes, ten o'clock Monday morning will suit me fine.
RICHARD: I look forward to seeing you then, Mr Gast. Goodbye.

19.2 Writing practice: preparing for the meeting

Before Hans Gast arrives, Richard Price spends some time preparing a list of what he will need to ask Hans. Start the list for him. You will be able to add to it in 19.5.

19.3 Document study

This is the business plan that Hans prepared. If you were preparing an advertisement for Hans to put in specialist food distributors' magazines, which points would you use to describe his transport service?

<u>Hans Gast</u>

<u>BUSINESS PLAN</u>

I wish to set up a refrigerated road transport business, with myself as *sole proprietor*.

Initially, I shall have one truck with a load capacity of 1.5 tonnes. It will be fitted with a mobile phone. I shall undertake deliveries for *chilled food* distributors, offering them a service on which they know they can rely at short notice and in case of emergency. I have made preliminary enquiries with a number of firms, which I contacted while following a marketing course at Cardiff Polytechnic. Their response was very favourable.

I shall drive the truck myself and also employ part-time drivers. My fiancée will help me with administration, book-keeping and telephone enquiries. Her parents have offered us the use of a room in their house as an office, until we can find a small office to rent.

To finance this venture, I have £10,000 capital. My start-up costs will total £25,000. I am therefore seeking a bank loan of £15,000. I can offer the truck (estimated value £20,000) as *security*.

I have prepared a detailed cash-flow forecast for the first year of operation, and this shows that *the break-even point* is reached after twenty-two months. This assumes a bank loan of £15,000 over five years at an annual percentage rate of 18.5%, with interest-only repayments during the first six months.

19.4 Listen and read

Hans is in Richard's office at the bank, discussing his plan. Listen to what they say. Who seems to be more concerned with expanding the business?

RICHARD Well, Mr Gast, it's an interesting idea, everything's very nicely presented, and you've obviously done your homework. Though some of your figures are perhaps *a little on the optimistic side*. And you appreciate the bank will need some kind of security for the loan?

HANS Naturally. But the only fixed asset I can offer you that's of any real value is the truck.

RICHARD Yes, I thought you might say that. Loans can be secured on motor vehicles.

HANS I've found a dealer who will sell me a brand-new one-and-a-half-tonne refrigerated truck for twenty thousand pounds. I think that ought to be acceptable as security for a fifteen-thousand-pound loan.

RICHARD Hm. Do you see this *road haulage* business of yours starting *to pay its way* in a couple of years?

HANS Well – if we just stay with one truck, yes.

RICHARD Ah! So *you might be looking to expand* in a year or two. If you're going to come back then to borrow more money, then obviously . . .

HANS To be honest, Mr Price, I want to see how the first year goes before I commit myself – and I'm sure the bank feels the same way.

RICHARD I see. Well, I'm happy to approve your application for a loan of fifteen thousand pounds, to be repaid over five years. You'll receive a letter of confirmation and a formal offer from the bank in a few days' time. Repayments will be monthly, by *direct debit*. But remember, our service doesn't stop there. You have twelve months' free banking – no bank charges – provided you stay in the black, and the turnover on your account doesn't exceed a hundred thousand pounds in the year. And when you are ready to make your next move, you let me know.

19.4
a little on the optimistic side a little too optimistic.
road haulage the business of moving goods by lorry.
to pay its way to make a profit.
you might be looking to expand you might consider expanding.
direct debit a means of making regular payments directly from one bank account to another.

19.5 Writing practice: following up the meeting

Richard Price can now complete his list from 19.2, and write short notes under each heading. Write the list and notes for him.

19.6 Find the word

This is the letter that Richard Price sent to Hans. Read through it, and write a word from the box to fill each of the gaps.

BARWEST

Dear Mr Gast

APPLICATION FOR ___a___ BUSINESS LOAN

Following our meeting on 17 October, I am glad to be able to ___b___ the Bank's offer of a Small Business Loan on the terms set out below.

___c___ of loan: £15,000
___d___ of loan: five years from 1 November 1992
Rate of ___e___ : 18.5%
Special ___f___ : interest-only payments for first six months
Monthly payments: £231.25 until 1 May 1993
Thereafter £509.03 until 1 November 1997.

The enclosed leaflet gives details of some of the Bank's services to new businesses. No bank ___g___ will be made during the first year of operation, provided ___h___ does not exceed £100,000 and the account remains in ___i___ .

If you will kindly check, complete and sign the acceptance form enclosed, we will arrange for the ___j___ of money shown above to be transferred to your account on 1 November. The loan will be ___k___ monthly over five years by direct ___l___ . On behalf of the Bank, I should like to wish you every success in your enterprise.

Yours sincerely

amount	charges
confirm	credit
debit	interest
period	repayable
small	sum
terms	turnover

Planning for growth

19.7
a limited company a company owned by shareholders.
30-tonners trucks with a load capacity of 30 tonnes.
the authorised share capital under UK company law, a limited company must state in its memorandum and articles of association what its maximum share capital will be; this is the **authorised share capital**. The **issued share capital** is usually less.

19.9
quite a different ball game very different from the previous situation.
articled to an accountant to enter a profession (such as accountancy or law), the student must have not only academic qualifications but also practical experience. Hans's wife will work as an articled clerk for at least two years while she studies for her final examinations.
goodwill a way of accounting for the extra value of a business from its name, brands or connections, in addition to its physical assets. In fact, the bank may not consider goodwill as security.
highly geared dependent on borrowed money, rather than shareholders' money.
take a charge over the assets obtain a legal document which will give the bank ownership of the assets if the company becomes bankrupt.
the numbers the figures; Hans's trading figures and the cash-flow forecast for the expanded business.

19.7 Listen and read

It is now a year later, and Hans meets Richard Price again. Listen to what they say. How does Hans want to finance the new company?

HANS Richard, I'd like to introduce a friend of mine – Andreas Tsoulas. Andreas, this is Richard Price.

ANDREAS How do you do, Mr Price. Hans and I were students together at Cardiff Polytechnic.

RICHARD How do you do. So, I understand from what Hans has been telling me that both of you think it's time to expand the business and set up *a limited company*?

HANS That's right. We want to transport chilled foods between the UK and Greece, via Germany. Eventually, of course, the network will extend much further. But to run a scheduled service between London and Athens, we need two *30-tonners*.

RICHARD Mhm. So you propose to put in twenty thousand pounds each as shareholders?

HANS As we show in our business plan, *the authorised share capital* will be fifty thousand pounds, and the *issued share capital* will be forty thousand.

RICHARD Mm. And on that basis you want the bank to lend you two hundred thousand?

ANDREAS I should explain perhaps that my family owns a road-haulage business in Greece. My uncle died last year, and I've been asked to take it over.

19.8 Writing practice: making notes

Richard Price needs to make notes on Hans and Andreas's new proposal. Start the notes for him. You can add to your list after you have read 19.9.

19.9 Listen and read

The meeting continues. Listen to what they say. What do Hans and Andreas offer as security for the loan?

RICHARD Um. Hans, this is certainly *quite a different ball game* from what you've been in so far.

HANS Yes, but we're confident we can make it work. And my wife is going to be *articled to an accountant* in Cardiff next year – eventually she will be our Financial Director.

RICHARD Is she going to be a shareholder?

HANS Yes, she can be a shareholder right away. In fact, she owns the house we are living in. We can offer that as our security for half the loan.

ANDREAS Mr Price, the business in Greece has been valued at the equivalent of half a million pounds. That includes stock, *goodwill*, everything.

RICHARD So although your company will be *highly geared*, you do seem to have acceptable security – provided the bank can *take a charge over the assets* in Greece. However, two hundred thousand is outside my limit as a branch manager. All I can do is to pass on your application to regional head office, with a recommendation. They'll want to see *the numbers*, so I hope you've got some good ones.

19.10 Reading for key words

Find the words or phrases in 19.7 and 19.9 that tell you the following:

1 Hans has already given Richard some information about what he and Andreas are planning.
2 Their trucks will run to a regular timetable.
3 Andreas is anxious that Richard may reject their proposal without even hearing about the Greek assets.
4 Richard did not expect Hans and Andreas to need so much money.
5 Richard thinks that Hans and Andreas will be relying rather heavily on borrowed capital.

19.11 Speaking practice: challenging a proposal

Listen to this conversation between a bank manager and a customer. Then listen again and speak the part of the bank manager.

CUSTOMER I've just bought this lovely old farmhouse in Tuscany. What I propose to do is to open a country hotel.

MANAGER Mm. To be honest, I haven't much experience of the hotel business. Have you?

CUSTOMER Well, not very much, but I believe I can make it work.

MANAGER I see. Let's try and assess its potential. How many bedrooms has it got?

CUSTOMER At the moment there are no bedrooms at all. I should explain that it needs complete renovation.

MANAGER I see. And how much money are you able to put into this?

CUSTOMER Not very much really. I was hoping the bank would be prepared to lend me the full amount.

MANAGER And when do you see the hotel starting to generate some income, so that you could repay the loan?

CUSTOMER I would think in about two or three years.

MANAGER And have you anything to offer as security in the meantime?

CUSTOMER Only the house itself, I'm afraid.

MANAGER I'd be interested to see the figures, but I'm not sure you've really thought this thing through.

19.12 Find the word

Read the text below about Hans and Andreas's business plans. Write a word from the box to fill each of the gaps.

Hans's transport business has done well in its first year and he wants to ___**a**___ it. His friend, Andreas, has been asked to take over the ___**b**___ firm in Greece, which is ___**c**___ (if we include stock and ___**d**___) at about £500,000. The two men plan to set up a ___**e**___ company, which will be independent of the Greek company. They want to ___**f**___ nearly £250,000 altogether, and the bank manager is not sure that they can ___**g**___ such a large sum. Their ___**h**___ capital will amount to only £40,000. Andreas proposes his Greek assets as ___**i**___ for a loan; but it is not always easy for a bank to take a ___**j**___ over property in another country, even within the EC, and the other Greek shareholders may object. The loan would make the company highly ___**k**___ – that is, the ratio of loan capital to share capital would be high – and head office may find this unacceptable.

charge	expand
family	finance
geared	goodwill
limited	raise
security	share
valued	

Raising capital

19.13
government grants money provided by the government to persuade companies to create new jobs, start up businesses in certain areas, etc.
tax holidays periods during which a new business does not pay the full tax due on its profits.
business rates a form of local taxation on business property in the UK.

19.14
finance . . . internally get the money you need from inside your business, by selling assets or using profits.
collateral something of value which a borrower promises to a lender, in case the borrower is not able to repay a loan or debt; security.
repackage it make it look like a new proposal, even if it is really the same as before.

19.13 Listen and read

Richard Price is meeting Hans and Andreas to tell them of the bank's decision. Liste to what they say. Why has the bank refused the loan?

RICHARD Briefly, gentlemen, the word from head office is that they have studied your proposals with great interest, but they feel you have not yet tried hard enough to exploit other sources of finance.
ANDREAS Other sources of finance?
RICHARD Well, this is a Development Area. I think they mean *government grants*.
HANS How can they say we're not taking advantage of government help? We located our business in South Wales because of *tax holidays*, low *business rates* . . .
ANDREAS I'm really surprised at the attitude of your head office, because they must know that we would only qualify for a very small grant. We're not creating many new jobs, we're not doing anything for the inner city . . .
RICHARD How about the European Regional Development Fund?
HANS We want two hundred thousand, not two million!
RICHARD Of course. Let me try regional head office again.

19.14 Listen and read

Hans and Andreas have another meeting with Richard Price. Listen to what they sa How do Hans and Andreas 'persuade' Richard to try again?

RICHARD Do you have to be so dependent on external finance? Can't you *finance* part of your expansion *internally*?
HANS My business is showing a good profit, but I haven't had time to build up any reserves . . .
RICHARD No, no, no, I was thinking of Mr Tsoulas. You said the family business was worth half a million. Can't you get any more out of it? Sell some property? Move some of your assets over here as *collateral*? Why not get some members of your family in as shareholders?
HANS I'm afraid that would not be acceptable. We agreed on equal representation of German and Greek shareholders.
ANDREAS Hans, I know how we can do it. We'll put in for an EC grant, and ask the bank for a short-term loan till it comes through.
RICHARD Well, I can try, but . . .
HANS He means a loan from a Greek bank.
RICHARD Oh! Well, I'm sure we can fix it for you. I'll put it up to region again, but we must *repackage it* somehow. Suppose some of your trucks, which at the moment are registered in Greece, could be re-registered in the UK? That might persuade them.

19.15 Find the word: financing a growing business

Read the text below about expanding a business. Write a word from the box to fill each of the gaps.

When an established company needs to ___**a**___ further expansion, it can often ___**b**___ its own internal resources. One way to do this is to use profit from previous years as capital; but Hans has not had time to build up any ___**c**___ . Another way is to sell off some of the firm's ___**d**___ for cash. Companies sometimes sell their own factories or offices and then lease them back from the buyer. If the company uses its assets as ___**e**___ for a bank loan, the bank will normally take a charge over the property.

New businesses, on the other hand, can often get government ___**f**___ , particularly if they are located in ___ **g** ___ areas. They may ___**h**___ for grants, or they may be eligible for tax ___**i**___ , low-interest ___ **j** ___ or low business ___**k**___ for a fixed number of years, or assistance with finding and training staff. In return, the company will ___**l**___ new jobs.

assets	collateral
create	
development	
exploit	finance
grants	holidays
loans	qualify
rates	reserves

19.16 Reading for key words

Find the words or phrases in 19.13 and 19.14 that tell you the following:

1 Find other ways of getting the money.
2 Richard partly agrees with head office that they should apply for a grant.
3 Hans is worried that the business he started may be taken over by Andreas's family.
4 Richard is not very optimistic about the idea of a short-term loan.
5 Richard suddenly becomes more co-operative.
6 We have to present the application in a different way.

19.17 Writing practice: making notes

Hans and Andreas must now make notes of what they have to do. Re-read the dialogues on these pages and write the notes for them.

Study record	
19.1	
19.2	
19.3	
19.4	
19.5	
19.6	
19.7	
19.8	
19.9	
19.10	
19.11	
19.12	
19.13	
19.14	
19.15	
19.16	
19.17	

Answer key and commentary for unit 19

19.1 Listen and read
Hans wants to set up a small business.

19.2 Writing practice
There are many things that Richard could ask; this is a list of some of them:
What type of business?
How much finance altogether?
How much does he want to borrow?
How much capital will he put into the business?

19.3 Document study
This is a model answer; there are many things you could choose.
– refrigerated road transport
– owner-managed
– radio control
– a specialist service for chilled food distributors
– reliable
– available at short notice and in emergencies
– always on call

19.4 Listen and read
Hans seems quite cautious, he says 'I want to see how the first year goes'. Richard seems more keen for Hans to expand, he says 'So you might be looking to expand in a year or two.'

19.5 Writing practice
This is a model answer.
What type of business? – Specialist road haulage: refrigerated delivery service for chilled food producers, on call for emergency deliveries, etc.
How much finance? – Start-up costs £25,000
How much does he want to borrow? – £15,000 over 5 years
How much capital will he put into the business? – £10,000 own money
Documents supporting loan application: Business plan, cash-flow forecast
Assets: Marketing degree (Cardiff Poly), knowledge of market (from research while studying), use of room in fiancée's parents' home as office
Performance forecasts: first year's turnover probably less than £100,000; time to break even 22 months
Long-term plans: expansion possible in a year or so?

19.6 Find the word
a small **b** confirm **c** amount
d period **e** interest **f** terms **g** charges
h turnover **i** credit **j** sum
k repayable **l** debit

19.7 Listen and read
Hans and Andreas will each put £20,000 into the new business, and they want to borrow £200,000 from the bank.

19.8 Writing practice
Customers: Hans Gast, Andreas Tsoulas
Type of business: limited company, specialist international road haulage
Start-up capital £250,000: £50,000 authorised share capital; £200,000 bank loan
Assets: one truck, Andreas's road-haulage business in Greece – no definite information

19.9 Listen and read
Hans and his wife are offering her house a security; Andreas is offering the Greek business
You should add this to your notes from 19.8

19.10 Reading for key words
1 I understand from what Hans has been tellin me
2 to run a scheduled service
3 I should explain perhaps that
4 this is certainly quite a different ball game
5 your company will be highly geared

19.12 Find the word
a expand **b** family **c** valued
d goodwill **e** limited **f** raise
g finance **h** share **i** security **j** charge
k geared

19.13 Listen and read
The bank refused the loan because it felt tha Hans and Andreas had not tried hard enough t find other sources of finance, especiall government grants.

19.14 Listen and read
They suggest that they will try to get a short-term loan from a Greek bank.

19.15 Find the word
a finance **b** exploit **c** reserves
d assets **e** collateral **f** grants
g development **h** qualify **i** holidays
j loans **k** rates **l** create

19.16 Reading for key words
1 exploit other sources of finance
2 Well, this is a Development Area
3 that would not be acceptable. We agreed o equal representation of German and Greek shareholders.
4 Well, I can try, but . . .
5 Well, I'm sure we can fix it for you.
6 we must repackage it somehow

19.17 Writing practice
This is a model answer; there are many possible ways of writing these notes.
– try to exploit other sources of finance.
– Andreas to see if he can transfer some of the assets from his Greek company to the UK, so tha they could be used as collateral for the loan. I particular, to see whether he can re-register some of his Greek trucks in the UK.
– Andreas to see if he can sell some propert to raise some more money, so that they would need to borrow less from the bank.
– prepare an application for an EC grant. The prepare an application for a short-term loan from a Greek bank, until the grant was paid.
– alternatively, repackage application to Richard's bank.

Unit 20: Investing in capital equipment

SITUATION

Kazaguruma Kitchen Equipment Ltd is a Japanese company which has a factory in South Wales. At a morning production meeting the Mouldings and Fittings team explain that they are having problems with one of the injection moulders which is producing faulty goods and keeps breaking down. The management committee then have to decide on the most cost-effective solution to the problem.

CHARACTERS

Yukio Inamura	is Production Manager. He is Japanese.
Anita	works on Mouldings and Fittings production. She is British.
Phil	works on Mouldings and Fittings production. He is British.
Frank Parkwich	is Works Manager. He is British.
Harry Evans	is Finance Manager. He is British.

All these characters work at Kazaguruma Kitchen Equipment Ltd.

LANGUAGE

Vocabulary	Machinery and production; investment decisions; investment finance.
Skills	Telephone conversations and meetings; making a point politely against opposition; signalling disagreement; using figures in discussion.
Documents	A logbook; a memo; notes.

Assessing a problem

20.1
(an) injection moulder a machine which forces liquid plastic into a mould. The plastic takes the shape of the mould, cools and becomes hard, producing a moulding.
gone down failed to work; broken down. This phrase is used only for heavy machinery in factories, and for computer systems.
defective mouldings mouldings which cannot be used because they are faulty.
Quality Control the part of the company which is responsible for checking the quality of its products.
what it comes down to what it means.
past it too old to do its job properly; an informal usage.
(a) logbook a record book, in this case recording the service history of a machine.

20.2
the Works Manager the factory manager.
reconditioned not new, but repaired in the factory so that it is nearly as good as new.
(a) hopper a container which holds raw materials, components or fastenings that the machine will use in its work. A **feed hopper** sends its contents to the machine as they are required.
stripped taken to pieces.
downtime time when the machine is not working.

20.1 Listen and read

In the Kazaguruma factory near Cardiff, each day starts with production tea meetings. Yukio Inamura, the Production Manager, is holding the Mouldings an Fittings team meeting. Listen to what they say. What problem are they discussin How does it affect them?

YUKIO OK, everybody. So what's new?

ANITA Well, this isn't new, because we've said it before, but it's getting t be a real problem, I mean it's that big *injection moulder*. You know, the one that makes all the plastic bits for the hinges and door catches.

YUKIO Has it *gone down* again?

ANITA Again? It's always going down. And even when it's not down, we're still getting *defective mouldings*. I'm constantly getting complaints from *Quality Control*.

PHIL That's right. And that means we're losing bonuses.

YUKIO Yes. And you have discussed ways to overcome this?

PHIL Well, yeah, we've talked about it. We've tried various things which help for a week or two, but *what it comes down to* is the machine's just too old. It's *past it*.

YUKIO We took over that machine with the factory; it's seven, eight year old. Very expensive to replace. Maybe even more expensive not t replace.

ANITA Well, surely we can work out what the costs would be. We could start by looking at the machine *logbook*.

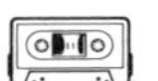

20.2 Listening practice

This is the logbook for the injection moulding machine. Read it carefully. Then liste as Yukio telephones Frank Parkwich, *the Works Manager*, to tell him about th problem. Listen to how he joins together the different bits of information. Then liste again, and, as you listen, write what Yukio says.

FRANK I see. Yeah, we evidently have a problem here. Do you have the machine logbook in front of you? Can you give me the details of the machine – serial number and everything – and tell me all the faults that have occurred since the beginning of May, and what was done in each case?

YUKIO Yes, of course . . .

MACHINE Injection Moulding Machine
MAKE Driscill
LOCATION Plastics Shop
TYPE IMP 36
SERIAL NO. 345912798

DATE	INCIDENT	ACTION	SUPERVISOR
4 May	Pressure regulator valve faulty	Reconditioned valve fitted and tested	A.K.
8th May	feed hopper hose loose due to excessive vibration	Hopper retaining bolts tightened.	J.L. H.R
11th May	– – ditto – –	Anti-Vibration washers fitted	A.S
28th May	Pump not working	Pump stripped reassembled and tested	A.S
29 May	Pressure lost in hoses	Hoses replaced	A.k

MACHINE DOWNTIME THIS MONTH 27 hours 45 minutes

20.3 Listen and read: estimating

Phil and Anita are trying to work out how much money they have lost because of the machine breaking down. Listen to how they explain their calculations.

PHIL — How much bonus *do you reckon* we're losing with that machine *packing up* all the time?

ANITA — Oh, I don't know. Well, let's work it out. Now, we work a five-day week, don't we, and 1 May was a Friday – how many working days was that, for the whole month?

PHIL — Well, according to this calendar – you've got four weeks, starting on the fourth, the eleventh, the eighteenth and the twenty-fifth, and *one odd day* – the first.

ANITA — So that's four times five is twenty, and one makes twenty-one. On average we work an eight-hour day, so eight twenty-ones makes a hundred and sixty-eight hours in the month.

PHIL — Right. Out of those hours, the machine was down for twenty-seven and three-quarters. What's that as a percentage?

ANITA — Oh, I could never get these right. It's twenty-seven and three-quarters – that's point seven-five – times a hundred, divided by a hundred and sixty-eight – that's right, isn't it? According to the calculator, that's sixteen point five one eight.

PHIL — Well, *round it up*, call it seventeen per cent. So we're losing, give or take a bit either way, seventeen per cent of our bonus. How much bonus did you get last week?

ANITA — Just under eighteen pounds, I think.

PHIL — Right, so let's see what you should have got.

20.3
do you reckon do you think; an informal usage. **Reckon** also means 'calculate', but that is not what Phil means here.
packing up failing to work; an informal usage.
one odd day one extra day.
round it up increase it to the next whole number; numbers above 0.5 are usually **rounded up**, and numbers below 0.5 are usually **rounded down**, decreased to the whole number below.

20.4 Listen and read: mental arithmetic

Phil and Anita continue their calculations. Listen to what they say. What answer did Anita get? What answer did Phil get?

PHIL — Now, you lost seventeen per cent of your bonus and you still got eighteen pounds.

ANITA — Well, seventeen per cent of eighteen pounds is three point oh six. Does that sound right?

PHIL — Well, seventeen hundredths is about one-sixth, near enough – because six times seventeen is a hundred and two – and one-sixth of eighteen is three. So, yes, about three pounds.

ANITA — It's not a lot of money, is it? Come to think of it, though, three pound a week . . .

PHIL — Right! Fifty-two weeks a year – that's more than a hundred and fifty pound you're losing.

20.5 Reading for key words

Find the words or phrases in 20.3 and 20.4 that show you the following calculations:

1 (4 x 5 = 20) + 1 = 21
2 8 x 21 = 168
3 27.75 x 100 ÷ 168 = 16.518
4 17% x £18 = 3.06
5 17/100 = 1/6
6 6 x 17 = 102, 1/6 x 18 = 3

20.6 Figure practice

Phil and Anita actually made a very common mistake when they were doing their calculations in 20.4. What was it? What bonus did Anita actually lose last week? How much does she really lose in a year?

Discussing the options

20.7
do our sums do some calculations.
see how it comes out see what the result is.
overstepped gone beyond.
(X) is one thing, (Y) is something else X may be acceptable, Y is not.
bending over backwards trying very hard to be helpful; in this case trying too hard.
leeway space or time to change things; in this case it means that the factory is not working to full capacity.
in-house by the factory's own staff.
Any slack here, any spare capacity which is not being used.
wrong-footed unprepared, not ready; here, unable to increase production to meet the increased demand.

20.9
a zero failure rate no failures at all.
over the top too much; an informal usage.

20.7 Listen and read

The management committee meet to discuss the injection moulder. Who wants t replace the machine? Who wants to keep the old machine?

YUKIO It's quite true that this machine is not scheduled for replacement under our capital investment programme until 1994. But it is costing us more than it's worth in lost production and unscheduled maintenance.

HARRY Well, perhaps we could *do our sums* on that and *see how it comes out*. We have agreed on several previous occasions that the spending limits on capital expenditure mustn't be *overstepped*.

YUKIO But these production shortfalls are quite unacceptable, especially when the market is just beginning to recover.

FRANK We may have to be a bit flexible on this one, Harry.

HARRY *Being flexible's one thing, bending over backwards is something else.* There's plenty of *leeway* in the production schedules – we've got two months' supply of hinge and door fittings stockpiled in the warehouse. And for the last five years, all the maintenance on that injection moulder has been done entirely *in-house*, and we haven't had to purchase a single spare part.

YUKIO Look – in today's 'Financial Times': 'The economy is on the upturn. *Any slack* in production capacity will soon be taken up'.

FRANK We can't afford to be *wrong-footed* if demand does start to recover.

20.8 Reading for key words

The management committee choose their words carefully to express disagreemer in a polite way. Find the words or phrases in 20.7 that show you the following:

1 I don't believe what you have just said is correct.
2 Don't you remember that we all said we wouldn't spend more money than w had planned?
3 We can't allow the factory to make fewer goods than we planned for.
4 Perhaps we should treat this as a special case.
5 It's not as special as you say it is.
6 We shall lose money if we aren't ready for an increase in orders.

20.9 Listen and read

Yukio explains to the Mouldings and Fittings team why it is acceptable for some o the fittings produced by the machine to be faulty. Listen to what he says. As yo listen, draw the diagram that Yukio sketches.

ANITA Surely we ought to be going for *a zero failure rate*? We don't want even one faulty moulding from that machine.

YUKIO It's not quite as simple as that. Absolute perfection every time isn't economic. What we want is the lowest failure rate we can get at an acceptable cost. Look.
[He sketches a rough diagram on a piece of paper.]
On a graph, the cost of rejects is a straight line – a hundred rejects cost twice as much as fifty. But the cost of preventing rejects is a curve. It is extremely high if you want none at all, then it comes down sharply if you allow a few, then it levels out. As you tolerate more and more rejects, the cost of preventing them falls more slowly. Now, if you work out the total cost, by adding the cost of rejects to the cost of prevention, you get another curve. You can see the total cost is lowest just about where the cost-of-rejects and cost-of-prevention lines cross. So what we try to do is to find the percentage of rejects that will give us the lowest total cost. This injection moulder is producing about eleven per cent of faulty mouldings, and that's definitely *over the top*. Quite apart from the breakdowns.

20.10 Find the right word

Read the text below on capital investment. Write a word from the box to fill each of the gaps.

Every machine has a ___**a**___ lifespan. Most companies have ___**b**___ investment programmes, but falling profits may impose tight ___**c**___ limits that prevent the ___**d**___ of machines at the proper time. The production manager has to decide what failure ___**e**___ can be accepted. What percentage of ___**f**___ work, how many ___ **g** ___, can be tolerated per month? A zero ___**h**___ rate is uneconomical; it would cost the company too much. If a machine is easy to ___**i**___ and there are plenty of ___ **j** ___ parts stockpiled in the company storeroom, it may be cheaper to go on ___**k**___ than to ___**l**___ it. In-house ___**m**___ can keep a machine working for years without the need for retraining operators and engineers or disrupting production schedules.

capital failure
faulty limited
maintenance rate
rejects repair
repairing replace
replacement spare
spending

20.11 Listen and read

Harry Evans and Yukio Inamura meet to discuss how they might finance a new machine. Listen to how Harry rejects each of Yukio's suggestions. Does Harry think that the company will be able to afford a new machine?

YUKIO Two hundred thousand – can we meet that out of *revenue reserves*?

HARRY You're joking. The total reserve is only *two fifty*, and we're holding a proportion of that against *deferred taxation*.

YUKIO Well, of course, I'm only a production engineer, so I don't pretend to understand these things. But I thought we could set off capital investment against tax, with a one hundred per cent *depreciation allowance* in the first year.

HARRY Not these days we can't. They've changed the rules. The thing is that our tax position for the last financial year is still very unclear. It may have *to go to arbitration*, and that could take months. We can't afford to get a big tax assessment if we've just spent all the money on a machine – even if the machine is tax-deductible in the long run.

YUKIO What about a grant? This is a Development Area! Look at all the jobs we have created!

HARRY We might be able to get a cheap loan from *the Welsh Office*.

YUKIO And we can sell the old machine. It must be worth something.

HARRY From what I've heard, it's only *fit for scrap*. Scrap value won't be more than five hundred – we'll probably end up paying someone to take it away. No, leave it with me, Yukio. I've got your payback figures, I may be able *to swing it*.

20.11

revenue reserves money kept from the company's profits.

two fifty here, this means two hundred and fifty thousand pounds, because of Yukio's earlier mention of two hundred thousand.

deferred taxation tax which is due this year but which will not be paid until next year or later.

depreciation allowance the amount by which the value of an asset falls each year. For tax purposes, it is sometimes possible to assume that a machine loses all its value as soon as it is bought (100% depreciation); the full cost of the machine can then be claimed at once against tax.

to go to arbitration to ask an independent person or organisation to decide an argument.

the Welsh Office the UK government department responsible for Wales.

fit for scrap of no further use; to be thrown away.

to swing it to get what we want; Harry means that this will be difficult, and he may have to cheat a little.

Considering the alternatives

20.12
the plastics industry note that **plastics** is used here; **plastic** would mean 'made of plastic'.

20.12 Document study

Yukio has read an article about a new machine. He sends his colleagues a mem about it. Read the memo carefully. In the memo Yukio uses the word 'this' thre times. What does it refer to each time?

MEMO

FROM Production Manager

TO Works Manager
R&D Manager
Finance Manager

DATE 25 June 1992

Announcement of new Injection Moulder

An important article has just come to my attention in a Japanese trade journal for *the plastics industry* (photocopy attached). This announces the development of an advanced new injection moulding machine. The machine is expected to be ready for shipment in about a year from now.

In the light of this, I wonder if we should consider leasing a moulder or even buying a reconditioned machine. Perhaps we can discuss this at the management committee meeting next week.

20.13 Listen and read

When he saw the article in a trade journal, Yukio immediately telephoned Fran Parkwich. Listen to what they say. What does Yukio have to do?

FRANK Hello.
YUKIO Hello. Is that Frank Parkwich?
FRANK Speaking.
YUKIO It's Yukio Inamura.
FRANK Hi, Yukio. What can I do for you?
YUKIO Somebody's just shown me an article in a Japanese trade journal for the plastics industry. It's about a new type of injection moulding machine.
FRANK Oh yeah? Sounds quite interesting. I'd like to see it.
YUKIO The article, you mean? I'm afraid it's in Japanese.
FRANK That's OK, we can get it translated. When's this machine going to be ready?
YUKIO They expect to be shipping them in about a year's time.
FRANK Oh, I don't think we can wait that long.
YUKIO It's a very advanced machine – a big improvement on what we're using now.
FRANK Mm, well. What do you suggest?
YUKIO I'd like the other members of the management committee to know about it.
FRANK Could we get it translated in time for next week's meeting?
YUKIO I think so. I thought I'd show the article first to people who are most concerned.
FRANK Yes, exactly. Why don't you tell R&D about it and Harry Evans – send them photocopies if you can.
YUKIO OK.

20.14 Listen and read

The management committee meet again to discuss the new machine. Listen to what they say. What is the problem with the new Japanese machine?

FRANK Now, that injection moulder in the plastics shop. I know Yukio's been making enquiries about a new machine that's due to be launched next year. Yukio, what's the score on this one?

YUKIO I've been on the telephone to people in the company who are developing it and to some other *contacts* of mine in Japan. The general feeling is that there are still some problems to be ironed out. It's an advanced piece of technology and the makers won't launch it until they are one hundred per cent sure they have got it right. That might be one year, or it might be two.

FRANK Right, well, I think, taking everything into account, the conclusion seems to be that we lease a machine, for two years in the first instance, renewable annually thereafter. Do we all agree?

HARRY I appreciate that we need to make a decision on this quickly – but there are one or two points I'd like to make . . .

20.14
contacts people you know who are able to give you help, advice or information about a particular subject.

20.16
(a) premium an additional amount of money; more than you would usually pay.

20.15 Reading for key words

Find the words or phrases in 20.14 that show you the following:

1 What is the present position on this matter?
2 Some useful people whom I know quite well.
3 To be solved or overcome.
4 To begin with.
5 After that.
6 I disagree, and I don't think we ought to make up our minds in a hurry.

20.16 Speaking practice: considering the options

Listen to this conversation. Then listen again, and speak the part of the man.

WOMAN There are one or two points I'd like to make. First, we don't know what this new machine will cost.

MAN I understand the cost will be comparable with that of machines currently on the market.

WOMAN That's about two hundred thousand pounds, which would have to come from our reserves, so we should lose interest payments.

MAN The machine will give a far higher rate of return than a deposit account does! What rate are we getting?

WOMAN Twelve per cent – on 200K that's twenty-four thousand a year.

MAN The machine will produce goods worth almost ten times as much as that.

WOMAN Yes, but we can buy in the same goods from another supplier at quite a low *premium* – only ten per cent.

MAN That means about twenty thousand pounds a year premium – quite apart from the cost of the goods.

WOMAN Not really – because at least half our requirements will be produced by the old machine.

MAN There are other factors to consider as well – staff morale, for instance. And what about tax relief?

20.17 Writing practice

These are some notes Harry Evans made after the management committee meeting. Read through them carefully. Use the notes and the dialogues on these pages to write a short memo in favour of leasing a new machine. Explain your reasons, using figures to support your argument.

```
INJECTION MOULDER
Max annual value of production: £180,000
Cost of labour and materials: £120,000 per year max
Current cost of new moulder: £200,000
Useful lifespan: 5 years
Likely cost of advanced machine next year: ???
Current cost of leasing: £40,000 per year
Corporation tax on profits: 35%
Premium on cost of components bought in: 10%
Capital reserve: £1.3m - on deposit at 12%

OPTIONS
1       Buy in mouldings from outside supplier
2       Buy a new or reconditioned moulding machine
3       Lease, indefinitely or until new machine available
```

Study record	
20.1	
20.2	
20.3	
20.4	
20.5	
20.6	
20.7	
20.8	
20.9	
20.10	
20.11	
20.12	
20.13	
20.14	
20.15	
20.16	
20.17	

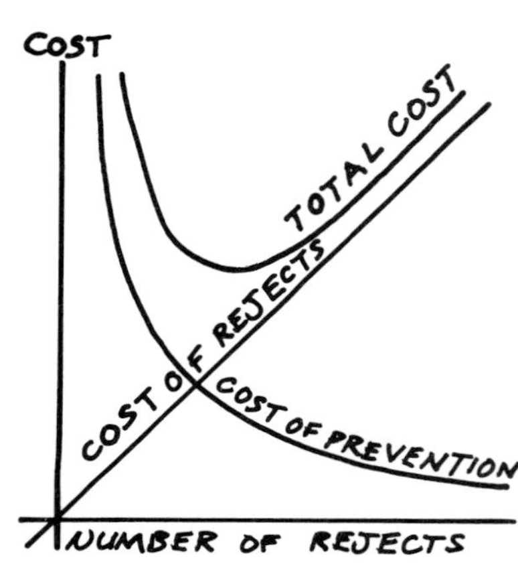

Answer key and commentary for unit 20

20.1 Listen and read
They are discussing the problem of a machine, the injection moulder, which keeps breaking down. It affects the production team because they lose bonuses.

20.2 Listening practice
Yes, of course. It's a Driscoll Injection Moulding Machine, type IMP36, serial number 345912798, and it's located in the plastics shop. On 4 May the pressure regulator valve was faulty. A reconditioned valve was fitted and tested. On 8 May the feed hopper became loose because of excessive vibration. The retaining nuts were tightened, but the same thing happened on 11 May, so anti-vibration washers were fitted. On 28 May the pump was not working, so it was stripped, reassembled and tested. The next day, pressure was lost in the hoses, and the hoses were replaced. The total downtime for the month was 27 hours 45 minutes.

20.4 Listen and read
Anita's answer, worked out on her calculator, was 3.06. Phil's answer, worked out in his head, was 3.

20.5 Reading for key words
1 four times five is twenty, and one makes twenty-one
2 eight twenty-ones makes a hundred and sixty-eight
3 twenty-seven and three-quarters – that's point seven-five – times a hundred, divided by a hundred and sixty-eight . . . that's sixteen point five one eight
4 seventeen per cent of eighteen pounds is three point oh six
5 seventeen hundredths is about one-sixth
6 six times seventeen is a hundred and two – and one-sixth of eighteen is three

20.6 Figure practice
Phil and Anita worked out 17% of £18. But £18 was the bonus that Anita actually got, not the bonus she should have got. £18 represents 83% of the full bonus (i.e. 100% minus the 17% she lost because of the machine). Their mistake, therefore, was to take £18 as being 100% of the full bonus. To calculate what Anita actually lost, work out what the full bonus should have been (i.e. £18 ÷ 83 x 100 = £21.69). Anita therefore lost £3.69 last week, which would mean £191.88 over a year.

20.7 Listen and read
Yukio and Frank want to replace the machine; Harry does not. Frank says 'We may have to be a bit flexible on this one', and 'We can't afford to be wrong-footed'; Harry says 'spending limits on capital expenditure mustn't be overstepped' and 'Being flexible's one thing, bending over backwards is something else'.

20.8 Reading for key words
1 Well, perhaps we could do our sums on that and see how it comes out.
2 We have agreed . . . that the spending limits . . . mustn't be overstepped.
3 production shortfalls are quite unacceptable
4 We may have to be a bit flexible on this one
5 Being flexible's one thing, bending over backwards is something else.
6 We can't afford to be wrong-footed if demand does start to recover.

20.9 Listen and read
See sketch on left.

20.10 Find the right word
a limited **b** capital **c** spending
d replacement **e** rate **f** faulty
g rejects **h** failure **i** repair **j** spare
k repairing **l** replace **m** maintenance

20.11 Listen and read
No, Harry does not think that the company will b able to afford a new machine. Although he says the end 'I may be able to swing it', he has argue against every suggestion that Yukio put forward

20.12 Document study
'This announces': 'An important article' in th trade journal.
'In the light of this': the fact that a new machin may be ready in a year.
'we can discuss this': the possibility of 'leasing moulder or even buying a reconditione machine'.

20.13 Listen and read
Yukio has to get the article translated, and sen photocopies of it to the members of th management committee.

20.14 Listen and read
The problem with the new machine is that it ma not be ready for another year or two.

20.15 Reading for key words
1 what's the score on this one?
2 some other contacts of mine
3 to be ironed out
4 in the first instance
5 thereafter
6 I appreciate that we need to make a decisio on this quickly – but there are one or tw points I'd like to make

20.17 Writing practice
This is a model answer; there are many possib ways of writing this memo.

The fixed costs of producing the necessar number of components will remain the same whether we buy in, buy a new machine, o lease.

If we buy in components from an outside supplier, it will cost £180,000 divided by two because we could still produce half of the components ourselves, so that's £90,000, but a a premium of 10%, so that's £99,000 per year but our staff would be idle for half the time, an that would have an effect on morale.

The new Japanese machine still ha problems and we don't know when it will b ready. If we buy a new or reconditione machine it will cost us £200,000, which wil have to come from our reserves. This means tha we will lose interest at the rate of £24,000 pe year, and the machine would depreciate ove the five years at the rate of £40,000 per year, s we are losing £64,000 per year.

If we lease a machine, it would cost £40,00 per year, and would keep the staff full employed.

Leasing seems to be the most attractiv option, in terms of the company's finances an staff.

Unit 21: Investing in the stock market

SITUATION

Francesca Amato has arrived in Cardiff to do a postgraduate marketing course at the University of Wales. Her father, a businessman in Milan, has given her £40,000 to cover her fees and expenses while she is studying in Britain. Francesca, however, has other, more ambitious, ideas about what to do with the money.

CHARACTERS

Yukio Inamura	
Richard Price	
Hans Gast	
Andreas Tsoulas	
Francesca Amato	is doing a marketing diploma at the University of Wales. She is Italian.

LANGUAGE

Vocabulary	Bonds, shares and other securities; investment management; financial journalism.
Skills	Giving advice and warnings; explaining concepts and calculations.
Structure	Giving advice.
Documents	A portfolio; a bank leaflet on investment; a newspaper stock market column; listed share prices.

Getting investment advice

21.1
speculative uncertain; a **speculative** purchase is one where you hope to make a lot of money, but you can't be sure of this, and you might in fact lose your money. This is why Richard Price calls it dangerous.
peanuts a very small amount; an informal usage.
the city pages the part of a newspaper that gives financial news about companies and lists share prices.
the market is bullish investors believe that share prices will rise. **Bulls** buy shares now and intend to sell them at a profit later. If the market is **bearish**, prices are expected to fall and so investors sell their shares.
playing the market buying and selling shares for quick profits.
a portfolio of investments a combination of different shares for a particular investor.
Junk bonds bonds which offer a high rate of interest, but which are often not supported by assets. **Junk bonds** are often issued by the new owners of a company after a leveraged buy-out in order to borrow money to pay off the loans. They are considered to be very high-risk investments. **Junk bonds** are a type of mezzanine finance.
mezzanine finance when a very large company is the target of a takeover bid, and the bidders cannot raise sufficient finance from the banks and other finance houses, they will try to raise **mezzanine finance**. They will offer a very high rate of return, but at very high risk, so that if the company fails, the providers of the **mezzanine finance** will be the last to be repaid.

21.1 Listen and read

Francesca Amato is a postgraduate student at the University of Wales. A few day after her arrival in Cardiff, she visits Richard Price, her new bank manager. Listen t what they say. Does Richard think that her ideas are sensible?

RICHARD I see. You've got forty thousand pounds to invest. And the aim is a high income?

FRANCESCA And capital growth. I was thinking of buying and selling on the currency market – that's how my father made his money – but . . .

RICHARD Whoa! That is highly *speculative* and very dangerous. Anyway, times have changed – forty thousand is *peanuts* in the foreign exchange market nowadays. Even on the stock market, it's frankly not a lot of money, but I think we can make it work for you.

FRANCESCA Every day I read *the city pages* in the newspaper. I think at the moment *the market is bullish.*

RICHARD Well, it's true that the one hundred share index has been rising this week, but that doesn't necessarily mean that the big investors think it will go on rising. Anyway, I would strongly advise you not to go *playing the market*. Leave that to the big financial institutions – the building societies, insurance companies, pension funds – they've got fund managers who are experts. What you want is *a portfolio of investments* which will give you a good return on your investment.

FRANCESCA Mm, yes! *Junk bonds – mezzanine finance* . . .

RICHARD No, no, no! The whole point of investment is to spread the risk. Look, I'll show you what I recommended the other day to a client in a somewhat similar position to yourself.

21.2 Listening practice: an investment portfolio

Richard Price telephoned his client to give her the details of the portfolio he ha arranged for her. Listen to what he says. As you listen, read the details of the portfoli in 21.3.

RICHARD I've now got the details of the bank's proposals for your investment portfolio, and here they are.

The capital to be managed amounts to fifty-seven thousand pounds, and we propose to split it like this: forty-four per cent cash, seventeen and a half per cent gilts, fourteen and a half per cent bonds, six per cent UK shares and eighteen per cent international shares and bonds. Now, I'll tell you what we propose to buy for you in each of those groups, starting with the cash: twenty thousand pounds will be put in a deposit account, five thousand will remain in your current account as a liquidity reserve. Gilts: five thousand in Treasury two per cent index-linked bonds redeemable in the year 2006; five thousand in Treasury nine per cent, in 1998. Bonds: two thousand six hundred James Dancey convertible preference; two thousand six hundred A and Z redeemable preference; three thousand Goodies convertible unit trust.

Next, the UK shares: twelve hundred pounds in Barwest Bank plc, twelve hundred in Foresight Insurance, twelve hundred in Annandale Glass. International shares and bonds: three thousand pounds in Pacific Assets Trust, two thousand in Trans-Siberian Railroad, and two thousand six hundred each in Europewide unit trust and European Space Development. Total, fifty-seven thousand pounds, excluding initial charges.

21.3 Document study

This is the portfolio Richard Price put together for his client. Read it carefully.

```
------------------------------------------------------------
Proposed portfolio for Mrs Johnson
------------------------------------------------------------
Holding and security

  5000.00 current account (liquidity reserve)
 20000.00 bank deposit account
        Total cash (44%)                              25000.00
  5000.00 Treasury 2% IL 2006
  5000.00 Treasury 9% 1998
        Total gilts (17.5%)                           10000.00
  2600.00 James Dancey convertible preference
  2600.00 A&Z redeemable preference
  3000.00 Goodies convertible unit trust
        Total bonds (14.5%)                            8200.00
  1200.00 Barwest Bank plc
  1200.00 Foresight Insurance Co
  1200.00 Annandale Glass Ltd
        Total UK shares (6%)                           3600.00
  3000.00 Pacific Assets Trust
  2000.00 Trans-Siberian Railroad
  2600.00 EuropeWide unit trust
  2600.00 European Space Development
        Total international shares/bonds (18%)        10200.00
------------------------------------------------------------
Portfolio total cost (excl. initial charges)          57000.00
------------------------------------------------------------
```

21.4 Listen and read

Richard explains the portfolio to Francesca. Listen to what they say. Notice how he explains many of the terms he uses. What is Richard trying to protect Francesca, and her money, from?

FRANCESCA But this is no good to me! Almost half of her money is still in cash! And seventeen per cent in gilts – those are government loan certificates, aren't they? I don't want to lend money to the government!

RICHARD Gilts are government bonds, yes, but remember they're called gilts because they're gilt-edged – the safest, most secure investment you can have, and very easy to sell at any time. You can't go putting everything into *equities* – suppose there's another *crash*! The principle of any portfolio is to spread your risk, so whatever happens in the future you can be fairly certain your capital will be protected.

FRANCESCA Mm. But these cash deposits are going to be *eroded by inflation*.

RICHARD Yes, but you can't afford to be caught without cash in an emergency, can you? You must keep some liquidity. If all your assets are tied up, you're exposed to risk. That is what sound investment is all about – limiting your exposure to risk, *covering your position*. Your father used to be an international exchange dealer, you said; he knows all about *hedging* a deal so he keeps himself covered.

FRANCESCA You haven't answered my question about inflation.

RICHARD Right. The loss of value of the cash due to inflation is compensated for by interest payments, and by the gain in value of the other investments – which should rise faster than *the RPI*, in addition, of course, to paying dividends. Now, I do have to warn all clients that share prices can go down as well as up. But I think you appreciate that . . .

21.5 Reading for key words

Find the words or phrases in 21.1 that tell you the following:

1 Extremely risky; you might win a lot, you would probably lose.
2 Very little money.
3 Organisations which act as savings banks, and lend people money to buy houses.
4 A collection of investments of different types.
5 Invest in several companies so as to reduce the possibility of losing money.

21.3
(a) Holding an amount of money invested.
(a) security an investment, i.e. what the money is invested in.
(a) liquidity reserve assets that can be quickly changed to cash.
Treasury 2% IL 2006 bonds issued by the government in exchange for loans. The annual rate of interest is low but IL means 'index-linked'; in this case interest is paid at 2% above the rate of inflation each year until 2006.
convertible preference convertible preference shares are a way of lending money to a company; they can be 'converted' into ordinary shares; **redeemable preference** shares can be bought back, or 'redeemed', by the company.
(a) unit trust an organisation which invests large sums of money in many different businesses, and then sells 'units' of that investment to smaller investors.
excl. initial charges excluding the charges made for setting up the portfolio and buying the shares and bonds.

21.4
equities ordinary shares; the total capital of a company funded by ordinary shares is also called its **equity**.
(a) crash a sudden and very large fall in prices on a stock exchange.
eroded by inflation gradually reduced by a rise in prices.
covering your position taking care that you are never at risk of losing large amounts of money.
hedging taking steps to protect yourself against losses by balancing one deal against another, e.g. a purchase against a sale.
the RPI the retail price index; the usual measure of inflation in the UK.

Reading about the stock market

FINANCE · STOCKMARKET 1991 Page 33

ICI RESCUE ACT AS SHARES NEAR *FIVE-MONTH LOW*

Imperial Chemical Industries came to the rescue of a *beleaguered* stock market.

The *FT-SE* share index had, for the first time since October, dipped below 2,600 points and shares on the first day of the account were in desperate need of a little encouragement.

ICI obliged. Its first-quarter results, expected by some to be no more than £340m, came out at £414, and the FT-SE quickly clambered back above 2,600. ICI rose 20p to 1,080p.

Bass, firm last week, was another *to turn in* a strong performance. County NatWest Wood-Mac estimate that Britain's biggest brewer has increased its market share to 24%. The group's progress last week stemmed from suggestions it was about to sell its Crest Hotels chain. Accor, the French group mentioned as a buyer, has denied any involvement, but appears to have left the door open for a related company to clinch the deal.

- Why not let Barwest look after your invested capital for you under its Investment Management Service?
- You can give Barwest investment experts discretionary powers to manage your securities on lines you yourself lay down.
- We will buy or sell to defend or improve your position at our discretion, though we can, if you wish, refer all proposed investment decisions to you for approval.
- Your dividends will be addressed to wherever you direct.
- The fee is 90p per £100 per annum (plus Value Added Tax if applicable) calculated on the market valuation of the investments at the time the fee is due. A minimum fee of £360 is payable.

SIX

21.6 Writing practice: dictation

Listen again to Richard Price reading th details of the investment portfolio i 21.2. As you listen, write what he says When you have finished, compare wha you have written with the printe version in 21.2.

21.7 Document study

These are two of the documents abou investments that Francesca reads. On is a leaflet which the bank gives t potential clients, the other is from th stock market column in a dail newspaper. Read through ther carefully, and then do the exercis which follows.

21.7
five-month low at the lowest point for five months.
beleaguered threatened; in trouble.
FT-SE Financial Times-Stock Exchange Index of 100 Shares; this is pronounced 'footsie'.
to turn in to announce.

21.8 Reading for key words

Find the words or phrases in 21.7 that tell you the following:

1 The ability to make decisions as they think best.
2 Buy or sell stocks and shares so that you are likely to make a profit.
3 If you are registered for VAT.
4 ICI did what the people who boug their shares hoped they would do.
5 Allowed the possibility to remain.
6 To make sure of the deal.

21.9 Find the right word

Read the text below about securities. Write a word from the box to fill each of th gaps.

bond convertible
gilts index
inflation lend
portfolio
preference price
prices redeemable
securities unit
value

Most investors seek, above all, security. They even call their investments '___a___'. By building up a ___b___ of investments, you can be pretty confident that, in the long run, the ___c___ of your shares will stay a little ahead of ___d___. Many small investors pay their money to a ___e___ trust, which can invest more securely and profitably than the individuals could if they acted separately.

Every stock exchange has its ___f___, to show how share ___g___ are moving from day to day; in London, the Financial Times-Stock Exchange 100-share index (known as the FT-SE 100 for short, or the Footsie) calculates the average ___h___ of shares of 100 major companies. This index started at 1000 on 1 January 1984.

Instead of buying shares in a business, you may prefer simply to ___i___ money to it. You receive in return a certificate, called a ___j___. The safest 'business' to lend money to is the government. UK government bonds are called '___k___' (because they are printed on gilt-edged paper). If you lend to a company, you may receive bonds or ___l___ shares. ___m___ preference shares give the holder the right to convert them into ordinary shares at a later date; ___n___ preference shares give the company the right to buy them back or redeem them.

21.10 Speaking practice: the bank's investment services

Listen to this conversation. Then listen again, and speak the part of the man.

WOMAN What exactly will the bank do for me, if I use their management service?
MAN First, they'll deal on your behalf. Remember, you can only buy and sell shares through *a stockbroker*.
WOMAN So you act as my stockbroker. Do I have to tell you what to do every time?
MAN You can do, if you want, but usually customers ask us to buy and sell at our discretion.
WOMAN OK, as long as you refer the decision to me for my approval.
MAN We also *keep you posted on* company news: new issues, takeover bids, that kind of thing.
WOMAN Why do I need to know about takeover bids?
MAN Because the bidder may be making an offer for your shares. You've got to decide whether to accept.
WOMAN And the money that comes in – does that have to go to my account?
MAN No, we can forward *dividends* and other income anywhere you want – in accordance with your instructions.

21.10
a stockbroker a person who sells stocks and shares for other people.
keep you posted on tell you about; keep you informed of the latest news.
dividends amounts paid to shareholders as their part of the profit of a company.

21.12
get in on the ground floor buy shares in a new company; it suggests the very beginning of something which looks like a good opportunity.

21.11 Writing practice: figures

Richard Price has to advise a customer who wants to invest £20,000. Look back at the dialogues and documents in this unit. What advice would you give the customer? What fee will the bank charge him per year under its Investment Management Service? Explain to the customer how to calculate the smallest investment he must make to justify the bank's minimum fee.

21.12 Listen and read

Francesca is at a party for local business people. Listen to what they say. Notice how the different people give advice, and make and decline offers.

YUKIO So, you have come to Cardiff to study? What subject?
FRANCESCA I'm doing a marketing diploma and I hope also a doctor's degree in business administration, but at the moment I'm studying the stock market.
HANS Really? Is that just for fun, or have you some money to invest?
FRANCESCA I'm very serious about it. I have to have an income so that I can continue to live in England.
HANS Really! Excuse me a moment – Andreas – I would like you to meet a friend of mine. Francesca, can I introduce you to my business partner, Andreas Tsoulas. Andreas, this is Francesca – she is doing a marketing diploma at the university.
ANDREAS Hello, Francesca, I'm pleased to meet you.
FRANCESCA How do you do.
HANS And she is looking for an investment with a good return. She has a large sum of money to invest.
ANDREAS Ah! Really! Well, we have a great opportunity – you could *get in on the ground floor*.
YUKIO You want her to put money into your road transport company? Huh! Don't you listen to them! They tried it on me last week. They know I'm only a production engineer so they think I don't understand money!
FRANCESCA Don't worry! I can look after myself. But I can see now why my bank manager warned me not to play the market!

Considering the options

21.13
blue-chip companies large companies, thought to be an absolutely safe investment.
an alpha stock the stock or shares of a blue-chip company.
closing price the price of a share when the Stock Exchange closes at the end of the day.
a par value the amount printed on the share certificate; its face value.
Discretion here, being discreet; not telling other people about something.

21.13 Listen and read

Francesca meets Richard Price again to talk about her investments. Listen to wh they say. Does Richard think that the p/e ratio is a useful way to value a compan

1991		Stock	Price	Change	Yield	P/E
High	Low					
1199	1024	*ICI	1080	+20	6.8	8.1

RICHARD You see, Miss Amato, it's a question really of knowing what to look for. With *blue-chip companies* like ICI your money is safe, but the market price of the shares is obviously high. You know, of course, that share prices are published every day in the newspaper. This is what it says about ICI in today's listing. Wher are we? Yes, here. Now, 'high and low' means the highest and lowest prices of this stock during the current year. The stock, of course, is ICI – stocks and shares are practically the same thing – and the star means that ICI is rated *an alpha stock* – as I said, a blue-chip company. Yesterday's *closing price* was 1080p, for a shar with *a par value* of one pound. That's 20p higher than the day before, so the change column says plus twenty. 'Yield' means the percentage of return on your investment – assuming you've had your shares for at least a year, you'll get a six point eight per cent return on what you paid for them. And the price-to-earnings rati – ah, now this is supposed to be the key to the whole thing. You take the price of the shares as quoted on the Stock Exchange and multiply by the number of shares issued; that gives you the market valuation of the company. Then you divide that valuatior by the company's earnings – that means its latest profit figure, after tax. In fact, of course, there are so many factors that influenc market valuation and how big companies account for their profit that, in my opinion, p/e ratios are pretty meaningless.

FRANCESCA Yes, it's not as easy as it looks, is it? Do you know, I met two young men at a party who wanted me to put all my money into their international road transport consortium?

RICHARD Oh, did they now?

FRANCESCA But I would rather the bank looked after my financial affairs. I know you're very discreet.

RICHARD Yes. *Discretion* is the name of the game for bankers.

21.14 Reading for key words

Find the words or phrases in 21.13 that tell you the following:

1 You must know precisely what information you require.
2 The amount you have to pay if you want to buy one share.
3 The amount you would have to pay if you wanted to buy all the shares.
4 A large international busine organisation.
5 Doing something without oth people knowing about it.
6 An essential quality in this job.

21.15 Listen and read

Francesca has another meeting with Richard Price to talk about her investments. Listen to what they say. How will Francesca be able to give her father the money back when she returns home?

RICHARD With your income from this portfolio, and the money you earn working part-time for that road transport company, I should think you'll have enough to live on quite comfortably. Probably won't have to dig into the capital at all.

FRANCESCA That's my intention. In three years' time I'll go back to Milan and say to my father: 'Here's your eighty million lire, I don't need it after all.'

RICHARD Hm, and what's his reaction going to be to that?

FRANCESCA He'll say: 'That's what I hoped you would do. You can keep the money, here's another eighty million – now start your own business!'

21.16 Structure practice: giving advice

Richard Price gives Francesca advice on her investments in a number of ways. Perhaps the most obvious is when he uses the verb 'advise':

I would strongly advise you not to go playing the market.

The pattern here is:

to advise (someone) to do (something).

You can also use the noun 'advice':

Let me give you some advice. Let me give you a piece of advice.

But there are many other ways of giving advice to people.

I suggest that you do . . .
If I were you, I'd do . . .
Why don't you do . . .
Why not do . . .
How about doing . . .
What about doing . . .

You meet a friend who has some money to invest. Give him some advice. Use each of the phrases listed above. Make sure that you use the right form of the verb with each.

I would advise you to go and talk to your bank manager.
Let me give you some advice – go and talk to your bank manager.

21.17 Find the right word

Read the text below on securities. Write a word from the box to fill each of the gaps.

Your bank can act as your ___**a**___ ; it will deal in ___**b**___ on your behalf, at its own ___**c**___ or in accordance with your instructions, referring decisions to you for ___**d**___ if you wish. It will also advise you if, for instance, one of the companies you hold shares in is the subject of a ___**e**___ bid. The only way a company can take over another is to buy a controlling ___**f**___ in it – that is, at least 51% of its ___ **g** ___ . This can happen to even the most successful companies, rated as '___**h**___ companies' or '___**i**___ stocks' on the Stock Exchange. A takeover is not necessarily a disaster; rumours of one usually send the share price ___ **j** ___ sharply, sometimes far above its ___**k**___ value.

A company that wants to increase its capital must normally ___**l**___ more shares. It may take the opportunity to reward and encourage its existing shareholders by giving them shares as a ___**m**___ , or by offering them the right to buy the new shares before they are offered on the open ___**n**___.

alpha	approval
blue-chip	bonus
discretion	equity
interest	issue
market	par
securities	
stockbroker	
takeover	up

Study record	
21.1	
21.2	
21.3	
21.4	
21.5	
21.6	
21.7	
21.8	
21.9	
21.10	
21.11	
21.12	
21.13	
21.14	
21.15	
21.16	
21.17	

Answer key and commentary for unit 21

21.1 Listen and read

No. He says 'That is highly speculative and very dangerous', 'I would strongly advise you not to go playing the market', and 'No, no, no!'

21.4 Listen and read

Richard is trying to protect Francesca and her money from exposure to risk.

21.5 Reading for key words

1 highly speculative
2 peanuts
3 building societies
4 a portfolio of investments
5 spread the risk

21.8 Reading for key words

1 discretionary powers
2 improve your position
3 if applicable
4 ICI obliged
5 left the door open
6 to clinch the deal

21.9 Find the word

a securities **b** portfolio **c** value
d inflation **e** unit **f** index **g** prices
h price **i** lend **j** bond **k** gilts
l preference **m** convertible
n redeemable

21.11 Writing practice

This is a model answer.

Frankly, I wouldn't advise you to buy shares at all. Twenty thousand isn't really enough to buy a well-balanced portfolio. If I were you I'd put some of the money in a deposit account – we can offer you a very good rate of interest – and the rest in a reliable unit trust. Again, the bank has a very good unit trust scheme if you want to make use of it. The important thing is to know that you can get at your cash quickly if you have to.

I'll be glad to advise you at any time, but don't join our Investment Management Service for the time being. The charges are ninety pence per hundred pounds' market value of your investment, but the minimum charge is £360. If you work that out, £360 divided by 90 pence is 400; so your investments have got to be worth at least 400 times £100, that's £40,000, if you're going to justify that minimum charge.

21.13 Listen and read

No, he doesn't. He says 'this is supposed to be th
key to the whole thing', but he also says 'there a
so many factors that influence market valuatio
and how big companies account for their profi
that, in my opinion, p/e ratios are pret
meaningless.'

21.14 Reading for key words

1 it's a question really of knowing what to lo for
2 the market price
3 the market valuation
4 international . . . consortium
5 Discretion
6 the name of the game

21.15 Listen and read

Francesca will be able to give her father th
money back because her portfolio will give h
enough interest for her to live on. She won't ha
to spend, or 'dig into', the capital sum at all.

21.16 Structure practice

These are model answers.

Let me give you a piece of advice – go and talk your bank manager.

I suggest that you go and talk to your ba manager.

If I were you, I'd go and talk to your ba manager.

Why don't you go and talk to your bank manage

Why not go and talk to your bank manager?

How about going to talk to your bank manage

What about going to talk to your bank manage

21.17 Find the word

a stockbroker **b** securities **c** discretion
d approval **e** takeover **f** interest
g equity **h** blue-chip **i** alpha **j** up
k par **l** issue **m** bonus **n** market

Unit 22: Boardroom decision making

SITUATION

Standard Can is a multinational corporation based in Dallas, Texas. Its latest acquisition is J.F. Hiltmann und Söhne AG of Dusseldorf, the makers of Maxy sauce. Standard Can's President, Jerome Fantam, intends to close Hiltmann and sell off its valuable property assets to improve his corporation's cash flow, but in the boardroom there is serious opposition to his plan.

CHARACTERS

Leo Schooler	is a senior executive at Standard Can. He is German.
Patricia Hart	is responsible for Wholesale Distribution at Standard Can. She is American.
Stephen Sablon	is European Marketing Director at Standard Can. He is British.
Jerome Fantam	is President of Standard Can. He is American.
Anton Hiltmann	is a senior executive at J.F. Hiltmann. He is German.

LANGUAGE

Vocabulary	Group dynamics: rivalry, alliance, challenge; corporate planning; takeovers and finance; marketing.
Skills	Intervening in a discussion; taking sides; defending a position.
Structure	Conceding a point.
Documents	Business journal article; a company annual report; a newspaper article; a business report and market survey.

Beginning a power struggle

BUSINESS JOURNAL

STANDARD CAN FINDS TASTE OF HILTMANN IRRESISTIBLE

J.F. Hiltmann, makers for the past century and a half of the popular Maxy brand savoury food flavouring, are themselves rumoured to be *flavour of the month* for US-based conglomerate Standard Can. Hiltmann directors are said to have recommended acceptance of StanCan's offer of one SC ordinary share plus DM 4.78 for each Hiltmann share, even though this values their company at a *puny* $37m. Whether the brand name, or indeed any trace of Hiltmann, will survive is problematical, given Standard Can's appetite for prime industrial locations which it can sell off for redevelopment. Hiltmann's factory was built in 1849 on what was then *a greenfield site* but is now a very expensive piece of real estate in *downtown* Dusseldorf.

22.1 Document study

This is an article from a business journ about an attempt by Standard Can t take over Hiltmann. Read through carefully. What does the writer thin may happen to Hiltmann if the takeov goes ahead?

22.1
flavour of the month something that is very popular at the moment, but probably only for a short time.
puny small and weak; **puny** is not normally used in this context, but journalists use words like this to add variety to their writing.
a greenfield site a site outside a town, which has no buildings on it.
downtown near the town centre, where property values are highest.

22.3
Wholesale dealing with retailers, not with shoppers.
the business in hand what we're doing or talking about at the moment.
it's in the bag we've succeeded; an informal usage.
sit on the fence refuse to decide which side you support.

22.2 Reading for key words

Find the words and phrases in 22.1 that tell you the following:

1. The current favourite.
2. Very uncertain.
3. In view of.
4. First-class places to build factories.
5. Journalists like to play with words. What words or phrases can you find in th article that were probably suggested by the nature of Hiltmann's product?

22.3 Listen and read

Leo, Patricia and Stephen are senior executives of Standard Can. They are about go into a meeting at their European head office in Vienna. What are Leo and Patric trying to do? Does Stephen agree with them?

LEO — Er – Patricia! Could we have a quick word before we go in? By th way, I'd like you to meet Stephen . . .

PATRICIA — Oh – you must be Stephen Sablon, the new European Marketing Director.

STEPHEN — That's right.

PATRICIA — I'm Patricia Hart, *Wholesale* Distribution. How do you do?

STEPHEN — I'm pleased to meet you, Patricia, I've heard . . .

LEO — Yes, I'm sure you have, but could we concentrate for the moment on *the business in hand*? Item five on the agenda for this meeting is the Hiltmann takeover. I've just heard from a very reliable source that we now have at least fifty-five per cent of the shares, so it looks as though *it's in the bag*!

PATRICIA — What Leo is saying is that we want to make certain the right decisions are taken at this meeting about the future of Hiltmann. Pressure is going to be brought to bear on the directors to close down the company and dispose of its assets.

LEO — Whereas I see Hiltmann becoming a nice little profit centre – under the right management, if you follow me. Now, Stephen, I assume that I can count on your support?

STEPHEN — Well, I think I'd like to hear the arguments on both sides before I make any decision.

LEO — You can't *sit on the fence*, Stephen.

STEPHEN — Shall we go in?

22.4 Speaking practice: looking for support

Listen to this conversation. Then listen again, and speak the part of the man.

WOMAN Could we have a quick word before the meeting begins?
MAN If it's about the takeover, I haven't made up my mind yet.
WOMAN We're going to be under a lot of pressure to sell off the company, and frankly I think that's rather short-sighted.
MAN Sell it off! We don't know the outcome of the takeover bid yet.
WOMAN I've just heard from a reliable source that we've got fifty-five per cent of the shares.
MAN Well, I just hope we can afford this takeover – considering our pressing cash-flow problems.
WOMAN Can we concentrate for a moment on the business in hand? I'm counting on you to back me up.
MAN I'm not so sure. What about that new man?
WOMAN I had a word with him yesterday. He says he's with me, but you can't keep sitting on the fence for much longer. The new company could do great things – with the right management!
MAN Hm. Oh! It's time to go in.

22.5
a shake-out a clear-out of unwanted, unproductive managers.
Chicken feed very little money; an informal usage.
a household word a name that is known to many people.
eighty-five per cent brand recognition 85% of people, when asked, recognised the brand name and knew what products it represented.

22.5 Listen and read

Two hours later, the meeting ends. What decision has been made about the future of Hiltmann? Why is Jerome Fantam, the President of Standard Can, so angry? Why does he mention motorcycles?

JEROME Stephen! Why didn't you support me over the closure of Hiltmann?
STEPHEN Because frankly, Mr President, I think your policy proposal is short-sighted. OK, get rid of the Hiltmann management – they need *a shake-out*. But they did turn over seventy-three million dollars last year.
JEROME *Chicken feed*, Stephen. You let me down.
STEPHEN You won't be saying that three years from now. The point about Hiltmann is their brand name is *a household word* in half the countries of Europe. Why do you want to throw away *eighty-five per cent brand recognition*?
JEROME We control the company, we can use the brand any damn way we like. We can use it to sell – motorcycles, if we want to.

22.6 Structure practice: conceding a point

In 22.1, the journalist writes:

> Hiltmann directors are said to have recommended acceptance of StanCan's offer of one SC ordinary share plus DM 4.78 for each Hiltmann share, even though this values their company at a puny $37m.

In 22.5, Stephen says:

> OK, get rid of the Hiltmann management – they need a shake-out. But they did turn over $73 million last year.

In both cases two statements are being made, and one of them is being presented as surprising in view of the other. You can use 'even though' or 'although' as in 22.1, or 'but' as in 22.5 to do this, but you must not use both.

Rewrite the pairs of sentences below, using 'although' or 'even though', and then rewrite them again using 'but'.

1 Hiltmann is in financial difficulties. It owns some valuable real estate.
Hiltmann is in financial difficulties, even though it owns some valuable real estate.
Hiltmann owns some valuable real estate, but it is in financial difficulties.
2 Leo believes Hiltmann could be profitable. It's in financial difficulties.
3 The offer undervalues the company. The board have recommended acceptance.
4 Fantam would like to sell off Hiltmann. It turned over $73 million last year.

A shareholders' meeting

The past year has been *particularly fruitful* in new acquisitions; *no fewer than six* new wholly- or part-owned subsidiary companies have been *incorporated into* the Group.

All takeovers and mergers are in line with our *corporate strategy* and every element in our growing family has a vital role to play in our development, guided always of course by the forces of the marketplace.

ANNUAL REPORT

25

22.7 Document study

Standard Can's Annual General Meetin is due. This is an extract from th President's address in the annual repor Read through it carefully. Th President's statement is intended t inform shareholders but also to reassu them. Which words in the extract a chosen specially to make th shareholders feel good about th company?

22.7
particularly fruitful especially profitable.
no fewer than six Jerome Fantam is saying that he thinks that six is a lot in this case.
incorporated into made part of.
corporate strategy the corporation's long-term financial plans for growth and investment.

22.8
Shame! a way of expressing strong disagreement with the speaker at a large formal meeting.

22.9
standing orders the rules which control the conduct of shareholders' meetings.
points of order formal objections to what someone has done or said, on the grounds that he or she has broken the rules of the meeting.
be ruled out of order be judged to have broken the rules.
to take you up on that to have a full discussion of that point with you.
your own equity Standard Can used their own ordinary shares.

22.8 Listen and read

At the shareholders' meeting, the President approaches the end of his speech. Liste to what is said. Why is Anton Hiltmann allowed to attend this meeting? Why is h allowed to speak?

JEROME	. . . a vital role to play in our development, guided always of course by the forces of the marketplace . . .
ANTON	*Shame!*
CHAIRMAN	Quiet, please – ladies and gentlemen! Order!
JEROME	If the gentleman who spoke just then wishes to raise a point of order, let him stand up and speak up!
ANTON	With great pleasure, Mr President!
CHAIRMAN	Stay where you are, please, sir, the steward will bring you a microphone. . . . Please identify yourself.
ANTON	Anton Hiltmann, ordinary shareholder. . . . In his annual report tc us, the owners of Standard Can, Mr Fantam says that the actions of the board of directors are guided by market forces. In my experience, Mr Chairman, these decisions are too often guided by the personal ambition and prejudices of members of the board!

22.9 Listen and read

The shareholders' meeting continues. Listen to what is said. Why do Antc Hiltmann and the chairman argue about orders and rules?

CHAIRMAN	Quiet, please! May I remind you, Mr Hiltmann, that under *standing orders* you are entitled to raise *points of order* but not to question the speaker.
ANTON	I ask, Mr Chairman, that the speaker should *be ruled out of order* for wasting the time of the meeting. The treatment of the management and employees of J.F. Hiltmann Söhne since the takeover six months ago shows that market forces have nothing to do with this company's decision making!
JEROME	I'd like *to take you up on that*, Mr Hiltmann – after the meeting!
STEPHEN	[To Patricia] This is what comes of paying for takeover bids with *your own equity*. Why didn't Standard pay cash for Hiltmann?
PATRICIA	[To Stephen] Because if you ask me they hadn't got it.

22.10 Writing practice: an eye-witness account

As a Standard Can shareholder, you attended the AGM. You are also a director/shareholder of a small company which Standard Can is interested in; it has already bought 12% of your company's shares. Write a short report for your colleagues, telling them what happened at the AGM, and what might happen to your own company.

22.11 Document study

This article appeared on the city pages of a daily newspaper the next day. Read through it carefully, then do the exercise that follows.

£MONEY PAGE

SHAREHOLDERS ON THE WARPATH AS STANDARD CAN AGM ENDS IN UPROAR

PRESIDENT ACCUSES *'INTERESTED PARTIES'*

Protestors interrupted the President of Standard Can during his address to shareholders at yesterday's Annual General Meeting in the Ballroom of the Dorchester Hotel, Park Lane.

Mr Anton Hiltmann, head of J.F. Hiltmann und Söhne AG, the internationally-known sauce manufacturers of Dusseldorf, led *hecklers* who accused Mr Jerome Fantam of putting 'personal ambition' and 'prejudice' before the true interests of the shareholders. Order was restored after Mr Fantam agreed to meet Mr Hiltmann and a group of shareholders in Germany next week. He accused 'interested parties' of stirring up trouble to achieve their own ends, which were not compatible with the Group's goals.

When I spoke to Mr Hiltmann after the meeting, he expressed disappointment and disillusion at the way his company had been treated since its takeover by Standard Can last year. He said a successful business and prestigious brand name were being 'sacrificed in return for *a fast buck*.'

Market gossip has it that StanCan is facing problems with over-manning, spiralling costs and falling profitability, particularly in its Food and Entertainment Divisions, and that the real wrangles at the top are about product mixes, brand management and the corporate image – which certainly did not benefit from yesterday's *shenanigans*. Despite the announcement of a slightly increased dividend of 18.3p (up 1%), SC shares fell 18p in quiet trading *to close at 207p*.

22.11

interested parties note that 'interested' here means 'having something to lose or gain'; such a person or group may not be fair or impartial in making decisions.

hecklers people who interrupt a meeting by shouting questions or comments at the speaker.

a fast buck a quick, easy profit, with no regard to long-term benefits; an informal usage.

shenanigans trouble or fighting, especially if dishonest; an informal usage.

to close at 207p this was the price of the shares when the Stock Exchange closed at the end of the day.

22.12 Writing practice: Stephen's notes

Stephen has attended all of the meetings and read all of the reports on these pages. He now has to write a report on what Standard Can should do with Hiltmann. Before he does this, he needs to organise his notes. What is Fantam's position? What is Hiltmann's position? What other information and speculation is there? Write these notes for Stephen from all of the things you have heard and read in this unit so far.

Making the best of a difficult situation

22.13
given him credit for believed him to be.
the upshot was the result was.
I was counting on I was relying on.
pressing urgent.

22.14
The recent spate the recent large number.
somewhat obscured forgotten about; Stephen shows his disagreement with Jerome's management by being sarcastic. What he means is 'We have been so busy taking over companies that we have totally forgotten about marketing.'
a diagnostic marketing strategy a course of action which will show us what is wrong with our marketing policy.
viability enough profitability for the company to survive.
optimising the marketing mix making sure that we use the best possible combination of marketing methods.

22.13 Listen and read

Stephen has a meeting with Jerome Fantam. Listen to what they say. What decisio has been made? What new information does Stephen learn about Standard Can

JEROME Stephen, thank you for coming in today. I guess you know what I want to discuss with you. I had a long talk yesterday with Anton Hiltmann, who turns out to be a cleverer businessman than I had *given him credit for*. I won't bore you with all the details, but *the upshot was* that he convinced me Hiltmann AG should not only continue trading but it should continue to exploit the Maxy brand name.

STEPHEN Good for him.

JEROME Hm. Yeah. Well, I think I ought to put you a little more fully in th picture. *I was counting on* the sale of Hiltmann assets, particularly in the real-estate department, to ease Standard's cash-flow problems, which I don't mind admitting are a little more *pressing* than you may realise.

22.14 Document study

Stephen's report and market survey is circulated to senior managers. H conclusions are printed below. Read through them carefully. Does the report prais or criticise Standard Can's policies?

The recent spate of acquisitions and takeovers has led to group marketing policy becoming *somewhat obscured*. This paper has attempted to outline *a diagnostic marketing strategy* which may, in the medium to long term, lead to restored *viability* for the Group as a whole.

A period of at least two years' consolidation and rationalisation of Group activities is required, during which capital investment must be restricted to the Group's own members.

A systematic evaluation of all the Group's products and markets, actual and potential, must be carried out, together with an in-depth study of our competitors.

As a first step, a subsidiary company should be selected to mount a pilot scheme aimed at determining marketing goals and *optimising the marketing mix* in a clearly-defined region of Europe.

22.15 Writing practice

The conclusions in Stephen's report are very brief, but they are also phrased in ve formal language so that it is sometimes difficult to understand. Rewrite h conclusions in simpler, less formal language so that it is easy to see what he mean

22.16 Listen and read

In another meeting in Jerome Fantam's office, Leo, Patricia, Stephen and Jerome discuss the report. Listen to what they say. Stephen's plan is good because it should succeed, but it's also good if it fails. Why?

LEO — I mean, this paper of Stephen's – it's just *so much hot air*. These are *platitudes*.

PATRICIA — Except, perhaps, the suggestion for a test-marketing exercise.

STEPHEN — Thank you. But if we mean to implement the proposal, we have to move fast.

JEROME — I agree the time-scale is short. Did you have any particular company in mind as *a test-bed* for this scheme of yours?

STEPHEN — Well, I hardly like to mention the name but, er, Hiltmann?

JEROME — Why Hiltmann?

STEPHEN — Good location. Good market position. Good product.

PATRICIA — And *if it came unstuck*, it would be easier for us to back out. We could say this was something that was already *in the pipeline* before the takeover.

22.17 Listen and read

The meeting continues. Why are Jerome Fantam and Stephen both willing to try the test-marketing exercise?

LEO — Hm. You want to run a marketing exercise based on a one-product, one-market company.

STEPHEN — No. We must diversify the product range, repackage it and establish a new brand image in *a market* that up till now Hiltmann *has never penetrated*. I suggest Greece.

LEO — Stephen, to launch a new product range takes years.

STEPHEN — It does in Standard Can, that's why we're in such deep trouble. There's so much red tape and bureaucracy in this organisation, people are scared to think for themselves. . . . *I'll put my job on the line*, Mr President: *second* me as *brand manager* to Hiltmann for six months, and I'll have every Greek kitchen loaded with Maxy products.

JEROME — And if you don't?

STEPHEN — If I don't . . . I'll resign my directorship.

JEROME — It's a deal.

LEO — Provided you can sell it to Anton Hiltmann.

JEROME — Oh, I'll sell it to him. Trust me.

22.18 Writing practice: Jerome Fantam's notes

Jerome Fantam also keeps notes of what has happened. Write notes about the things that have happened in 22.13–22.17. Remember that you must present what has happened from Jerome Fantam's point of view, and say what he thinks about them. Read the documents again, and listen to the dialogues – they will help you to work out what Jerome's attitude is.

22.16
so much hot air meaningless words.
platitudes statements which are true but are rather boring and meaningless; they don't add anything new but are simply meant to sound impressive; a formal usage.
a test-bed somewhere to test a plan or carry out a trial.
if it came unstuck if it failed.
in the pipeline on its way through the organisation's procedures; if the test marketing scheme had already been planned or started before the takeover, Standard Can could deny responsibility for it if it fails.

22.17
a market . . . has never penetrated an area where we have never been successful.
I'll put my job on the line if I fail I will resign.
second transfer.
brand manager the manager who is responsible for all aspects of developing, manufacturing and marketing the product or products sold under a particular brand name.

Study record	
22.1	
22.2	
22.3	
22.4	
22.5	
22.6	
22.7	
22.8	
22.9	
22.10	
22.11	
22.12	
22.13	
22.14	
22.15	
22.16	
22.17	
22.18	

Answer key and commentary for unit 22

22.1 Document study

The reporter thinks that Standard Can will take over Hiltmann, paying a very low price for it, and will then sell off its valuable property. The brand name Maxy, and perhaps Hiltmann itself, will disappear.

22.2 Reading for key words

1 flavour of the month **2** problematical
3 given **4** prime industrial locations
5 taste . . . irresistible; flavour; appetite

22.3 Listen and read

Leo and Patricia are trying to get Stephen to support them over the future of Hiltmann. Stephen does not say whether he agrees with them or not.

22.5 Listen and read

Hiltmann will continue to exist, although the management will be replaced. Jerome Fantam is angry because he wanted to sell Hiltmann. Jerome mentions motorcycles because he thinks that the important thing about Hiltmann is the brand name 'Maxy', not the product. He thinks that Standard Can could use the Maxy brand name to sell any product at all, even something that has nothing to do with food.

22.6 Structure practice

These are model answers.

2 Leo believes Hiltmann could be profitable, even though it is in financial difficulties.
Hiltmann is in financial difficulties, but Leo believes it could be profitable.

3 Although the offer undervalues the company, the board have recommended acceptance.
The offer undervalues the company, but the board have recommended acceptance.

4 Fantam would like to sell off Hiltmann, even though it turned over $73 million last year.
Hiltmann turned over $73 million last year, but Fantam would like to sell it off.

22.7 Document study

The words which are used to make people feel good about Standard Can are: 'fruitful', 'no fewer than', 'in line with', 'our growing family', 'a vital role', 'our development', 'guided'. These all provide a very positive image of the company.

22.8 Listen and read

Anton Hiltmann is allowed to attend the Annual General Meeting because he is a Standard Can shareholder. He is allowed to speak because he wants to raise a point of order; that is, to comment on how the meeting is being conducted.

22.9 Listen and read

Anton Hiltmann and the Chairman argue about orders and rules because an important formal meeting must be run strictly according to rules of procedure. If it is not, decisions may be made which are not valid or legal.

22.10 Writing practice

This is a model answer.

I've just attended the Standard Can AGM. There was a row between the President, Jerome Fantam, and Anton Hiltmann, who is the boss of J.F. Hiltmann, the people who make Maxy sauce. You know Standard took over Hiltmann a few months ago. Just as Fantam was reaching the climax of his speech, Hiltmann stood up and started complaining about the treatment of their managers and staff since the takeover. A lot of people in the room seemed to be on his side. There was a great deal of shouting; finally th chairman restored order, and Fantam an Hiltmann agreed to meet in private afterwards. can't help thinking that we shall have to b careful. StanCan already has 12% of our share and they're rumoured to be interested in takeover. I think we should discuss what our ow strategy will be if they make a serious bid.

22.12 Writing practice

This is a model answer.

Fantam's position: wants to close Hiltmann ar dispose of its assets.

Hiltmann's position: wants to save Hiltman thinks that Fantam is not acting in Hiltmann's be interests.

Information: Hiltmann has valuable brand nam and a valuable site.

Speculation: problems at StanCan over-manning, rising costs, falling profitability.

22.13 Listen and read

The decision has been made that Hiltmar should continue trading, and should continue exploit the Maxy brand name. Stephen learns th Standard Can has a big cash-flow problem.

22.14 Document study

Stephen's report is critical of Standard Can policies.

22.15 Writing practice

This is a model answer.

Because of all the companies Standard Can h bought recently, we no longer have a clear grou marketing policy. I have tried to write a marketi strategy that will, in time, make Standard Ca financially strong again.

There must be no more takeovers for at lea two years. In that time we must concentrate c investing in the companies we already own.

We must look at our products, and at th products of our competitors, now and in th future, and work out what we will be able to se in different markets.

We need to test a product and a marketi plan in one market in Europe.

22.16 Listen and read

If the plan fails, Standard Can can say that it w planned before the takeover, so that it doesn look as though they have failed.

22.17 Listen and read

Jerome is willing to try because Stephen h offered to resign if he fails. Stephen is willing to t because he needs to show that he can b successful.

22.18 Writing practice

This is a model answer.

We discussed Sablon's confidential mark survey. Everyone agreed that its contents we worthless. However, there was support for proposal to test-market a single product in clearly-defined region. Sablon wants to sell Ma in Greece. I like this idea. If it comes unstuck, will be a good reason for getting rid of Sablon and, publicly, we can save face by saying th scheme was in the pipeline before the takeov He proposed to diversify the product, repacka it, etc. Then he lost his head and offered to resi if Maxy wasn't a hit in Greece inside six month I look forward to this. He demanded to b seconded to Hiltmann as brand manager.

Unit 23: Test marketing

SITUATION

The test marketing results suggest that to increase sales Maxy sauce needs to be redeveloped and repackaged as a more up-market product. Stephen Sablon and Anton Hiltmann have been given the task of making it work within six months. Can they do it?

CHARACTERS

Anton Hiltmann

Jerome Fantam

Stephen Sablon

Patricia Hart

Leo Schooler

Michael Tsatsos is a marketing consultant. He is Greek.

LANGUAGE

Vocabulary	Market research; retail promotion and merchandising; the marketing mix: advertising, packaging, pricing, etc.
Skills	Questioning proposals in detail; negotiating a management decision; listening to figures being spoken.
Documents	A questionnaire; bar charts; a line chart; a pie chart; a memo.

Planning a campaign

23.1
broken down analysed.

23.1 Listen and read

In Anton Hiltmann's office in Dusseldorf, Michael Tsatsos, a Greek marketin consultant, presents his findings to the Hiltmann management. Listen to what the say. What was the purpose of Michael's enquiries in Greek supermarkets? What so of results would Hiltmann regard as encouraging?

MICHAEL First, the good news – we've got the results of the supermarket survey. You should have received a copy yesterday.

ANTON On the face of it, I thought these figures looked encouraging. What exactly was the procedure, Mr Tsatsos?

MICHAEL Twenty interviewers visited altogether one hundred supermarkets in five large towns on different days of the week, at different times of day. They interviewed a total of five hundred and thirty-seven women and twenty-four men.

ANTON You say this is a summary – but you've also analysed these figures in more detail, haven't you?

MICHAEL Well, yes, if you look on the second sheet you'll see we have got the computer to do a bar chart of the responses to question seven, *broken down* according to age. That's the bad news!

23.2 Document study

This is the questionnaire, and the bar chart of the responses to question 7. Wh good news for Hiltmann can you find in these figures? What bad news appears i the bar chart?

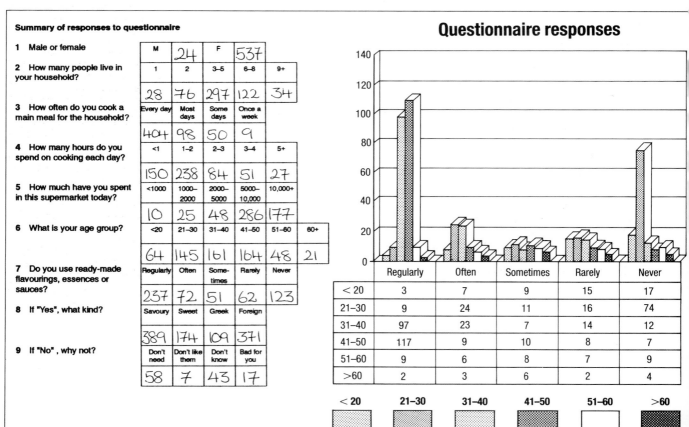

Summary of responses to questionnaire

Question						
1 Male or female	M	24	F	537		
2 How many people live in your household?	1	2	3–5	6–8	9+	
	28	76	297	122	34	
3 How often do you cook a main meal for the household?	Every day	Most days	Some days	Once a week		
	404	98	50	9		
4 How many hours do you spend on cooking each day?	<1	1–2	2–3	3–4	5+	
	150	238	84	51	27	
5 How much have you spent in this supermarket today?	<1000	1000–2000	2000–5000	5000–10,000	10,000+	
	10	25	48	286	177	
6 What is your age group?	<20	21–30	31–40	41–50	51–60	60+
	64	145	161	164	48	21
7 Do you use ready-made flavourings, essences or sauces?	Regularly	Often	Sometimes	Rarely	Never	
	237	72	51	62	123	
8 If "Yes", what kind?	Savoury	Sweet	Greek	Foreign		
	389	174	109	371		
9 If "No", why not?	Don't need	Don't like them	Don't know	Bad for you		
	58	7	43	17		

Questionnaire responses

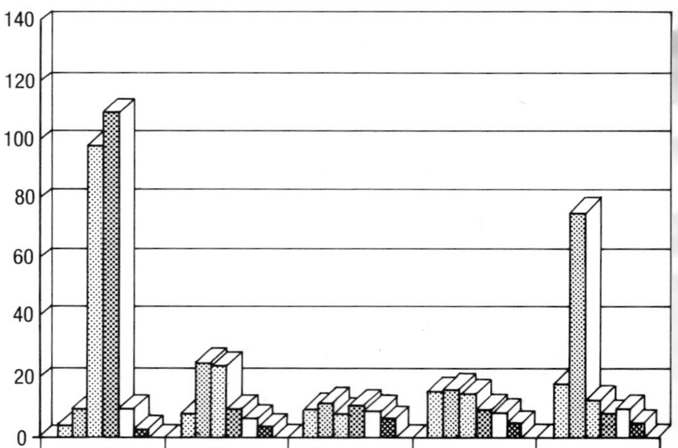

	Regularly	Often	Sometimes	Rarely	Never
< 20	3	7	9	15	17
21–30	9	24	11	16	74
31–40	97	23	7	14	12
41–50	117	9	10	8	7
51–60	9	6	8	7	9
>60	2	3	6	2	4

< 20 | 21–30 | 31–40 | 41–50 | 51–60 | >60

23.3 Writing practice: a customer profile

A profile is simply a short, factual description. Write a profile of the typical Gree food shopper, based on all the relevant information you can extract from th summary of responses and the bar chart.

23.4 Listen and read

The presentation continues. Listen to what they say. How is Michael going to try to reach the typical Greek food shopper as described in your profile in 23.3?

ANTON — All right, Mr Tsatsos, *the marketing mix*. Let's hear what you propose.

MICHAEL — *The main thrust* of our campaign will be through television commercials. Some of these will be *at peak viewing times* in the early evening, but many will be screened during the afternoon when rates are low, but many housewives watch.

ANTON — Mhm. You've *costed* the whole thing, I suppose?

MICHAEL — Yes, and we expect *to come in at ten per cent below budget*, even *allowing for contingencies*.

ANTON — *I've heard that one before.* What are you doing *apart from* TV?

MICHAEL — We obviously have to target the housewife. So, *to soften up the market*, a series of half-page ads in the four most popular women's magazines, running from mid-March through to the middle of April.

23.4

the marketing mix the combination of marketing techniques that will achieve increased demand for Maxy.
The main thrust the main part; the greatest activity.
at peak viewing times when most people will be watching television.
costed estimated the cost. Be careful not to confuse this with the verb **cost** meaning 'have a price of'.
to come in at ten per cent below budget to spend 10% less than we have available.
allowing for contingencies putting aside some money for unexpected expenses.
I've heard that one before Anton is saying here that he doesn't believe Michael.
apart from here, this means 'as well as' or 'in addition to'. But it can also mean 'except for': 'I have visited every EC country, **apart from** Greece' means that I have not been to Greece.
to soften up the market to get people used to the idea of Maxy before we start advertising a lot on television.

23.5 Listen and read

The presentation continues. Listen to what they say. Apart from advertising, what does Michael want to spend money on?

ANTON — Just that? Nothing else?

MICHAEL — That's it as far as the media are concerned – except for *some interviews I've got lined up* on some local radio stations' cookery programmes. They're going to mention Maxy in their 'new products' feature, you know the sort of thing. That won't cost us anything.

ANTON — What about *in-store promotion*?

MICHAEL — Naturally, there'll be *point-of-sale merchandising*: show cards, special display stands – where we can find room for them. You must remember floor space in supermarkets is *at a premium*.

ANTON — Can't you slip the manager something – *a little backhander*?

MICHAEL — Well, there are ways of offering little incentives, yes. And talking of incentives – we have allowed for a certain amount of *below-the-line expenditure*.

23.5

some interviews I've got lined up some interviews that I have arranged.
in-store promotion advertising inside shops and stores.
point-of-sale merchandising advertising next to the goods in shops and stores.
at a premium in great demand, therefore expensive.
a little backhander a small bribe.
below-the-line expenditure money spent on promoting the product, in addition to normal advertising, free offers, competitions, etc. This might include gifts or the cost of a party to entertain shop managers.

23.6 Reading for key words

Find the words or phrases in 23.1–23.5 that tell you the following:

1. Anton Hiltmann thinks the questionnaire results look good, but he doesn't want to appear too enthusiastic in case they turn out to be not so good after all.
2. The most important part of our effort.
3. The times of day when the largest numbers of people watch TV.
4. In my experience, statements like that are usually not true.
5. That's all.
6. Give somebody a small bribe.

Presenting the results

23.7 Document study

The test-marketing exercise produced many figures. The diagrams below shov some of the results. Which of the diagrams is a bar chart? Which is a bar and lin chart? Which is a line chart? Which is a pie chart? Which of the diagrams show trend over a period of time? Which show an analysis at a given point in time?

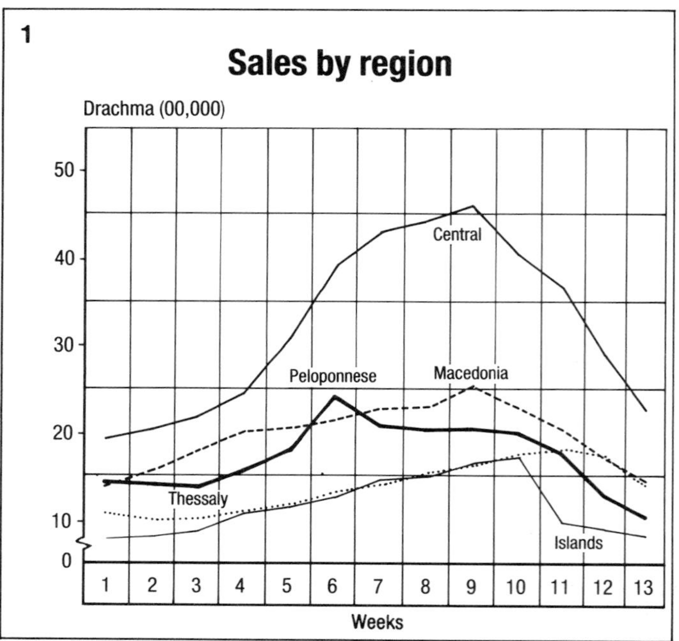

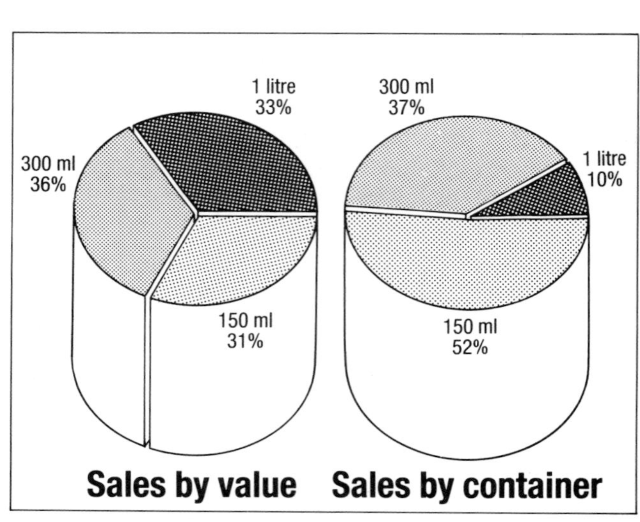

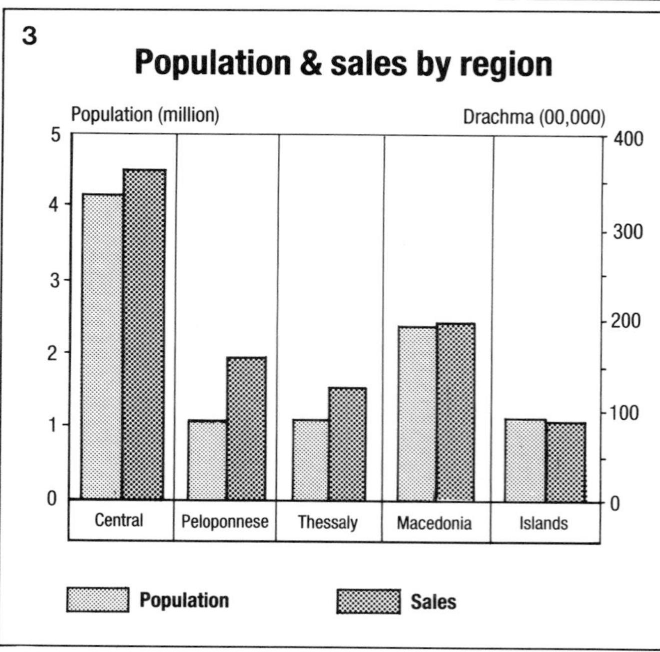

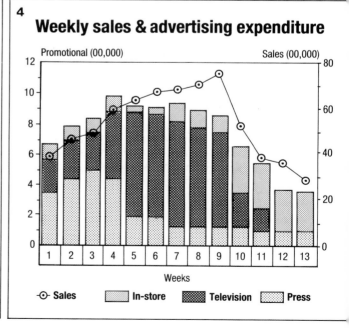

4

Weekly sales & advertising expenditure

Promotional (00,000)

Sales (00,000)

12
10
8
6
4
2
0

80
60
40
20
0

1 2 3 4 5 6 7 8 9 10 11 12 13

Weeks

Sales In-store Television Press

23.8 Find the word: tendencies and trends

Choose the most suitable word from the box to fill each gap.

If we look at Figure 4, overall the message is pretty clear. A marked ___a___ in sales to begin with, then a ___b___ in week 9, and then a ___c___ . The sales figures seem to follow the advertising expenditure, with a small ___d___.

Some of the regional figures ___e___ considerably, however. For example, if we look at Figure 1, sales in the small shops in the islands build up gradually. They ___f___ steadily until week 10, then they ___g___ sharply in week 11, and finally ___h___ to almost nothing. The figures for Thessaly show a more gradual ___i___ and decrease. At the end of the period they're ___j___ than they were at the beginning.

If we look at Figure 3, there seems to be a strong ___k___ between population and sales.

Figure 2 shows that although the greatest ___l___ of sales came from the 150ml containers, the greatest ___m___ of sales came from the 300ml containers.

collapse	
correlation	
fall	fluctuate
higher	increase
lag	number
peak	rise
rise	slump
value	

23.9 Listen and read

Stephen telephones Jerome Fantam to tell him about the test-marketing results. Listen to what they say, and to how Jerome asks for the figure to be broken down.

JEROME Fantam.

STEPHEN Stephen Sablon here. I've got the Maxy test-marketing results from Tsatsos.

JEROME Oh, have you! So how do the results look?

STEPHEN Quite promising.

JEROME Oh, yeah? What was the retail sales total?

STEPHEN Just over ninety million drachmas.

JEROME Ninety million? How many people are there in Greece?

STEPHEN A little under ten million.

JEROME Oh, not as many as I thought. How does your sales figure break down, regionally? How many sales regions are there?

STEPHEN There are five. Central Greece, with the capital, Athens, . . .

JEROME Just tell me which region got the highest sales total.

STEPHEN Central Greece, easily. It's got nearly half the population. Sales were thirty-six million.

JEROME And how about the other four regions?

STEPHEN Well, Macedonia was about twenty million, Peloponnese sixteen million, Thessaly twelve million, and the Islands nine million.

JEROME Are those the results you'd expect, taking into account the population of each region? Which regions got the best results per head?

STEPHEN The Peloponnese did very well indeed. Thessaly did well. The other three were pretty similar.

JEROME Uh-huh. That's interesting, Stephen, I look forward to seeing the detailed figures very shortly. I have to hang up now, I've got Tokyo on the other line. Bye.

Key decision making

23.10
on the table on offer.
to let you off the hook to let you get out of a difficult position.

23.11
go down market reduce the price so that the product appeals to people with less money.
product differentiation in this case making a single product into a range of products, each different from the others.
at the outset at the beginning.

23.12
to see some light at the end of the tunnel to come to the end of a bad situation.
carte blanche complete freedom.
there are strings attached there are things that Anton has to do in return.

23.10 Listen and read

Patricia, Stephen and Leo are having a telephone conversation with Jerome Fantan Listen to what they say. Does Jerome think that the test-marketing exercise has bee a success? How do you know?

PATRICIA Good morning, Mr President. Can you hear me? We have some figures for the Maxy test-marketing scheme in Greece.

JEROME I hear you, you don't need to shout. And I've seen the results. First of all I have to ask, is Sablon's resignation still *on the table*?

STEPHEN My offer to resign from the board still stands, of course. However, I . . .

JEROME Ah . . . I'm not going *to let you off the hook* that easy. Leo, can we have your comments on the exercise?

LEO Obviously the problem is the lack of repeat orders. We must, of course, bear in mind that this was only a three-month trial, of a product which the market perceived as being quite a high-priced luxury item.

STEPHEN Right. Where we failed was we didn't get them using it every day.

23.11 Listen and read

The telephone conversation continues. Listen to what they say. What solutions t the problem of Maxy's future are proposed?

PATRICIA So, Stephen, you think we should *go down market*, knock twenty o thirty per cent off the price?

LEO Just a minute. On Anton's behalf, as he can't be with us today, may I point out that Maxy is a quality product. It's produced in small batches from high-grade materials, and the overheads are correspondingly high. They can't cut the price just like that.

JEROME They can sell at a loss for up to three years if that's what it takes tc get established in the market. Also they could manufacture somewhere else than that expensive site in the middle of Dusseldorf – that would bring their overheads down.

STEPHEN I agree we may have got it wrong over pricing. But I'd suggest just the opposite from Patricia. Let's take Maxy up market, but make sure people buy every flavour in the Maxy range.

LEO Ah, *product differentiation* – that's what you're suggesting, is it?

STEPHEN I said *at the outset*, you remember, that we ought to diversify the product, but everyone said we didn't have time. Now we've got even less time, but we're just going to have to do it.

23.12 Listen and read

The telephone conversation continues. Listen to what they say. What solution ha been chosen? What benefit is Jerome Fantam hoping to gain?

JEROME OK. I think we're beginning *to see some light at the end of the tunnel* here. This is what I'm prepared to recommend to the board. Stephen and Anton can have *carte blanche* to redesign, redevelop and repackage the product any way they see fit. They've got six months to do it in.

STEPHEN I think Anton will accept that offer.

JEROME It's not an offer. And *there are strings attached*. He's going to have to relocate. The new Hiltmann factory and offices will be sited at Essen. You've seen the site, Stephen, you agreed it was ideal, it's got laboratories, everything.

STEPHEN Well, I think . . .

JEROME Let me know how you get on.

23.13 Find the right word: the marketing mix

Read the text below on the marketing mix. Write a word from the box to fill each of the gaps.

The marketing ___**a**___ is the combination of all the factors that affect the sale of a product. One of the most important is the product itself, its design, ___**b**___ and price. A lot depends on how the consumer perceives the product. ___**c**___, like soap powder, are just as hard to sell as ___**d**___ items, like liqueur chocolates, but the problems are not the same.

Maxy, as a food flavouring, is somewhere in between these two extremes. People have to cook, and a high- ___**e**___, low-___**f**___ product that makes cooking easier should bring the customers back for more and bring plenty of ___**g**___ orders from the distributors. Patricia therefore assumes that Stephen wants go for the ___**h**___ end of the market, bringing the price ___**i**___. But Stephen in fact wants to go ___**j**___ market. People who buy this type of product will go on buying it even if it ___**k**___ more; the problem is to make them buy another bottle before the first one is empty. This in turn means product ___**l**___ : Hiltmann must produce a range of sauces and flavourings under a name that already has excellent brand ___**m**___.

cost costs
differentiation
down lower
luxury mix
necessities
packaging quality
recognition repeat
up

23.14 Speaking practice: making a proposition

Listen to this conversation. Then listen again, and speak the part of the president.

MAN Good morning, Mr President. What can I do for you?

PRESIDENT Good morning. I have a proposition to put to you which I think will interest you.

MAN I see.

PRESIDENT You'll be pleased to hear that the board have given the go-ahead on your plans for product diversification.

MAN That is good news.

PRESIDENT We said at the outset, you remember, that we ought to have a range of different flavoured sauces.

MAN On the face of it, it certainly sounds like a sensible idea. But what about the time scale?

PRESIDENT Yes, you're going to have to work fast, especially as you're also going to be relocated.

MAN Oh. To that splendid new factory at Essen. Yes, I remember, we agreed it was ideal.

23.15 Document study

Jerome Fantam sends this memo to Standard Can's managers world-wide. Read it carefully. Why do you think Jerome wrote point 3?

MEMO

from the desk of Jerome D. Fantam, President

to *mailing list D*

MAXY

1 Members of the Board of Directors have agreed on a project to re-launch this product as a range of ready-made sauces.

2 The launch date is proposed for March next year, subject to further tests and market studies and to revised production schedules at Hiltmann's new factory at Essen.

3 Stephen Sablon is appointed Vice-President, Group Food Products (Europe), *with immediate effect.*

JDF

23.15
mailing list D Jerome's assistant has a number of different mailing lists stored on the computer; this means that Jerome does not have to list all of the names.
with immediate effect at once.

Study record	
23.1	
23.2	
23.3	
23.4	
23.5	
23.6	
23.7	
23.8	
23.9	
23.10	
23.11	
23.12	
23.13	
23.14	
23.15	

Answer key and commentary for unit 23

23.1 Listen and read
Michael's purpose was to assess the potential market for Maxy sauce in Greece. Hiltmann would like to see figures that showed that a large number of Greeks buy products similar to Maxy.

23.2 Document study
The good news for Hiltmann is that a large percentage of people cook, and spend quite large amounts of money on food. They have only a limited amount of time to spend on cooking. They use ready-made flavourings, and prefer imported brands.

The bad news is that the regular users of sauces are mostly over 30; younger people use them much less.

23.3 Writing practice
This is a model answer.
The typical food shopper in Greece is female, aged 20–50, and lives in a household of three to five people. Larger households are common, and few people live alone. When she goes to a supermarket, she spends between 5000 and 10,000 drachmas. She cooks every day but does not usually spend more than two hours in the kitchen. She uses ready-made savoury sauces and flavourings often, and prefers imported brands.

23.4 Listen and read
Michael is going to reach the target audience mainly through television advertising, but he will also use magazine advertising to soften them up first.

23.5 Listen and read
Michael wants to spend some money on in-store promotion and 'below-the-line expenditure': gifts and other incentives for the shopkeepers.

23.6 Reading for key words
1 On the face of it, I thought these figures looked encouraging.
2 The main thrust of our campaign
3 peak viewing times
4 I've heard that one before.
5 That's it
6 slip . . . a little backhander

23.7 Document study
Figure 3 is a bar chart. Figure 4 is a bar and lin chart. Figure 1 is a line chart. Figure 2 is a pi chart. Figures 1 and 4 show a trend over time Figures 2 and 3 show an analysis at a given poir in time.

23.8 Find the word
a rise **b** peak **c** slump **d** lag
e fluctuate **f** rise **g** fall **h** collapse
i increase **j** higher **k** correlation
l number **m** value

23.10 Listen and read
Jerome does not think that the test-marketin exercise has been a success. He asks if Stephen still offering to resign.

23.11 Listen and read
One solution is to reduce the price of Maxy an move down market. Another is to move th factory to reduce production costs. A third optio is to increase the price, move Maxy up marke and diversify the product.

23.12 Listen and read
The chosen solution is to diversify the produ and move up market. One of the conditions of th investment is that the factory relocates, so Jerom should benefit from the sale of the city-centre sit

23.13 Find the word
a mix **b** packaging **c** necessities
d luxury **e** quality **f** cost **g** repeat
h lower **i** down **j** up **k** costs
l differentiation **m** recognition

23.15 Listen and read
Jerome wants Stephen to be closely associate with the re-launch of Maxy, because he expects i and therefore Stephen, to fail.

Unit 24: Assessing company performance

SITUATION

Intrigue is brewing in the boardroom at Standard Can, and the future of J.F. Hiltmann and Stephen Sablon continues to hang in the balance. Will Jerome Fantam allow a management buy-out that could save them all?

CHARACTERS

Jerome Fantam

Leo Schooler

Patricia Hart

Anton Hiltmann

Stephen Sablon

Commentator — on the radio. He is British.

LANGUAGE

Vocabulary	Business journalism; food processing; doubt and suspicion; the end of a company's life.
Skills	Discussing sales figures; congratulating someone; expressing criticism and disappointment.
Structures	Analysing a long sentence; the next, the last.
Documents	A press release; a magazine article; notes for a letter.

Assessing the prospects

24.1
(a) press release a document sent to newspapers, magazines and trade journals in the hope that they will print it or quote it, thus giving the company some free advertising.
convenience food food that can be bought and cooked quickly without any preparation.
haute cuisine food cooked to a very high standard.

24.3
food additives substances added to food to make it last longer, look different, taste different, etc.
leaked shown a document to somebody who wasn't meant to see it.
to fill us in on the details this suggests that you know what the speaker is talking about but have forgotten the details. It is a useful expression when you have no idea what the speaker is talking about, but don't want to admit it.
anti-oxidants substances that are put in processed foods to prevent the ingredients combining with oxygen in the air; without anti-oxidants, the colour or the taste of the food might be affected.
take care this is not a warning, but a friendly way of saying goodbye. It is common in the US.

24.1 Document study

This is one of the press releases for the new Maxy product range. Read through it carefully. Has Maxy gone up market or down market? How do you know?

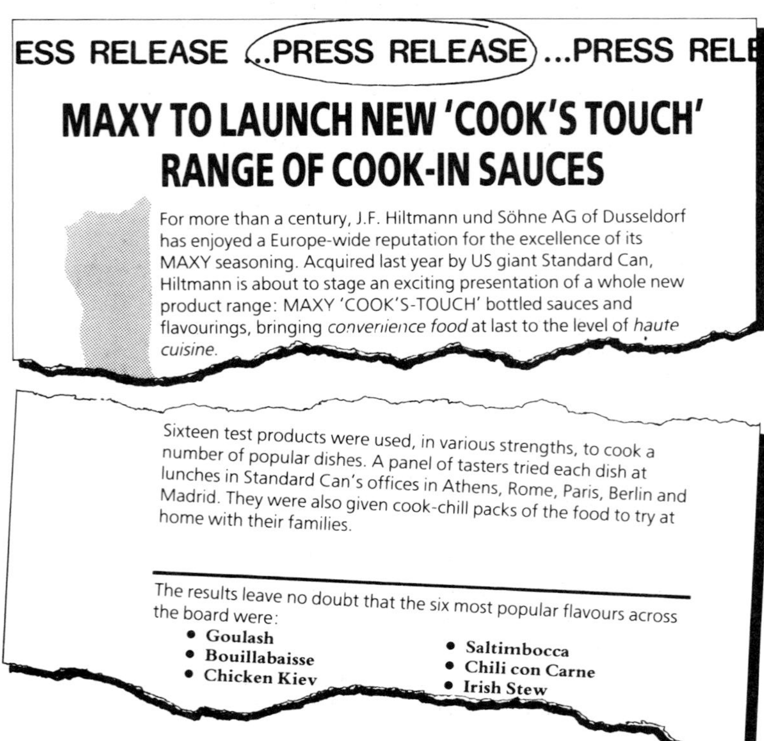

ESS RELEASE ...PRESS RELEASE ...PRESS REL

MAXY TO LAUNCH NEW 'COOK'S TOUCH' RANGE OF COOK-IN SAUCES

For more than a century, J.F. Hiltmann und Söhne AG of Dusseldorf has enjoyed a Europe-wide reputation for the excellence of its MAXY seasoning. Acquired last year by US giant Standard Can, Hiltmann is about to stage an exciting presentation of a whole new product range: MAXY 'COOK'S-TOUCH' bottled sauces and flavourings, bringing *convenience food* at last to the level of *haute cuisine*.

Sixteen test products were used, in various strengths, to cook a number of popular dishes. A panel of tasters tried each dish at lunches in Standard Can's offices in Athens, Rome, Paris, Berlin and Madrid. They were also given cook-chill packs of the food to try at home with their families.

The results leave no doubt that the six most popular flavours across the board were:

- Goulash
- Bouillabaisse
- Chicken Kiev
- Saltimbocca
- Chili con Carne
- Irish Stew

24.2 Reading for key words

Find the words or phrases in 24.1 that tell you the following:

1 To make public.
2 Food which can be prepared and cooked in a few minutes.
3 A group of people who were asked to try the food and say what they thought of it.
4 Boxes of refrigerated, cooked food.
5 In each area or department.

24.3 Listen and read

Leo, Patricia and Jerome Fantam are meeting in New York. Listen to what they say. Why is Patricia surprised and suspicious?

JEROME — Leo, Patricia – could I have a word with you before you go? What do you make of this story from Geneva?
LEO — From Geneva?
JEROME — About *food additives*. Somebody's *leaked* a government analyst's report.
PATRICIA — You'll have *to fill us in on the details*.
JEROME — I don't know any details. It seems there are reports of a new link between certain *anti-oxidants* and cancer. I wondered if you'd heard anything. No? Well, thank you both for being here today – I'll see you in Dallas in September. You *take care*, now.

. . . . . .

PATRICIA — What do you make of that?
LEO — It's not like him to ask about rumours. He generally starts them. Likes to keep the opposition guessing.
PATRICIA — Mm. Precisely!

24.4 Speaking practice: starting a rumour

Listen to this conversation. Then listen again, and speak the part of the man.

WOMAN Did you read that analyst's report that I sent you last week?
MAN Er – oh yes, I remember. Could you just remind me of the details?
WOMAN Well, briefly, it said that our claim that the product contained certain vitamins was unjustified.
MAN That's strange. Who was this analyst working for?
WOMAN We don't know. Apparently, the report was leaked. I wondered if you'd heard any more about it.
MAN No. But I find it very hard to believe. They've always been very strict about these things in Germany.
WOMAN Well, the boss seems very keen to tell everyone about it. Now why should he do that?
MAN It's not like him to spread a rumour, especially if it hasn't been confirmed.
WOMAN No, but he's quite capable of starting one if it suits him!

24.5 Listen and read

Anton Hiltmann is having a telephone conversation with Stephen Sablon. Listen to what they say. Which area had the lowest sales? Why is this surprising?

ANTON Stephen? I've got the print-out here for the first month's sales figures for the new Maxy range. *Hot off the computer*.
STEPHEN Uh-huh. How do they look?
ANTON Well, you'll be able to access the data direct within the next half hour, but, briefly, total turnover was nineteen million dollars, equal to the best month we ever had with the old Maxy. In Germany alone we shipped one point three million dollars' worth of stock, and the lowest sales were point three six of a million in, guess where, Greece!
STEPHEN Fantastic. Well done, Anton – I really do congratulate you.
ANTON I've got Patricia here, by the way – says she'd like a word.
STEPHEN Oh, great. *Put her on*.
PATRICIA Stephen? Just glancing through these print-outs, I'm a bit worried about France – new Maxy is under-achieving in the northern and western regions.
STEPHEN Yes. I understand there was a hitch with the TV commercials for that area. Just a hiccup, it's all sorted out now. Oh, but since you're there – do you know anything about this leaked analyst's report?
PATRICIA No. Should I? What is it?
STEPHEN Something about anti-oxidants. Jerome Fantam was saying something about them yesterday. Does Hiltmann use anti-oxidants?
PATRICIA Er – I think I'd better *hand you back* to Anton.

24.5
Hot off the computer Anton means that the figures have only just been printed; they are very new.
Put her on give her the telephone. Note also what Patricia says when she wants to give the phone back to Anton; 'I'd better **hand you back** to Anton.'

24.6 Writing practice: Stephen Sablon's notes

Stephen keeps notes on the progress of Maxy. Write his notes for him after his conversation with Anton and Patricia.

Assessing the damage

24.7
hitherto up to now; a formal usage.
Foremost among one of the most important of.
hyperactivity constant, excessive activity, which eventually damages a child's health.
rancid and toxic sour-tasting and poisonous.

24.7 Document study

This is the article that appeared in a popular consumer magazine on the food industry. Read through it carefully. Why would Anton Hiltmann be concerned about the article? What effect would the article have on consumers?

ADDITIVES SCARE HITS FOOD MANUFACTURERS AND DISTRIBUTORS

Confidential reports originating from government laboratories in three European countries suggest that certain synthetic food additives may not be as harmless as was *hitherto* supposed, even in the low concentrations permitted by EC regulations.

Foremost among the alleged offenders is BHX, a compound used in many cooked foods and branded food flavourings such as the popular 'Maxy' sauce. BHX has long been suspected of causing *hyperactivity* in children. Now there is evidence linking it to certain types of cancer – even though it is thought to give protection against other types. It is known to raise blood cholesterol levels and in some circumstances to destroy vitamins that the body needs.

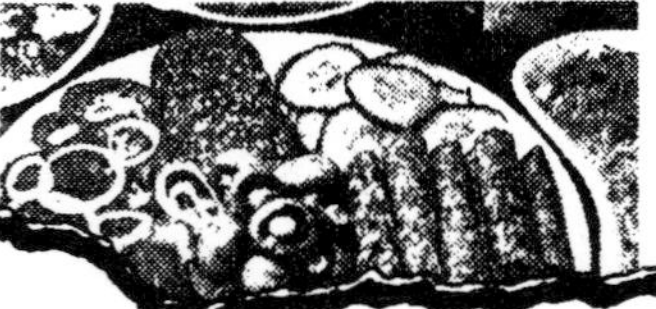

BHX is an anti-oxidant: it inhibits oils and fats from becoming *rancid and toxic.* Because it is heat-resistant and can withstand cooking, it is hard for the food processing industry to find an adequate substitute at an acceptable price.

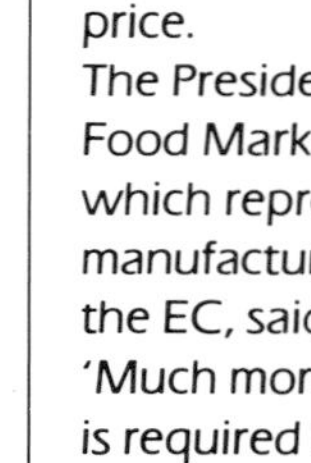

The President of the European Food Marketing Federation, which represents manufacturers throughout the EC, said last night: 'Much more thorough testing is required before we can say there is any scientific basis for banning BHX and similar compounds.'

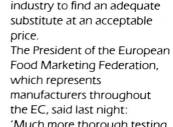

24.8 Reading for key words

Find the words or phrases in 24.7 that tell you the following:

1 Very small amounts.
2 The things which are said to cause the trouble (though it has not yet been proved).
3 It is not damaged by being heated or cooked.
4 Something else that will do the job just as well.
5 A price that the manufacturers are willing to pay.

24.9 Structure practice: analysing a long sentence

The first paragraph of the magazine article in 24.7 is a long, complex sentence. It contains several separate ideas and pieces of information. Rewrite it as a series of short, simple sentences that will communicate the same ideas and information.

24.10 Listen and read

Anton Hiltmann telephones the editor of the magazine. Why does he also become angry with Stephen?

ANTON This is outrageous. Why is Maxy the only brand name mentioned in your article? *Countless* other brands use BHX. And the least you could have done is spoken to me about it first. I intend to consult my company's lawyers this morning, and you may expect to hear from them very shortly. Goodbye!

PATRICIA I'm afraid the damage has been done, Anton.

ANTON Of course. Even if the magazine prints *a retraction*, no one ever reads it – *let alone* believes it.

STEPHEN Well, at least Maxy was the first brand name the journalist thought of – and he obviously knew his readers would recognise it.

ANTON You think so? I think this is deliberate *sabotage*.

STEPHEN *You're being paranoid*, Anton. However – speaking as a Standard Can director – I owe it to my colleagues on the board to ask what you intend to do to restore public confidence in your product.

ANTON Speaking as a – Stephen, don't you get tired jumping over that fence all the time! You offered to resign rather than see Hiltmann *go to the wall*. You were appointed Food Products Vice-President – *Maxy is your baby* just as much as it is ours.

PATRICIA Wait a minute! I'm just remembering a conversation Leo Schooler and I had with Jerome Fantam when we saw him in New York in July. Is it possible he'd deliberately start a rumour to wreck one of his own subsidiaries?

STEPHEN He might.

ANTON There, sabotage, you see. Who's being paranoid now?

24.10
Countless so many that they cannot be counted.
a retraction an announcement where a magazine or newspaper states that what it said was inaccurate.
let alone Anton uses this to say that not many people will read the article, and even fewer would believe it.
sabotage deliberate damage.
You're being paranoid you're being more suspicious than is reasonable.
go to the wall be driven out of business.
Maxy is your baby you have a special interest and responsibility for Maxy; an informal usage.

24.11 Writing practice: a letter to the press

Anton Hiltmann decides to write a letter to the magazine that published the article about BHX and Maxy. The letter is polite but very firm. Write this letter for him. Use the notes below to help you.

Errors
We do use BHX.
So does every other manufacturer.
BHX preserves goodness and flavour of sauces.
Shelf-life without BHX only a few days or weeks.
Without BHX prices would rise.
Products may disappear.
Substitutes cause similar problems.
Two points:
No proof that BHX causes cancer.
Why mention Maxy?
Retraction and apology!

Assessing your chances

24.12
interim results results published part of the way through the financial year.
holding company a company that owns one or more subsidiary companies.
ailing unhealthy; not progressing as it should be.
synthetic chemicals chemicals which are manufactured, not natural.
the last straw the last in a series of problems. Although it may itself be a small problem, it may cause the company to fail.
go into receivership to stop trading. A **receiver** is a person who takes over the company's affairs, and who collects money which is owed to the near-bankrupt company and pays off as many of its debts as possible.

24.14
leveraged buy-outs takeovers financed by a lot of borrowing.
turned us down flat refused even to consider our proposal.
to get cold feet to become nervous or frightened because of the risk of failure.
back out withdraw from the deal.
to wind up to pay its debts, sell its assets and end the existence of the company.

24.12 Listen and read

This is a radio report on the financial troubles at Standard Can. Listen to it carefully. What does the commentator think will happen to Hiltmann?

COMMENTATOR Next on Financial World Tonight, company news: and disappointing *interim results* for multinational giant Standard Can gave strength to rumours that the US *holding company* may be having second thoughts about its most recent acquisition, *ailing* German food manufacturer J.F. Hiltmann. StanCan bought up Hiltmann last year, and there was a vigorous management shake-out that left former sales director Anton Hiltmann as the only surviving member of the Hiltmann family in an executive position. But in the last six months nothing has gone right, and a scare over dangerous *synthetic chemicals* in the product may turn out to be *the last straw*. Hiltmanns could *go into receivership* in the next few weeks, unless current moves to stage a management buy-out can succeed.

24.13 Reading for key words

Find the words or phrases in 24.12 that tell you the following:

1 Half-year trading figures that were less good than expected.
2 About to reverse a previous decision.
3 The last company that was taken over.
4 Getting rid of a large number of the company's managers.
5 Things that are being done at the moment.
6 A takeover of the company by its own managers, who buy all (or a majority of) the shares.

24.14 Listen and read

Anton and Leo are trying to find a solution to Hiltmann's problems. Listen to what they say. Is Leo optimistic or pessimistic? What about Anton? How do you know?

ANTON But as I was saying, Leo, the era of junk bonds and *leveraged buy-outs* is past. The banks have *turned us down flat*. Stephen keeps talking about 'mezzanine finance', whatever that is.

LEO I am confident in the end you'll succeed in negotiating very reasonable terms with Jerome Fantam. The idea of management plus workers buying out the company together makes extremely good sense.

ANTON Yes, of course. But if we can't raise the money within the next few days, our workforce are going *to get cold feet*, and if Fantam thinks they may *back out* then he's liable *to wind up* Hiltmann and sell Maxy to the highest bidder.

24.15 Listen and read

Leo is reporting back to Jerome Fantam about what he thinks is happening in Germany. Listen to what they say. Will Standard Can make or lose money if it sells Hiltmann now?

LEO I think the people at Hiltmann are moving towards the idea of a buy-out – management and workers together. How would we react to that?

JEROME Yeah, I guess Standard Can might agree to *a demerger*. We didn't actually pay a great deal to buy Hiltmann, but their marketing adventures over the past twelve months have cost us a small fortune.

LEO They seem very confident they can make it work.

JEROME Well, I know they think they can *make a go of it*, but what about all that investment we put in? Are we supposed *to write that off as a bad debt*?

LEO Stephen Sablon appears to be quite willing for that to happen. He hasn't said anything about Hiltmann giving Standard Can any kind of compensation.

JEROME Tell Stephen I am very disappointed in him. I expected something more from him.

> **24.15**
> **a demerger** the separating of a subsidiary from its parent company; the opposite of a **merger**.
> **make a go of it** make it a successful company.
> **to write that off as a bad debt** to agree that the debt will not be repaid.

24.16 Structure practice: *the next, the last*

When we use 'next' and 'last' with a plural noun, we also need to use a number, or a word like 'few'. Anton says 'you'll be able to access the data direct within the next half hour', but the radio commentator says 'Hiltmanns could go into receivership in the next few weeks' and 'in the last six months nothing has gone right'.

Write answers to the questions below, using 'next' or 'last':

1 When will that letter be ready? [ten minutes]
Oh, in the next ten minutes.
2 Has anyone been in here recently? [twenty minutes]
3 Jerome Fantam is sixty. When's he going to retire? [ten years]
4 And when will Stephen Sablon be leaving the corporation? [a few minutes]
5 Someone told me Standard Can has taken over thirty companies. [fifteen years]
6 Do they sell off the assets every time? [a few times]
7 So Standard Can itself could be in serious trouble? [a year or two]
8 The Standard Can story seems to have been going on for ages. [three units]

24.17 Listen and read

Stephen is talking to a meeting of the European directors. Listen to what is said. Are the other directors as confident as Stephen that his new plan will work?

STEPHEN OK, quiet everyone, this is my proposal – we repackage the whole Maxy range in cubes in airtight foil wrappers, each cube individually wrapped. That gets rid of the anti-oxidant, we don't need it any more. It also gets rid of bottles and glass jars, which are perceived as environmentally unfriendly and which are fragile and heavy and generally bad news. Then a big advertising campaign to rebuild our image as green, wholefood, nature freaks.

PATRICIA Oh Stephen, you know as well as any of us that means at least another year's R&D and maybe twenty million dollars' advertising . . .

24.18 Writing practice: Stephen Sablon's notes

Once again, Sablon is writing his notes, trying to work out what courses of action are open to him at this moment. Write the notes for him, using whatever information you have from this unit. What options does he really have?

Study record	
24.1	
24.2	
24.3	
24.4	
24.5	
24.6	
24.7	
24.8	
24.9	
24.10	
24.11	
24.12	
24.13	
24.14	
24.15	
24.16	
24.17	
24.18	

Answer key and commentary for unit 24

24.1 Document study
Maxy has definitely gone up market. We know this because of the reference to 'haute cuisine' in the press release.

24.2 Reading for key words
1 to launch
2 convenience food
3 a panel of tasters
4 cook-chill packs
5 across the board

24.3 Listen and read
Patricia is surprised and suspicious because she knows that Jerome Fantam likes to start rumours, and she doesn't know what is going on.

24.5 Listen and read
Greece had the lowest sales. This is surprising because Greece is where the old Maxy sauce was test marketed, and so the Maxy brand name already had a presence.

24.6 Writing practice
This is a model answer.
Anton telephoned with the first month's sales figures for the new Maxy range. More or less as I had expected; $19 million overall for the month. Of course I congratulated him with great enthusiasm – he really seemed to be very pleased with himself. Patricia then took the phone from him and started complaining about poor sales in France. When I asked her about the anti-oxidant reports she handed me back to Anton – she obviously didn't want to discuss the matter.

24.7 Document study
Anton would be concerned because the article appears to link Maxy sauces with cancer. The effect of the article would be to discourage people from buying Maxy sauces.

24.8 Reading for key words
1 low concentrations
2 the alleged offenders
3 heat-resistant and can withstand cooking
4 an adequate substitute
5 an acceptable price

24.9 Structure practice
This is a model answer; there are many possible ways of rewriting the sentence.
EC regulations control the use of food additives. They allow only very low concentrations. At these low levels, the additives were believed to be safe. Government laboratories in three European countries have done research into certain synthetic additives. They have now issued confidential reports. These reports suggest that some additives may not be entirely safe after all.

24.10 Listen and read
Anton becomes angry with Stephen because Stephen tries to suggest that the problem is not his concern, and that Hiltmann must do something about it. He shows this by saying 'as a Standard Can director.'

24.11 Writing practice
This is a model answer; there are many possible ways of writing this letter.
Sir,
As the Managing Director of J.F. Hiltmann, the manufacturers of Maxy sauces and seasonings, I am writing to correct certain errors in your recent article. We do, of course, use the synthetic compound BHX in our product. So does virtually every other manufacturer of similar products. It is done to protect the public by preserving the goodness and flavour of our sauces. Without this anti-oxidant, they would have a shelf-life of only a few days or weeks. The price would become unacceptably high, and the products would soon disappear from the market. The same thing would happen if we attempted to replace BHX with any effective substitute. Two points in particular disturb me regarding your article. First, there is no conclusive proof that BHX, even in large amounts, can cause cancer. There are only the allegations of leaked reports from some unspecified government laboratories. Second, I do not understand why my firm's product is named by you although countless other products make use – quite properly – of the same additives. I hope that in your next issue you will publish a retraction and an apology.
Yours, etc., A. Hiltmann.

24.12 Listen and read
The radio commentator's view is that Hiltmann is a company in great difficulty, and that unless the management buy-out succeeds, the company will go into receivership.

24.13 Reading for key words
1 disappointing interim results
2 having second thoughts
3 its most recent acquisition
4 a vigorous management shake-out
5 current moves
6 a management buy-out

24.14 Listen and read
Leo is quite optimistic. He says he is 'confident'. Anton is pessimistic. He thinks the workforce will 'get cold feet' and Jerome Fantam will close Hiltmann.

24.15 Listen and read
Standard Can is likely to lose money. They will get money from the management buy-out, but will lose money because they will have to write off their investment as a bad debt.

24.16 Structure practice
These are model answers; there are many possible answers to these questions.
2 Not in the last twenty minutes.
3 Some time in the next ten years.
4 Some time in the next few minutes, probably.
5 Yes, in the last fifteen years it has taken over thirty companies.
6 Well, the last few times they have.
7 Not for the next year or two.
8 Only for the last three units!

24.17 Listen and read
The other directors do not seem to be as confident as Stephen. They seem alarmed at the thought of another large investment programme.

24.18 Writing practice
This is a model answer.
Options for Hiltmann: raise money however we can and continue with plans for the buy-out; try to find large corporation to take over Hiltmann on acceptable terms; give up and wait for Fantam to wind up the company.
Options for Maxy: go back to original product; keep marketing new range and rely on public relations to convince people BHX is safe; repackage the range in airtight wrappers so that we avoid BHX altogether.

Index and glossary

This index and glossary lists words, phrases and structures that are explained in the word notes in the units and/or practised in exercises. It includes both business terms and everyday idiomatic language. It also lists documents that are illustrated in the book.

References are to units and exercises: 18.5 means unit 18, exercise 5. References in ordinary type are usually to examples of the word or phrase in use. References in **bold type** indicate where the word or phrase is explained, or where more information is provided. Entries in *italic type* show vocabulary items. Explanations, where given, appear in brackets. They are intended as quick reminders of the meaning of a word or phrase, not full and exact definitions.

D

T